Site
Engineering
for Landscape
Architects

Site Engineering for Landscape Architects

Steven Strom
Landscape Architecture Program
Rutgers—The State University of New Jersey
New Brunswick, New Jersey

Kurt Nathan P.E.
Conservation Engineering, P.A.
Somerset, New Jersey

 VAN NOSTRAND REINHOLD
—————————— New York

Page 14, problem 1.3 is adapted with permission from V.C. Finch et al., *The Earth and Its Resources*, Third Edition, © 1959, by the McGraw-Hill Book Company, Inc., New York.

Page 80, quote from *The Pennine Dales* by Arthur Raistrick is reprinted by permission of Methuen London Ltd. Publishers.

Page 138, the runoff coefficients for urban areas are taken with permission from Chapter 3, Storm Drainage, by Paul Theil Associates Ltd., in *Modern Sewer Design*, First Edition, © 1980 by the American Iron and Steel Institute.

Page 138, the runoff coefficients for rural and suburban areas are taken with permission from G.O. Schwab et al., *Elementary Soil and Water Engineering*, © 1971, by John Wiley & Sons, Inc., New York.

Page 147, Table 6.2 is taken with permission from H.G. Poertner, *Practices in Detention of Urban Storm Water Runoff*, American Public Works Association, Special Report No. 43, 1974.

Page 172, Figure 6.26 is redrawn with permission from Chapter 3, Storm Drainage, by Paul Theil Associates Ltd., in *Modern Sewer Design*, First Edition, © 1980 by the American Iron and Steel Institute.

Page 241, Table 8.1 is adapted with permission from K. Lynch, *Site Planning*, Second Edition, published by the MIT Press, © 1971 by the Massachusetts Institute of Technology

Copyright © 1985 by Van Nostrand Reinhold
Library of Congress Catalog Card Number 85-1326
ISBN 0-87055-471-9

Printed in the United States of America

Van Nostrand Reinhold
115 Fifth Avenue
New York, New York 10003

Chapman & Hall
2-6 Boundary Row
London SE1 8HN, England

Thomas Nelson Australia
102 Dodds Street
South Melbourne, Victoria 3205, Australia

Nelson Canada
1120 Birchmount Road
Scarborough, Ontario M1K 5G4, Canada

16 15 14 13 12 11 10 9 8 7 6

Library of Congress Cataloging in Publication Data

Strom, Steven.
    Site engineering for landscape architects.

    Bibliography: p.
    Includes index.
    1. Building sites. 2. Landscape architecture.
I. Nathan, Kurt.   II. Title
TH375.S77 1985   690'.11   85-1326
ISBN 0-87055-471-9

To
Gladys and Clifford Strom
and
Barbara and Bernard David Nathan

Contents

CHAPTER 1 Contours and Form

CHAPTER 2 Interpolation and Slope

CHAPTER 3 Slope Formula Application

Contents Continued

Preface

The shaping of the earth's surface is one of the primary functions of site planners and landscape architects. This shaping must not only display sound understanding of esthetic and design principles, but also ecological sensitivity and technical competency. The last point, the technical ability to transform design ideas into physical reality, is the focus of this text. Specifically the book emphasizes principles and techniques of basic site engineering for grading, drainage, earthwork, and road alignment. The authors strongly believe that, in most cases, it is difficult to separate the design procedure from the construction and implementation process and that technical competency ultimately will lead to a better finished product. In this regard the authors also feel that collaborative efforts between the landscape architecture and engineering professions will result in the most appropriate solutions to design and environmental problems.

Although appropriate as a reference for practitioners, the book has been developed primarily as a teaching text. Based on the authors' experience the material, numerous examples, and problems have been organized to provide students with a progressive understanding of the subject matter. First, landform and contour lines are discussed descriptively. This is followed by explanations of interpolation and slope formulas and examples of their application. Chapters 4 and 5 are concerned with environmental and functional constraints and design opportunities which guide site engineering decisions and a procedure for developing grading solutions. The integrated relationship between site design and site engineering is also emphasized in these chapters. Storm water management and the design and sizing of management systems are discussed in Chapter 6. Earthwork terminology, construction sequence, and the computation of earthwork volumes are presented in Chapter 7. The procedures for designing horizontal and vertical road alignments are presented in the last two chapters. In summary, the authors believe that the book presents an environmentally sensitive and intellectually stimulating approach to site development.

Acknowledgments

Many sources have contributed to the authors' interest and growth in the field of site development and landscape construction. The classic text by Parker and MacGuire and the work of David Young and Donald Leslie deserve special mention among them. Publications of the USDA-Soil Conservation Service, particularly in the areas of storm water management and swale design, have been invaluable.

Thanks are due to the Department of Horticulture and Forestry of Cook College, Rutgers University, for the use of facilities and equipment, to Laura Sesta for typing the manuscript, to Elizabeth Grady and Karneel Thomas for their help with the illustrations, and to Vincent Abbatiello and Guy Metler for their fine photographic processing.

Robert Moore supplied Figure 6.19b, and Leland Anderson and Lee Holt of the Soil Conservation Service reviewed several portions of the manuscript in preparation. David Lamm, also of the S.C.S., reviewed the entire text. Their assistance is gratefully acknowledged.

CHAPTER 1

Contours and Form

DEFINITION

A clear understanding of what a contour represents is fundamental to the grading process. Technically defined, a *contour* is an imaginary line that connects all points of equal elevation above or below a fixed reference plane or datum. This datum may be mean sea level or a locally established bench mark. A *contour line* is the graphic representation of a contour on a plan or map. Within this text, however, the terms contour and contour line will be used synonymously.

A difficulty with understanding contours arises from the fact that they are imaginary and therefore cannot be easily visualized in the landscape. The shoreline of a pond or lake is the best example of a naturally occurring contour and illustrates the concept of a closed contour. A *closed contour* is one that reconnects with itself. All contours eventually close on themselves, although this may not occur within the boundaries of a particular map or plan.

A single, closed contour may describe a horizontal plane or level surface, again illustrated by a pond or lake. However, more than one contour is required to describe a three-dimensional surface. It is important to emphasize here that contour drawings are two-dimensional representations of three-dimensional forms. A basic skill that landscape architects and site designers must develop is the ability to analyze, interpret, and visualize landforms from contour maps and plans, commonly referred to as *topographic maps*. Designers must not only understand *existing* contours and landforms, but they must also understand the implications of changes, both esthetically and ecologically, which result from *altering* contours. The series of illustrations in Fig. 1.1 demonstrates how contours define form and how the form is altered by changing the contours.

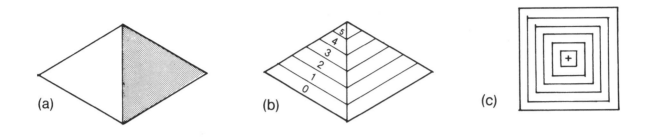

(a)   (b)   (c)

Fig. 1.1.   RELATIONSHIP OF CONTOUR LINES TO THREE-DIMENSIONAL FORM
   a. Isometric drawing of pyramidal form
   b. Contour lines illustrated on the isometric drawing
   c. Contour plan of pyramid (concentric squares)
   d. Small terraces created for spectators at the site of the 1972 Olympic kayak
      run provide an excellent example of contour lines as they appear on the
      ground.

The contour plan of the pyramid results in a series of concentric squares. By changing the squares to circles, the form is redefined from a pyramid to a cone. Figure 1.2 illustrates this transformation, starting with the contour plan.

Another aspect of contours and form is illustrated by Fig. 1.2b and 1.2c, and Fig. 1.3. A *gradual* rather than abrupt change is assumed to occur between adjacent contours. In Fig. 1.3, a section (see definition in following section) has been taken through the center of the cone. (Note that a section taken through the center of the pyramid results in the same two-dimensional form.) The steplike form that results from stacking the successive planes is indicated by the dashed line and the smoothing effect that results from assuming a gradual transition is indicated by the shaded triangles. It is this smoothing effect that gives the cone and pyramid their true form.

These examples are oversimplistic in their approach, since they deal with basic geometric forms and straightforward alterations. However, the landscape consists of numerous geometric shapes occurring in complex combinations. The ability to dissect landforms into their various component shapes and to understand the relationship of the shapes to each other will make the task of analyzing, interpreting, and visualizing the landscape easier.

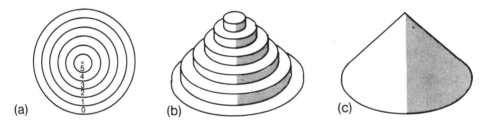

(a)   (b)   (c)

Fig. 1.2. ALTERATION OF FORM BY CHANGING CONTOUR LINES
    a. Square contour lines of pyramid altered to concentric circular contour lines
    b. Horizontal planes of circular contours stacked in layer cake-like manner
    c. Isometric of resultant conical form.

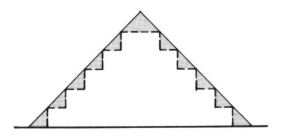

Fig. 1.3. SURFACE SMOOTHING
              BETWEEN ADJACENT
              CONTOUR LINES

The difference in elevation between adjacent contour lines as illustrated by the steps in Fig. 1.3 is defined as the *contour interval*. In order to interpret a topographic map properly, scale, direction of slope, and contour interval must be known. The most common intervals are 1, 2, 5, 10, and multiples of 10 ft. Selection of a contour interval is based on the roughness of the terrain and the purpose for which the topographic plan is to be used. It is obvious that as the map scale decreases (for example, changing from 1 in. = 20 ft to 1 in. = 100 ft for the same area) or the contour interval increases, the amount of detail, and therefore the degree of accuracy, decreases (Fig. 1.4).

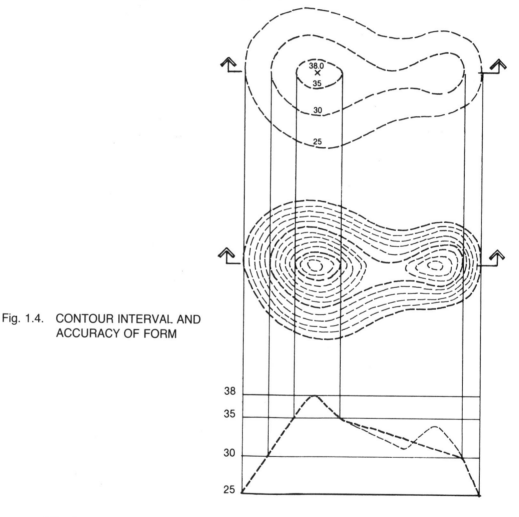

Fig. 1.4. CONTOUR INTERVAL AND
ACCURACY OF FORM

CONSTRUCTING A SECTION

Analyzing topography and landform can be accomplished by constructing a section. A *section* is a drawing made on a plane, which vertically cuts through the earth, an object like a building, or both. The ground line delineates the interface between earth and space and illustrates the relief of the topography. To draw a section, follow the procedure outlined in Fig. 1.5.

In Fig. 1.5 the highest elevation of the landform occurs between the 13 ft and the 14 ft elevations. Therefore a peak, or high point, must occur between the two intersections along the 13 ft elevation line. A similar condition, and how it may be misinterpreted due to degree of accuracy, is illustrated in Fig. 1.4.

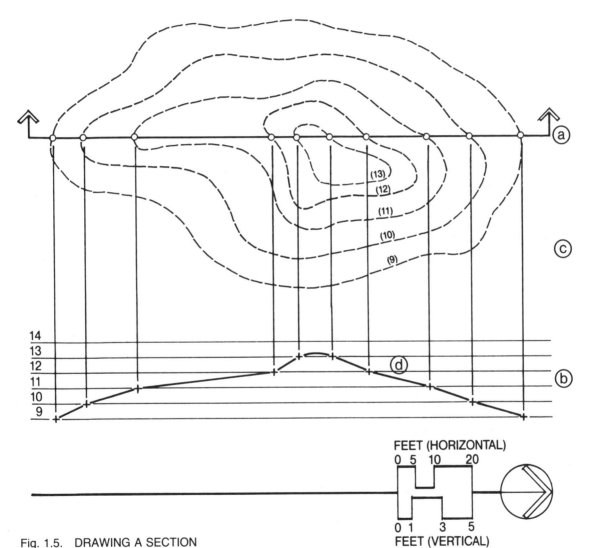

Fig. 1.5. DRAWING A SECTION
    a. Indicate cutting plane
    b. Draw parallel lines according to contour interval and proposed vertical scale.
    c. Project perpendicular lines from the intersection of the contour line with the cutting plane to the corresponding parallel line.
    d. Connect the points to complete the section and delineate the ground line.

CONTOUR SIGNATURES AND LANDFORM

It becomes apparent in analyzing landform that certain geomorphic features are described by distinct contour configurations. These configurations may be referred to as *contour signatures*. The characteristics of a variety of signatures are presented here accompanied by typical contour maps (Figs. 1.6 and 1.7).

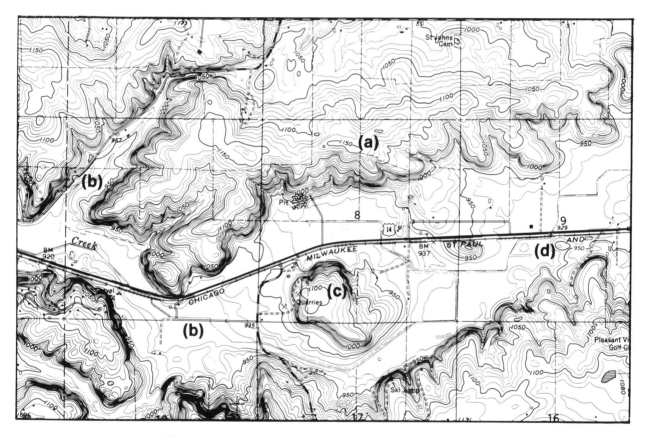

Fig. 1.6.   CONTOUR SIGNATURES
      a. Ridge
      b. Valley
      c. Summit
      d. Depression

Fig. 1.7.   CONTOUR SIGNATURES ▶
      a. Concave slope
      b. Convex slope
      c. Summit

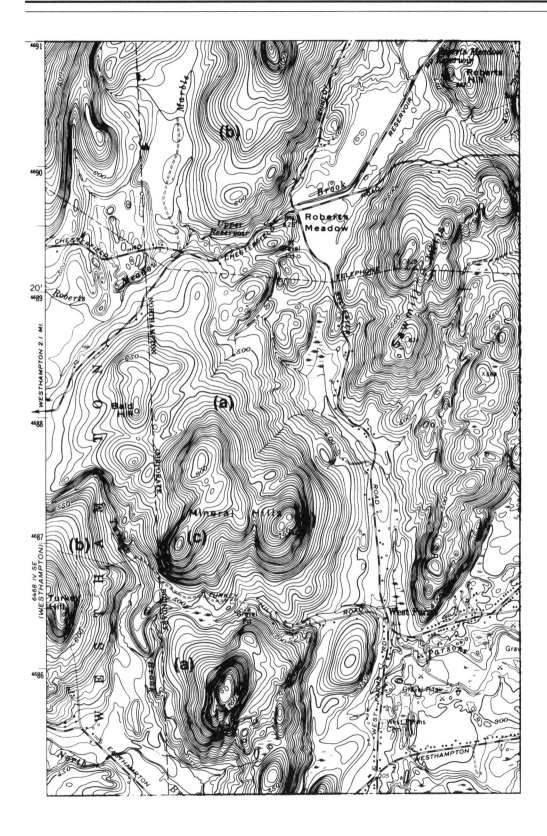

Ridge and Valley

A ridge is simply a raised elongated landform. At the narrow end of the form the contours point in the downhill direction. Typically, the contours along the sides of the ridge will be relatively parallel and there will be a high point or several high points along the ridge.

A valley is an elongated depression that forms the space between two ridges. Essentially valleys and ridges are interconnected, since the ridge side slopes create the valley walls. A valley is represented by contours that point uphill.

The contour pattern is similar for both the ridge and valley; therefore, it is important to note the direction of slope. In each case the contours reverse direction to create a U or V shape. The V shape is more likely to be associated with a valley, since the point at which the contour changes direction is the low point. Water collects along the intersection of the sloping sides and flows downhill, forming a natural drainage channel at the bottom.

Summit and Depression

A summit is a landform such as a knoll, hill, or mountain, which contains the highest point relative to the surrounding terrain. The contours form concentric, closed figures with the *highest* contour at the center. Since the land slopes away in all directions, summits tend to drain well.

A depression is a landform that contains the lowest point relative to the surrounding terrain. Again the contours form concentric, closed figures, but now the *lowest* contour is at the center. To avoid confusion between summits and depressions it is important to know the direction of elevation change. Graphically, the lowest contour is often distinguished by the use of hachures. Since depressions collect water, they typically form lakes, ponds, and wetlands.

Concave and Convex Slopes

A distinctive characteristic of concave slopes is that the contour lines are spaced at *increasing* distances in the downhill direction. This means that the slope is steeper at the higher elevations and becomes progressively more flat at the lower elevations.

A convex slope is the reverse of a concave slope. In other words, the contour lines are spaced at *decreasing* distances in the downhill direction. The slope is flatter at the higher elevations and becomes progressively more steep at the lower elevations.

Uniform Slope

Along a uniform slope, contour lines are spaced at *equal* distances. Thus, the change in elevation occurs at a constant rate. Uniform slopes are more typical in constructed rather than natural environments.

CHARACTERISTICS OF CONTOUR LINES

The points listed below summarize the essential characteristics associated with contour lines. Since many of the concepts and principles discussed in subsequent chapters relate to these characteristics, a thorough understanding must be achieved before proceeding.

1. By definition, all points on the same contour line are at the same elevation.
2. Every contour line is a continuous line, which forms a closed figure, either within or beyond the limits of the map or drawing (Fig. 1.8).
3. Two or more contour lines are required to indicate three-dimensional form and direction of slope (Fig. 1.9).
4. The steepest slope is perpendicular to the contour lines. This is a result of having the greatest vertical change in the shortest horizontal distance.

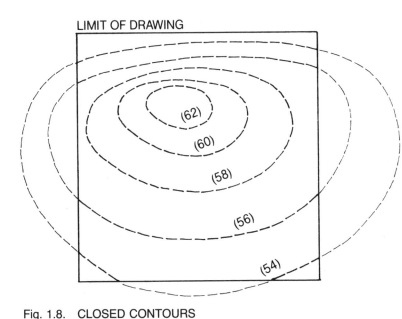

LIMIT OF DRAWING

(62)
(60)
(58)
(56)
(54)

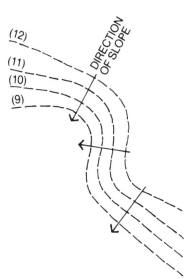

(12)
(11)
(10)
(9)

DIRECTION OF SLOPE

Fig. 1.8. CLOSED CONTOURS
Contours are continuous lines creating closed figures. However, closure may not always occur within the limits of a drawing or map.

Fig. 1.9. DIRECTION OF SLOPE
The steepest slope is perpendicular to the contour lines. Consequently, surface water flows perpendicular to contour lines.

5. Consistent with the preceding point, water flows perpendicular to contour lines.
6. For the same scale and contour interval, the steepness of slope increases as the map distance between contour lines decreases.
7. Equally spaced contour lines indicate a constant, or uniform, slope.
8. Contour lines never cross except where there is an overhanging cliff, natural bridge, or other similar phenomenon.
9. In the natural landscape, contour lines never divide or split. However, this is not necessarily true at the interface between the natural and built landscape as illustrated in Fig. 1.10.

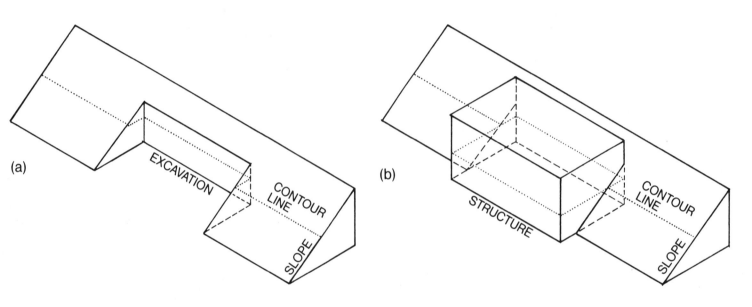

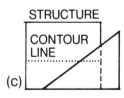

Fig. 1.10.   Technically, contour lines never divide or split where they are used to represent the surface of the *earth*. However at structures, contour lines may also be drawn across the face of the constructed object, thus providing a split appearance.
a. The contour line follows along the face of an excavation made in a slope.
b. The contour line follows along the face of the excavation as well as along the face of the structure placed in the excavated area.
c. End section illustrating the relationship between the slope and the structure.

PROBLEMS

1.1. The intent of this two-part problem is to develop your ability to visualize landform from contours. (a) Draw a contour plan of the land form. This is the reverse procedure of interpreting topographic maps, but will help establish the visual relationship between contour lines and form. Use a minimum of eight contour lines to depict the form.

(b) Draw an oblique aerial perspective of the landform represented by the contour plan on the following page.

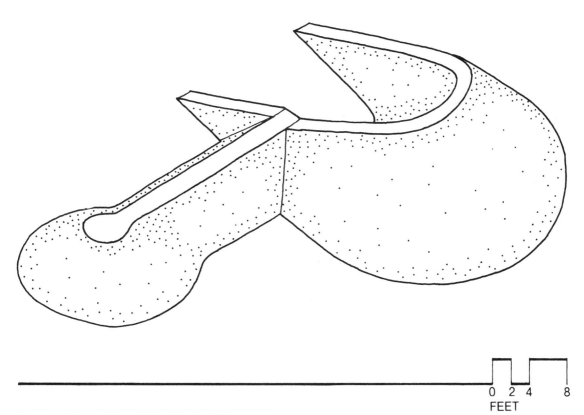

0 2 4   8
FEET

Problem 1.1a   AXONOMETRIC OF LANDFORM

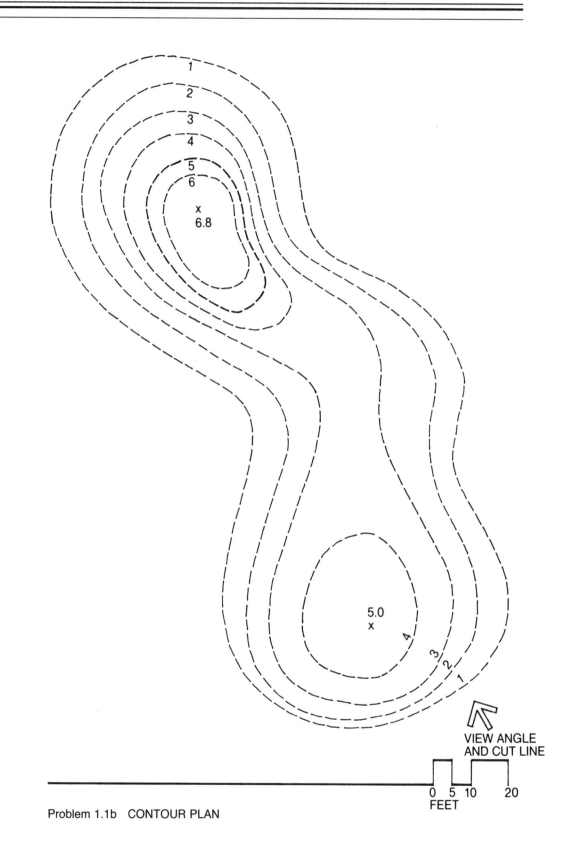

Problem 1.1b   CONTOUR PLAN

1.2. Problem 1.1 required the visualization of landforms and contour lines using two-dimensional graphics. An easier, but more time consuming method for interpreting contours is through the use of three-dimensional models.

Construct two models: the first of the contour plan in Problem 1.1b and the second of the more architectural landform illustrated here. Once constructed, these models may be used to analyze various contour line relationships, such as relative steepness, concave and convex slopes, etc.

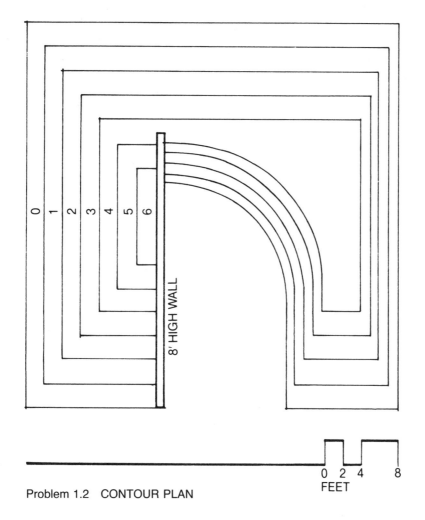

Problem 1.2   CONTOUR PLAN

1.3. As an alternative to Problem 1.2 mold an oval mound of wax 6½ in. high in an open tank, steeply sloping at one end and gently sloping at the other. Fill the tank with 6 in. of water, thus leaving ½ in. of the mound protruding. With a sharp point outline the position of the edge of the water on the wax. Next lower the level of the water by 1 in. stages, outlining the position of the water at each stage until all water has been removed. The marks made will now appear as contour lines on the wax mound, the lowest being 1 in. from the bottom of the tank, the next 2 in. and so on. If the mound is viewed from directly above, the arrangement of the lines is exactly like that of a contour map. Notice that where the slope of the mound is steep the contour lines are close together and that as the slope becomes more gentle they are more widely spaced.

1.4. The first two exercises address the issue of understanding the three-dimensional forms created by contour lines using graphic and model techniques. However, these methods are still somewhat abstract, since they are not related directly to the landscape. There are two techniques that may be used to place contour lines and form in a realistic context: (a) to "draw" contour lines directly on the ground by the use of lime, etching lines in snow (if the weather is appropriate), or by the use of string or surveyor's flagging and, (b) drawing contour lines on a map from an on-site visual analysis. Select a small area with a variety of topographic conditions and attempt one or both of these techniques. As a clue to laying out contour lines, there are numerous features in the landscape that can help to determine relative differences in slope and elevation. These include stairs, brick courses on buildings, door heights, vegetation, people, etc. Keying on these features will make this task easier.

1.5. Construct a section of the landform in Problem 1.1b along the cut line indicated. Use 1 in. = 10 ft for the horizontal scale and 1 in. = 5 ft for the vertical scale.

CHAPTER 2

Interpolation and Slope

TOPOGRAPHIC DATA

The previous chapter discussed contour lines from a descriptive viewpoint; that is, what contour lines portray. This chapter introduces the basic mathematical equations associated with plotting and manipulating contour lines.

In order to make informed design decisions as well as to execute construction drawings accurately, landscape architects require topographic data for all site development projects. This information is usually provided by a licensed land surveyor in the form of a topographic map or plan. However, there are occasions when a landscape architect may be required to gather topographic data or the data furnished by the surveyor are merely spot elevations, usually on a rectangular grid. This section discusses the latter two points.

Typically, topographic data are collected by laying out a grid pattern over the site to be surveyed. The size of the grid selected depends on the extent of the area, the degree of topographic variation, and the purpose for which the survey will be used. Generally 20, 25, 50, or 100 ft squares are used. For large rectangular areas, laying out the grid is a relatively simple task. Two rows of stakes may be placed along each of two sides of the rectangle, as illustrated in Fig. 2.1, thus allowing the rodman to locate the remaining grid intersection points by aligning the leveling rod with two pairs of stakes. Leveling proceeds as in differential leveling except that a number of foresights can be taken for each instrument setup. If the elevation of the area does not vary more than 10 or 12 ft, it may be possible to obtain all necessary data with one instrument setup. For referencing purposes, the grid intersections are labeled with letter and number coordinates.

For more complex sites, either in configuration, topographic variety, or both, the same basic principles may be applied with modifications, such as additional setups, more foresights, or a grid geometry compat-

15

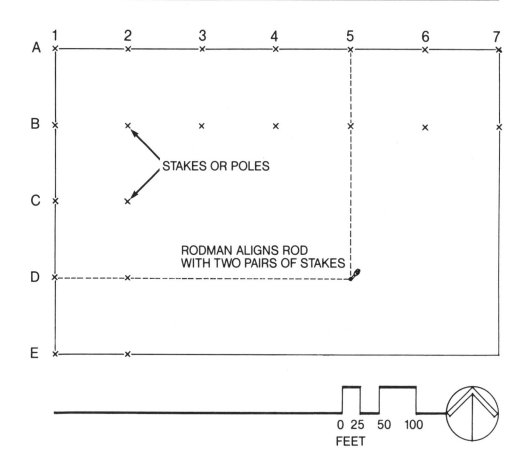

Fig. 2.1. PLAN OF STAKE LAYOUT FOR COLLECTING TOPOGRAPHIC DATA.
As discussed in Chapter 7, the grid of spot elevations is particularly helpful
when using the borow pit method of determining cut and fill volumes. However, irregular grids or selected points may also be used to collect topographic
data.

ible with the shape of the site. Further foresights may be necessary
where a high or low point exists between grid intersections, since, as
discussed in the next section, the assumption is that there is a constant or
uniform change in elevation from one grid corner to the next.

Once the elevations for each of the grid corners have been determined,
they are plotted on a plan at a desired or specified scale. The next step in
the process is to draw the contour lines (Fig. 2.6) since, as discussed in
Chapter 1, this allows for easier visualization and understanding of the
three-dimensional form of the landscape. Before drawing the contour
lines, however, it is necessary to introduce the concept of interpolation.

INTERPOLATION

Interpolation, by definition, is the process of computing intermediate values between two related known values. For the purpose of topographic surveys, interpolation is the process of locating whole number elevations (assuming that contour lines with a 1 ft vertical interval are desired) between the elevations of the grid intersections. Interpolation may be performed by constructing a simple proportional equation

$$\frac{d}{D} = \frac{e}{E} \tag{2.1}$$

where d = distance from one grid intersection to an intermediate point, in ft

D = total distance between grid intersections, in ft

e = elevation change between the same grid intersection and the intermediate point, in ft

E = total elevation change between grid intersections, in ft

Interpolation between Spot Elevations

The sample grid cell in Fig. 2.2 and accompanying calculations illustrate the interpolation process. The change in elevation along side a of the cell is from 97.3 to 95.3 for a total difference of 2.0 ft. Between these two points are the 97.0 and 96.0 elevations, which must be located in order to draw the whole number contours for the cell. The difference in elevation from 97.3 to 97.0 is 0.3 ft. Together with the knowledge that the cell measures 100 ft on each side, three parts of the equation are known. Substituting into the proportional equation the unknown value, which is the distance d from the 97.3 spot elevation to the 97.0 spot elevation, can be calculated.

$$\frac{d}{100} = \frac{0.3}{2.0}$$

$$d \times 2.0 = 0.3 \times 100$$

$$d = \frac{0.3 \times 100}{2.0} = 15.0 \text{ ft}$$

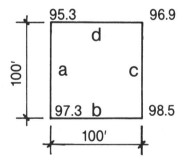

Fig. 2.2. SAMPLE GRID CELL

Measuring 15.0 ft from 97.3 with the appropriate scale will locate the 97.0 elevation along side a.

The difference between 97.3 and 96.0 is 1.3 ft. Substituting into the equation, the distance from the 97.3 spot elevation to the 96.0 spot elevation is 65.0 ft.

$$\frac{d}{100} = \frac{1.3}{2.0}$$
$$d \times 2.0 = 1.3 \times 100$$
$$d = \frac{1.3 \times 100}{2.0} = 65.0 \text{ ft}$$

Note that the distance also could have been determined from the 95.3 spot elevation. The difference in elevation from 95.3 to 96.0 is 0.7 ft, which computes to a distance of 35.0 ft, but now measured from the 95.3 intersection. As a check, the two distances calculated for the 96.0 spot elevation when added together must total the dimension of the side of the grid cell (65.0 + 35.0 = 100.0 ft).

The calculations for the remaining three sides are summarized below and the completed cell is shown in Fig. 2.3.

Side b:

$$98.5 - 97.3 = 1.2 \text{ ft (total elevation change, } E)$$
$$98.5 - 98.0 = 0.5 \text{ ft (elevation change, } e)$$
$$\frac{d}{100} = \frac{0.5}{1.2}$$
$$d = \frac{0.5 \times 100}{1.2} = 41.67 \text{ ft from the 98.5 intersection.}$$

Side c:

$$98.5 - 96.9 = 1.6 \text{ ft } (E)$$
$$98.5 - 98.0 = 0.5 \text{ ft } (e)$$
$$\frac{d}{100} = \frac{0.5}{1.6}$$
$$d = \frac{0.5 \times 100}{1.6} = 31.25 \text{ ft from the 98.5 intersection.}$$
$$98.5 - 97.0 = 1.5 \text{ ft } (e)$$
$$\frac{d}{100} = \frac{1.5}{1.6}$$
$$d = \frac{1.5 \times 100}{1.6} = 93.75 \text{ ft from the 98.5 intersection.}$$

Side d:

$$96.9 - 95.3 = 1.6\,\text{ft}\,(E)$$
$$96.9 - 96.0 = 0.9\,\text{ft}\,(e)$$
$$\frac{d}{100} = \frac{0.9}{1.6}$$
$$d = \frac{0.9 \times 100}{1.6} = 56.25\ \text{ft from the 96.9 intersection.}$$

Rather than calculating each elevation, interpolation may be done graphically as illustrated in Fig. 2.4. Along side b of the grid cell there is a difference in elevation of 1.2 ft. By dividing the side into 12 equal spaces (each space representing 0.1 ft of elevation change), counting either seven spaces from the 97.3 spot elevation or five spaces from 98.5, the 98.0 spot elevation is located. The side of any grid cell may be divided into the desired number of *equal* spaces by placing a scale *at any angle* with the appropriate number of divisions (usually the same as desired number of equal spaces) between perpendicular lines extended from the two end points of the side of the grid cell. From the appropriate point on the scale, a line perpendicular to the side of the grid cell is extended back to the cell, thus locating the desired spot elevation. This is a common technique for graphic proportioning and may be applied to the other three sides of the grid cell.

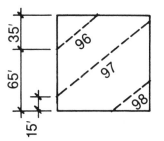

Fig. 2.3. SAMPLE GRID CELL WITH CONTOUR LINES LOCATED.

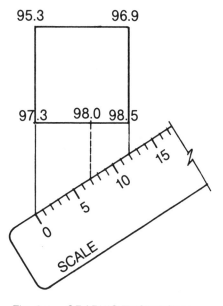

Fig. 2.4. GRAPHIC TECHNIQUE FOR INTERPOLATION.

Figure 2.5 represents the completed grid for the layout illustrated in Fig. 2.1. The process of interpolation may be applied to each of the grid cells to locate all the whole number spot elevations. (The sample grid cell is taken from the northwest corner of the grid.) Connecting the points of equal elevation may be left until the locations of all the whole number elevations have been determined for the entire grid, since contours are usually smooth curves rather than a series of straight line segments. The completed contour plan is shown in Fig. 2.6. Construction lines, including the grid, commonly are not shown on the completed plan. The closed 95 ft contour in Fig. 2.6 is a depression, which is depicted by the use of hachures, as illustrated.

With practice, contour lines can be drawn quite rapidly on a grid, with much of the interpolation done mentally and visually. It should be noted here that computers in conjunction with digitizers and plotters may be used to generate contour plans, thus eliminating the need for tedious calculations or drafting time.

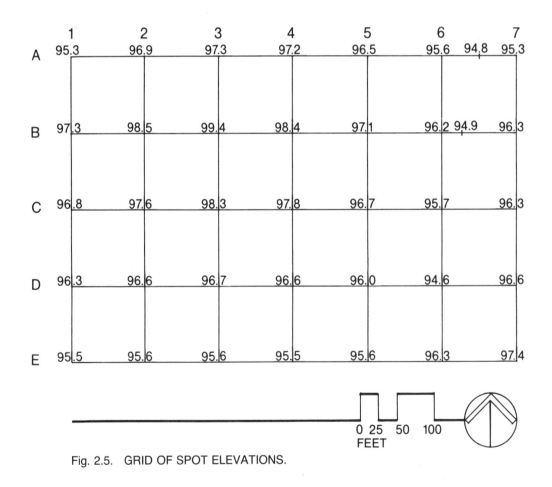

Fig. 2.5.   GRID OF SPOT ELEVATIONS.

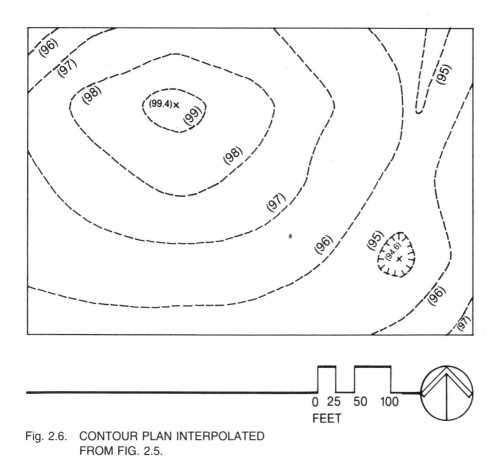

Fig. 2.6.   CONTOUR PLAN INTERPOLATED
            FROM FIG. 2.5.

Interpolation between Contour Lines

Interpolation may also be used to determine the elevation of points between contour lines. The information needed to compute these points includes the contour interval, the total distance between the contour lines, and the distance from one contour line to the point in question. With this information, the difference in elevation from the contour line to the point can be calculated by the following equation:

$$\frac{\text{distance from point to contour line}}{\text{total distance between contour lines}} \times \frac{\text{contour}}{\text{interval}} = \frac{\text{elevation}}{\text{difference}}$$

Example 2.1.   Determine the spot elevation for point A in Fig. 2.7. The contour interval is 1 ft, and the distances are as indicated on the drawing.

Solution   The difference in elevation between point A and the 67 ft contour line is calculated by substituting into the equation

$$\frac{4.0 \text{ ft}}{10.0 \text{ ft}} \times 1.0 \text{ ft} = 0.4 \text{ ft}$$

The spot elevation at point A is then determined by adding the elevation difference to the elevation of the contour line used as the point of reference:

$$67.0 + 0.4 = 67.4 \text{ ft (elevation point } A)$$

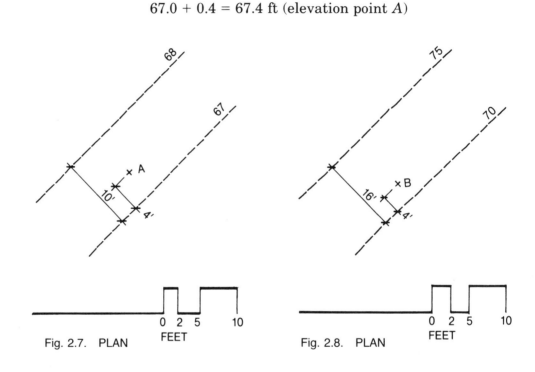

Fig. 2.7. PLAN   Fig. 2.8. PLAN

Example 2.2   Determine the spot elevation for point B in Fig. 2.8. The contour interval is 5 ft, and the distances are as indicated on the drawing.

Solution   Using the same procedure as Example 2.1, the difference in elevation is calculated as follows:

$$\frac{4.0 \text{ ft}}{16.0 \text{ ft}} \times 5.0 \text{ ft} = 1.25 \text{ ft}$$

By adding the difference in elevation to the 70 ft contour line, the spot elevation at point B is determined.

$$70.0 + 1.25 = 71.25 \text{ ft (elevation point } B)$$

Finally it must be emphasized that the interpolation process is valid only if there is a constant slope between two points, whether those points are contours or spot elevations.

CALCULATING SLOPE

Most often, changes in grade are described or discussed in terms of percentage of slope. Describing slope in this manner provides a common basis of understanding for the professionals associated with manipulating and changing the earth's surface, including landscape architects, engineers, and architects. Slope, expressed as percentage, is the number of feet of rise or fall in 100 ft of horizontal distance. In addition to being expressed as a percentage, slope may also be described by a decimal number. For example, a 12% slope may also be called a 0.12 slope but *not* a 0.12% slope. The terms *grade* and *gradient* are commonly used synonymously with slope.

A generalized definition of slope then is the number of feet of fall or rise in a horizontal distance or $S = DE/L$, where S is the slope and DE is the difference in elevation between the end points of a line of which the horizontal or map distance is L (Fig. 2.9). To express S as a percentage, multiply the value by 100.

One problem that commonly arises is realizing that L is measured *horizontally* rather than along the slope. To reinforce this point, it should be remembered from surveying that all map distances are measured horizontally and *not* parallel to the surface of sloping ground.

With the slope formula, three basic computations may be accomplished.

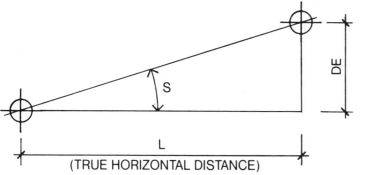

$$S=\frac{DE}{L}$$

DE = DIFFERENCE IN ELEVATION IN FT
L = HORIZONTAL DISTANCE IN FT
S = GRADIENT, EXPRESSED AS PERCENTAGE

Fig. 2.9. DIAGRAM OF SLOPE FORMULA

1. Knowing the elevations at two points and the distance between the points, *slope S* can be calculated.
2. Knowing the difference in elevation between two points and the percentage of slope, the *horizontal distance L* can be calculated.
3. Knowing the percentage of slope and the horizontal distance, the *difference in elevation DE* can be calculated.

The following sample problems illustrate the three basic applications of the slope formula.

Example 2.3   Two spot elevations are located 120 ft apart (measured horizontally). One spot elevation is 44.37 ft, while the other is 47.81 ft. Calculate the percentage of slope S.

Solution   First determine the difference in elevation DE between the spot elevations.

$$DE = 47.81 - 44.37 = 3.44 \text{ ft}$$

Then substitute the known values into the slope formula:

$$S = \frac{DE}{L} \tag{2.2}$$

$$= \frac{3.44}{120.0} = 0.0287 = 2.87\%$$

Example 2.4   Determine the location of the whole number spot elevations (i.e., 45.0, 46.0, 47.0) in the previous problem.

Solution   Since the horizontal distance L is the unknown, the slope formula may be rearranged as follows:

$$L = \frac{DE}{S} \tag{2.3}$$

With S previously determined in Example 2.3, the next step is to calculate the difference in elevation between the known and desired spot elevations and substitute the values into the above equation.

$$DE = 47.81 - 47.00 \ \ = 0.81 \text{ ft}$$
$$L = \frac{0.81}{0.0287} = 28.26 \text{ ft}$$
$$DE = 47.00 - 46.00 = 1.00 \text{ ft}$$
$$= 46.00 - 45.00 = 1.00 \text{ ft}$$
$$L = \frac{1.00}{0.0287} = 34.88 \text{ ft}$$
$$DE = 45.00 - 44.37 = 0.63 \text{ ft}$$
$$L = \frac{0.63}{0.0287} = 21.98 \text{ ft}$$

As a check, the sum of the partial distances should equal 120 ft. (Note that in computing these distances, the value used for S was not rounded.)

$$28.26 + 34.88 + 34.88 + 21.98 = 120.00 \text{ ft}$$

Example 2.5 Determine the spot elevation of a point 40 ft uphill from elevation 44.37. Use the slope calculated in Example 2.3.

Solution Since the difference in elevation DE is the unknown, the equation may be rearranged as follows:

Therefore,
$$DE = S \times L \qquad (2.4)$$

$$DE = 0.0287 \times 40 \text{ ft} = 1.15 \text{ ft}$$

The difference in elevation is then added to 44.37 to determine the desired spot elevation.

$$44.37 + 1.15 = 45.52 \text{ ft}$$

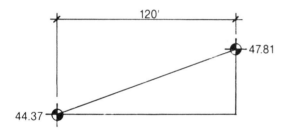

Fig. 2.10. SECTION

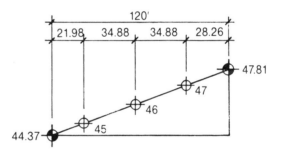

Fig. 2.11. SECTION

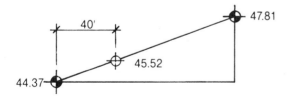

Fig. 2.12. SECTION

SLOPES EXPRESSED AS RATIOS AND DEGREES

Often slopes are expressed as ratios such as 4:1. This means that for every 4 ft of horizontal distance there is a 1 ft vertical change either up or down. On construction drawings, particularly sections, ratios may be shown graphically using a triangle as illustrated in Fig. 2.13a. In expressing ratios, the horizontal number should always be placed first. Conversely, ratios may be expressed by their percentage equivalents. A 4:1 ratio is equivalent to a 25 ft vertical change in 100 ft, or a 25% slope.

Civil engineers and surveyors may express slope in degrees rather than percentage, although this terminology is rarely used by landscape architects. However, the conversion from one system to the other is quite simple, since the slope formula is a basic trigonometric function. The percentage of slope is actually the tangent of the angle of inclination as illustrated in Fig. 2.13b. It should be noted that the rate of change between percentage and degrees is not arithmetically constant. For example, a 100% slope equals 45°, whereas a 50% slope equals 26°34'.

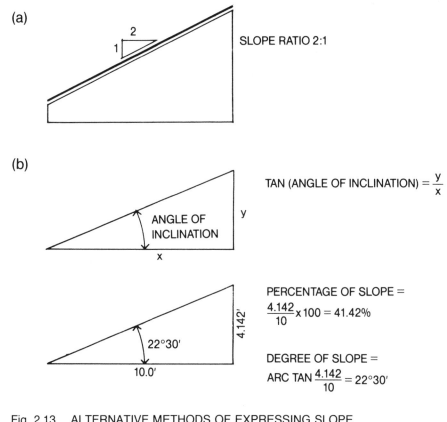

Fig. 2.13. ALTERNATIVE METHODS OF EXPRESSING SLOPE
            a. as a ratio
            b. in degrees

PROBLEMS

2.1.   At a scale of 1 in. = 100 ft plot the following spot elevations on a rectangular grid. The grid cells are 100 ft on each side, and the coordinate letter indicates the row, while the coordinate number indicates the column.

A1 70.2, A2 69.5, A3 69.2, A4 68.0, A5 67.5, A6 65.1
B1 75.8, B2 75.8, B3 74.2, B4 73.8, B5 72.6, B6 73.1
C1 74.9, C2 74.5, C3 73.3, C4 72.1, C5 71.4, C6 70.5
D1 73.8, D2 73.6, D3 72.5, D4 71.9, D5 73.2, D6 72.4
E1 75.0, E2 74.1, E3 73.9, E4 73.8, E5 73.2, E6 72.9

2.2.   Draw contour lines at a 1 ft vertical interval for the grid constructed in Problem 2.1. Analyze the landform represented by the contours and list the landform features which are present.

2.3.   From the scale and contour intervals given here, interpolate the elevations for the points indicated on the contour plans.

(a)

(b)

Problem 2.3.   CONTOUR PLANS

2.4.   At a 3.6% slope, how far down hill is the 47 ft contour line located from a 47.72 spot elevation?

2.5.   Two trees are located 87 ft apart (measured horizontally) on a slope with a 0.04 gradient. If the elevation of the higher tree is 956.58 ft, what is the elevation of the lower tree?

2.6.   The dropoff point at a hospital entrance is 3.2 ft lower than the door elevation.How long must a ramp be to maintain an 8% slope? What is the length of the ramp measured *along the slope*?

2.7.   Two drain inlets are located 140 ft apart, measured horizontally, on a road with a 0.053 gradient. If the elevation of the lower drain is 72.83, what is the elevation of the upper drain?

2.8   Convert the following slopes to ratios:

a. 5%   b. 33%   c. 50%   d. 20%

2.9   Convert the slopes a through d in Problem 2.8 to degrees and minutes.

CHAPTER 3

Slope Formula Application

The purpose of this chapter is to demonstrate, by example, the variety of uses of the slope formula. Several problems are presented, which, in addition to illustrating the mechanics of manipulating the formula, also introduce concepts that are basic to the grading process.

SLOPE ANALYSIS

To determine the best areas for placing buildings, roads, parking lots, and other activities on a particular site, landscape architects often conduct an analysis of the steepness of the terrain. This process, commonly referred to as *slope analysis*, provides information that can be used in conjunction with other considerations such as economics, vegetation, drainage, soils, etc., in making site planning decisions.

In order to conduct a slope analysis on a map, the following information is required: horizontal scale, contour interval, and percentage of slope categories. The scale and contour interval are established by the contour map used for the analysis. The slope categories are selected by the evaluator based on the amount of change in elevation, the complexity of the landforms, and the types of activities to be accommodated. An example of slope categories can be found in the soil classification system of the USDA Soil Conservation Service for land use.

Example 3.1. The task for this problem is to analyze the slopes illustrated by the contour plan in Fig. 3.1. The scale is noted on the figure, and the contour interval is 2 ft. The slope categories are divided into three groups: less than or equal to 5%, greater than 5% but less than 15%, and equal to or greater than 15%. To execute the analysis, the allowable horizontal distance between contours for each slope category must be determined.

Solution For the first category the range is from 0 to 5%. The unknown variable in the slope formula is the distance L, whereas the known variables are the difference in elevation (the contour interval, or 2 ft) and the slope, in this case the range from 0 to 5%. Substituting into the slope formula $L = DE/S$, at 0% the contours must be infinitely far apart, while at 5% the distance between contours equals 40 ft.

$$L = \frac{2.0}{0.05} = 40 \text{ ft}$$

Therefore, any adjacent contours closer than 40 ft represent a slope greater than 5%.

For the next category, greater than 5% and less than 15%, the maximum distance between adjacent contours is the 40 ft already determined by the first category. The minimum distance, or the steepest slope, is determined by substituting the upper limits of the category (15%) into the formula.

$$L = \frac{2.0}{0.15} = 13.3 \text{ ft (or 13 ft)}$$

Thus, slopes ranging from greater than 5% to less than 15% are represented by contours which range from 13 to 40 ft apart. (Due to the small map scale the 13.3 ft may be rounded to 13 ft.)

The third category, slopes equal to or greater than 15%, is represented by adjacent contours that are not more than 13 ft apart.

A simple technique to determine the percentage of slope between contours is to construct a wedge-shaped piece of paper indicating the critical dimensions between slope categories drawn to the proper map scale.

Fig. 3.1. CONTOUR PLAN ▶

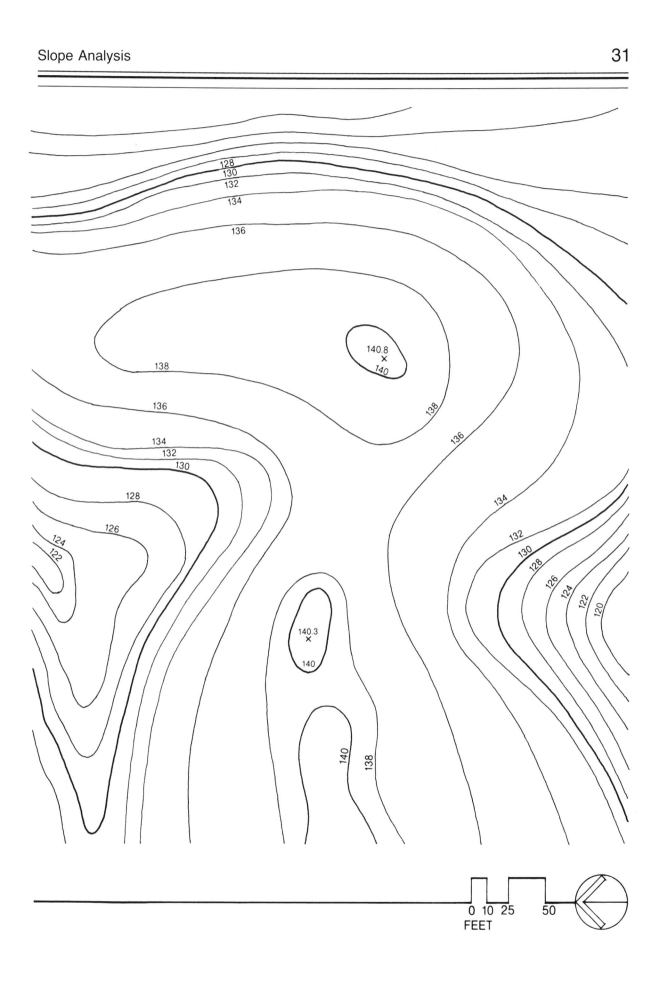

The wedge in Fig. 3.2 is a graphic interpretation of the information illustrated by the scales to the right. By moving the wedge over the contour map, it is easy to determine the distance between adjacent contours and the corresponding slope category. For ease of visualization and evaluation, the slope analysis is usually presented graphically on the topographic map as in Fig. 3.3. It should be noted that computers can be used very effectively to produce slope analysis maps.

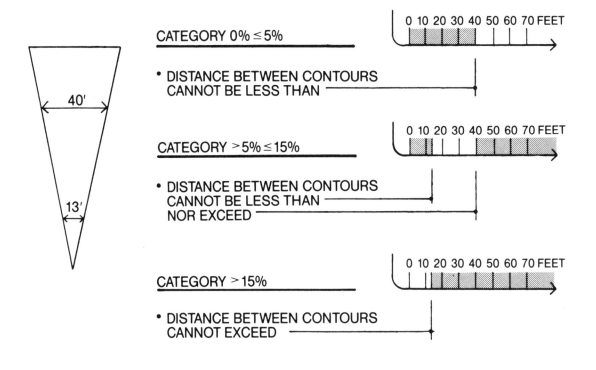

Fig. 3.2. WEDGE AND GRAPHIC SCALES FOR CONDUCTING SLOPE ANALYSIS

Fig. 3.3. GRAPHIC PRESENTATION OF SLOPE ANALYSIS ▶

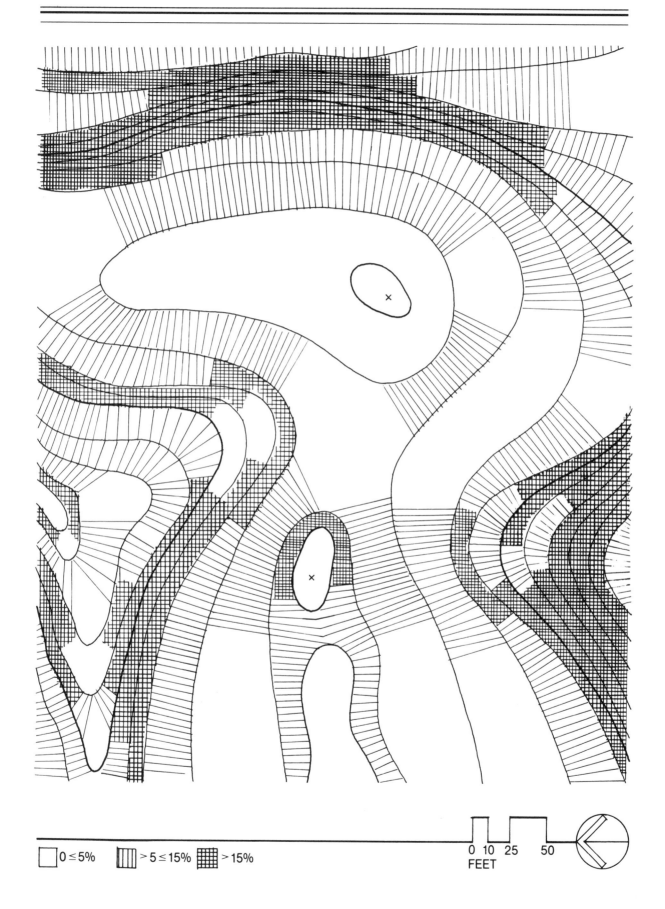

0 ≤ 5%   > 5 ≤ 15%   > 15%

0 10 25   50
FEET

SLOPES FOR SURFACE DRAINAGE

A primary objective in grading, in most instances, is to slope the ground surface away from buildings to insure proper drainage of storm water. Storm water is directed away from buildings to avoid potential leakage into interior spaces, the saturation of soils which reduces bearing capacity, and potential adverse effects of moisture on building materials.

Example 3.2   To illustrate the concept of drainage away from a structure, often referred to as *positive drainage*, the rectangle in Fig. 3.4 represents a building measuring 30 ft by 50 ft. The objective of the problem is to locate and draw the *25* and *26* ft contour lines so that a 3% slope away from the building is achieved. The spot elevations at the exterior corners of the building are as indicated.

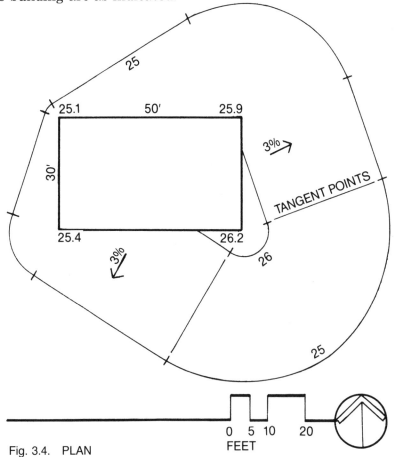

Fig. 3.4. PLAN

Solution   The first step in the solution is to determine the distance from the spot elevations to the whole number contour lines. Along the south face of the building there is a change in elevation from 25.4 to 26.2. Thus a 26.0 ft spot elevation exists between these points and is easily located using the following proportion:

$$\frac{x \text{ (hor. dist. from 26.2 to 26.0)}}{50 \text{ (hor. dist. from 26.2 to 25.4)}} = \frac{0.2 \text{ (elev. change from 26.2 to 26.0)}}{0.8 \text{ (elev. change from 26.2 to 25.4)}}$$

$$\frac{x}{50} = \frac{0.2}{0.8}$$

$$x = \frac{0.2 \times 50}{0.8} = 12.5 \text{ ft}$$

Therefore, the 26.0 ft spot elevation is located 12.5 ft (or ¼ the length of the south face) from the southeast corner.

The same process is applied to the east face, again to locate the 26.0 ft spot elevation.

$$\frac{x \text{ (hor. dist. from 25.9 to 26.0)}}{30 \text{ (hor. dist. from 25.9 to 26.2)}} = \frac{0.1 \text{ (elev. change from 25.9 to 26.0)}}{0.3 \text{ (elev. change from 25.9 to 26.2)}}$$

$$\frac{x}{30} = \frac{0.1}{0.3}$$

$$x = \frac{0.1 \times 30}{0.3} = 10 \text{ ft}$$

As a result, the 26.0 ft spot is located 10 ft, or ⅓ the distance, from the northeast corner.

The next step is to determine the distance that the 26 ft contour line must be located in any direction from the southeast corner in order to fulfill the requirement of a 3% slope away from the building. The known values are $S = 0.03$, and $DE = 0.2$ ft, which may be substituted into the equation $L = DE/S$ or $L = 0.2/0.03$. The computed distance is 6.67 ft or approximately 6.7 ft. An arc with a radius of 6.7 ft is constructed to the proper scale around the southeast corner and lines are drawn tangent to this arc from the previously determined 26.0 ft spot elevations. The 26 ft contour line is now complete.

The same method described above is used to compute the distance from each of the four corners to the 25 ft contour line. These computations are as follows:

$$\text{northeast corner:} \quad \frac{0.9}{0.03} = 30 \text{ ft}$$

$$\text{southeast corner:} \quad \frac{1.2}{0.03} = 40 \text{ ft}$$

$$\text{southwest corner:} \quad \frac{0.4}{0.03} = 13.3 \text{ ft}$$

$$\text{northwest corner:} \quad \frac{0.1}{0.03} = 3.3 \text{ ft}$$

Using these distances as radii, arcs are constructed around the appropriate corners and the 25 ft contour line is completed by connecting the arcs with tangent lines as illustrated in Fig. 3.4.

TERRACE GRADING

Another common grading problem is the construction of relatively level areas, or terraces, on sloping terrain. Most hillside development, whether it be for outdoor living areas, recreation facilities, or circulation systems, requires some form of terracing. In section, terraces may be graded in one of three ways: completely on fill, completely in cut, or partially on fill and partially in cut. Fill is soil that has been added to raise the elevation of the ground, while cut is a surface from which soil has been removed to lower the ground elevation. For further discussion see Chapter 7, particularly Fig. 7.2. The three terrace conditions are illustrated in Fig. 3.5. A grading technique for the first two conditions is explained in the next two examples.

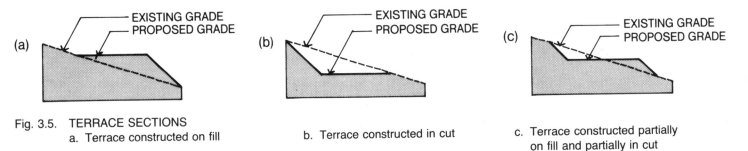

Fig. 3.5.   TERRACE SECTIONS
   a. Terrace constructed on fill   b. Terrace constructed in cut   c. Terrace constructed partially
                                                                                       on fill and partially in cut

Example 3.3   Terrace on Fill   A terrace measuring 25 ft by 40 ft is to be constructed with its south edge at elevation 220.0 as shown in Fig. 3.6. The terrace will slope downward at 3% toward the north for drainage and the side slopes will be graded at a ratio of 3 to 1 (1 ft drop in 3 ft horizontal distance). The purpose for making the side slopes quite steep is to return to the existing grade in the shortest distance possible. This reduces the amount of disturbance caused by grading and reduces cost. From the information provided, draw the proposed contour lines.

Solution   The first step in solving this problem is to determine the elevation along the north, or lower, edge of the terrace. From the equation $DE = S \times L$, the north edge is 0.03×25 ft $= 0.75$ ft lower than the south edge or 219.25 ft (220.0 − 0.75).

The next step is to determine the distance from the north edge of the terrace to the 219 ft contour line. Since the side slopes are to be graded at 3:1, the horizontal distance from the terrace edge to the 219 ft contour line is 0.75 ft as calculated by the following proportion:

$$\frac{x \text{ (horizontal distance from } 219.25 \text{ to } 219.0)}{0.25 \text{ (elevation difference from } 219.25 \text{ to } 219.0)} = \frac{3}{1} \text{ (proposed ratio)}$$

$$x = \frac{0.25 \times 3}{1} = 0.75 \text{ ft}$$

This distance is marked off along lines drawn perpendicular to the terrace at the northeast and northwest corners as shown in Fig. 3.6. (It is advisable to study Figs. 3.6 and 3.7 carefully while following the procedure outlined in the text.) From the point of the 219 ft spot elevation, the remaining whole number spot elevations (i.e., 218, 217, 216, etc.) can be located by progressing along the line in 3 ft increments, since for every 3 ft of horizontal distance there is a 1 ft vertical drop. These points are used for the construction of the proposed contour lines.

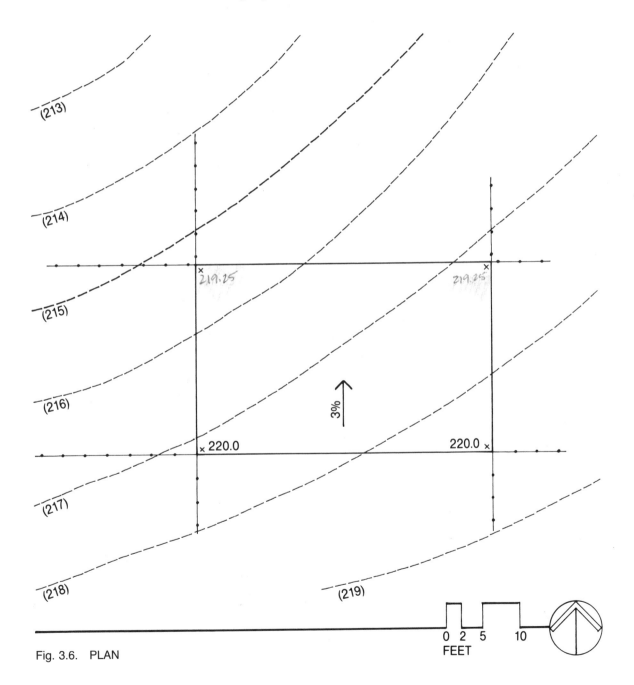

Fig. 3.6. PLAN

The same procedure is followed at the south edge of the terrace where, again, lines are drawn perpendicular to the terrace at the southeast and southwest corners. Since the elevation of the south edge is already at a whole number (220), the remaining whole number spot elevations can be located by progressing out from the edge in 3 ft increments.

Beginning with the 219 ft contour line, draw straight lines through the 219 ft spot elevations until the lines of adjacent sides intersect. The proposed 219 ft contour line is a closed contour, since it never intersects with the 219 ft contour line already existing on the site. Proceeding with the proposed 218 ft contour line and following the same technique, the new 218 ft contour line intersects the existing 218 ft contour line at two points. To continue the proposed contour line beyond the intersection point would result in cut that is unnecessary, since the terrace is entirely on fill. Therefore, the new contour lines are drawn only to the point where they intersect the corresponding existing contour lines. This is the point at which the grade returns to the original or existing ground surface. This is referred to as the point of no fill (or no cut). The procedure is continued for successively lower contour lines (217, 216, 215, etc.) until the point is reached where existing contours are no longer disturbed as shown in Fig. 3.7.

Frequently the points of no fill (or cut) are delineated by a line which also serves as the limit line for the grading contractor's work. Where there is no intersection of existing and proposed contour lines of equal elevation to delineate the no fill (or cut) line easily, a section showing the proposed and existing grade lines may be constructed. The point of no fill (or cut) occurs where the two grade lines intersect.

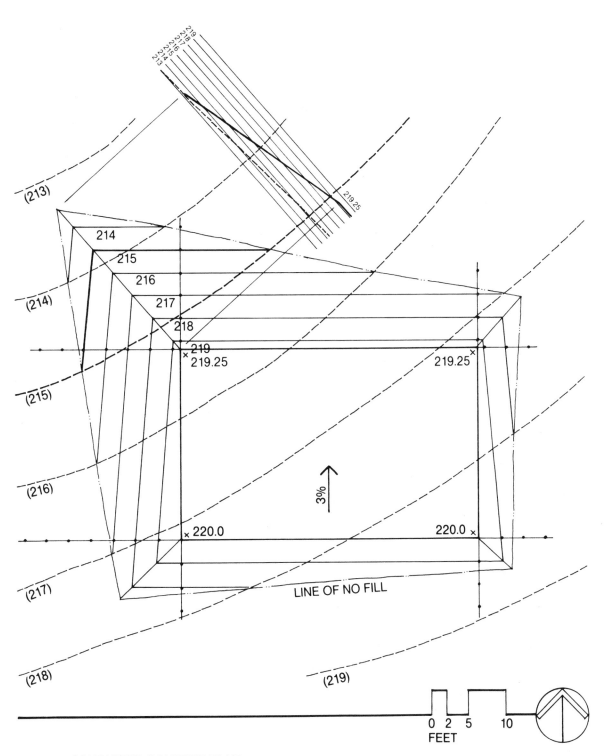

Fig. 3.7. COMPLETED CONTOUR PLAN
The section is used to determine the location of the
no cut-no fill line between contour lines 214 and 213.

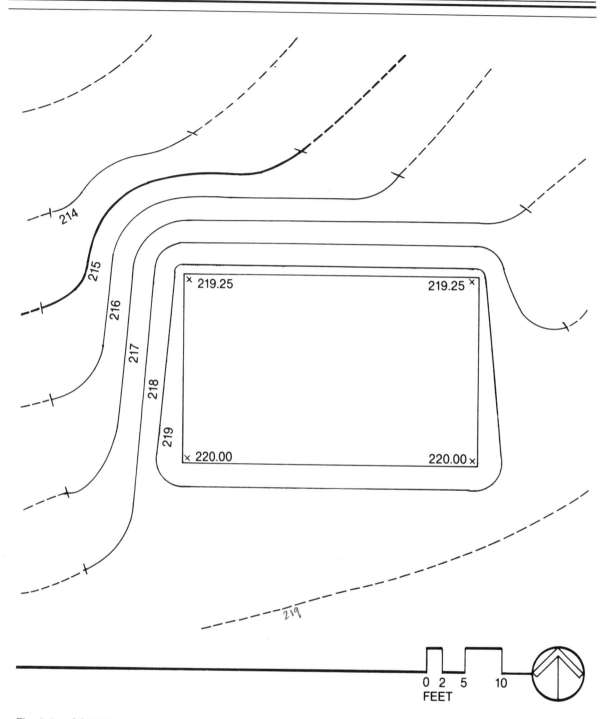

Fig. 3.8.   CONTOUR LINES ADJUSTED TO PROVIDE A SMOOTHER AND MORE
            ROUNDED APPEARANCE

With regard to the shape of the side slopes constructed in this example, two points must be made. First, the side slopes in plan view form planes with distinct intersections. This is difficult to construct and maintain and, within a natural context, usually does not blend well with the surrounding landscape. For these reasons, the contours are given a smoother and more rounded appearance as shown in Fig. 3.8.

The second point pertains to the relationship of the rather steep side slopes to the edge of the terrace and where the side slopes meet existing grade. As constructed there is an abrupt change in grade at the top and bottom of slope as shown in section in Fig. 3.9a. Again, not only is this condition difficult to maintain, it is also subject to erosion, particularly at the top of the slope. An alternative is to provide additional space at the top and bottom of the slope to allow for a smoother transition as illustrated in Fig. 3.9b.

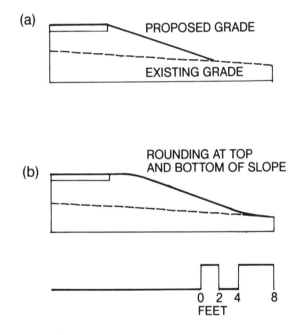

Fig. 3.9. SLOPE SECTIONS
a. Abrupt transition at top and bottom of slope
b. Rounded transition at top and bottom of slope. Note that providing a transition area requires additional horizontal distance.

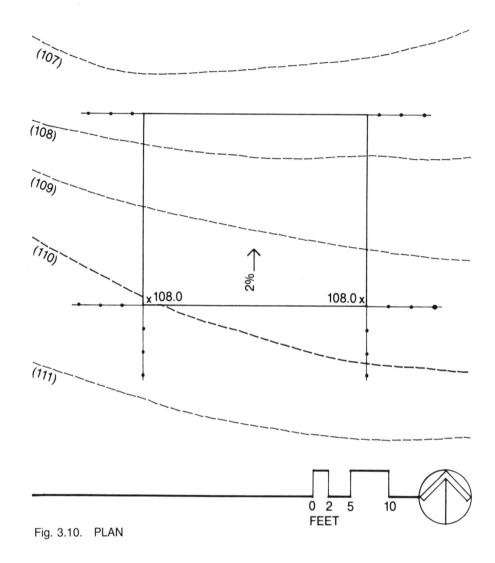

Fig. 3.10. PLAN

Example 3.4 Terrace in Cut A terrace measuring 25 ft by 30 ft is to be built with the southern, or higher, edge at elevation 108.0 ft as shown in Fig. 3.10. The surface of the terrace will slope toward the north at 2%. The proposed side slopes, which are in cut, will have a 3 to 1 slope. From the information given, locate the proposed contour lines.

Solution The procedure for solving this problem is similar to the previous example. First, the elevation of the northern edge of the terrace is determined to be 107.5 ft (0.02 × 25 = 0.5 ft and 108.0 − 0.5 = 107.5

ft). From analyzing the relationship between the existing and proposed elevations, essentially grading is not required along the northern edge, since the proposed and existing grades correspond. Along the southern edge there is between 1.5 and 2.0 ft of cut. This means that the ground must slope uphill from this edge at the proposed 3:1 ratio in order to return to the existing or original grade. The solution is shown in Fig. 3.11.

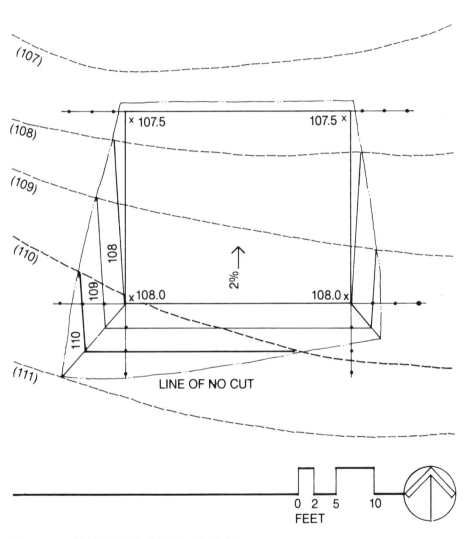

Fig. 3.11 COMPLETED CONTOUR PLAN

PATH LAYOUT WITH A MAXIMUM GRADIENT

Often the design of roads, walks, and paths may not exceed a specified gradient or slope. Slope criteria may be established by building and zoning codes, highways departments, accessibility for the handicapped, or common sense constraints such as climatic conditions and age of anticipated users. The following example illustrates, within a natural landscape, how a path may be designed not to exceed a specified gradient, while at the same time minimizing the amount of grading required.

Example 3.5 In Fig. 3.12 the objective is to construct a path from the road pull-off to the lake dock at a desired maximum slope of 4%. Both the horizontal scale of the plan and the contour interval must be known in order to proceed with the problem. In this example the scale is shown on the figure, and the contour interval is 1 ft. The path begins at point A along the 238 ft contour line.

Solution First, the known values must be substituted into the equation $L = DE/S$ to determine the length of the path between adjacent contours in order to satisfy the 4% criterion.

$$L = \frac{1.0}{0.04} = 25 \text{ ft}$$

By drawing an arc with a radius of 25 ft at the proper scale with point A as its center, two intersection points are obtained along the 237 ft contour line. A line drawn from point A to either of these two points will have a gradient of 4%. Any line drawn within the shaded triangle formed by the two path alternatives will be shorter than 25 ft and, therefore, steeper than 4%. Conversely, lines drawn beyond the boundaries of the triangle will be less than 4%. Selecting one of the previously established points on the 237 ft contour line as the center point, another arc is drawn with a radius of 25 ft. This arc intersects the 236 ft contour line at two points. Deciding which path direction to select is based on a number of considerations, such as overall design intent, views, location of trees, soil stability, etc. Progressing down hill on a contour by contour basis, the entire alignment for the path sloping at 4% may be established.

An alternative to the process described above is to simply take the difference in elevation between point A and the lake dock. By dividing by the desired percentage of slope, the total length of the path is determined. Assuming constant gradients, a path of shorter length will exceed 4%, while a longer path will be less than 4%.

$$238 - 229 = 9 \text{ ft}$$

$$\frac{9}{0.04} = 225 \text{ ft}$$

Thus, any combination of curves and straight lines with a total length of 225 ft and a constant gradient will meet the desired 4% criterion. However, this method does not necessarily relate as well to the natural topography of the land as the first method does.

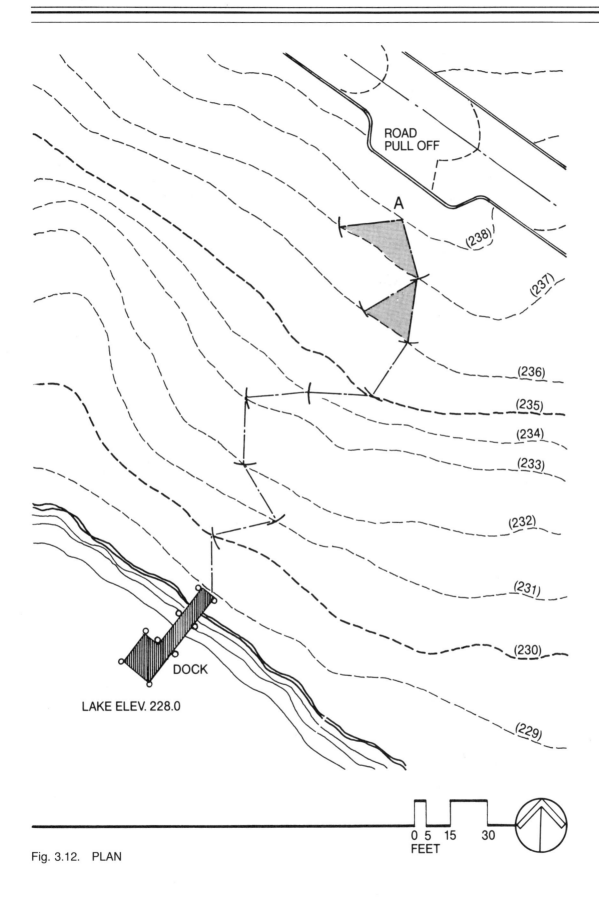

ROAD
PULL OFF

A

(238)

(237)

(236)

(235)

(234)

(233)

(232)

(231)

(230)

DOCK

LAKE ELEV. 228.0

(229)

0 5 15   30
FEET

Fig. 3.12.   PLAN

GRADING A ROAD

A road represents a microcosm of most grading problems found in landscape architecture. These include ridges (crowns), valleys (swales), slopes in two directions (cross pitch), and vertical planes (curbs). Developing the ability to grade a road, and to visualize this process in three dimensions will measurably improve one's understanding of manipulating contours. However, before discussing how to grade a road, it is necessary to define the terminology associated with road construction.

Definitions

Crown. Crown is the difference in elevation between the edge and the center line of a roadway. The primary purpose is to increase the speed of storm runoff from the road surface. A secondary purpose is to separate visually opposing lanes of traffic. Crown height may be expressed in inches or inches per foot. In the latter case, the total crown height is calculated by multiplying half the road width by the rate of change. For example, the crown height for a 24 ft wide road with a crown of ¼ in./ft is 3 in. (12 ft × ¼ in./ft = 3 in.) There are three basic types of road crown sections (Fig. 3.13).

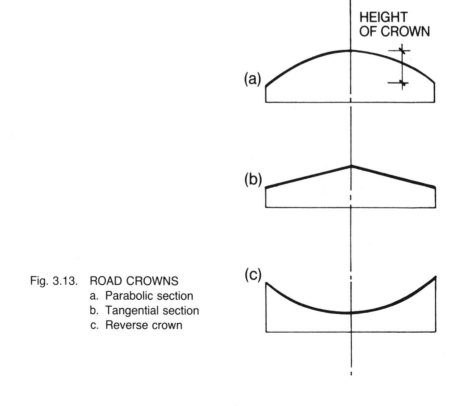

Fig. 3.13. ROAD CROWNS
    a. Parabolic section
    b. Tangential section
    c. Reverse crown

Parabolic Section. A parabolic crown is commonly used in asphalt construction. The change in slope direction at the roadway center line is achieved by a rounded transition. Contour lines point in the downhill direction (similar to a ridge contour signature).

Tangential Section. A tangential crown is most often found with concrete surfaces, since it is easier to form. The centerline of the roadway is visually emphasized due to the intersection of the sloping planes along this line. Again the contour lines point in the downhill direction, but are V-shaped rather than rounded in appearance.

Reverse Crown. A reverse crown may be either parabolic or tangential in section. It is typically used where it is not desirable to direct storm runoff to the edge of the road or in restricted conditions such as urban alleys.

It should be noted that not all roads have crowns. Some roads are cross-sloped; in other words storm runoff is directed from one side of the road to the other. This type of road section is used also to bank road curves to counteract overturning forces (see Chapter 8).

Curb. A curb is a vertical separation at the edge of the roadway. It is usually 6 in. high but may range from as low as 3 in. to as high as 9 in. Curbs are used to direct and restrict storm runoff and to provide safety for pedestrians along the road edge. In addition to vertically faced curbs, beveled or rounded cross-sections may also be used (Fig. 3.14).

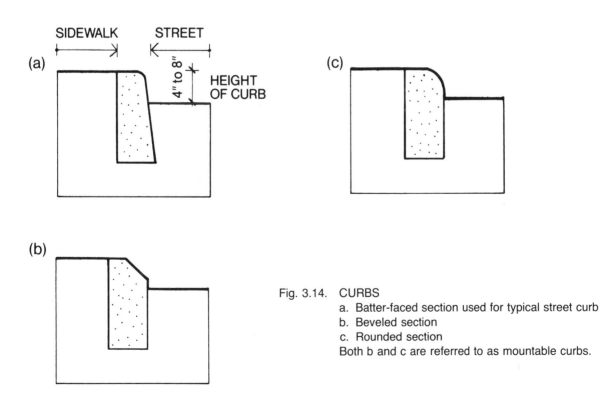

Fig. 3.14.   CURBS
a. Batter-faced section used for typical street curb
b. Beveled section
c. Rounded section
Both b and c are referred to as mountable curbs.

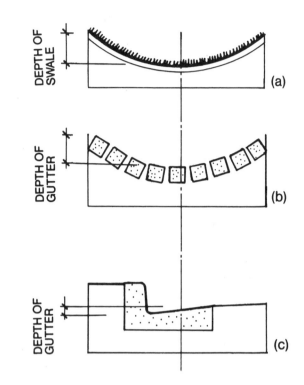

Fig. 3.15.   SWALES AND GUTTERS
a. Vegetated parabolic swale
b. Paved gutter
c. Combination curb and gutter

Swale.   A swale is a constructed or natural drainage channel which has a vegetated surface (usually grass). A *gutter* is a paved swale. The depth of swales (but not necessarily gutters) is usually measured as the difference in elevation between the center line and a point at the edge of the swale on a line taken perpendicular to the center line (Fig. 3.15). Since swales are depressions similar in form to valleys, the contour signatures are also similar. Swales are commonly used to intercept, direct, and control storm runoff and will be discussed in more depth in Chapter 6.

Example 3.6   Figure 3.16 illustrates in plan and section a variety of conditions found in conjunction with road and streets including crown, curb, sidewalk, and swale. From the established spot elevation of 25.42 ft at point A the location of the 25 ft contour line is to be determined based on the following criteria: a 6 in. crown height, a 6 in. curb height, a 4 in. swale depth, a 3% slope parallel to the direction of the street, and a 2% slope across the sidewalk perpendicular to and downward toward the street. The process of locating the 25 ft contour line is explained in this example.

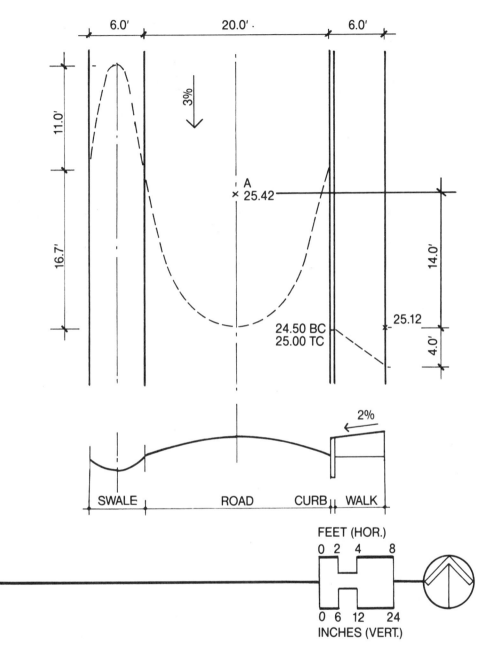

Fig. 3.16. PLAN AND SECTION FOR EXAMPLE 3.6

The first step is to locate the 25.0 ft spot elevation along the road center line. Since the difference in elevation is 0.42 ft and the slope is given at 3%, the distance between 25.42 and the 25.0 spot elevations equals 14.0 ft (0.42/0.03 = 14.0 ft). Based on the stated criteria, the crown height is 6 in. Therefore, the spot elevation at the edge of the road opposite the 25.0 ft spot elevation is 6 in. (0.5 ft) lower than the center line, or 24.5 ft. The 25.0 ft spot elevation at the edge of the road is located uphill from this point. The difference in elevation is 0.5 ft, therefore the distance from 24.5 to 25.0 is 16.7 ft (0.50/0.03 = 16.7 ft).

On the east side of the road, the edge is a 6 in. high curb. This means that the elevation at the top of the curb is always 0.5 ft above the elevation of the edge of the road pavement. Where the edge of the road is elevation 25.0 ft, the top of the curb is 25.5 and, where the road is 24.5 ft, the top of the curb is 25.0. Therefore, the 25.0 ft contour line follows along the face of the curb until it emerges at the 25.0 ft spot elevation as illustrated in plan (Fig. 3.16) and isometric (Fig. 3.17).

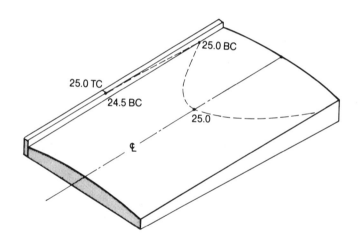

Fig. 3.17. PATH OF CONTOUR LINE ALONG FACE OF CURB

Adjacent to the curb is a sidewalk that slopes toward the road at 2%, while at the same time sloping 3% parallel to the direction of the road. As a result, the far edge of the sidewalk is higher than the edge along the curb. The difference in elevation between the two edges of the walk is the width, 6 ft, multiplied by the slope, 2%, or 0.12 ft. Thus, the elevation at the far edge of the sidewalk directly opposite the 25.0 ft spot elevation at the top of the curb is 25.12 ft. The 25.0 ft spot elevation along this edge is located downhill parallel to the direction of the road at a slope of 0.03. The distance is computed by dividing the difference in elevation, 0.12 ft, by the slope 3% (0.12/0.03 = 4.0 ft). Therefore, the 25.0 ft spot elevation is located 4.0 ft from the 25.12 ft spot elevation in the downhill direction.

The 25 ft contour line is constructed across the sidewalk by connecting the 25.0 ft spot elevation at the top of the curb with the 25.0 ft spot elevation at the edge of the sidewalk.

On the left side of the road is a swale that is 6 ft wide and 4 in. deep. Therefore, the center line of the swale is 4 in. or 0.33 ft lower than the two edges. As a result, where the edge of the road is at elevation 25.0 ft, the elevation at the center line of the swale is 24.67 ft. The 25.0 spot elevation along the swale center line is located by dividing the difference in elevation, 0.33 ft, by the slope of the swale center line, which is the same as that of the road, 3% (0.33/0.03 = 11.0 ft). Measuring 11 ft uphill along the center line from the 24.67 ft spot elevation locates the 25.0 ft spot elevation. The 25 ft contour line is constructed as shown in Fig. 3.16. Note that the crown of the road and the bottom of the swale are indicated by rounded contours which reflect the rounded shape of these elements in section, and both are shown symmetrical about their respective center lines.

Grading by Proportion

Grading a road provides an excellent opportunity for illustrating the use of visual and graphic techniques to locate proposed contour lines. The key to this process is to remember that there is a direct proportional relationship between change in elevation and horizontal distance between contour lines. This is demonstrated in Example 3.6 where a 1.0 ft change in elevation at a 3% slope requires a distance of 33.3 ft. For a 0.5 ft change in elevation only one-half that distance is required, or 16.7 ft, while a 0.33 ft change requires one-third the distance, or approximately 11 ft.

Figure 3.18 outlines a graphic technique which may be used to lay out the contour lines for a symmetrical road crown. Once this technique is fully understood it can be applied to *any* grading situation and can facilitate a quick, visual approach to solving grading problems.

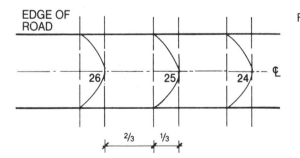

Fig. 3.18. GRAPHIC TECHNIQUE FOR ESTABLISHING CONTOUR LINES FOR CROWNED ROADS
a. Locate whole number spot elevations along road centerline.
b. Express crown height as fraction of a foot (e.g., 6 in. = ½ ft, 4 in. = ⅓ ft).
c. Divide space between whole spot elevations according to fraction
d. Draw smooth curve from spot elevation to where fraction lines cross the edge of the road.

Example 3.7   The final example of this chapter combines several of the points made in previous examples. For this problem only a portion of a proposed road is illustrated in Fig. 3.19. The objective of the problem is to locate and draw the proposed contour lines with a 1 ft interval according to the given criteria and to connect the corresponding proposed and existing contour lines where appropriate. The design criteria are as follows: a 4% slope toward the south parallel to the direction of the road, a 4 in. crown height, a 6 ft wide swale along the west edge of the road, 6 in. deep and also sloping at 4%; a 6 ft wide shoulder along the east edge that slopes at 2% perpendicular to and away from the road; and side slopes perpendicular to the center line of the road at a ratio of 3 to 1 in cut and fill. The spot elevation at point *A* has been established as 69.0 ft.

Solution   The first step is to locate the whole number spot elevations along the road center line. From the equation $L = DE/S$ the distance required for a 1.0 ft change in elevation at 4% is 25 ft. Spot elevations 68.0, 67.0, and 66.0 are marked off along the center line at 25 ft intervals. Because of the crown, points on both edges of the road on a line perpendicular to the center line, will be 4 in., or 0.33 ft, lower than a point at the center. Thus, each whole number spot elevation at the edge will be located 8.25 ft in the uphill direction from the same elevation at the center of the road. This distance was calculated by dividing the difference in elevation, 0.33 ft, by the slope, 4% 0.33/0.04 = 8.25 ft. From this information spot elevations 69.0, 68.0, 67.0, and 66.0 can be located on both edges of the road.

By examining the existing grades and the proposed spot elevations, it is determined that the west edge of the road is in cut and the east edge is in fill. The swale that has been proposed along the west edge is necessary in order to intercept the storm runoff from the cut slope. The swale is 6 in. (0.50 ft) deep, which means that a point on the center line of the swale is 0.50 ft lower than the edge of the road. Each whole foot spot elevation along the swale center line is 12.5 ft uphill from the corresponding elevation at the road edge (0.50/0.04 = 12.5 ft). The whole foot spot elevation along the far edge of the swale is opposite the whole foot spot elevation at the edge of the road.

A 6 ft wide shoulder, which slopes away from the road, is proposed along the east edge. The far edge of the shoulder is 0.12 ft *lower* than the edge of the road. This is determined by multiplying the slope by the shoulder width (0.02 × 6 ft = 0.12 ft). Again, the whole foot spot elevation at the edge of the shoulder must be located in the uphill direction from the whole foot spot elevation at the edge of the road. The distance uphill is calculated by dividing the difference in elevation, 0.12 ft, by the slope, 4%, which equals 3.0 ft.

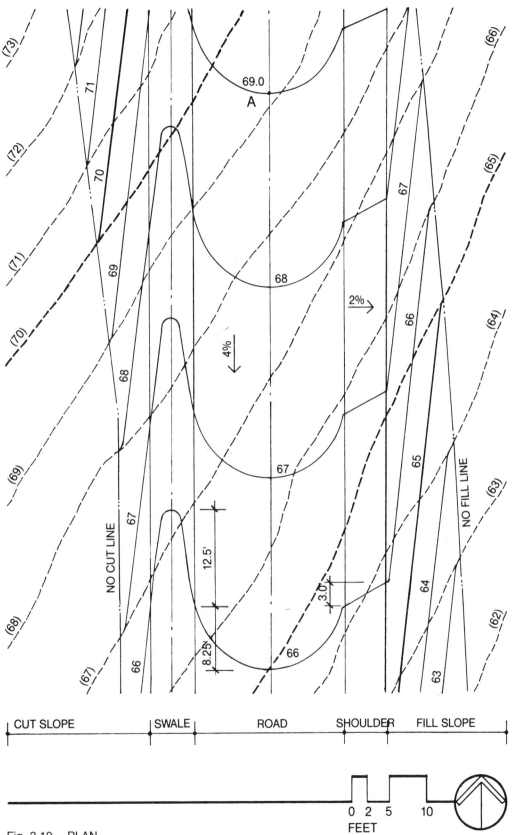

Fig. 3.19.   PLAN

The 3 to 1 side slopes begin at the outside edges of the swale and the shoulder. Using a method similar to that in Example 3.3, lines are drawn perpendicular to the road center line through the full foot spot elevations at the outside edges of the swale and the shoulder. Beginning at the respective edges, points are located at 3 ft intervals along the lines, since each 3 ft horizontal distance results in a 1 ft change in elevation. The proposed contour lines are located by connecting all the points of equal elevation determined in each of the previous steps. The proposed contour lines are drawn to the point where they intersect the corresponding existing contour lines. This is the point of no cut or fill, since beyond this point the existing contour line does not change.

VISUALIZING TOPOGRAPHY FROM CONTOUR LINES

Occasionally, it may be somewhat confusing to interpret contour maps or to construct new contour lines for proposed grading projects. One of the most common problems among students is drawing contour lines in the proper direction for proposed crowns, curbs, and swales. The following simple technique provides a visual aid in these situations.

By turning the plan so that the viewer is looking in the downhill direction (i.e.,the higher elevations are closer to the eye than the lower elevations), the proposed contour lines if drawn correctly resemble the proposed profile, i.e., a cross-section with an exaggerated vertical scale. Using Fig. 3.19 as an example, turn the page so that the plan is viewed from the north. Following the proposed 67 ft contour line, it can be seen that the contour plan of each of the proposed components reflects its respective cross-section: the swale looks like a valley, the crown looks like a ridge, and the shoulder slopes away from the road. The existing contour slopes down toward the swale on the right (west) indicating cut, and slopes away from the shoulder on the left (east) indicating fill.

PROBLEMS

3.1.   In each of the two drawings, a plane sloping at 2% has been placed on existing topography. Provide the missing spot elevations, plot all proposed contour lines, and connect them to the existing contour lines. All cut and fill side slopes are to be graded at 4 to 1.

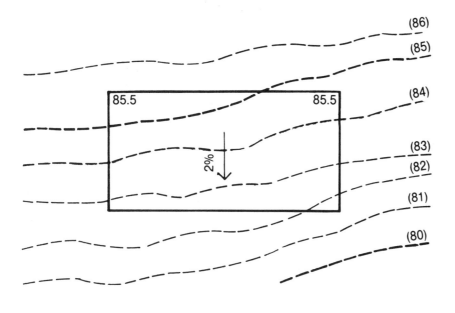

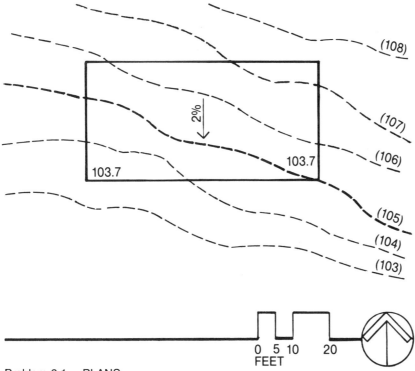

Problem 3.1   PLANS

3.2.   Draw the proposed contour lines at 1 ft intervals for the four road conditions illustrated below.

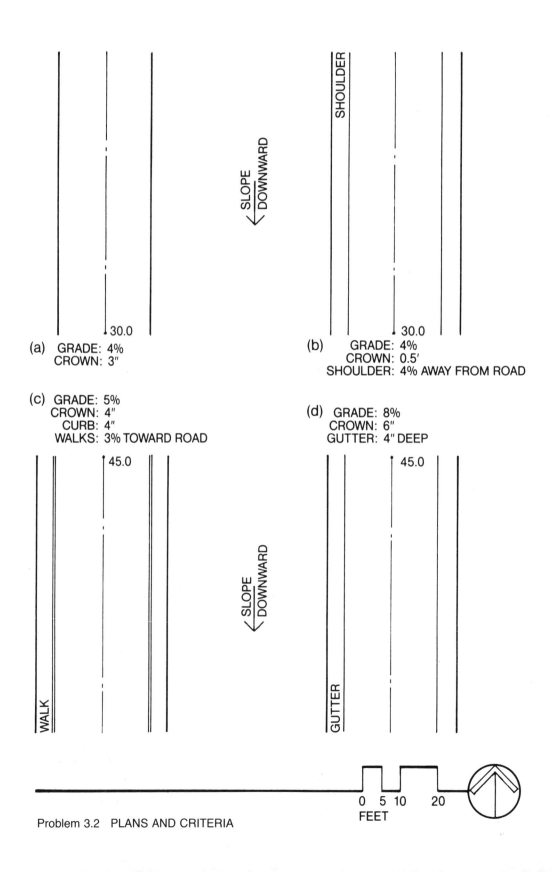

(a) GRADE: 4%
     CROWN: 3"

(b) GRADE: 4%
     CROWN: 0.5'
     SHOULDER: 4% AWAY FROM ROAD

(c) GRADE: 5%
     CROWN: 4"
     CURB: 4"
     WALKS: 3% TOWARD ROAD

(d) GRADE: 8%
     CROWN: 6"
     GUTTER: 4" DEEP

Problem 3.2 PLANS AND CRITERIA

3.3.   For the two road plans provided, draw the proposed contour lines at 1 ft intervals according to the criteria given and connect the proposed and existing contour lines where appropriate.

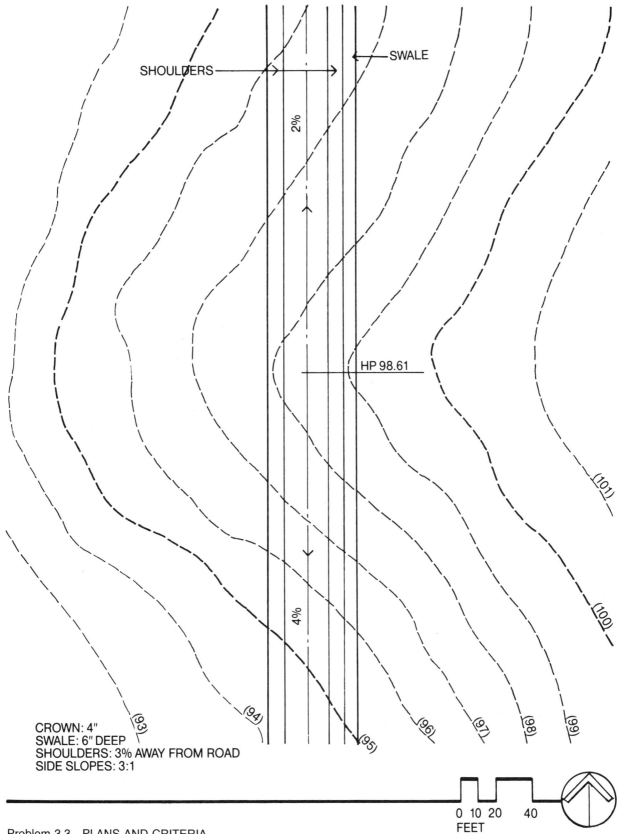

CROWN: 4"
SWALE: 6" DEEP
SHOULDERS: 3% AWAY FROM ROAD
SIDE SLOPES: 3:1

0 10 20   40
FEET

Problem 3.3   PLANS AND CRITERIA

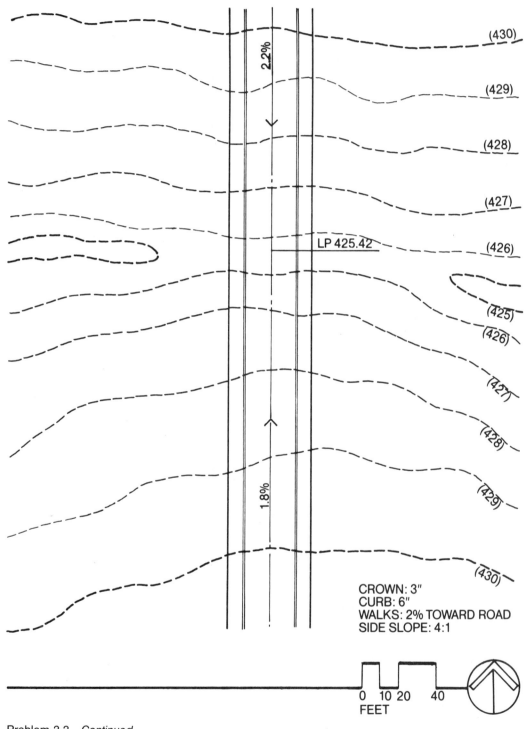

CROWN: 3"
CURB: 6"
WALKS: 2% TOWARD ROAD
SIDE SLOPE: 4:1

0   10 20   40
FEET

Problem 3.3   *Continued*

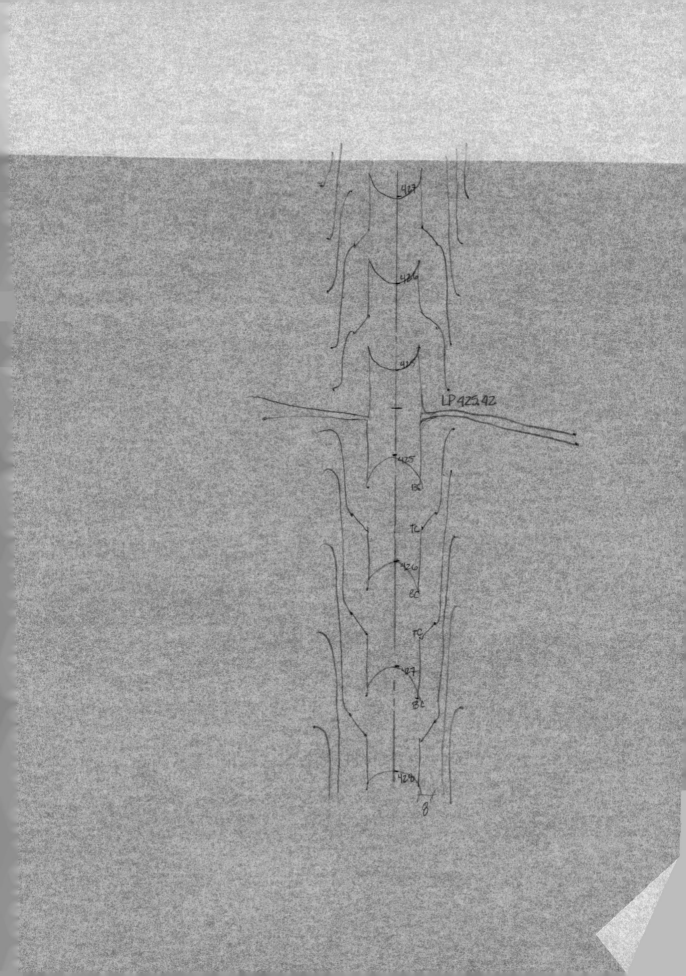

CHAPTER 4

Grading Constraints

The problems presented in the last chapter were highly structured, since all grading criteria such as proposed spot elevations, slopes, crown and curb heights, etc., were provided. However, grading is more than a mechanical process dictated by a predetermined set of criteria. Designing an appropriate grading scheme is a decision-making process based on a variety of constraints and opportunities.

The grading process must be viewed as a response to program concerns, design intent, and contextual conditions. The latter consist primarily of the existing physical conditions and the regulations that govern the development of a site. These establish the framework within which the program and design concept may be formulated. In turn, all three elements (program, site, and intent) create constraints that guide the decision-making process.

Although difficult to classify neatly, constraints may be placed in two broad categories: environmental and functional. Environmental constraints are those that deal with the natural conditions of the site. Functional constraints relate to the requirements of the activities that must be accommodated and other restrictions including laws and regulations such as building and zoning codes. The following discussion examines each of the categories in more detail.

ENVIRONMENTAL CONSTRAINTS

Topography

The most obvious constraint is the existing topography. The existing landform should be analyzed carefully in order to guide the design of the proposed development. High and low points should be located, percentages of slope inventoried, and extent of relatively level and steep areas determined. Coordinating the proposed grading with the existing conditions, in most cases, will reduce development costs and result in a more desirable final product.

59

Drainage

It is difficult to separate the act of grading from the act of accommodating and controlling storm water runoff, since one directly affects the other. This section briefly discusses storm drainage as a grading constraint. A more complete discussion of storm runoff and drainage systems is presented in Chapter 6.

A good rule of thumb to follow in order to reduce impacts and potential problems is to conform as closely as possible to the established natural, as well as constructed, drainage pattern within the proposed development. Before conforming, however, it is important to evaluate the existing system to determine whether it is functioning correctly both ecologically and hydraulically and whether it has the capacity to absorb any anticipated changes. Hydrologic problems that result from changes in the character of the environment have been well documented. Increased use of impervious surfaces such as pavements and roofs, channelization of streams, and floodplain encroachment, particularly in urban and suburban areas, have lowered water tables, increased the fluctuation of water levels in streams, ponds, and wetlands, and increased potential flood hazards. The impacts of these problems are also obvious. Flooding is a threat to safety, health, and personal well-being, while lowering the water table directly affects water supply. Fluctuation of water levels will have an impact on plant and animal habitats, since such conditions require a high degree of tolerance to ensure survival. Acknowledging and understanding these problems will lead to a more sensitive handling of storm water runoff.

Vegetation

Disturbing the earth around existing vegetation generally has a detrimental effect on the health of plants. The impacts are often not readily apparent. There have been instances where architects and landscape architects have developed areas quite close to specimen trees. The photographs taken immediately after completion of the project provided an excellent and sensitive impression, but the reality of the design became apparent 2 or 3 years later when the dead trees were removed. Although not necessarily assuring survival, protection of existing plant material is best accomplished by avoiding grade changes within the drip line of the plants. Cutting soil within the drip line removes surface roots, while filling within the same area reduces the amount of air available to the root system. The consequence of any changes will depend on the plant species and soil conditions.

Protective systems, as illustrated in Fig. 4.1, may be used where it is

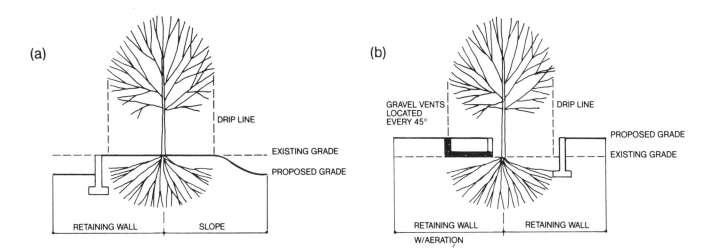

Fig. 4.1. GRADE CHANGES AT EXISTING TREES
    a. For cut conditions either a slope or retaining wall can be used beyond the drip line to attain the desired grades.
    b. In fill situations a retaining wall can be placed beyond the drip line or within the drip line if proper aeration measures, such as gravel vents, are provided.
    c. A wood retaining wall used to protect a tree in a fill condition.

necessary to change the elevation around existing vegetation, particularly trees. However, these systems increase the cost of a project and still do not guarantee plant survival. A better approach is to develop a grading system that minimizes these types of disturbances.

Existing vegetation may also be affected by changes in drainage patterns. Directing storm runoff to areas that are normally dry, draining areas that are typically wet, or lowering the water table alter the environmental conditions to which plants have adapted. These alterations may cause severe physiological stress and result in a change in the plant community that inhabits the area.

Soils

In any building process, it is important to understand the nature of the construction material used. In the case of grading, the construction material is soil. For landscape architects some knowledge of its engineering, as well as edaphological and pedological properties is necessary, since soil is used both as building material and growing medium. Properties such as bearing capacity, angle of repose, shear strength, permeability, erodibility, frost action potential, pH level, and organic content establish the capabilities and limitations of a soil. As part of the preliminary planning process for any major project, an investigation of the soil and geologic conditions must be conducted and an engineering report prepared by qualified professionals. Such a report will help determine the feasibility of a project and will form the basis for structural design decisions. Even for small-scale projects, it is advisable to consult a soils or foundation engineer, particularly if poor or unfamiliar soil conditions are anticipated.

Bearing Capacity. Bearing capacity refers to the size of the load, usually expressed as pounds per square foot, which a soil is able to support. Hard, sound rock has the highest bearing capacity, while saturated and organic soils have the lowest. If the bearing capacity of an existing soil cannot support the proposed load or structure, the soil must be removed and replaced with suitable material, or other engineering measures must be taken. Such measures include piles, spread footings, floating slabs, etc.

Angle of Repose. This is the angle at which an unconsolidated soil will naturally slope. The angle varies with the soil grain size, grain shape, and moisture content. To maintain stability, cut or fill slopes should not exceed this angle, or slippage of the soil may occur.

Permeability. Permeability pertains to the ease with which water can flow through soil or any other material. The permeability of a soil is one of the factors that directly affects the design of a storm drainage system. Where permeability is high, and the infiltration capacity of the soil is sufficient, water easily penetrates the soil, and the amount of storm runoff is relatively low unless the soil is saturated. Where permeability is low, the volume of runoff is higher, and the design of the drainage system becomes a more critical concern. Ecologically, it is good practice to maintain as much permeable surface on a site as possible. This not only maintains the level of the water table, but also normally results in lower site development costs.

Soil permeability also affects the location and design of septic systems and the need for, and method of, dewatering excavations during construction.

Shear Strength. Shear strength determines the stability of a soil and its ability to resist failure under loading. Shear strength is a result of internal friction and cohesion. Internal friction is the resistance to sliding between soil particles, while cohesion is the mutual attraction between particles due to moisture content and molecular forces. Under typical conditions, sand and gravel are considered cohesionless. Clay soils, on the other hand, have high cohesion but little internal friction. As a general rule, the slopes for cohesive soils require flatter angles as the height of the slope is increased. Due to their internal friction, the shear strength of sand and gravel increases in relation to increased normal pressure; therefore, the angle of slope does not decrease with increased height.

Slope failure occurs when shear stress exceeds shear strength. The reasons for failure are either increased stress or decreased strength brought about naturally or induced by human activity. Examples of increased stress are increasing the load at the top of a slope or removing the lateral support at the base of a slope through excavation or erosion. Decreased strength, as well as increased stress will occur when the moisture content of the soil is increased. In conclusion, care must be taken when developing at the top or bottom of relatively large slopes and particular attention must be given to the handling of storm water runoff.

Erodibility. All soils are susceptible to erosion. This is especially true during the construction process, since stabilizing surface material such as vegetation is removed and soils become unconsolidated due to excavating and scraping. Erosion not only results in the loss of soil but also causes problems by depositing the soil in undesirable places such as lakes, ponds, and catch basins. Many communities now require the submission of a soil erosion and sedimentation control plan prior to the start of construction. The plan indicates the temporary control measures to be taken during construction and often includes the permanent measures that will remain once construction has been completed. An extremely important step is to strip and stockpile properly the existing topsoil layer in order to prevent unnecessary loss of this important resource. After regrading has been completed, the topsoil can be replaced on the site.

Topographic factors influencing erosion are the degree and length of slopes. The erosion potential increases as either or both of these factors increase. Knowing the erosion tendency of a soil, therefore, will influence the proposed grading design by limiting the length and degree of slope.

Frost Action. In northern climates silty soils and soils with a wide, fairly evenly distributed range of particle sizes, referred to as a well-graded soil, are subject to frost action. Soils that exhibit these characteristics will influence footing and foundation design for structures and base course design for pavements. Two problems associated with frost action are soil expansion, which occurs during freezing, and soil saturation, which occurs during thawing.

Organic and Nutrient Content and pH Level. Tests to determine the nutrient and organic content and pH are performed to assess the ability of a soil to support plant growth, since slope stabilization is often achieved through vegetative means. If the chemical condition of the soil prevents vegetation from becoming established, erosion will occur. By knowing the pH, nutrient level and the amount of organic matter, corrective steps can be easily taken to improve the growing environment.

FUNCTIONAL CONSTRAINTS

Functional constraints have been broadly interpreted to include not only the limitations resulting from the uses that must be accommodated, but factors such as maintenance, economics, and existing restrictive conditions.

Restrictive Conditions

The first set of functional constraints is determined by legal controls and physical limitations. Property lines establish legal boundaries beyond which a property owner does not have the right to modify or change existing conditions. Therefore grades along property lines cannot be altered and thus become a controlling factor. In urban situations where land is expensive and sites are relatively small, costly grade change devices may be necessary along property lines to maximize the usability and development potential of a site.

In addition to prohibiting physical change, it is usually illegal to increase the rate of flow of storm water runoff from one property to adjacent properties. To be in compliance, the rate of runoff after completion of construction must not exceed the rate prior to construction.

Most design projects come under the jurisdiction of a political authority, whether it be at the municipal, state, or federal level, and usually must comply with a variety of building and zoning code regulations. In order to obtain permits, approvals, and certificates of occupancy, it is necessary to meet the criteria and standards set by these regulatory authorities. Items that typically may be regulated include maximum allowable cross slope for public sidewalks, maximum height of street curbs, acceptable riser/tread ratios for stairs, maximum number of stair risers without an intermediate landing, maximum slope for handicapped ramps, slope protection, drainage channel stabilization, retention ponds, vegetative cover, etc. Before starting a project, the designer should become familiar with all applicable regulations.

Existing as well as proposed structures establish controls that affect grading design. Door entrances and finished floor elevations must be met, window openings may limit the height of grades, and structural conditions may limit the amount of soil that can be retained or back-filled against a building. The ability to waterproof or not waterproof a particular structure may determine whether soil can be placed against it. The response to these various conditions will influence the form of the grading design.

Utility systems, particularly those that flow by gravity or gravity-induced pressure such as storm drainage, domestic water supply, and sanitary sewers, established additional criteria that may control the grading process. If a proposed storm drainage system is connected to an existing system, then obviously the elevation of the existing system cannot be higher than proposed system at the point of connection or pumping stations will be required. To prevent this from occurring, it is wise to work back from the known elevation at the outlet when establishing grades along the new drainage system. Also, the capacity of the existing system, including pipes and swales, must be evaluated to determine if additional storm runoff can be accommodated. Domestic water and sanitary sewer connections also may require pumping if the required flow cannot be achieved naturally by gravitational pressure.

Activities and Uses

The two most prevalent uses that must be accommodated by grading are buildings and circulation systems. Typically, these create the most difficult problems and the most limiting constraints that must be dealt with in the grading process. In a holistic sense, the placement of buildings in the landscape and the resultant pedestrian and vehicular access patterns should work in concert with each other as well as with the natural and cultural context in which they are placed. This has not always been the case.

Quite often the decision to locate a building is based on a singular criterion such as zoning setbacks, initial cost, or view from the site, without a complete understanding of how this placement will affect the construction of roads, parking areas, and walks. The criterion may be achieved, but at the expense of increased construction costs, high visual and/or natural impacts, user inconvenience, and increased long-term maintenance costs.

The reverse condition is also common. The grid street patterns of many North American cities were plotted with little regard for existing natural and topographic features. The consequences have been the loss of landscape character and uniqueness and the development of a rather homogenized environment. There are exceptions, San Francisco perhaps being the most noteworthy. San Francisco serves not only as an example of lack of coordination between development and environment, it also serves as an excellent example of contradiction and happenstance. If the city were laid out according to current environmental principles, it may have been denied the charm, drama and attraction it displays today. The lesson to be learned here is that all principles, even those described in this text, must be viewed as guidelines. A successful designer applies these principles with flexibility and even knows when it is appropriate to bend or break the rules.

Fitting buildings into the landscape is related to the type of structural foundation, method of construction, and ultimately the form of the architecture employed. There are three general types of structural foundations: slab, continuous wall, and pole (Fig. 4.2). A *slab* foundation forms a horizontal plane with a relatively thin profile which results in the least amount of grading flexibility. Depending on the length of the building, slopes up to 3% may typically be achieved along the building face. A *continous wall* foundation forms a line that provides for a moderate degree of flexibility. Depending on the height of the foundation wall,

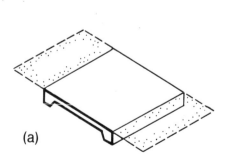

(a)

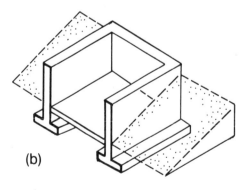

(b)

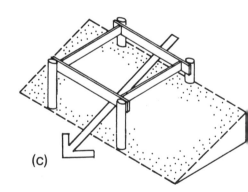

(c)

Fig. 4.2. FOUNDATION SYSTEMS   a. Slab
                                 b. Continuous wall
                                 c. Pole

grade changes of a story or more may be achieved. *Pole*, or pier, construction provides the greatest amount of grading flexibility and potentially the least amount of grading impact, since there is a minimum amount of ground disturbance. This technique uses poles or piers as the primary method of transferring the structural load to the ground. The poles form points rather than lines where they meet the ground and the building is placed above the landscape, thus allowing drainage to continue uninterrupted. This normally reduces the amount of grading required to redirect storm runoff around structures.

The method of connection between the foundation and the wall system, and the material composition of the wall may also create grading constraints. As illustrated in Fig. 4.3a, soil should not be placed directly against wood frame construction. To reduce moisture problems an 8 in. space is recommended as a minimum between the wood frame and the exterior grade. It should be noted that pressure-preservative-treated lumber may come in contact with soil, but usually this material is used for conditions and purposes other than wood frame construction detailing. Concrete and masonry when properly waterproofed will allow somewhat more flexibility in varying the exterior grade. This is particularly true when the foundation and wall are an integral system as indicated in Fig. 4.3c.

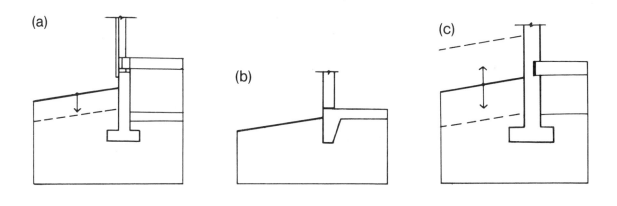

Fig. 4.3. EXTERIOR WALL DETAILS
   a. Standard wood frame construction places wood floor joists on top of a concrete foundation and the exterior siding material extends below the joist/foundation connection. The grade at the foundation should be at least 8 in. below the siding material. If a continuous wall foundation is used, there is obviously some flexibility downward with the grades.
   b. Walls are normally constructed directly on slab foundations. Since it is very difficult to waterproof this connection, this condition offers the least amount of flexibility.
   c. Where the exterior wall forms a continuous plane uninterrupted by floor connections, greater grading flexibility, both up and down, can be achieved.

At the risk of considerable oversimplification, architectural design may be categorized as either flat-site buildings or sloping-site buildings with respect to grading. Flat-site buildings are characterized by the fact that there is relatively little change in grade from one side of the building to the opposite side. Sloping-site buildings, on the other hand, attempt to accommodate any existing changes in topography by stepping or terracing the structure with the slope. Each building type is appropriate when used in the proper context. However, an example of an actual case where these simple building-site relationships have been disregarded either through oversight or by the establishment of other functional or esthetic priorities is illustrated in Fig. 4.4. In this situation, a three-story townhouse complex with garages on the first level was placed on a sloping parcel of land. Entrances to the garages were placed at the rear of the units, which went against the slope and required additional excavation. This decision may have been based on esthetic concerns by placing the garage doors behind the units out of view from the street and creating the traditional image of a large green lawn in front of the units. Alternatively, if the garage doors had been placed at the front of the units, less excavation would have been necessary, more of the existing vegetation could have been preserved, and a private area could have been provided at the back of each unit at the second floor level, thus allowing the building to step with the site. This example also illustrates that grading and design are an integral process and that the decision-making process may result in trade-offs or compromises.

Often the framework for building placement and development is established by street patterns. There are three basic ways in which street layout is related to topography. The first is to locate the street parallel to the contours. As indicated in Fig. 4.5, buildings placed parallel to the road create obstacles, or dams, for the natural drainage pattern since there is little pitch in the longitudinal direction. To compensate for this obstruction the proposed grading must direct the storm water runoff around the buildings. The section that normally results from this arrangement is a terraced condition formed by cutting on the uphill side and filling on the downhill side. The advantage of this layout is that it normally results in easy access between circulation system and building.

The second way is to locate the street perpendicular to the contours. Since the most common practice is to place the long axis of the building parallel to the street, the task of directing storm water around the structure is made somewhat easier by this configuration. However, three potential problems arise from this arrangement. The first is that the gradient of the road may be excessive, since the steepest slope occurs perpendicular to the contours. The second is the awkward relationship that may result at access points from the street, since paths or drives placed perpendicular to the direction of the road must be cross-sloped.

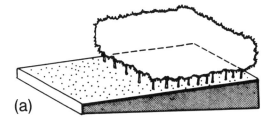

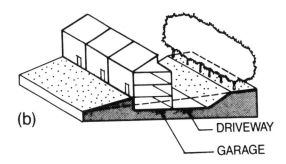

Fig. 4.4.   RELATIONSHIP OF BUILDING TO TOPOGRAPHY
a. Wooded, sloping site prior to construction
b. Site as constructed, creating a valley across the slope
c. An alternative site design that reduces the amount of excavation and preserves more of the wooded area

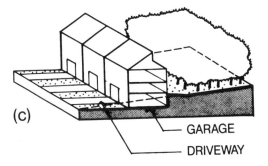

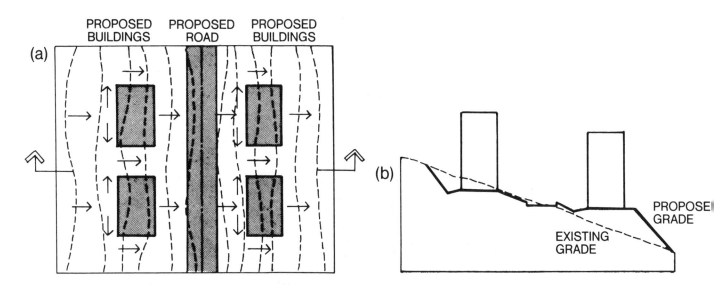

Fig. 4.5.   ROAD AND LONG AXIS OF BUILDINGS PLACED PARALLEL TO CONTOURS
a. Plan indicating the proposed drainage pattern
b. Section indicating the typical terrace conditions for this configuration

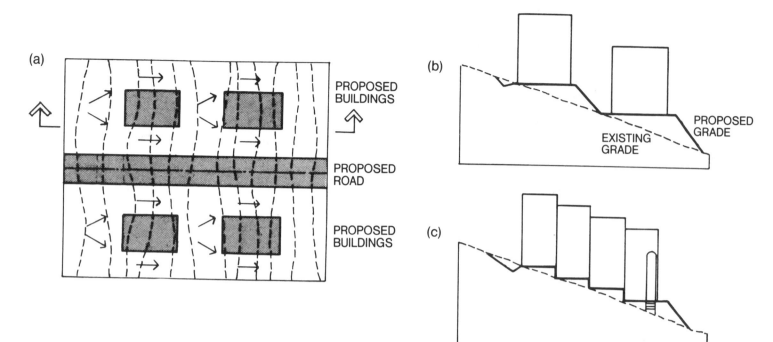

(a)

PROPOSED
BUILDINGS

PROPOSED
ROAD

PROPOSED
BUILDINGS

(b)

EXISTING
GRADE

PROPOSED
GRADE

(c)

Fig. 4.6.   ROAD AND LONG AXIS OF BUILDINGS PLACED PERPENDICULAR TO
CONTOURS.
   a. Plan indicating proposed drainage pattern
   b. Section indicating stepped terraces
   c. Section indicating stepped buildings
   d. Elevation illustrating the cross-slope condition at entrances
   e. Height varies along first riser where stair meets steep cross-slope.

(d)

CROSS SLOPE
ALONG STEPS
AT FRONT DOOR

(e)

Finally, costly grade changes may be required between buildings as illustrated in Fig. 4.6b. Part of this problem may be alleviated by stepping the architecture as shown in Fig. 4.6c.

The third option for street layout is to place the street diagonally across the contours. This arrangement usually results in a more efficient storm drainage design, a better relationship between access and structure, and less steep gradients than those of the perpendicular arrangement. It should also result in the least amount of disturbance to the landscape, since this option should minimize the amount of regrading required.

More than likely, most development situations will be a composite of the three layout options. The actual grading criteria applied to the grading of any pedestrian or vehicular circulation system depend on many factors. For both systems, such factors as type, volume, and speed of traffic, climatic conditions, existing topography, etc., must be addressed.

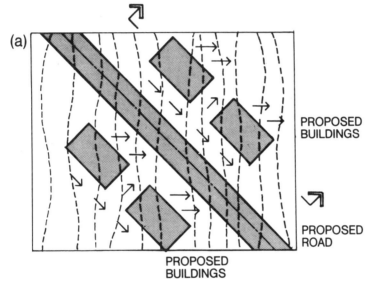

(a)

PROPOSED
BUILDINGS

PROPOSED
ROAD

PROPOSED
BUILDINGS

Fig. 4.7. ROAD AND LONG AXIS OF BUILDINGS PLACED DIAGONALLY TO CONTOURS.
   a. Plan indicating proposed drainage pattern
   b. Section illustrating a reduced amount of required grade change compared to Fig. 4.5 and Fig. 4.6

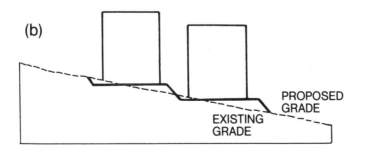

(b)

PROPOSED
GRADE

EXISTING
GRADE

Specific activities and land uses also establish limits and constraints on the grading process. Athletic facilities, including playfields and game courts, are excellent examples. Facilities like football and soccer fields, baseball and softball diamonds, and tennis courts have specific guidelines for layout, orientation, and grading (Fig. 4.8). The preciseness of these guidelines is determined by the anticipated level of play (e.g., international vs. intramural competition or professional baseball vs. Little League) and the governing athletic association. Guidelines and standards extend beyond the world of sports. Highway departments, zoning ordinances, and city, state, and federal agencies have a variety of regulations and standards that must be adhered to in the design and grading process. Table 4.1 lists a number of site conditions and the suggested range of acceptable slopes for each. These guidelines are based on experience and represent common uses under average conditions. They should be applied with flexibility, particularly in unique or atypical situations.

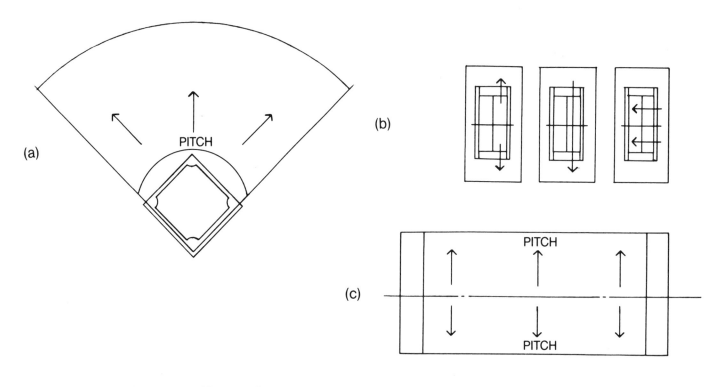

Fig. 4.8.   GRADING FOR SPORTS FACILITIES
a. Baseball and softball fields are normally pitched toward the outfield.
b. Court sports such as tennis and basketball may be pitched from the center to both ends, from one end to the other, or from one side to the other. They may also be diagonally cross-sloped.
c. Playfields like football and soccer are crowned at the center and pitched to both sides.

TABLE 4.1. Grading Standards and Critical Gradients

Type of Use	Extreme Range (%)	Desirable Range (%)
Public Streets	0.5 − 10	1 − 8
Private Roads	0.5 − 20	1 − 12
Service Drives	0.5 − 15[a]	1 − 10[a]
Parking Areas	0.5 − 8	1 − 5
Parking Ramps	up to 20	up to 15
Collector Walks	0.5 − 12	1 − 8
Entrance Walks	0.5 − 8	1 − 4
Pedestrian Ramps	up to 12	up to 8
Stairs	25 − 50	33 − 50
Game Courts	0.5 − 2	0.5 − 1.5
Play Fields	1 − 5[b]	2 − 3[b]
Paved Gutters	0.25 − 100	1 − 50
Grassed Swales	0.5 − 15	2 − 10
Terrace and Sitting Areas	0.5 − 3	1 − 2
Grassed Banks	up to 50[c]	up to 33[d]
Planted Banks	up to 100[c]	up to 50[c]

[a]Preferred gradient at loading/unloading areas is 1 to 3%.

[b]Playfields such as football may be level in the longitudinal direction if they have a 2 to 3% cross slope.

[c]Dependent on soil type.

[d]Maximum slope recommended for power mower. 25% is preferred.

General Comments

1. Minimum slopes should be increased based on drainage capabilities of surfacing materials.
2. Maximum slopes should be decreased based on local climatic conditions, such as ice and snow, and maintenance equipment limitations.
3. All standards should be checked against local Building Codes; Public Work and Highway Departments; and other governing agencies.

Economics and Maintenance

Economic constraints relate to both initial construction costs and long-term maintenance and operational costs. As an approach to grading design, an optimum solution is one that balances the amount of cut and fill on site. This means that soil does not have to be imported to or exported from the site. If this cannot be achieved, usually the less costly option is to have an excess of cut material. This will be discussed in more detail in Chapter 7.

The types of equipment and labor required during the construction process directly affect cost. Historically, earth moving was accomplished primarily by extensive human effort with the aid of animals and rudimentary machinery. The gardens at Versailles and New York's Central

Park are both excellent examples of landscape designs that required large-scale earth moving and grading, executed to a great extent by hand labor. It is only in this century that labor-intensive grading became costly as wages increased and human energy was replaced by powerful, efficient earth-moving equipment. The development of this equipment increased the feasibility for large-scale earth-moving projects, since construction time was reduced and the ratio of the amount of work achievable per dollar spent was greatly increased. Even with the current trends of increased equipment operation costs due to higher energy prices, earth moving still remains one of the most cost-effective construction processes. Generally, grading designs that utilize standard construction equipment and a minimum of hand labor in their implementation will be the least costly. Factors influencing the actual method of construction include the configuration of the site and of the proposed landforms, available maneuvering and staging space, and the preciseness of the grading required.

Grading designs that require elaborate storm drainage systems will be more expensive than designs that conform to natural drainage patterns. In urban areas, it may be difficult to avoid such conditions. In these instances both the grading and storm drainage design must be evaluated for unnecessary intricacy. Simplification, but not at the expense of the over-all design concept, will result in the most cost-effective system.

Once a project is completed, it must be maintained. Obviously each design requires a different level of maintenance. Understanding a client's expertise, staffing and budget capabilities, and attitudes toward maintenance at the beginning of a project will influence design decisions. Providing a client with a design that cannot be maintained due to impracticality or budget constraints will, in the long run, destroy the project and one's credibility as a design professional. However, there must be a balance between maintenance demands and other esthetic and functional design criteria.

One of the primary maintenance concerns in grading design is the extent and steepness of sloped areas. Where turf must be mowed, steep slopes will require handmowers rather than tractor or gang mowers. Improperly maintained steep slopes may also result in soil erosion. This is not only unsightly, but the transported sediment may clog storm drainage structures. This, in turn, creates a safety problem and an additional maintenance concern.

In northern climates, steep slopes along circulation routes may increase the amount of snow removal required and may result in an excessive use of salt or sand to reduce slippery conditions. Also, in these climates, where stairs are used extensively and intricate or constricted sidewalk patterns occur, the amount of snow removal done by hand is increased. This slows the clearing process and increases snow removal budgets.

SUMMARY OF CRITICAL CONSTRAINTS

Various constraints and factors influencing grading design decisions have briefly been presented in this chapter. At this point, a few are worth repeating because of their importance.

1. To avoid moisture and structural problems, storm water must be drained away from buildings. This is referred to as positive drainage.
2. Grade changes should be avoided within the drip line of existing trees in order to protect the health of the plants.
3. Legally, grades cannot be changed beyond the property lines of the site.
4. The rate of storm runoff leaving the site after construction has been completed should not exceed the pre-construction rate.
5. The proposed grading and landform design should respond to the function and purpose of the activities and uses to be accommodated.

PROBLEMS

4.1.   As part of their design vocabulary it is important for landscape architects to be able to visualize different percentages of slope and understand how these percentages affect use. One method that aids in developing this skill is to measure percentages of slope for a variety of

$$(\text{HI-x}) \times 5 = \% \text{ SLOPE}$$

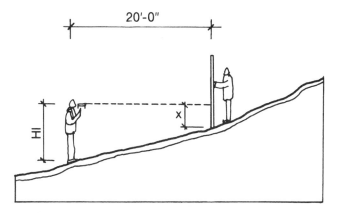

Problem 4.1.   FIELD TECHNIQUE FOR QUICKLY APPROXIMATING SLOPES.
A hand level is used to determine the reading on the rod placed 20 ft away. The difference in elevation is obtained by subtracting the rod reading from the height of the instrument, which in this case is the height of the person's eye. The percentage of slope is obtained by multiplying the difference in elevation by 5.

landscape conditions as they actually appear on the ground. Survey a variety of slopes using the technique illustrated. Try to develop the ability to predict percentages of slope from visual inspection.

4.2.   As discussed in the text, there is a relationship between street pattern, building access, and topography. To develop a better understanding of this relationship, examine your surrounding community. Look at how topography may have influenced street patterns and how the means of building access change as topographic conditions change.

4.3.   Grading around buildings is related to the type of structural foundation, method of construction, and building form. Examine a variety of building conditions to see how grading is handled with respect to building entrances, construction materials, and types of foundation. Look at how the building has been adapted to, or imposed, on the topography (i.e., flat-site vs. sloping-site building).

4.4.   During a rain storm, examine how grading directs the flow of surface runoff. Also examine how surface conditions (paved, unpaved, roofs, etc.) influence the rate and amount of runoff. In addition, look for drainage problems. Analyze why they occur and how improvements could be made.

CHAPTER 5

Grading Design and Process

GRADING DESIGN

It is extremely important to realize that grading is one of the primary design tools available to the landscape architect. Every site design project requires some change in grade. How these grade changes are integrated into the overall design concept will influence the success of the project both functionally and visually. The necessity for grade changes goes beyond the constraints discussed in Chapter 4 to include esthetic, perceptual, and spatial considerations.

Esthetics

The visual form of grading may be broadly categorized into three types. The selection of a particular type is appropriate within a given landscape or design context, but it is possible to combine types within the same project. The three categories are geomorphic, architectonic, and naturalistic (Fig. 5.1).

Geomorphic The proposed grading blends ecologically and visually with the character of the existing natural landscape. It reflects the geologic forces and natural patterns that shape the landscape by repeating similar landforms and physiographic structure. Generally, the intent of this category is to minimize the amount of regrading necessary in order to preserve the existing landscape character.

Architectonic The proposed grading creates uniform slopes and forms, which usually are crisply defined geometric shapes. The line along which

Fig. 5.1. VISUAL FORM OF GRADING
    a. Geomorphic. The geologic formation of Manhattan Island is expressed in the grading design for New York's Central Park.
    b. Architectonic. The sloping grassed plane is used to reinforce the architectural edge of this space.
    c. Naturalistic. In this large urban park the land was manipulated to create a meadow within a valley-like space.

planes intersect is clearly articulated, rather than softened by rounded edges. This type of grading is appropriate where the overall impact is man dominated or where a strong contrast is desired between the built and natural landscape.

Naturalistic This last category is perhaps the most common type of grading particularly in suburban and rural settings. It is a stylized approach in which abstract (or organic) landforms are used to represent or imitate the natural landscape.

Perception

Slope The perception of slope is influenced by the texture of the surface material and the relationship to surrounding grades. The coarser the texture, the less noticeable the slope. For example, the slope of smooth pavement, such as troweled concrete, is more noticeable than coarse pavement like cobblestone. Generally, slopes of 2% or greater on pavements can easily be perceived. However, horizontal reference lines, such as brick coursing or the top of a wall, increase the awareness of slope even in unpaved situations.

The relationship of one slope to another will also influence perception of steepness. For example, when traveling along a walk with an 8% slope, which then changes to a 4% slope, the 4% slope will visually appear to be less than half the original slope.

Topography, landform, and change in grade break the landscape into comprehensible units, which establish a sense of scale and sequence. The manner in which these grade changes occur affect spatial and visual perception and image of a place.

Elevation Change Being at a higher elevation relative to the surrounding landscape is potentially dramatic for a variety of reasons. First, a rise in grade may provide a feeling of expansiveness by extending views and overall field of vision. Also, being at a higher elevation may provide a sense of superiority, which may contribute to a feeling of control or dominance of a place. In addition, an upward change in elevation can provide an opportunity to contrast or exaggerate the steepness or flatness of the surrounding landscape. The abruptness of the elevation change will affect how space is perceived. The more gradual the ascent the more subtle the experience. The steeper the grade the greater the sense of enclosure at the lower elevations, while the opportunity for drama and excitement is increased at the higher elevations.

Convex and Concave Slopes   Generally a plane is visually less pleasing than a convex or concave landform, although this depends on scale and contrast (Fig. 5.2). In comparing the two rounded forms, the concave appears more graceful from the downhill side, since it exhibits an uplifting quality. From the downhill side both forms foreshorten the view, with the foreshortening much more abrupt with the convex slope. From the uphill side of a convex slope the sense of height is accented. Also, the sense of distance appears compressed, since the middle ground is foreshortened. The following quote, which appeared in *The Sense of Place* by Fritz Steele, illustrates the influence landform can have on experience.

> The most impressive approach to a view of one of the dales is to come upon it from the high moors—what the dalesfolk call, so expressively, from off the 'tops'. One has spent the day, perhaps, up in this world of heather, with grouse or curlew providing a commentary to one's every movement, and with wide view of moorland cut by faint runnels and gullies, many of which are, in fact, the gaps of the dale lip seen in foreshortened perspective. The high ground begins to decline and one may come to the edge of the heather and peat and enter a world of benty grass and occasional stream heads. Then comes the moment when one looks 'over the edge'—the convexity of the hill has reached the point where one can look back up the gentler slope of mooreland, or forward down what often appears to be an almost precipitous slope into the valley.

Arthur Raistrick
The Pennine Dales

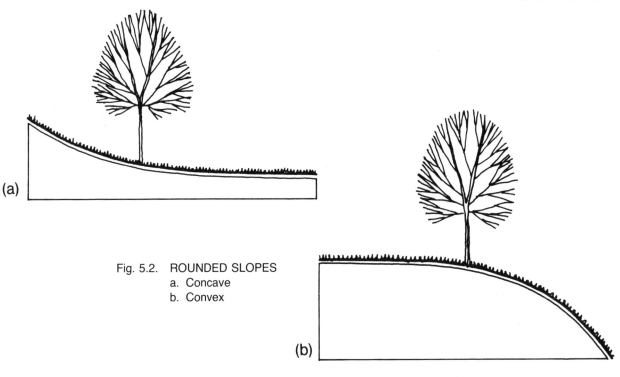

Fig. 5.2. ROUNDED SLOPES
   a. Concave
   b. Convex

(a)

(b)

Enhancement From analyzing the existing topography and landscape character, proposed landforms, grade changes, and design elements may be constructed or placed to emphasize, negate, or have little impact on the visual structure of the landscape. The basic considerations when proposing design alternatives are whether they will enhance, complement, contrast, or conflict with that particular landscape context (Fig. 5.3).

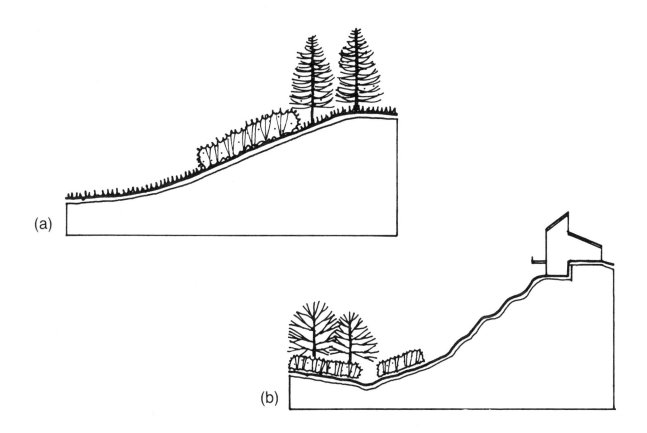

Fig. 5.3. ENHANCING TOPOGRAPHY WITH DESIGN ELEMENTS
   a. Planting
   b. Architecture

Spatial Considerations Proposed grade changes may perform a variety of spatial functions. The appropriateness of the application of these functions is determined by a careful analysis of the potentials of the site and the demands of the design program. Several grading design applications are discussed and illustrated in this section.

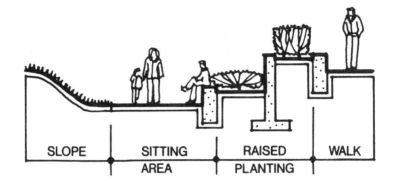

Fig. 5.4. LEVEL CHANGES FOR PRIVACY
Raised planting separates and visually screens the sunken sitting area from the sidewalk. The slope is used to add to the spatial enclosure of the sitting area.

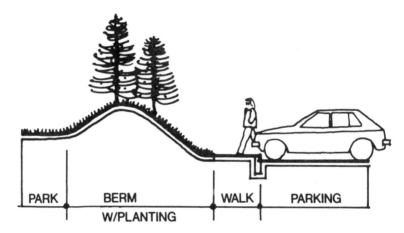

Fig. 5.5. VISUAL SCREEN
Topography, particularly in conjunction with planting, can be used to screen or block undesired views. In the illustration, a planted berm is used to screen the view of a parking lot from a park area.

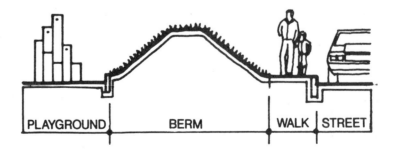

Fig. 5.6. ENCLOSURE FOR SAFETY
In the section a berm is used to separate a playground from a street.

Enclosure Enclosure may be used to perform several tasks including containment, protection, privacy, and screening. Seclusion, intimacy, and privacy may be achieved through the use of containment as in the section of the sitting area illustrated in Fig. 5.4. Screening is a form of visual containment, since it terminates sight lines and eliminates undesirable views (Fig. 5.5).

Enclosure, possibly in the form of a berm as illustrated in Fig. 5.6, also may be used to provide safety and protection like restraining children from running into the street from a playground or serving as a backstop for various types of athletic activities. However, this type of application should be used with caution for two reasons. First, it may inadvertently promote careless recreational uses, and, second, the enclosure reduces visibility into the area creating a potentially unsafe condition. It should be noted that properly designed and placed landforms can be an excellent outlet for creative play.

Berms are vegetated or paved embankments, somewhat dike-like in appearance, commonly used by landscape architects for enclosure and separation purposes. However, the use of these devices must be carefully evaluated, since there are many examples where the scale and proportion of berms have been insignificant or inappropriate with regard to the surrounding context.

Enclosure may also provide protection from climatic elements (Fig. 5.7). Properly placed landforms can control drifting snow and significantly reduce the impact of wind on structures and even over large areas such as playfields and parking lots.

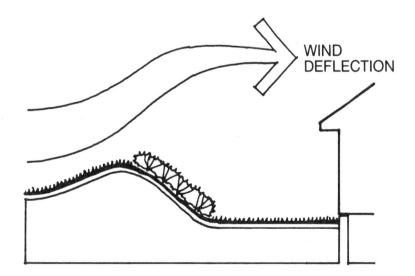

Fig. 5.7. MICROCLIMATE MODIFICATION
        Topography can be used to channel or deflect winds, capture solar radiation, and to create cold or warm pockets.

Fig. 5.8.   SEPARATION OF ACTIVITIES
   a. Along a riverfront promenade a grade change, which incorporates seating,
      is used to separate the pedestrian walk from the bicycle and service lane.

Separation A very basic application of grading is the separation of activities to reduce potential conflicts like separating auto traffic from pedestrians and bicyclists, bicyclists from pedestrians, sitting areas from walkways, etc. In the design of New York's Central Park, Olmstead and Vaux showed great vision in using grade changes and overpasses to separate the traffic on the transverse roads from the park. Even a change in grade of only a few inches may sufficiently define the territory in which an activity may occur. Separation may be accomplished by a variety of techniques, one of which is illustrated in Fig. 5.8.

Fig. 5.8 (*Continued*)
    b. An underpass is used to separate pedestrian and vehicular circulation in New York's Central Park.

Fig. 5.9. AMPHITHEATERS
There are many good examples where topography has been used effectively to
create a theater setting, two of which are presented on these pages.
a. A Roman amphitheater built in Caesarea, Israel, about 25 BC. The theater
   has been reconstructed and is in use today.

Channeling Landform may be used to direct, funnel, or channelize
auto and pedestrian circulation. It may also be used to direct and control
viewing angles and vistas as well as wind and cold air drainage. An

amphitheater is a special use of landform to both focus attention and enclose space. See Fig. 5.9.

It must be realized that in all the applications listed above, the functions of landform and grade changes are reinforced and strengthened by the use of plantings and structural elements like walls and fences.

Fig. 5.9 (*Continued*)
　　　　　b. An amphitheater constructed at the site of the 1972 Olympics in Munich. Note how the edge of the theater has been blended into the surrounding earth form.

GRADE CHANGE DEVICES

Accommodating changes in elevation in outdoor environments is one of the basic functions of a landscape architect. There are many devices that can accomplish these changes, including stairs, ramps, perrons, walls, slopes, and terraces. Concern for the experiential, functional, and visual manner in which these grade transitions are executed should result in good landscape design.

Stairs

Stairs are the most common technique used to accommodate pedestrian circulation where an abrupt change in grade is necessary or desired. The width of a stair depends on the design intent, but should be a minimum of 3 ft. A desirable minimum width to allow two people to pass comfortably is 4 ft.

The proportion of riser height to tread width is critical to the ease and comfort of the user. A standard rule of thumb that has evolved for *exterior* stairs is that two risers plus one tread should equal 24 to 26 in. Two commonly used ratios are 6 in. riser with 12 in. tread and 5 in. riser with 15 in. tread. Preferably, there should be a minimum of three risers and a maximum of 10 to 12 risers for a set of stairs. The minimum number is suggested to make the stair more visible to prevent tripping. Where the number of risers exceeds 12, an intermediate landing is recommended to reduce the apparent scale of the stair and provide a comfortable resting point. Again, both of these guidelines must be applied with flexibility. Handrails are normally required on stairs with five or more risers, although this must be checked against local building code requirements. Stair treads should pitch $\frac{1}{8}$ in./ft in the downhill direction to insure proper drainage. Low curbs, referred to as *cheek walls*, are commonly used along the edges of stairs for safety and maintenance purposes. See Fig. 5.10.

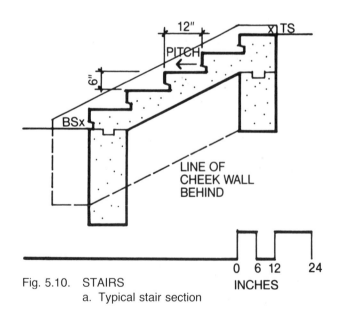

Fig. 5.10.   STAIRS
a. Typical stair section

Fig. 5.10 (*Continued*)
b. Stair spiraling up a steep slope. Both the stair and path are pitched to a gutter on the uphill side, which also intercepts the runoff from the slope.

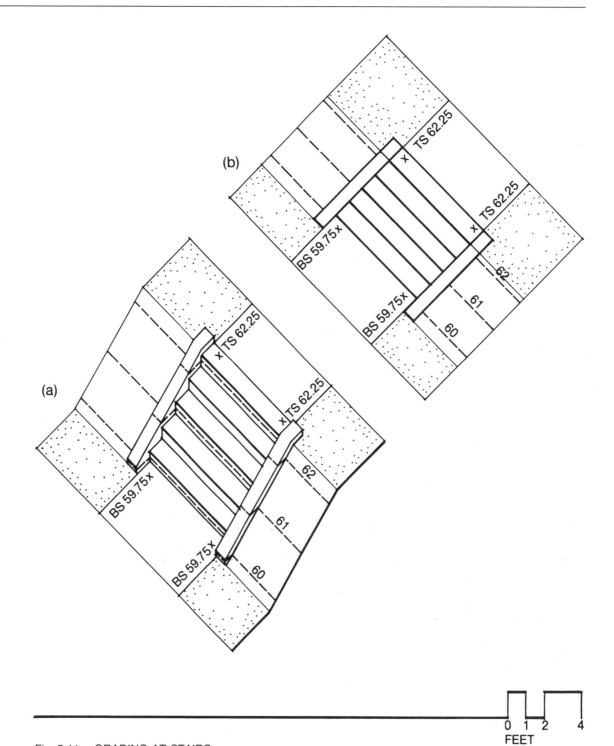

Fig. 5.11.   GRADING AT STAIRS
   a. Plan oblique illustrates how contour lines follow along the face of the stair
      risers.
   b. On construction drawings the contour lines are drawn only to the edge of
      the stairs or cheek walls. Spot elevation are given at the top and bottom
      of the stairs and *not* for each step.

The configuration of contour lines where they cross stairs is illustrated in Fig. 5.11. However, contour lines are drawn only to the outside edge of the cheek walls on grading plans, and the grade at the top and bottom of the stair is indicated by spot elevations. It is not necessary to indicate the spot elevation for each step, since this information is provided by dimensions on construction detail drawings.

Ramps

Ramps are simply inclined sidewalks or driveways usually at a uniform slope. Typical slopes range from 5 to 8% for pedestrian use and can be as great as 15% where handicapped access is not a constraint. Again, 4 ft is a recommended minimum width to allow people to pass. Handrails, particularly for handicapped use, are normally required on ramps of 5% and greater slopes. Where ramps exceed 30 ft in length, an intermediate landing is usually required. Ramps may be graded to slope perpendicular to the direction of travel (or cross pitched) for drainage purposes. Contours are drawn across ramps on grading plans and spot elevations are used to indicate top and bottom of ramp.

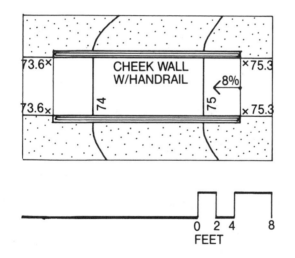

Fig. 5.12.   GRADING AT RAMPS
Spot elevations are indicated at the top and bottom of a ramp and contour lines are drawn across the ramp. An arrow, normally pointing downhill, is shown with the slope of the ramp. It should be noted that the slope on ramps to be used by the handicapped cannot be more than 8%. This is approximately 1 in. vertical change for each 1 ft of horizontal distance. Thus the length of a ramp sloped at 8% will be 12 ft for each foot of elevation change.

Stairs and ramps may be used in combination. The arrangement may be sets of stairs alternating with ramps as illustrated in Fig. 5.13a or lengthened and ramped treads as in Fig. 5.13b. Many examples of the latter arrangement can be found, most of which are uncomfortable to use. Not only are the height of the risers and the distance between risers important in this situation, but also the percentage of slope between risers, since in the uphill direction the slope shortens a person's stride and lengthens it in the downhill direction.

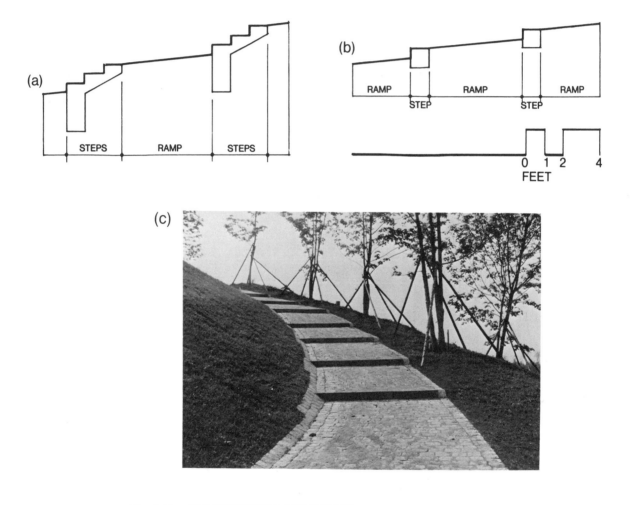

Fig. 5.13.   COMBINATION RAMP STAIRS
a. Sets of stairs connected by a short ramp
b. Alternating arrangements of ramp and step
c. Photograph illustrates the condition in part b. Again, the walk has been pitched toward the uphill side.

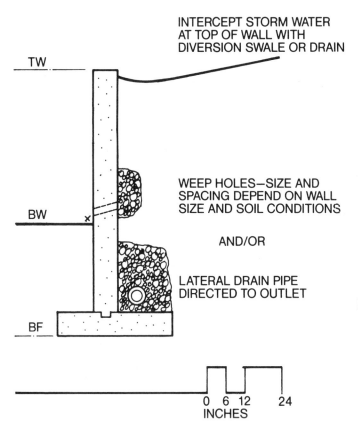

INTERCEPT STORM WATER
AT TOP OF WALL WITH
DIVERSION SWALE OR DRAIN

TW

WEEP HOLES—SIZE AND
SPACING DEPEND ON WALL
SIZE AND SOIL CONDITIONS

BW

AND/OR

LATERAL DRAIN PIPE
DIRECTED TO OUTLET

BF

0 6 12   24
INCHES

Fig. 5.14. RETAINING WALL SECTION
Depending on the conditions, weep holes,
a lateral drain, or both, may be
required to prevent a buildup of water
pressure behind a wall.

Retaining Walls

Retaining walls allow for the greatest vertical change in elevation in the shortest horizontal distance. They are also the most expensive method for accommodating grade changes, but may be necessary where space is at a premium such as urban or small sites or where the use of walls is an integral part of the design concept.

Walls must be structurally designed to support the weight of the earth being retained, but the discussion is beyond the scope of this book. However, proper drainage of retaining walls is critical to their stability. There are two primary issues related to drainage. The first is the buildup of water pressure behind the wall, which, if not alleviated, will cause the wall to slide or overturn. To prevent the buildup of water pressure, drain holes, referred to as *weepholes,* are constructed near the base of the wall or a lateral drain pipe is placed behind the wall to collect and dispose of excess ground water. The second issue is the saturation of the soil under the wall, which can cause overturning due to reduced bearing capacity. This is prevented by intercepting storm runoff on the uphill side of the wall and can be accomplished through the use of swales or drains, which also reduces potential staining of the face of the wall by preventing runoff from flowing over the wall.

Fig. 5.15. CONTOUR LINES AT RETAINING WALLS
   a. Similar to curbs and stairs, the contour
      lines again follow along the face
      of the structure.
   b. On construction drawings contour lines
      are drawn to the edges of the wall but *not*
      along the face of the wall. Spot elevations
      are provided at appropriate places.

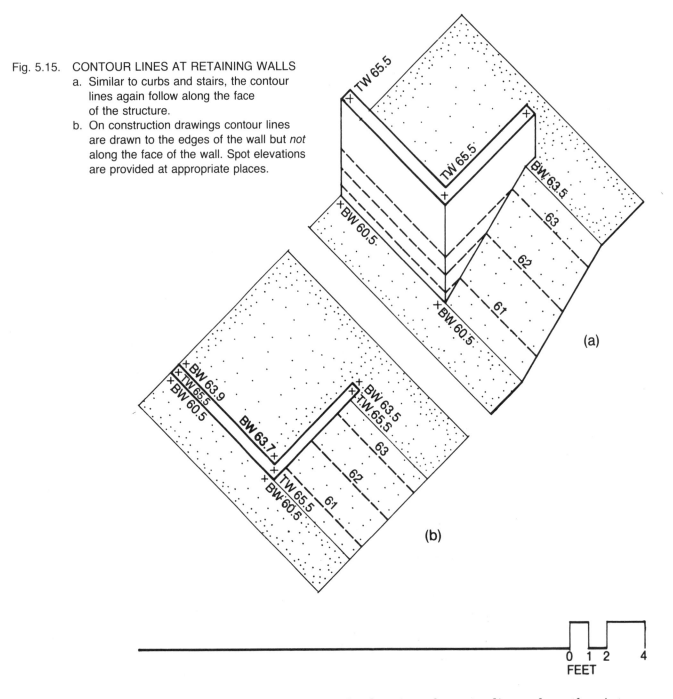

(a)

(b)

0 1 2   4
FEET

Figure 5.15 illustrates the drawing of contour lines where they intersect a vertical surface such as a retaining wall. On a grading plan, the
contour lines are drawn to the face of the wall, but *not* along the face. Top
and bottom of wall spot elevations are typically indicated at the ends and
corners of walls.

Several ways in which sloping ground and retaining walls may interface are illustrated in Fig. 5.16. A slightly exaggerated pitch at the base of retaining walls to insure positive drainage is indicated by the contour lines where they abut the wall. The condition illustrated in Fig. 5.16e is unacceptable because of erosion and maintenance problems, unless the wall is quite thick.

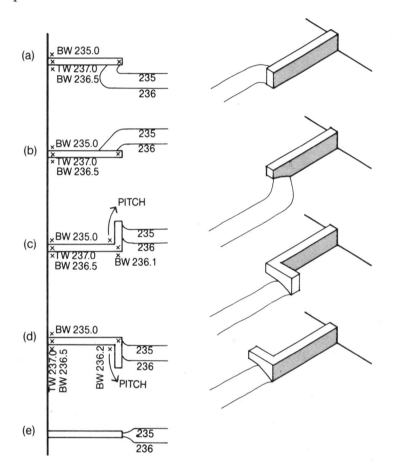

Fig. 5.16.   GRADING OPTIONS AT RETAINING WALLS
a. A slope is created along the uphill face of the wall, thus making the end of the wall more visually apparent.
b. A slope is created along the downhill face, somewhat reducing the scale of the wall visually.
c. The wall is shaped in the form of an L, with the L pointing in downhill direction. A niche is formed on the downhill side and again the end of the wall protrudes as in part a.
d. Again, the L form is used, but now pointing in the uphill direction. As a result the outside corner of the L becomes more apparent.
e. Except for wide walls, this condition is unacceptable due to erosion, maintenance, and safety problems.
In the options in parts c and d, the grading must be handled to prevent the trapping of storm water at the inside corner of the L.

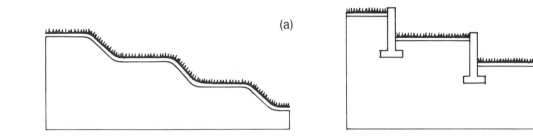

(a)

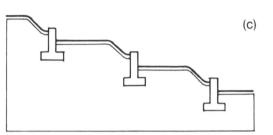

(b)

Fig. 5.17.   TERRACE SECTIONS
          a. Terraces created by slopes.
          b. Terraces created by retaining walls
          c. Terraces created by combining slopes
             and retaining walls
          d. An example of part c

(c)

(d)

Slopes

Slopes are the least costly technique for changing grade but require more space than retaining walls. To be visually significant, slopes should not be less than 5 to 1. Generally, planted slopes should not exceed 2 to 1, but paved slopes may be 1 to 1 or greater. Mowed lawn areas should not exceed 3 to 1, although 4 to 1 is the preferred maximum. The use of slopes and the selection of a desired gradient are based on the design intent, soil conditions, susceptibility to erosion, and type of surface cover. All slopes must be stabilized by vegetative or mechanical means to reduce erosion potential.

Terraces

Terraces provide a series of relatively flat intermediate levels to accommodate a change in grade. The reasons for terracing may be visual, functional, or structural. Terraces may be created by the use of slopes or walls or a combination of both (Fig. 5.17). Where both the slope and the level portion, known as a *bench*, are relatively small in area and grade change, it is possible to pitch the bench in the downhill direction. However, where grade changes and area of slope are considerable such as in a highway cut or fill, the bench must be pitched back from the slope to reduce erosion (Fig. 5.18). The storm runoff from the bench must be properly disposed of to prevent saturation of the toe of the uphill slope, which could cause the slope to slump.

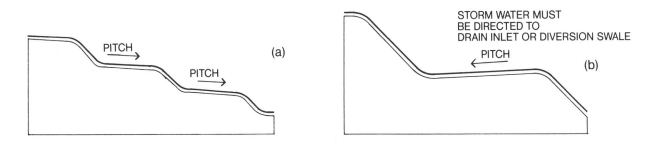

Fig. 5.18.   DRAINAGE FOR SLOPES AND TERRACES
   a. For relatively small terraces the bench may be pitched in the downhill direction so that storm runoff flows across the slopes.
   b. For large terraces or steep slopes the bench should be pitched back from the top of the slope. It is important, however, to prevent saturation of the bench by properly disposing of storm runoff.

GRADING PROCESS

The grading procedure presented in this text is best described as a *controlled intuitive process.* Unfortunately, there is no precise sequence to follow in order to arrive at a correct grading solution, since every grading problem is different and in most cases there is more than one appropriate solution to a particular problem. This lack of preciseness is often a source of frustration to students. This frustration may be reduced through continued practice and by following a generalized three-phased approach. These phases include (1) an inventory and analysis of the site and development program, (2) design development, and (3) design implementation.

Phase 1: Inventory and Analysis

The initial phase of any landscape architectural design problem is to inventory the existing physical and cultural conditions of the site and its surroundings. Both the inventory and the development program (i.e., what is to be placed on the site) are analyzed and evaluated to identify conflicts, constraints, and opportunities that will guide the design development and the proposed grading scheme. This phase relates directly to the discussion in chapter 4 and the preceding sections of this chapter.

Phase 2: Design Development

During this phase the observations and evaluations of the first phase are synthesized into a design concept that may generate one or more design solutions. As a result of the compartmentalization of the educational system, which typically separates courses in grading technology from courses in design, this phase is often overlooked by students. From experience and observation, many students wrongly conclude that, because grading is taught as an engineering subject, design is of secondary importance. The reverse situation is commonly found in the design studio.

With regard to grading and design, three points must be emphasized. First, grading and site design are two highly related and dependent processes. To achieve an appropriate as well as successful final product, both must be integrated in a holistic manner at the outset of the project. Second, before manipulating contours on a grading plan it is important to have a clear understanding of the form of the desired final product. Without this knowledge the manipulation of contours is an aimless and futile act. To reinforce this point, any appropriate three-dimensional form can be expressed by contours on a grading plan. However, without a preconception of what that form should be, it can never be attained. Finally, a change in grade must be purposeful, whether for functional or esthetic reasons, and not arbitrary. The intent to change a grade 2 in. is no less important than the intent to change a grade 20 ft.

Phase 3: Design Implementation

At this point the design solution is translated into a workable and buildable scheme through the development of construction drawings and specifications. Although not always applicable or necessary, four steps may be followed to make the task of developing accurate, concise, and correct grading plans easier. Based on a process developed by David Young and Donald Leslie at Pennsylvania State University, these steps include (1) development of section criteria, (2) application of section criteria, (3) development of slope diagrams, and (4) evaluation of slope diagrams.

Since grading is the change upward or downward of the ground surface, plans alone are normally inadequate to study vertical relationships properly. Therefore, sections should be drawn at critical points and section criteria developed to establish relative vertical relationships, approximate slopes, and select appropriate grade change devices like walls, slopes, and steps. Once the section criteria have been developed, they may be applied to the plan in order to establish key spot elevations.

The purpose of slope diagrams is to outline the extent of areas to be graded to relatively the same slopes, indicate the direction of proposed slopes, establish drainage patterns by outlining proposed drainage areas and locating proposed high points and collection points, and, finally, to establish spot elevations at critical points such as building corners and entrances, top and bottom of stairs and walls, high points of swales, etc. For evaluation purposes, a check list may be established to determine whether the slope diagrams maintain the integrity of the overall design concept; respond appropriately to identified constraints; provide positive, efficient, and ecologically sensitive drainage; and maintain a relative balance between cut and fill, if possible. Slope diagrams should be revised where problems or conflicts are identified.

It should be noted that in the steps outlined above no contour lines have been manipulated or drawn. Only areas to be regraded, approximate slopes, and critical spot elevations have been determined. These now provide a controlled framework within which the proposed contour lines may be located.

It is important to realize that very rarely is a grading plan completely correct or appropriate on the first try. The development of a grading plan is to some degree a trial and error process often requiring numerous adjustments. These adjustments are usually minor; however, in some instances the entire grading approach may need to be reexamined. Finally, although the overall design concept is established during the design development phase, many detailed design decisions made at the implementation phase will contribute to the ultimate success of a project.

Example 5.1   The following example is presented to illustrate a typical sequence of events associated with a grading design problem. In this problem a small, L-shaped office building with a slab foundation is to be constructed on a suburban corner lot. The development program requires a seven-car parking area with potential for expansion, an entrance court, and handicapped access. The site is to be designed and the grading plan developed.

Site Analysis

As can be seen in Fig. 5.19, there are no major natural constraints on the site. The high point located in the northeast corner is at elevation 44.8 ft, while the low point, elevation 35.8 ft, is located on the property line in the southwest corner. The steepest slope is approximately 10% with the average slope across the site just over 6%. The existing surface drainage pattern is primarily sheet flow with approximately half directed toward Third Street and half toward Oak Street. The most significant feature on the site is the grove of mature red oak trees.

The adjacent land uses include a bank on the north and a single-family residence on the east. The residence is screened from the property by a hemlock hedge. The heaviest vehicular traffic is along Oak Street, while most pedestrians will approach the site from the southwest.

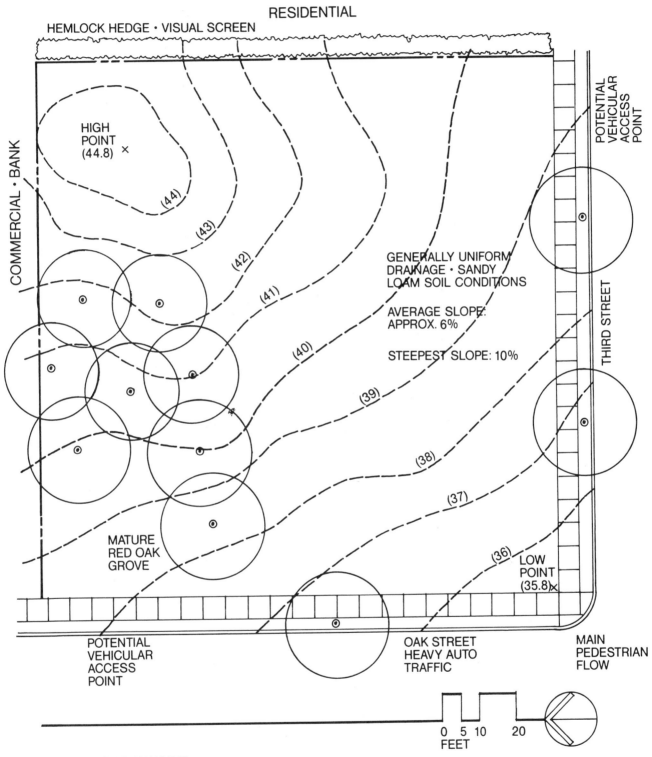

Fig. 5.19.   SITE ANALYSIS

Design Development

As shown in Fig. 5.20, both the building and parking are located as far from the oak trees as possible to insure their preservation. The building is placed with the open part of the L toward the street corner in order to orient the building entrance toward the primary pedestrian approach and to maximize the amount of glazing facing south to increase energy efficiency. The entrance court is developed within the open space of the L. The parking area is located so as to maximize the distance between the driveway entrance and the street intersection as well as to take advantage of the visual screen already provided by the adjacent hedge. The parking entrance is not located on Oak Street in order to preserve the existing oak grove and to avoid possible conflicts with the bank traffic.

Design Implementation

In developing the grading plan the four major elements of the design including the parking area, building, entrance court, and oak grove are analyzed. Where appropriate, section criteria and grading diagrams are developed for each component and alternative solutions are presented and explored.

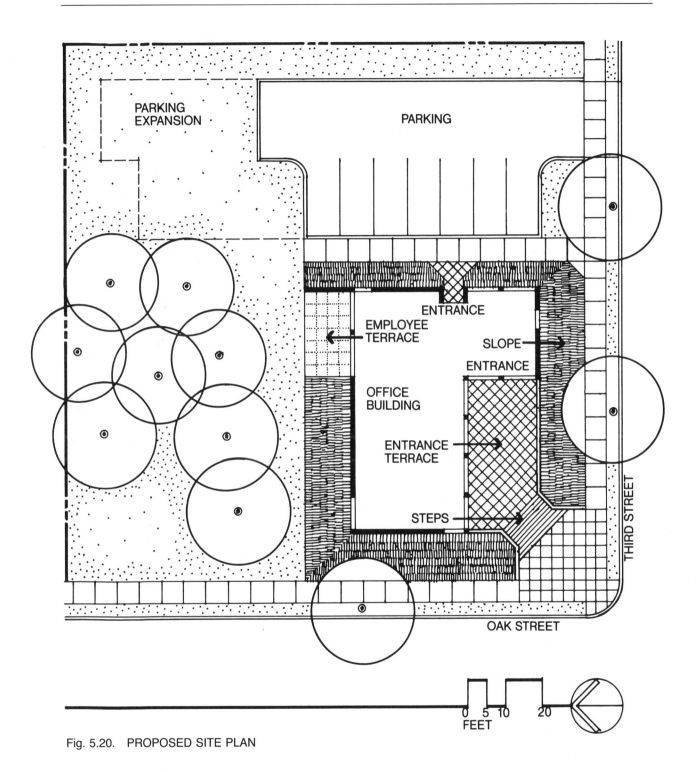

Fig. 5.20.   PROPOSED SITE PLAN

Parking Area   The existing grade slopes downward toward Third Street along the longitudinal axis of the parking area. To be consistent, the proposed grading for the parking area should slope in the same direction. There are four basic approaches to grading the parking area, as illustrated by the sections and slope diagrams in Fig. 5.21. The first is to cross-pitch the pavement toward the building and collect the storm water runoff in the southwest corner of the lot. The second is to cross-pitch the pavement away from the building and collect the runoff in the southeast area of the lot. The third combines the first two options resulting in a valley down the center of the parking area. The fourth alternative again combines the first two options to create a ridge down the center of the parking area. Runoff is collected in both the southeast and southwest corners of the lot.

Generally, cross-sloping small parking areas in one direction is the most efficient and visually least disturbing method of grading. However, in working through the four options for this problem, it was determined that pitching toward the center was the best alternative. Cross-pitching the parking area toward the building placed the catch basin too close to the building and in an inconvenient location for pedestrians, particularly if it clogged. Cross-pitching away from the building resulted in more cut in the northeast corner of the lot. The ridge alternative did not result in significant grading advantages and would be more costly because of the additional storm drainage structure. Other factors that influenced this decision are the accessibility for the handicapped at this end of the building and the limited change in grade that can occur along the face of the building owing to the slab construction. The controls for selecting the proposed elevations and gradients within the parking area are based on the above factors in conjunction with the existing grades along the east property line and at the entrance to the parking area.

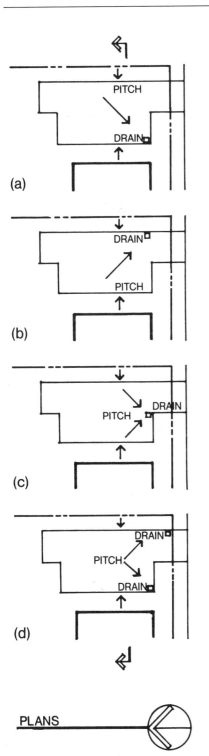

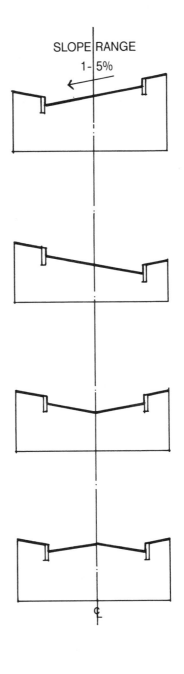

PLANS

SECTIONS

Fig. 5.21. ALTERNATIVE SLOPE DIAGRAMS AND SECTIONS FOR PARKING AREA
     a. Cross-pitched toward building
     b. Cross-pitched away from building
     c. Pitched to center, creating a valley
     d. Pitched to edges, creating a ridge

Building   There are several concerns that must be addressed in establishing a finished floor elevation for the building. First, positive drainage away from the building must be maintained on all sides. A second concern is the elevation of the east entrance and its relationship to the proposed parking lot grades. The elevation of the southwest entrance and its relationship to existing sidewalk grades must also be considered. In addition, the proposed finished floor elevation must be evaluated. A basic slope diagram for the building is illustrated in Fig. 5.22.

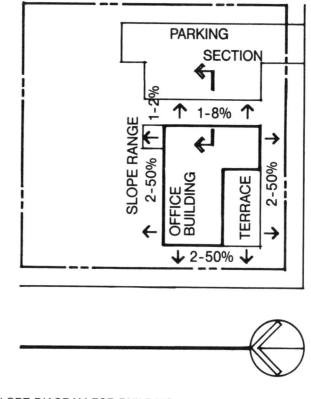

Fig. 5.22.   SLOPE DIAGRAM FOR BUILDING
          The primary objective is to maintain positive drainage away from the building. Except for the east side where handicapped access must be maintained, there are very few slope restrictions.

In examining the relationship of the building to the existing grades, a finished floor elevation of approximately 38.0 ft would seem appropriate, since the 38 ft contour line roughly bisects the building. This is a typical strategy since it strikes a balance in the grade change from one end of the building to the other and potentially produces a more balanced cut and fill condition. However, when examining the relationship of the east entrance to the parking area, there are two basic alternatives. The first is to create a positive drainage condition; thus the elevation at the edge of the building must be higher than the elevation at the top of the curb at the edge of the parking lot as shown in Fig. 5.23a. If the finished floor elevation is established at 38.0 ft, the elevation of the parking lot adjacent to the east entry must be lower than 38.0 ft. This results in approximately 2 ft of cut in the parking lot. A second alternative would be to construct the walk and edge of the parking area at an elevation above the finished floor elevation as illustrated in Fig. 5.23b. This results in more costly construction and may cause drainage problems, since a low area is created directly adjacent to the building.

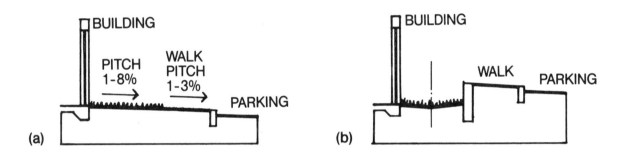

Fig. 5.23.   SECTION AT EAST FACE OF BUILDING
a. Floor elevation set higher than parking lot elevation
b. Floor elevation set lower than parking lot elevation.

In the third and final analysis, perhaps the finished floor elevation (FFE) should be raised *above* 38 ft, thus insuring good drainage, reducing cut, and reducing construction costs. In raising the elevation of the building, however, most of the foundation slab will be placed on fill. Purchasing and properly placing the fill material can add to the cost of the project. Also, if not constructed properly, future soil settlement may cause cracking and structural problems within the building. As can be seen from these three conditions, a number of factors must be explored and assessed in making grading decisions. In this case, since the scale of the building is small, it is felt the third alternative (i.e., raising the FFE) represents the best option and could be properly constructed.

Entrance Court There are several ways in which the entrance court could be designed, each directly related to grading decisions. Three schematic plans and accompanying sections are illustrated in Fig. 5.24. By establishing the finished floor elevation above elevation 38.0 ft, it is necessary to provide stairs at the southwest entrance. Also, along the south and west faces of the building slopes are needed, since the floor elevation is above the existing grades of the sidewalk. The three solutions illustrated respond to these conditions. It should be realized that these solutions were studied during the design development phase in order to reach a design decision. Again there is not always a distinct separation between the work to be performed in each of the phases. The third option (Fig. 5.24c) was selected for several reasons. The entrance courts in Fig. 5.24a and b were considered too large in relationship to the size of the building. The option in Fig. 5.24c provides a transitional space between the street corner and the building entrance and, by continuing the slopes along the edges of the entrance court, the relationship of the building to the street corner is more clearly defined. The other two solutions are also correct and could be implemented if different design objectives were desired.

Oak Grove In order to preserve the oak grove, there should be as little regrading and soil disturbance as possible within the drip line of the trees. Minimizing grading restricts the extent to which the existing contour lines may be altered on the north side of the building. As a result, the intent is to return to the existing grade in as short a distance as possible beyond the building. To be consistent with the treatment of the south and west sides, a slope is used along this edge of the building.

Fig. 5.24. DESIGN ALTERNATIVES FOR ENTRANCE TERRACE ▶

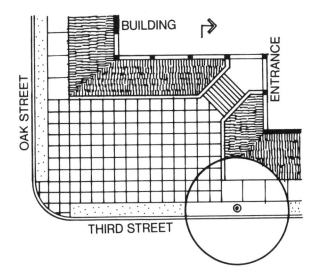

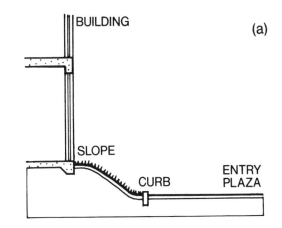

(a)

BUILDING

SLOPE

CURB

ENTRY PLAZA

OAK STREET

BUILDING

ENTRANCE

THIRD STREET

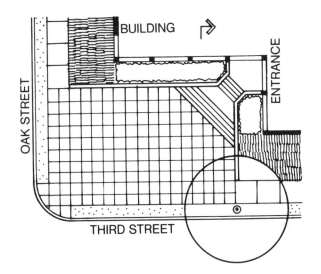

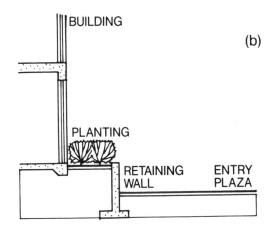

(b)

BUILDING

PLANTING

RETAINING WALL

ENTRY PLAZA

OAK STREET

BUILDING

ENTRANCE

THIRD STREET

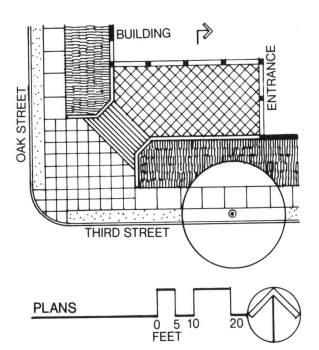

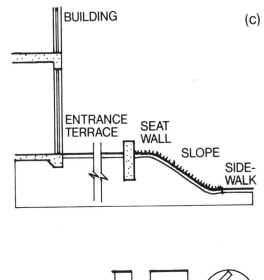

(c)

BUILDING

ENTRANCE TERRACE

SEAT WALL

SLOPE

SIDE-WALK

OAK STREET

BUILDING

ENTRANCE

THIRD STREET

PLANS

0 5 10   20
FEET

SECTIONS

0 2.5 5   10
FEET

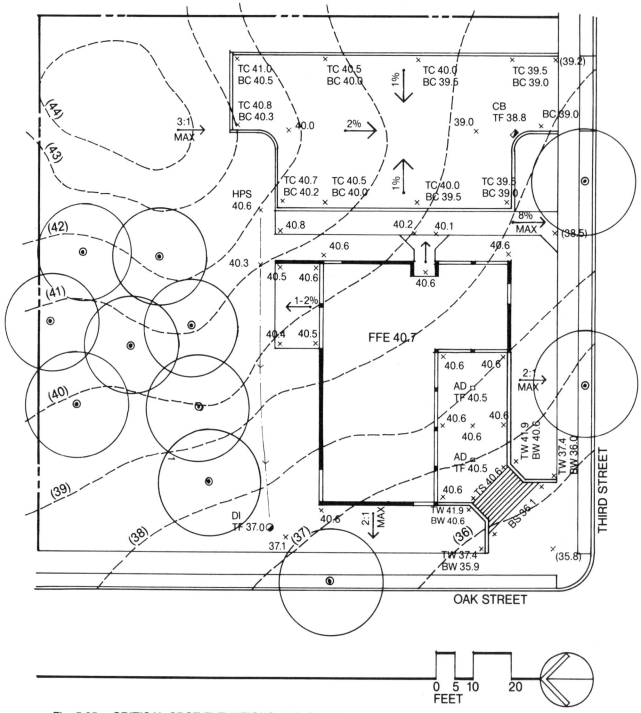

Fig. 5.25.   CRITICAL SPOT ELEVATIONS AND GRADIENTS

Synthesis

The rationale and criteria presented in the previous sections are synthesized into a final grading plan. Figure 5.25 illustrates the placement of critical spot elevations and proposed gradients, while Fig. 5.26 illustrates the final grading plan. From this drawing a grading contractor should be able to execute his portion of the project. Again it must be emphasized that this is *a* solution, not *the* solution, to this problem.

GRADING PLAN GRAPHICS

There are two basic types of grading plans. The first is the conceptual grading plan which communicates the design intent but is not usually an accurate or engineering representation of the ground form (Fig. 5.20). The audience for this plan is normally the client who may be an individual, architect, public agency, etc., and its purpose is to make the proposed concept easily understandable. The second is the grading plan executed as part of a set of construction documents (Fig. 5.26). The purpose of this drawing is to interpret accurately the design intent and communicate effectively this information to the grading contractor. The plan, in conjunction with the technical specifications, must provide complete instructions as to the nature and scope of work to be performed as well as a solid basis for estimating the cost involved. The success of a project depends on the *accuracy*, *completeness*, and *clarity* of the construction drawings.

Construction Grading Plan

The grading plan should show all existing and proposed features of the site. This includes all buildings; structures like walls, walks, steps, roads, etc.; utilities like water, sewer, storm drainage, electrical lines, etc.; utility structures like manholes, meter pits, junction boxes, etc.; and all other underground structures like vaults, septic systems, fuel storage tanks, etc. Proposed features are normally drafted as solid lines and the existing features are shown as dashed lines or photographically screened to appear lighter. In addition, of course, both existing and proposed contour lines and spot elevations are shown.

Spot elevations are used to supplement contours in the following situations:

1. To indicate variations from the normal slope or gradient between contour lines.
2. To indicate elevations of intersecting planes and lines like corners of buildings, terraces, walks, etc.
3. To indicate elevations at top and bottom of vertical elements like walls, steps, and curbs.
4. To indicate floor and entrance elevations.
5. To indicate elevations of high and low points.
6. To indicate top of frame (rim) elevations and inverts for utility systems.

With the above list in mind, examine the use of spot elevations in Fig. 5.26. In some cases only spot elevations are shown on highway plans and contour lines are omitted.

LEGEND FOR FIG. 5.26

(42)	EXIST. CONTOUR	BS	BOTTOM OF STAIR
42	PROP. CONTOUR	HPS	HIGH POINT OF SWALE
x(42.1)	EXIST. SPOT ELEV.	AD	AREA DRAIN
x 42.1	PROP. SPOT ELEV.	CB	CATCH BASIN
FFE	FINISHED FLOOR ELEVATION	DI	DRAIN INLET
		TF	TOP OF FRAME
TW	TOP OF WALL	℄	CENTER LINE OF SWALE
BW	BOTTOM OF WALL		
TS	TOP OF STAIR	- - - -	PROPERTY LINE

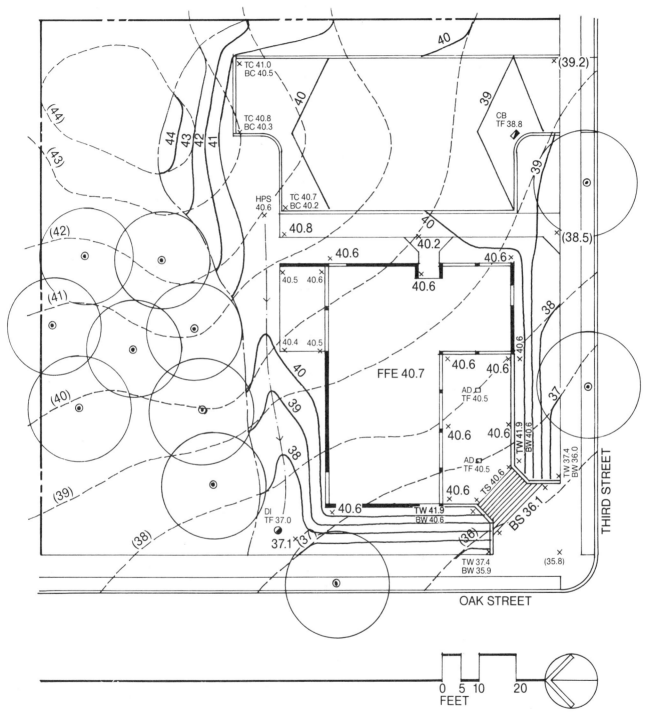

Fig. 5.26.   FINAL GRADING PLAN

The following elements should appear on all grading plans:

1. *Written and/or Graphic Scale.* The scale at which a grading plan is drawn depends on the scope of the project and the nature of the available topographic data. Scales for site plans usually range from ⅛ in. = 1 ft to 1 in. = 40 ft.

2. *North Arrow.* A north arrow is provided for orientation purposes. It should be indicated whether this is assumed, magnetic, or true north.

3. *Notes.* Notes include general or explanatory information as well as descriptions of any unique conditions of the plan. All plans should contain a note describing the source from which the existing conditions were taken as well as bench marks and reference datum.

4. *Legend.* All symbols and abbreviations used on the drawing should be identified in a legend. Examples of typical symbols and abbreviations are presented in Fig. 5.27. It should be pointed out that convention varies in different regions of the country and even between design offices within the same region. This fact only reinforces the need for a legend. The conventions used in this text include dashed lines for existing contours, solid lines for proposed contours, parenthetic labels for both existing contours and existing spot elevations, labeling contours on the *uphill* side, and using a wider line for every fifth or tenth contour line. Generally, contour lines are drawn freehand for unpaved areas and drafted for paved areas.

5. *Title Block.* Information such as project name, location of project, name of client, name of design firm, drawing title, drawing number, scale, and date should be arranged in an orderly and easily readable manner, normally in the lower right-hand corner of the sheet.

The readability of construction drawings is dependent on the clarity and legibility of the graphic technique. Variation in line thickness, referred to as line weight, the line type (e.g., solid, dashed, and dotted) are used to indicate a hierarchy of importance, a change in level, or a change in material. The organization of the information also contributes to the readability of a drawing. Development of a consistent, clear lettering style will also add to the quality of the drawing. Lettering guidelines should be used to contain letters within the same lines and to prevent separate lines of lettering from diverging.

_ _ (24) _ _ _ _ _ _ _	EXISTING CONTOUR	⎤ LABEL UPHILL SIDE/EVERY 5TH OR
24 _____	PROPOSED CONTOUR	⎦ 10TH CONTOUR LINE HEAVIER
x (24.21)	EXISTING SPOT ELEVATION	⎤
x 24.71	PROPOSED SPOT ELEVATION	
FFE	FINISHED FLOOR ELEVATION	
TW/BW	TOP OF WALL/BOTTOM OF WALL	
TC/BC	TOP OF CURB/BOTTOM OF CURB	
TS/BS	TOP OF STAIR/BOTTOM OF STAIR	INCLUDE SPOT
BF	BOTTOM OF FOOTING	ELEVATION
HP/LP	HIGH POINT/LOW POINT	
HPS	HIGH POINT OF SWALE	
TF or RE	TOP OF FRAME OR RIM ELEVATION	
INV. EL.	INVERT ELEVATION	⎦
☐ CB	EXISTING CATCH BASIN	⎤
◪ CB	PROPOSED CATCH BASIN	
◯ DI	EXISTING DRAIN INLET	REQUIRE TOP OF
◓ DI	PROPOSED DRAIN INLET	FRAME AND INVERT
◯ MH	EXISTING MANHOLE	ELEVATIONS
● MH	PROPOSED MANHOLE	⎦
◪ AD	PROPOSED AREA DRAIN	⎤ REQUIRES TOP OF ⎦ FRAME ELEVATION
CIP	CAST IRON PIPE	⎤
RCP	REINFORCED CONCRETE PIPE	
CMP	CORRUGATED METAL PIPE	INCLUDE PIPE SIZE
VCP	VITRIFIED CLAY PIPE	
PVC	POLYVINYL CHLORIDE (PLASTIC) PIPE	⎦
STA. 0+00	STATION POINT	
⎯P⎯ _ _ ___	PROPERTY LINE	
___CLL__ _ ___	CONTRACT LIMIT LINE	
___℄___ . ___	CENTER LINE	
___℄___ . ⟶	CENTER LINE OF SWALE	⎤ INDICATE FLOW DIRECTION ⎦

Fig. 5.27.   TYPICAL GRADING PLAN SYMBOLS AND ABBREVIATIONS

PROBLEMS

5.1.   Develop a sketch book catalog of different types of grade-change devices.

5.2.   Evaluate a variety of stairs and ramps in terms of walking comfort. Measure risers, treads, and slopes to determine comfortable (and uncomfortable) relationships.

The problems in Chapter 3 provided all the criteria necessary to plot proposed contour lines. The following problems are less structured and, therefore, allow for the development of an approach to grading and the consideration of constraints which affect grading decisions.

5.3.   A residence has been placed on a site as illustrated on the facing page. Using the finished floor elevations noted on the plan, regrade the site and indicate all proposed contour lines and spot elevations. The proposed exterior grades adjacent to the building cannot be less than 0.5 ft nor more than 1.0 ft below the established FFE, except at the garage door.

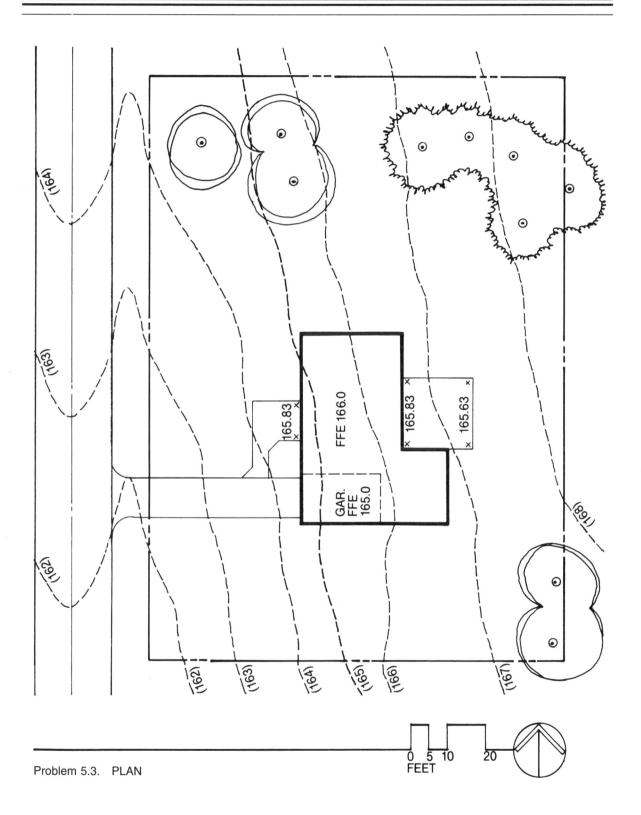

Problem 5.3.   PLAN

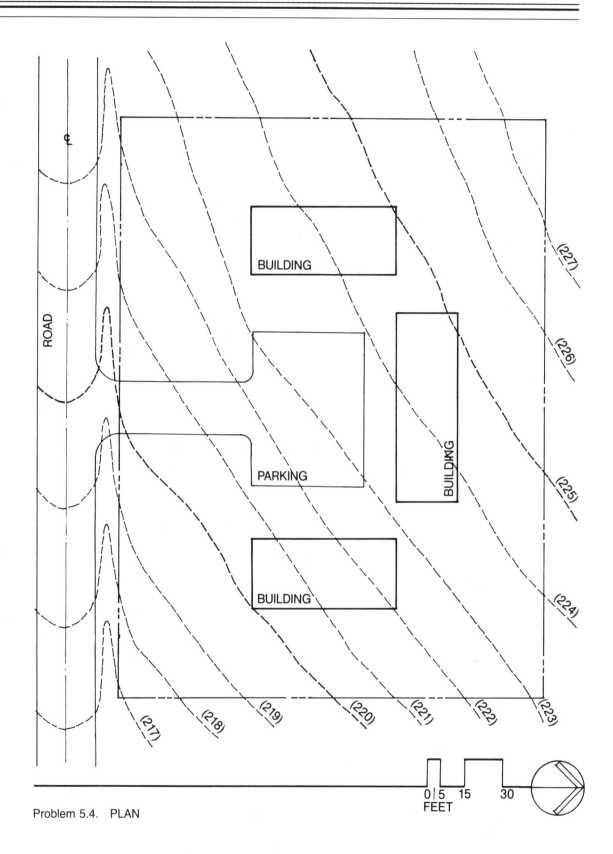

Problem 5.4. PLAN

5.4. Several buildings and a parking lot have been placed on a site (see p. 118). Establish the FFE for each building, regrade the site, and indicate all proposed contour lines and spot elevations. The proposed exterior grades adjacent to the building cannot be less than 0.5 ft nor more than 1.5 ft below the established FFE at each building. The curb along the driveway and parking lot is 0.5 ft high.

5.5. For this problem six townhouse units have been placed on a sloping site (see plan on p. 120). The architectural unit has been designed to accommodate the cross-slope by providing the following features:

a. The rear entry is 4.0 ft above the front entry elevation.

b. Each *pair* of units must have the same FFE, however, elevations of the units may change a maximum of 4.0 ft up or down at the fire walls.

c. The exterior grade at the front entry may equal the FFE; however, the exterior grade at the rear entry must be 0.5 ft below the rear FFE.

Regrade the site indicating all proposed contour lines and spot elevations. Provide a usable outdoor living space for a distance of 8 to 10 ft at the rear of each unit.

5.6. This problem deals with four attached dwelling units, walks, parking lot, and entry drive (see plan on p. 121). The FFE for all units must be the same and the rear entrances must be 9.0 ft below the front entrance elevations. There should be a 10.0 ft by 10.0 ft usable area adjacent to the rear entrance of each unit. The finished exterior grade at each entrance should be 2 in. below the proposed FFE. Grade-change devices (steps and walls) may be necessary to solve this problem. The existing contour lines are shown at a 2 ft interval. However, the proposed contour lines should be indicated at a 1 ft interval.

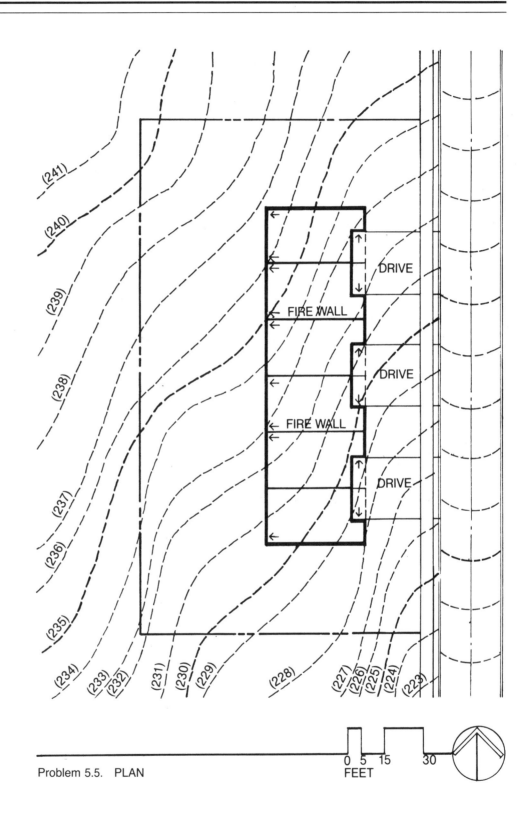

Problem 5.5. PLAN

0 5 15   30
FEET

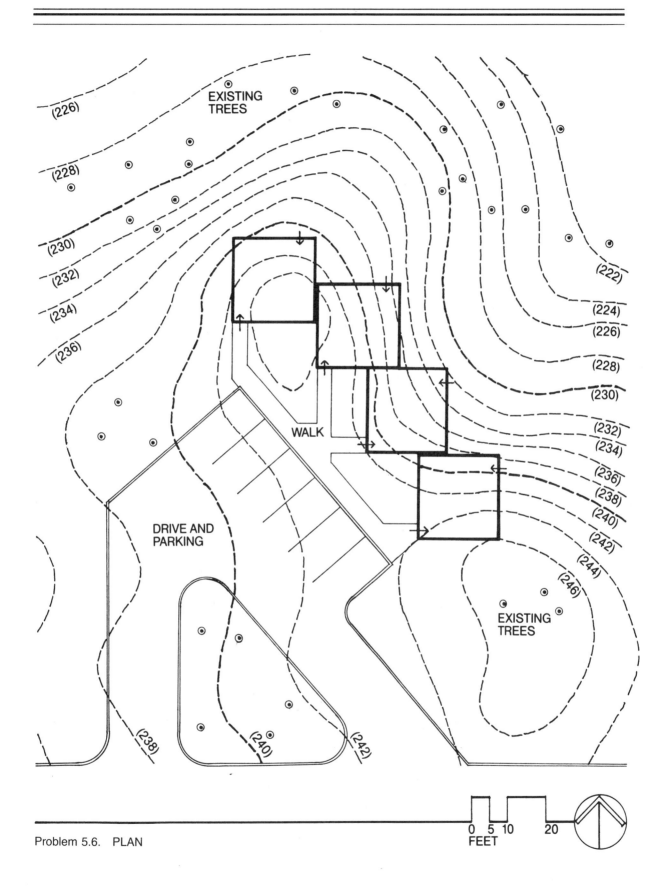

EXISTING
TREES

(226)

(228)

(230)

(232)

(234)

(236)

WALK

DRIVE AND
PARKING

(238)

(240)

(242)

(222)

(224)

(226)

(228)

(230)

(232)

(234)

(236)

(238)

(240)

(242)

(244)

(246)

EXISTING
TREES

0 5 10   20
FEET

Problem 5.6.   PLAN

CHAPTER 6

Storm Water Management

STORM RUNOFF

Surface runoff is storm water that moves on the ground by gravity and flows into streams, rivers, ponds, lakes, and oceans. For impervious surfaces like pavements and roofs, runoff occurs almost immediately. For pervious surfaces, the intensity of precipitation must exceed the infiltration rate, that is, the surface must be saturated before runoff will occur. *Subsurface runoff* is storm water that infiltrates and moves through the soil both horizontally and vertically. The rate of movement is influenced by soil permeability and typically occurs at a much slower rate than surface runoff.

Storm water (whether in the form of rain, snow, sleet, or hail), recharges ground water, replenishes water in the root zone of plants, and maintains the water level of streams, rivers, ponds, lakes, and reservoirs, which in turn support wildlife habitats, domestic water supplies, recreational activities, etc. Landscape development affects these relationships as a result of surface changes, which modify permeabilities, infiltration rates, and runoff volumes and rates. In low density developments and rural areas, a certain amount of change can be accommodated with little or no impact. However, high density and urban situations normally result in a more pronounced degree of change, which often requires elaborate and costly storm water management techniques. Typically in these situations, the area of pavement is increased while the vegetative cover is reduced. These conditions increase both the volume and rate of storm runoff.

There are several environmental impacts that may result from changes in the storm drainage pattern. These include increased flood potential due to increases in peak flow rates; decreased ground water supply due to reduced infiltration; increased soil erosion and sedimentation caused by greater runoff volumes and velocities; increased petrochemical pollution from street and highway runoff; and the addition of salt and sand to winter runoff in colder regions. Addressing these and other issues in the design and implementation phases will result in a more environmentally responsive management system.

MANAGEMENT SYSTEMS

The purpose of managing runoff is to ameliorate safety and health hazards including flooding and property damage, stagnation, earth slides, and reduced soil bearing capacity; to increase the usability of areas through the elimination of unwanted water; to provide better growing conditions for plants by increasing soil aeration and reducing soil saturation; and to prevent erosion by reducing the rate of flow and volume of runoff. There is a variety of management techniques that may be used to control storm water runoff. The context, i.e., the purpose and environmental conditions, will influence the selection of appropriate techniques.

The selection of an appropriate drainage system is based on a variety of factors. The scale and intensity of development, the amount and location of paved and unpaved surfaces, the proposed uses, and esthetic concerns must be addressed in making a choice. Physical factors such as soil erodibility, extent and steepness of slopes, expected rainfall intensities, etc., must also be considered. In addition, the availability and suitability of a potential drainage outlet and the character of existing local systems may help determine the type of proposed system. Building and environmental codes or other regulatory requirements such as maximum rate and volume of runoff, water quality, method of connection to an existing system, etc., must be met. The ultimate objective in designing most storm drainage systems is not to exceed the rate of flow that existed prior to the development of a site.

Components of Storm Water Management Systems

A brief explanation is provided here of the various components of storm water management systems. See Figs. 6.1–6.6.

Catch Basin A structure, typically concrete block or precast concrete rings, 2.5 to 4 ft in diameter, used to collect and divert surface runoff to an underground conduction system. A general rule of thumb is that one catch basin may be used for each 10,000 ft^2 of paved surface. At the base of the catch basin is a sump or sediment bowl to trap and collect debris.

Drain Inlet A structure that allows surface runoff to enter directly into a drain pipe. It does not contain a sump.

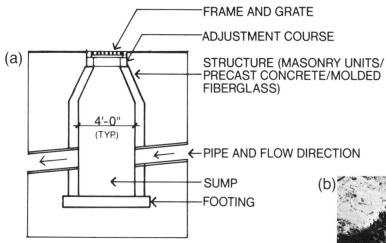

Fig. 6.1. CATCH BASIN
a. Section
b. Catch basin with curb inlet under
   construction

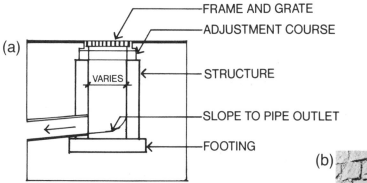

Fig. 6.2. DRAIN INLET
a. Section
b. Grate and frame for drain inlet

Area Drain   A prefabricated structure, similar to a floor drain, that collects runoff from paved areas. Usually one is used for each 1000 to 2000 ft^2 of pavement.

Trench Drain   A linear inlet structure used to collect sheet flow runoff in paved areas.

Manhole   A structure, often 4 ft in diameter, made of concrete block, precast concrete, or fiberglass-reinforced plastic rings, which allows a person to enter a space below ground. For storm drainage purposes, manholes are used where there is a change in size, slope, or direction of underground pipes. It is more cost effective if catch basins and manholes are combined.

Culvert   Any structure not classed as a bridge, which allows a water course to flow beneath a road, walk, or highway. A *pipe culvert* has a segmental, full circular, or elliptical arch cross-section, while a *box culvert* has a rectangular cross-section.

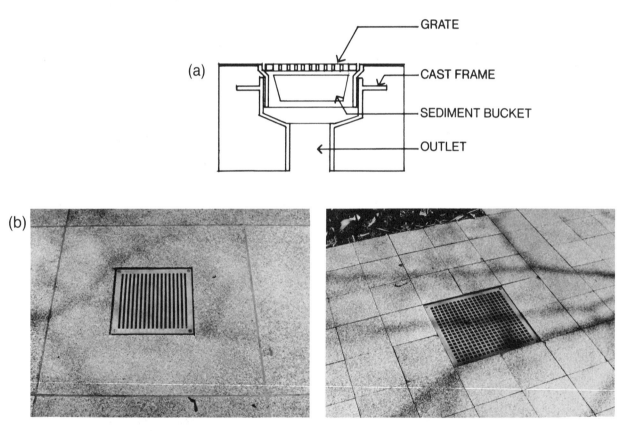

Fig. 6.3.   AREA DRAIN
    a. Section
    b. Area drain grates. Notice how the placement of the grates is coordinated with the paving pattern.

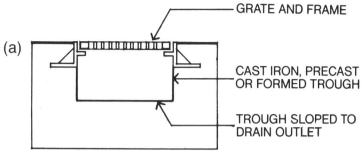

Fig. 6.4. TRENCH DRAIN
  a. Section
  b. Trench drain under construction
     A prepared base course (see
     Chapter 7) and grade stake
     are also illustrated.

Fig. 6.5. CULVERT
  Twin culverts carry the flow under a street along a large parabolic grassed
  swale.

Detention (Retention) Basin   An impoundment area constructed to collect storm runoff from a managment system for the purpose of reducing peak flow and controlling the rate of flow. A retention basin may be defined as having a permanent pool, while a detention basin is normally dry.

Sediment Basin   An impoundment area or structure that slows the velocity of runoff in order to allow sediment particles to settle out. Retention basins also function as sediment basins, although the reverse

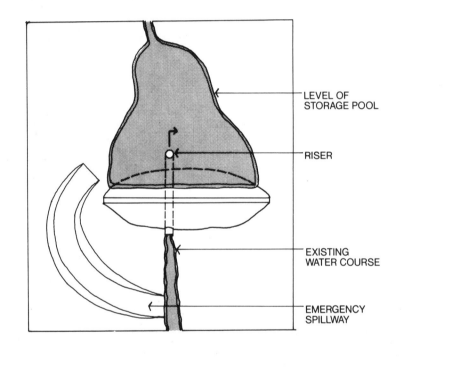

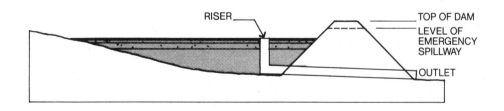

Fig. 6.6.   DETENTION/RETENTION BASIN
Level of storage pool is controlled by the height of the principal spillway. The principal spillway may be a riser (as illustrated) or a constructed spillway which allows water to flow across the dam. An emergency spillway is provided to allow for overflow when the design capacity is exceeded.

is not necessarily true. Retention, detention, and sediment basins require periodic cleaning to remove sediment.

Swale A constructed or natural drainage channel used to direct surface flow. (See Chapter 3.)

Open Drainage System

In an open drainage system (Fig. 6.7a) all surface runoff from paved and unpaved areas is collected and conveyed on the ground, primarily by swales. The system is discharged or directed to an on- or off-site drainageway, stream, or other natural water course, an existing street or municipal storm drainage system, or an on-site retention or sediment pond. The components of a system may include swales, gutters, channels, culverts, and detention, retention, or sediment basins. In designing the system, consideration must be given to the volume and velocity of runoff to prevent swale erosion, and to the means of controlling discharge at the outlet in order to collect sediment and, if necessary, to dissipate flow energy to prevent erosion.

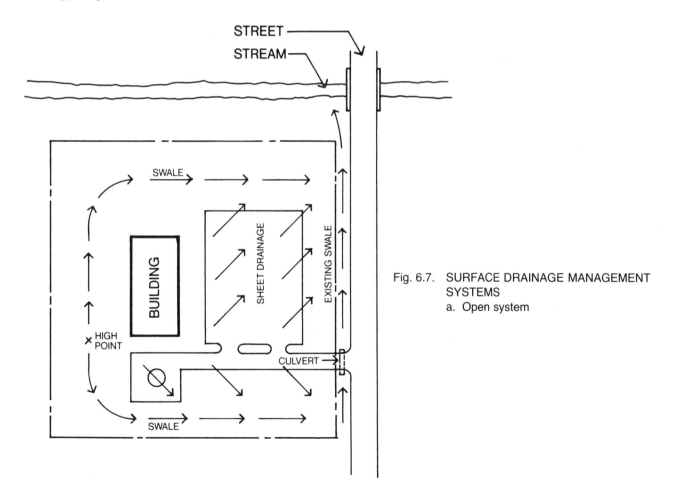

Fig. 6.7. SURFACE DRAINAGE MANAGEMENT
SYSTEMS
a. Open system

Closed Drainage System

For this system, surface runoff from paved and unpaved areas is collected at surface inlets and conveyed by underground pipes to an outlet either on or off the site (Fig. 6.7b). The advantage of this system is that the runoff may be intercepted before the volume and velocity increase to the point of causing erosion. Disadvantages include increased cost and complexity of the system, potential for erosion at the discharge point due to the greater concentration of runoff, and reduced filtering of sediment because of increased velocity of the storm water in the pipes. Structures commonly associated with closed systems are catch basins, drain inlets, area drains, trench drains, manholes, and piping. There are various piping materials including reinforced concrete, vitrified clay, corrugated metal, and plastic.

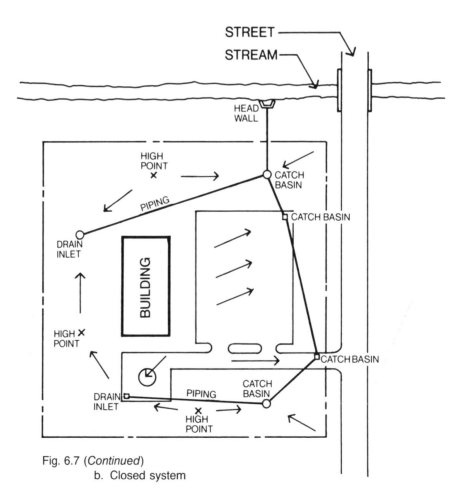

Fig. 6.7 (*Continued*)
    b. Closed system

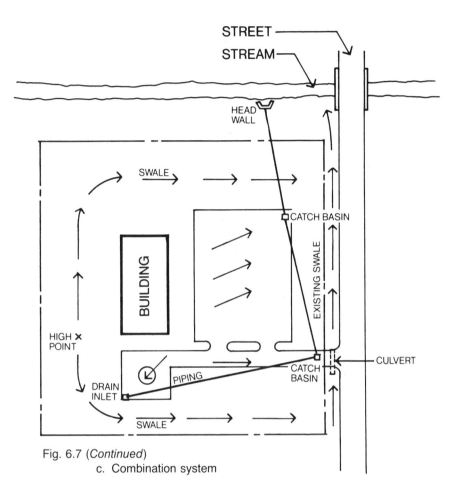

Fig. 6.7 (*Continued*)
   c. Combination system

Combination System

In many cases, the system is a combination of open and closed drainage (Fig. 6.7c). Typically, the open system is used in unpaved areas with the intent of providing more opportunity for the storm water to infiltrate the pervious surface, whereas the closed system is used in paved areas. The advantages of this system are reduced construction costs compared to a totally closed system, lower potential for soil erosion because of reduced volumes of surface runoff, and lower potential for erosion problems at the outfall because of lower volumes in the pipes.

Subsurface Drainage

The purpose of subsurface drainage is to maintain the water table at a level that provides desirable plant growth conditions and increases the usability of areas for recreational or other purposes. Subsurface drains remove only *excess* water and not water plants can use. Water available to plants is held in the soil by capillary, or surface tension, forces, while excess water flows by gravity into the drains. Subsurface drainage is accomplished by means of clay tile or perforated or porous pipe laid in a continuous line at a specified depth and grade (Figs. 6.8 and 6.9). Free water enters the drains through the joints, perforations, or porous walls of the pipe and flows out by gravity. Although somewhat similar to a closed system, it must be emphasized that subsurface drainage differs in principle from surface drainage in that water percolates through the soil and is then removed by drains placed below the ground surface.

The major components of a subsurface drainage system are mains, submains, laterals, and drainage outlets. The laterals collect the free water from the soil and carry it to the submains and mains. These, in turn, conduct the water to the drainage outlet. The installation procedure for perforated pipe is to place the perforations at the bottom of the pipe to minimize the amount of soil particles entering the pipe. For clay tile a small gap is left between pipe segments. Tar paper is placed over the top of the gaps or permeable filter strips are wrapped around the pipe to minimize the entrance of silt particles into the pipe. Finally, under certain conditions, surface inlets may be used in conjunction with a subsurface drainage system.

Underdrainage is a specific type of subsurface drainage used to maintain proper structural conditions. Examples include footing and foundation drains and lateral drains placed behind retaining walls (see Chapter 5). Pavements placed over clay soils or rock or at the bottom of steep slopes may need underdrains to reduce the possibility of perched water and hydrostatic pressure (Fig. 6.10).

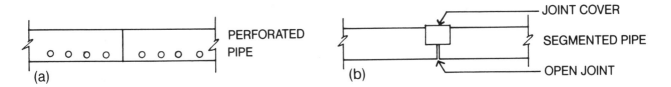

Fig. 6.8. PIPE INSTALLATION FOR SUBSURFACE DRAINAGE
    a. Perforated pipe with perforations placed toward the bottom of the pipe
    b. For segmented pipe, such as clay tile, a gap is left between pipe segments.
       A cover or filter is placed over the open joint to prevent sediment from
       entering the pipe.

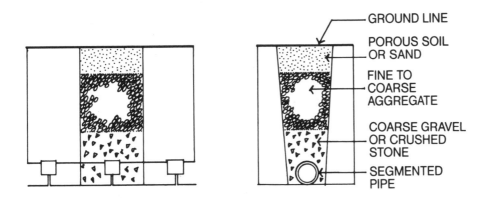

Fig. 6.9. FRENCH DRAIN WITH SUBSURFACE DRAINAGE
    A french drain is a trench filled with porous material which is used to collect
    and conduct surface runoff. French drains may also be used in conjunction with
    subsurface drainage as illustrated.

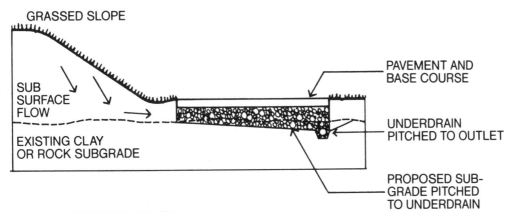

Fig. 6.10. UNDERDRAINAGE
    The section illustrates a condition where a build-up of water could occur
    beneath the pavement, thus causing damage by pressure or frost action. To
    reduce these problems the new subgrade is sloped to an underdrain which
    carries off the excess water.

DESIGN AND LAYOUT OF DRAINAGE SYSTEMS

Surface Drainage

The three basic functions of any storm drainage system are to *collect*, *conduct*, and *dispose* of storm runoff. In order to proceed with the design of a system, each of these functions must be appropriately analyzed as follows.

Collection To determine where runoff is coming from, it is necessary to analyze the existing and proposed drainage patterns. To begin with, it is important to analyze *off*-site patterns, since very few sites exist as isolated entities. The extent of the surrounding drainage area, its effect on the site, and the effect of the proposed site development must be evaluated. The character of the drainage area including soils, slopes, and surface cover has to be determined.

The character of the existing and proposed *on-site* patterns must also be investigated. This includes the location of high points, low points, ridges, valleys, swales, points of concentration, streams, etc. Also by analyzing the on-site patterns, the critical areas where runoff should be collected or intercepted may be determined. Drainage structures such as catch basins, drain inlets, and area drains and interception measures such as diversions and trench drains must be located at these critical points. By understanding the nature, direction, and extent of these patterns it is possible to estimate the rate of runoff expected from the individual drainage areas. The analysis of where runoff is coming from also provides an opportunity to reexamine the grading scheme to determine whether it is functioning properly with regard to storm drainage. Remember that to insure positive drainage all surfaces must slope and that, in most cases, it is illegal to increase the rate of flow of runoff across adjacent property.

Disposal The question of where the water is going must be answered before the question of how it is going to get there, because the outlet will have a direct influence on the method of conduction. It must first be determined whether the runoff will be disposed of on or off the site and whether the connection is to a natural system (e.g., stream, river, lake) or an engineered system (e.g., drainage channel, storm sewer, retention basin). Failure to consider the suitability of the outlet and the nature of the connection has, in some cases, resulted in systems that do not function properly, a waste of money, or even litigation brought about by damage caused by concentrated water flowing from drainage pipes or channels onto adjacent properties. Finally, the connection and means of disposal must comply with all building codes, zoning ordinances, and environmental regulations.

Conduction Storm runoff may be conducted in an open, closed, or combination system. Some factors that could influence the type, layout, components, and extensiveness of a system have been previously mentioned. These include surface cover and soil type; type of land use (e.g., urban plaza, park or playfield); and visual appearance. This last point is particularly important to landscape architects and site planners. In addition, rainfall characteristics like frequency, duration, and intensity of storms have to be considered. In most cases it is not difficult to develop a storm drainage management system that functions properly hydraulically. However, to develop a system that is integrated with the overall design concept and does not become visually distracting requires a certain amount of care, finesse, and understanding of basic engineering principles. A general rule of thumb is to make the management system as inconspicuous and unobtrusive as possible. This does not mean that costly measures should be taken to disguise or hide a system or that in some designs it is not appropriate to use the management system as an element that is significant to the design concept. It does mean that generally, for open systems, swales should be broad with gentle, rounded cross sections rather than narrow and ditch-like. For closed systems, structures should be placed logically and inlet openings not oversized unnecessarily. Where drainage inlets are placed in pavement, the location should be coordinated with the paving pattern, and the sloping of the planes of pavement to direct runoff should be minimized to reduce the warped appearance of the surface.

Whether an open, closed, or combination system is used, the typical conduction pattern will be tree-like in appearance. This pattern results from a hierarchical collection of runoff from a series of small drainage areas which, in most instances, will terminate at one disposal point. Also it must be realized that generally the conduction component (swales or pipes) must increase in size as it progresses toward the outlet point, since the volume of runoff continues to increase.

In laying out piping patterns for closed systems, it is important to avoid buildings, subsurface structures such as other utilities, retaining walls, and trees. For most small-scale site development projects, pipes are designed as straight lines, since this reduces the potential for clogging and makes the system easier to clean. It is possible, however, to lay out pipe using curved alignments, particularly for large size pipe (36 in. diameter and larger). Since pipes are placed underground, they are independent of the surface slope. However, avoid running pipe contrary to the surface slope, since this increases the amount of trench excavation required. Finally, storm water flows through pipes by gravity, therefore all pipes must *slope*.

SIZING MANAGEMENT SYSTEMS

The Rational Method

The first step in determining the size of a management system is to calculate the expected rate of runoff. The relationship between rate of runoff to rainfall is affected by such factors as intensity of rainfall, slope, type of surface cover, soil type, and size of drainage area. The extent of the drainage area is determined by connecting the high points and ridge lines on a topographic map or grading plan until a closed system is developed (Fig. 6.11). Drainage areas may vary in size from several hundred square feet for an area drain, or several square miles for a stream, up to thousands of square miles for a large river, in which case it is called a *watershed*. It must also be realized that drainage area boundaries are independent of property lines. It is important to include all parts of a drainage area, even if they are beyond the property line.

A generally accepted formula for computing the peak rate of runoff from small drainage areas (i.e., less than one square mile) is the "Rational method." The equation is

$$Q = CIA \tag{6.1}$$

where Q = peak runoff rate in cubic feet per second (cfs)
C = dimensionless runoff coefficient (between 0 and 1)
I = rainfall intensity in inches per hour (iph) for the design storm frequency and for the time of concentration of the drainage area
A = area of drainage area in acres

The equation is based on the theory that the peak rate of runoff from a small area is equal to the intensity of rainfall multiplied by a coefficient that depends on the characteristics of the drainage area, and by the size of the drainage area. One acre-inch per hour of water may be converted to cubic feet per second as follows:

$$1 \text{ acre} \times \frac{1 \text{ in.}}{\text{hr}} \times \frac{43560 \text{ ft}^2}{\text{acre}} \times \frac{1}{12 \text{ in./ft}} \times \frac{1}{3600 \text{ sec/hr}} = 1.008 \text{ cfs}$$

The rate computed by the rational method is therefore dimensionally incorrect by 0.8%. This is generally ignored, since the field of hydrology is not an exact science.

The *runoff coefficient C* is a value between 0 and 1. Zero represents a completely pervious surface from which there is no runoff, while 1 represents a completely impervious and wetted surface from which there

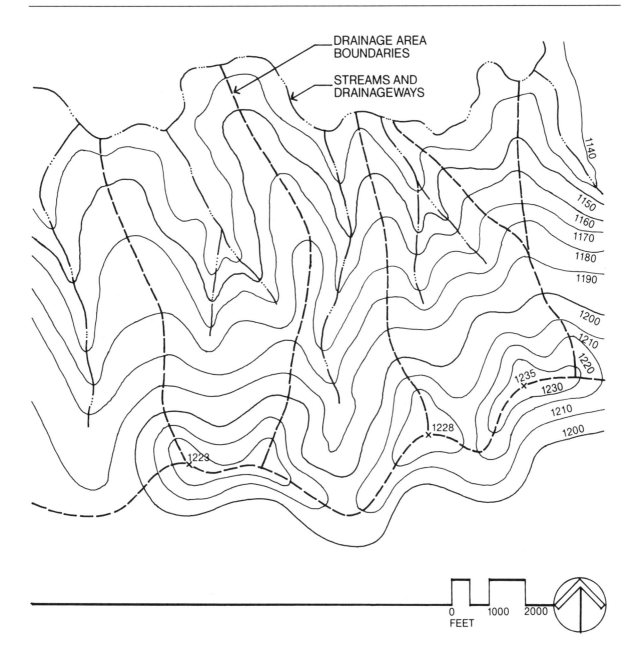

Fig. 6.11. DRAINAGE AREAS
Boundaries for drainage areas are determined by locating ridge lines and
high points.

is total runoff. Table 6.1 contains suggested C values for a variety of surface conditions. For unpaved areas the C value would increase as the soil becomes saturated. Most drainage areas will consist of a variety of surfaces with different C values. Runoff volumes may be computed for each surface separately or an average C value can be computed for the entire drainage area, if the locations of the various land uses are mixed throughout the area.

TABLE 6.1.   Recommended Runoff Coefficients (C)

Urban areas[a]	
Downtown Business	0.70−0.95
Neighborhood Business	0.50−0.70
Single-family Residential	0.30−0.50
Detached Multi-Unit Residential	0.40−0.60
Attached Multi-Unit Residential	0.60−0.75
Suburban Residential	0.25−0.40
Apartment	0.50−0.70
Light Industry	0.50−0.80
Heavy Industry	0.60−0.90
Parks, Cemeteries	0.10−0.25
Playgrounds	0.20−0.35
Railroad Yards	0.20−0.35
Unimproved	0.10−0.30
Urban surfaces	
Roofs	0.80−0.95
Asphalt and Concrete Pavements	0.75−0.95
Gravel	0.35−0.70

	Soil Texture		
Rural and suburban areas[b]	Sandy loam	Clay and silt loam	Clay
Woodland			
flat (0−5% slope)	0.10	0.30	0.40
rolling (5−10% slope)	0.25	0.35	0.50
hilly (10−30% slope)	0.30	0.50	0.60
Pasture and Lawns			
flat	0.10	0.30	0.40
rolling	0.16	0.36	0.55
hilly	0.22	0.42	0.60
Cultivated or No Plant Cover			
flat	0.30	0.50	0.60
rolling	0.40	0.60	0.70
hilly	0.52	0.72	0.82

[a] From American Iron and Steel Institute (1980)
[b] From Schwab et al. (1971)

Example 6.1 The drainage area for a grassed waterway is an 8.2 acre site for a small industrial plant. As shown in Fig. 6.12, several different surfaces are dispersed throughout the site. These surfaces include 4.4 acres of relatively flat lawn with a silt loam soil, 2.8 acres of pavement, and 1 acre of roof surface. The assumed rainfall intensity is 2 iph. Calculate the peak rate of runoff for this drainage area.

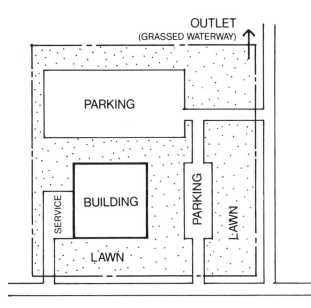

Fig. 6.12. SCHEMATIC SITE PLAN

Solution 1

A = 4.4 acres of lawn, 2.8 acres of pavement, 1 acre of roof.

$I = 2$ *iph*.

From Table 6.1

$$C_{\text{flat lawn}} = 0.30$$
$$C_{\text{pavement}} = 0.85$$
$$C_{\text{roof}} = 0.95$$

Using Eq. (6.1), substitute the known values.

$$Q_{\text{lawn}} = 0.30 \times 2.0 \times 4.4$$
$$= 2.64 \text{ cfs}$$
$$Q_{\text{pavt.}} = 0.85 \times 2.0 \times 2.8$$
$$= 4.76 \text{ cfs}$$
$$Q_{\text{roof}} = 0.95 \times 2.0 \times 1$$
$$= 1.90 \text{ cfs}$$
$$Q_{\text{total}} = 2.64 + 4.76 + 1.90 = 9.30 \text{ cfs}$$

Solution 2

$$A_{\text{total}} = 4.4 + 2.8 + 1.0 = 8.2 \text{ acres}$$
$$I = 2 \text{ iph}$$

$$C_{\text{ave}} = \frac{(4.4 \times 0.30) + (2.8 \times 0.85) + (1.0 \times 0.95)}{8.2}$$
$$= 0.567$$

Again, substitute the known values into Eq. (6.1)

$$Q_{\text{total}} = 0.567 \times 2.0 \times 8.2$$
$$= 9.30 \text{ cfs}$$

Note that the total Q value is the same whether it is computed separately or using an average C value. However, for this example the average C value is a better representation of the actual runoff conditions.

Rainfall intensity I is the rate of rainfall in inches per hour for the design storm frequency and for the time of concentration of the drainage area. The *storm frequency* is the number of years during which the design storm, or a storm exceeding it, statistically may be expected to occur once. It must be pointed out that the frequency is based on long-term probabilities and that, for example, a 10-year frequency storm could conceivably occur several times during a period shorter than 10 years. This might be compared to throwing a die for which the overall probability of coming up 6 is one out of six throws, but which could come up 6 several times in succession. The *design storm* is a storm with a frequency and duration for which the management system is designed. The selection of a design storm is based on economics, environmental context, and the ultimate consequences should the system overflow. Rainfall intensities for various durations may be obtained from National Weather Service publications and charts.

The *time of concentration* is the time for water to flow from the hydraulically most remote part of the drainage area to the section under consideration. It is important to realize that this is not necessarily the longest distance, since overland and channel flow time is dependent on slope, surface, and channel characteristics. Assuming a theoretical storm of uniform intensity falling uniformly over the entire drainage area with a duration equal to or exceeding the time of concentration, the peak runoff is reached at the time of concentration. At this time, all parts of the drainage area are contributing simultaneously to the runoff at the section under consideration. Convenient charts which are used to estimate time of concentration are illustrated in Fig. 6.13 for overland flow time, as demonstrated in Example 6.2 and Fig. 6.14 for channel flow time, as applied in Example 6.3.

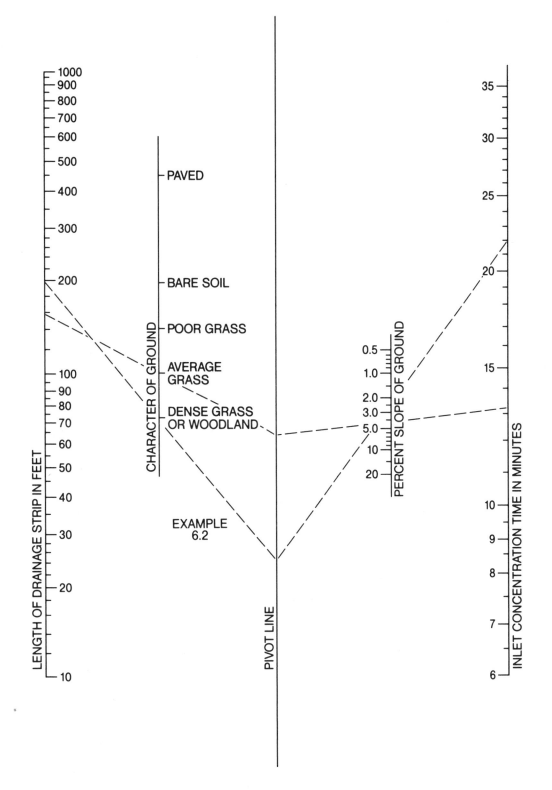

Fig. 6.13. NOMOGRAPH FOR OVERLAND FLOW TIME

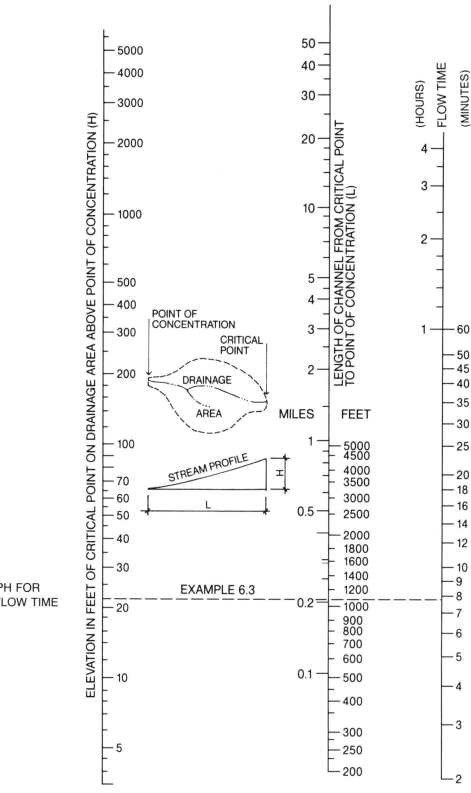

Fig. 6.14. NOMOGRAPH FOR
           CHANNEL FLOW TIME

Example 6.2   The 1.5 acre drainage area illustrated in Fig. 6.15 consists of 0.14 acre of pavement, 0.20 acre of woodland, and 1.16 acres of lawn. The soil is a silt loam and the slopes range up to 5%. Calculate the peak rate of runoff leaving the site at the southwest corner. A 10-year design storm is to be used.

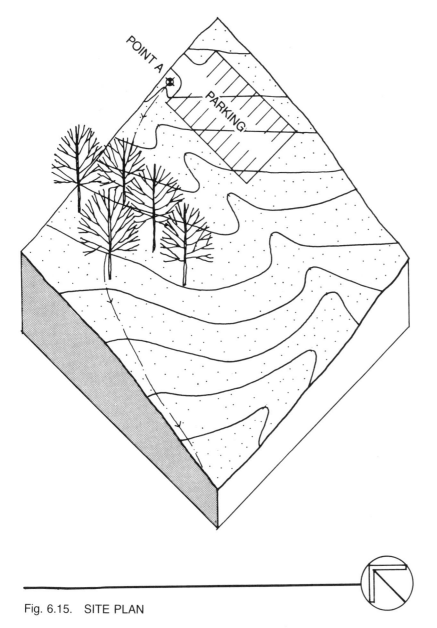

Fig. 6.15.   SITE PLAN

Solution   The first step in this problem is to determine the time of concentration in order to establish the rainfall intensity value I. Additional information is required to compute the overland flow time. From visual inspection, it is determined that point *A* is the hydraulically most remote point on the site. The *distance* that a drop of water must travel to reach the outlet point from point *A*, the *slope* of its path of travel, and the *surface character* of the path must also be determined. This is summarized below for this problem.

Length	Character	Slope	Time of concentration
200 feet	Woodland	2%	22 minutes
160 feet	Average grass	4%	13 minutes
			35 minutes total

The time of concentration is determined from the chart in Fig. 6.13. First, the travel distance is located along the length line, then the surface character is located on the character of ground line. A straight line is drawn through these two points until it intersects with the pivot line. Next the slope of the path is located on the percent slope line and a straight line is drawn from the point on the pivot line through the point on the slope line until it intersects with the inlet concentration time. This point of intersection represents the time of concentration in minutes. No additional time needs to be computed, since there is no channel flow involved in this example.

The intensity of the design storm can then be obtained from the chart in Fig. 6.16. Locate the 35 min storm duration along the horizontal axis of the chart and extend a vertical line until it intersects with the 10-year frequency curve. From the point on the curve extend a horizontal line to the left until it intersects with the vertical axis. The value obtained, 3.0 iph, is the rainfall intensity for the storm duration. The chart in Fig. 6.16 applies to New Jersey. The appropriate charts or similar information for other states may be obtained from the State Department of Conservation, Water Resources, or other similar agency or from the National Weather Service.

The next step is to select an appropriate runoff coefficient from Table 6.1 for the various surfaces.

$$C_{\text{pavement}} = 0.90$$
$$C_{\text{woodland}} = 0.30$$
$$C_{\text{lawn}} = 0.30$$

The last step is to substitute all the known values into Eq. (6.1)

$$Q_{\text{total}} = (0.90 \times 3.0 \times 0.14) + (0.30 \times 3.0 \times 0.20) +$$
$$(0.30 \times 3.0 \times 1.16)$$
$$= 3.0 (0.90 \times 0.14 + 0.30 \times 0.20 + 0.30 \times 1.16)$$
$$= 3.0 \times 0.53 = 1.60 \text{ cfs}$$

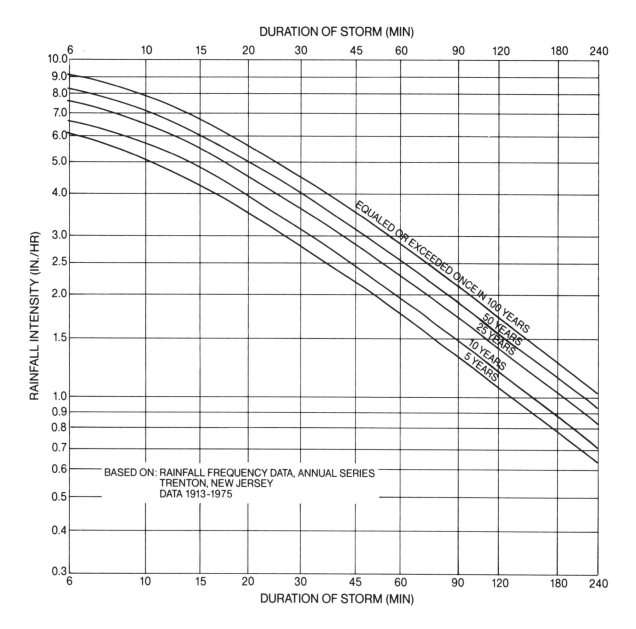

Fig. 6.16. RAINFALL INTENSITY CURVES

The following example demonstrates the determination of the time of concentration when overland flow and stream flow are involved.

Example 6.3   Figure 6.17 shows a 95 acre drainage area which is completely wooded with a stream flowing through the center. The soil survey report indicates a silt loam. The topographic map shows that the average drainage area slope is 6%, while the stream slope is 2%. A road culvert is to be installed at the outlet from this drainage area and must be designed for a 50-year frequency storm. What is the peak rate of runoff for which the culvert must be designed?

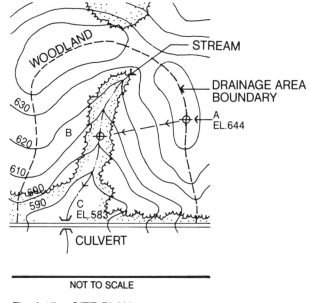

NOT TO SCALE

Fig. 6.17.   SITE PLAN

Solution   An examination of the topographic map shows that A is the hydraulically most remote point. From A to B the water flows overland for 970 ft along a 4% slope. (The *average* drainage area slope is 6%.) From B to C there is 1100 ft of stream flow with a 2% slope. Using Fig. 6.13 as before, the overland flow here is determined as 35 min. To obtain the stream flow time Fig. 6.14 must be used. To calculate H, which is the elevation of the critical point above the point of concentration, i.e., the elevation of point B above point C, distance B−C is multiplied by the slope:

$$H = 1100 \times 0.02 = 22 \text{ ft}$$

A straight line is drawn from 22 ft on the H scale on the left through 1100 ft on the L scale to the T scale on the right which yields about 8 min. (Note the rapidity of the streamflow compared to overland flow.) Then the total time of concentration is overland flow time + streamflow time, or 35 + 8 = 43 min. The intensity for a 50-year 43 min. storm is about from Fig. 6.16. The C value for woodland on silt loam with an average slope of 6% is 0.35 from Table 6.1. The design peak rate of runoff is thus:

$$Q = CIA$$
$$= 0.35 \times 3.5 \times 95$$
$$= 116 \text{ cfs}$$

Therefore, the culvert must be sized to accommodate 116 cfs.

As pointed out earlier, surface runoff cannot take place until the ground is thoroughly wetted and all surface depressions have been filled. If this has already been done by an earlier storm event, more runoff can be expected from a specific design storm. In recent years, it has been recognized that allowance should be made in the Rational formula for this *antecedent precipitation*. Less frequent events are more likely to be part of a prolonged and extensive storm system and thus are more likely to occur under high antecedent moisture conditions. To adjust the peak runoff rate as determined by the Rational formula, an antecedent precipitation factor, C_A, is included so that the formula becomes

$$Q = CC_A IA \tag{6.2}$$

Recommended values for C_A are listed in Table 6.2. The product $C \times C_A$ must never exceed 1, since otherwise the computed runoff rate would be greater than the intensity of the design storm, which is incongruous.

TABLE 6.2.   Recommended Antecedent[a] Precipitation Factors

Frequency (years)	C_A
2 to 10	1.0
25	1.1
50	1.2
100	1.25

[a] From American Public Works Association (1974)

Example 6.4   What is the peak runoff rate for Example 6.3 if allowance for antecedent precipitation is made?

Solution   The peak runoff rate for a 50-year frequency was previously determined as $Q = 116$ cfs. The antecedent precipitation factor for a 50-year frequency is 1.2 from Table 6.2. $C \times C_A = 0.35 \times 1.2 = 0.42$, which is less than 1 and can be used. The required peak runoff rate is

$$Q = CC_A IA$$
$$= 0.35 \times 1.2 \times 3.5 \times 95$$
$$= 139.65 \text{ } or \text{ } 140 \text{ cfs.}$$

As demonstrated by the following examples, common sense should be applied when determining time of concentration, particularly with regard to the location of different surface types (C values) on a site.

Example 6.5a Figure 6.18a schematically illustrates a drainage area consisting of 3 acres of pavement ($C = 0.80$) and 3 acres of lawn ($C = 0.30$). As contrasted with Example 6.1 where the different surfaces were mixed throughout the site, these two surfaces are concentrated and segregated. Determine the peak rate of runoff at the point of discharge from the site for a 10-year storm frequency. Assume a 6 min time of concentration for the pavement and a 30 min time of concentration for the lawn. The runoff from the pavement flows across the lawn area to the discharge point.

Solution Since it takes the hydraulically most remote drop of water 6 min to flow across the pavement and an additional 30 min to flow across the lawn before reaching the discharge point, the total time is 36 min (6 + 30). Entering the chart in Fig. 6.16 with a storm duration of 36 min, a rainfall intensity of approximately 2.9 iph is determined from the 10-year storm frequency curve. From the Rational formula, the peak rate of runoff is calculated as follows:

$$\begin{aligned}
Q_{\text{lawn}} &= 0.30 \times 2.9 \times 3.0 \\
&= 2.61 \text{ cfs} \\
Q_{\text{pavt.}} &= 0.80 \times 2.9 \times 3.0 \\
&= 6.96 \text{ cfs} \\
Q_{\text{total}} &= 2.61 + 6.96 = 9.57 \text{ cfs}
\end{aligned}$$

Example 6.5b All the conditions of this example, including times of concentration, are the same as in Example 6.4a, except the relationship of pavement to lawn has been reversed. Now the runoff from the lawn flows across the pavement to the discharge point as illustrated in Fig. 6.18b. Again, calculate the peak rate of runoff from the site using a 10-year storm frequency.

Solution In the previous example the lawn attenuated the velocity of flow from the pavement, since it was located between the paved area and the point of discharge. However, in this example the overland flow is not attenuated and the runoff from the pavement concentrates at the discharge point in 6 min. Therefore, the storm duration for determining the rainfall intensity is 6 min for the pavement. Again referring to Fig. 6.16, the rainfall intensity is 6.6 iph on the 10-year storm frequency curve. Thus, the peak rate of runoff from the pavement is:

$$\begin{aligned}
Q_{\text{pavt.}} &= 0.80 \times 6.6 \times 3.0 \\
&= 15.84 \text{ cfs}
\end{aligned}$$

The runoff rate from the pavement alone is considerably greater than the runoff rate for the entire drainage area in Example 6.5a. Due to its much longer time of concentration and relatively small contribution, the runoff

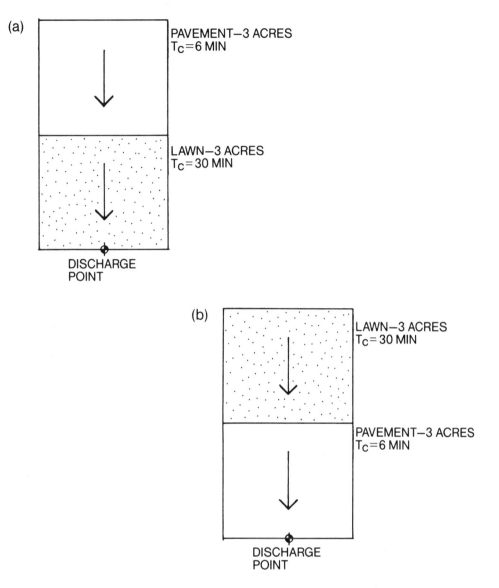

Fig. 6.18.   SCHEMATIC PLANS

from the lawn area for this example can be disregarded when peak flow is determined.

The Rational method is not applicable to large drainage areas because it assumes that the rainfall duration is at least equal to the time of concentration and that the rate of runoff does not increase after the time of concentration has been reached. It also assumes precipitation that is uniform in intensity and amount over the entire drainage area. These assumptions are not valid for larger areas.

Designing and Sizing Grassed Swales (Waterways)

Grassed swales are a common component of open drainage systems. Generally, grassed swales should not carry continuous flows or even be continuously wet. Where this might occur, an alternative method such as a lined waterway or the use of subsurface drains, which leave the swale to carry flow only during and after storms, is preferable. When designing the layout of a management system, it may be possible to retain an existing natural drainageway or it may be necessary to construct new waterways. New waterways generally have a smooth, shallow, and relatively wide cross-section, which is called *parabolic*, since it represents part of a parabolic curve. Although the discussion here will be limited to parabolic waterways, there are other cross-sectional shapes that are applicable. The dimensions of the cross-section are specified by the width W and the depth D as illustrated in Fig. 6.19. Typically, swales are seeded with the same seed mixtures that would be used for lawns in that particular location or with native grasses if a naturalized effect is desired. Newly constructed vegetated waterways should be protected from the erosive effect of flowing water until a good stand of grass has been established.

Grassed waterways are constructed to a design slope that is staked out and controlled during construction by profile leveling. In engineering terms, it is preferable to design swales so that the velocity of the water flowing in them will not be decreased, since a reduction in flow velocity will result in siltation. Velocity could be reduced by a change in slope from steep to flat, by enlarging the cross-section without also increasing the slope, or by an increase in the frictional resistance of the surface caused by tall vegetation being placed down slope from a stand of short vegetation. However, there are situations where a decrease in velocity, which filters out sediment, is desired. It must be realized, however, that sedimentation changes the character and capacity of a swale, thus increasing the level of maintenance. Generally, grassed waterways are maintained in the same way as any turf area. Two points of critical concern, though, are the prompt repair of any erosion damage and the removal of accumulated sediment.

(a)

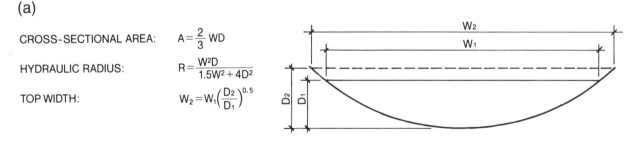

CROSS-SECTIONAL AREA: $A = \frac{2}{3} WD$

HYDRAULIC RADIUS: $R = \dfrac{W^2 D}{1.5W^2 + 4D^2}$

TOP WIDTH: $W_2 = W_1 \left(\dfrac{D_2}{D_1}\right)^{0.5}$

Fig. 6.19. PARABOLIC SWALES
a. Elements of parabolic swales

(b)

(c)

(d)

Fig. 6.19 (*Continued*)
b. A parabolic swale flowing full
c. A diversion swale with drain inlet
d. A swale which is not functioning properly. A broader cross-section or longer stand of grass could be used to slow the velocity of flow and reduce the potential for erosion.

151

The required dimensions for grassed swales may be determined analytically or by a variety of published nomographs or other design aids. To determine the required dimensions of a swale, the rate of runoff to be handled must be known. This may be computed from the Rational formula, $Q = CIA$, as previously discussed. With the runoff rate known, the next step is to determine the slope for the proposed swale and the design velocity of flow. The slope is generally determined by the proposed grading plan, the elevation of the outlet point, and the existing topography. The permissible maximum design velocity depends on the type and condition of the vegetation, the erodibility of the soil, and the slope of the swale. Recommended velocities for various conditions may be found in Table 6.3.

TABLE 6.3.   Permissible Velocities for Vegetated Swales and Channels[a]

Cover	Slope range (%)[b]	Permissible velocity (fps)	
		Erosion-resistant soils	Easily eroded soils
Bermudagrass	0–5	8	6
	5–10	7	5
	over 10	6	4
Reed canarygrass Smooth bromegrass Tall fescue Kentucky bluegrass	0–5	7	5
	5–10	6	4
	over 10	5	3
Grass–legume mixtures	0–5	5	4
	5–10	4	3
Red fescue Redtop Lespedeza sericea Alfalfa	0–5[c]	3.5	2.5
Common lespedeza[d] Sudangrass	0–5[e]	3.5	2.5

[a]Use velocities exceeding 5 fps only where good cover and proper maintenance can be obtained.

[b]Do not use on slopes steeper than 10% except for vegetated side slopes in combination with stone, concrete, or highly resistant vegetative center sections.

[c]Do not use on slopes steeper than 5% except for vegetated side slopes in combination channels.

[d]Annuals—use on mild slopes or as temporary protection until permanent cover is established.

[e]Use on slopes steeper than 5% is not recommended.

TABLE 6.4. Retardance Factors for Grassed Swales[a]

Range of vegetation height during different periods of the year	Vegetative retardance factors	
	For determining minimum capacity	For determining maximum allowable velocity
Good stand		
between 6 in. and less than 2 in.	D	E
between 10 in. and 2 in.	C	D
between 24 in. and 2 in.	B	D
Fair or poor stand		
between 10 in. and less than 2 in.	D	E
between 24 in. and 2 in.	C	D
between 30 in. and 2 in.	B	D

[a]From New Jersey Association of Conservation Districts (1982)

Since the friction, or resistance to flow, of the vegetation varies with its length (which is short right after mowing and relatively long just before mowing), the range of heights must be determined. Also, as the flow depth increases, long vegetation will bend over and offer less resistance to flow than it would with only a shallow depth of flow.

For this reason various resistance, or retardance factors have been experimentally determined and are listed in Table 6.4.

If the length of vegetation changes, the final design should always be checked for channel stability with maximum velocity (short vegetation) and capacity with minimum velocity (long vegetation). As a minimum, swales should be designed to carry the peak flow for a 10-year storm frequency.

Swale Design by Hydraulics

There are two formulas, Manning's equation and the continuity equation, which are used in determining the dimensions of open channels, including swales. *Manning's equation* is used to calculate the velocity of flow in open channels and is stated as:

$$V = \frac{1.486}{n} R^{0.67} S^{0.50} \tag{6.3}$$

where V = velocity of flow in fps
    n = dimensionless roughness coefficient (see Table 6.5)
    R = hydraulic radius in ft = (cross-sectional area in ft^2 ÷ wetted perimeter in ft)
    S = slope in ft/ft

TABLE 6.5.   Roughness Coefficients for Pipes and Channels

	n
Pipe Material	
Concrete	0.012–0.015
Cast Iron	0.013
Corrugated Metal	0.024
Plastic (smooth)	0.012
Vitrified Clay	0.010–0.015
Channel Surface	
Asphalt	0.013–0.016
Concrete	0.012–0.018
Riprap	0.020–0.040
Vegetated	0.030–0.080

The *continuity equation* relates the cross-sectional area to the design flow and the average flow velocity and is defined as

$$Q = AV \qquad (6.4)$$

where Q = flow in cfs
       A = cross-sectional area of flow in ft^2
       V = velocity of flow in fps

If the hydraulic radius and the required cross-sectional area are known, the design dimensions can be determined.

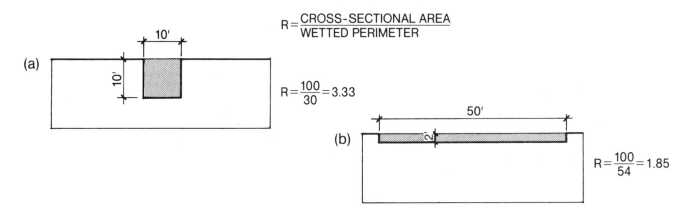

Fig. 6.20.   HYDRAULIC RADIUS
For the same given cross-sectional area, R varies inversely with the wetted perimeter. Although the cross-sectional area in (b) is the same as in (a), the surface area exposed per unit length of channel is much greater, resulting in greater friction between the channel and the water. Consistent with the increased friction, the R value is less than in (a) and the velocity of flow is reduced.

Example 6.6   A grassed waterway with a slope of 4% must carry 50 cfs of runoff. The soil is easily eroded. Design a vegetated drainageway with a parabolic cross-section. The vegetative cover will be a good stand of bluegrass sod that will be kept mowed to a 2.5 in. height.

Solution   From Table 6.3 the permissible velocity for the given conditions is determined as 5 fps, while the roughness coefficient (Table 6.5) is taken as 0.04. The known values are substituted into Manning's equation:

$$5 = \frac{1.486}{0.04} R^{0.67} 0.04^{0.50}$$

$$R^{0.67} = \frac{5 \times 0.04}{1.486 \times 0.04^{0.50}}$$

$$= 0.67$$

$$R \quad = 0.67^{1/0.67}$$

$$= 0.67^{1.5}$$

$$= 0.55$$

The minimum cross-sectional area is determined by substituting the runoff volume, 50 cfs, and the permissible velocity, 5 fps, into the continuity equation:

$$50 = A \times 5$$

$$A = \frac{50}{5} = 10 \text{ ft}^2$$

At this point, the required cross-section for the drainageway is obtained by successive approximations. For small parabolic swales, an initial trial depth may be taken as $1.5R$, which in this case is 1.5×0.55 or 0.825 ft. As indicated in Fig. 6.16, the *area* of a parabolic cross-section is

$$A = 2/3 \; WD \qquad\qquad (6.5)$$

where A = cross-sectional area in ft^2
$\quad\;\; D$ = depth in ft at the center
$\quad\;\; W$ = top width in ft

Substituting into the equation, a trial width of 18.18 ft is obtained as follows:

$$10 \text{ ft}^2 = 2/3 \; W \times 0.825 \text{ ft}$$

$$W = \frac{10 \times 3}{0.825 \times 2} = 18.18 \text{ ft}$$

The *hydraulic radius* of a parabolic channel is expressed as

$$R = \frac{W^2 D}{1.5\,W^2 + 4D^2} \tag{6.6}$$

where R = hydraulic radius in ft
  W = top width in ft
  D = depth in ft at the center

For this problem a trial hydraulic radius is obtained by substituting $D = 0.825$ and $W = 18.18$ into the equation.

$$R = \frac{18.18^2 \times 0.825}{(1.5 \times 18.18^2) + (4 \times 0.825^2)}$$
$$= 0.547 \text{ ft (or approximately 0.55 ft)}$$

Since this agrees with the hydraulic radius for a velocity of 5 fps, the design dimensions of $W = 18.18$ ft and $D = 0.825$ ft are satisfactory. In any approximation, the final area should be close to but *not* less than the calculated area (in this case 10 ft^2) and the final hydraulic radius should be close to but *not greater* than the calculated hydraulic radius (0.55 ft, in this problem). Thus, the final design dimensions for this example are $W = 18.18$ ft (or 18 ft) and $D = 0.83$ ft (or 10 in.). If the first trial dimensions do not accomplish this, new dimensions must be assumed and tested.

Swale Design with Charts

Since the hydraulic design of swales is somewhat involved and since the n-value of vegetation is variable, charts for the solution of Manning's equation have been developed. These charts aid in finding the required hydraulic radii for various vegetative retardance classes, and maximum permissible velocities and are shown in Fig. 6.21. An example will illustrate their use.

Example 6.7 Storm water runoff from part of a townhouse development is to be conducted through a vegetated waterway (swale). The area in which this swale is located will be mowed twice during the growing season so that the height of the vegetation, which will be a good stand of grass mixture, will vary between 2 and 10 in. The soil survey report shows the existing soil to be easily eroded. The site plan indicates that the swale will have a 3% gradient and it is to be designed to carry 36 cfs.

Solution. The maximum permissible velocity for this swale with a grass mixture on a 3% gradient and on an easily eroded soil is determined to be 4 fps from Table 6.3. In Table 6.4, the vegetative retardance factor for the maximum allowable velocity is specified as D and for minimum

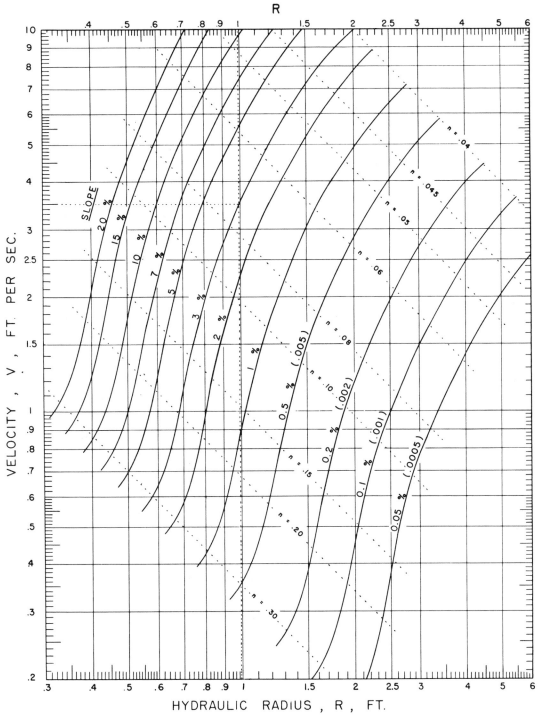

Fig. 6.21. SOLUTION OF MANNING'S EQUATION FOR SWALES WITH VARIOUS
VEGETATIVE RETARDANCE FACTORS
(From New Jersey Association of Conservation Districts 1982)
a. Retardance B (high vegetative retardance)

capacity as C. To design for stability Fig. 6.21 (retardance factor D) is used. Entering horizontally from the left with 4 fps velocity until the 3% slope line is intersected, a vertical line is extended upward from the point of intersection and the required hydraulic radius is determined as 0.56 ft.

As in the previous example, the minimum required cross-sectional area is determined from $Q = AV$:

$$36 = A \times 4$$
$$A = 36/4 = 9 \text{ ft}^2$$

The trial depth is again $1.5 \times R$ or 1.5×0.56 which is 0.84 ft. From $A = 2/3WD$, $9 = 2/3W \times 0.84$. Solving for W

$$W = \frac{9 \times 3/2}{0.84} = 16.1 \text{ ft}$$

The dimensions $W = 16.1$ ft and $D = 0.84$ ft are satisfactory for stability with the vegetation in the mowed condition.

When the grass is long, retardance factor C is indicated. Since the velocity will be reduced below the allowable 4 fps, the cross-sectional area will have to be increased, so that the swale will still be able to handle 36 cfs. This is done by deepening and widening the swale, retaining the same parabolic shape. A trial and error procedure must be employed. Assume a flow depth of 1.0 ft. Then the hydraulic radius from $D = 1.5 R$ is $D/1.5 = R = 0.67$ ft. Entering Fig. 6.21 (retardance C) vertically with $R = 0.67$ until the 3% slope line is intersected and then extending a horizontal line to the left, a velocity of 3.9 fps is obtained.

From the equation of a parabola, the width is proportional to the square root of the depth, and thus the new top width is computed as $W_2 = W_1 (D_2/D_1)^{0.5} = 16.1 \times (1.0/0.84)^{0.5} = 17.6$ ft. The new area is $2/3WD = 2/3 \times 17.6 \times 1 = 11.7$ ft^2. From $Q = AV$, the swale under these conditions will handle $11.7 \times 3.9 = 45.6$ cfs, which is more than required.

This solution would be satisfactory. However, it is possible that a smaller section would accommodate the design flow rate. If the trial depth is reduced to 0.9 ft, $R = 0.6$, $V = 3.1$, $W_2 = 16.7$, and $A = 10.0$. Q is 31 cfs, which is less than the required design Q. Therefore, the final design dimensions are $W = 17.6$ ft and $D = 1.0$ ft.

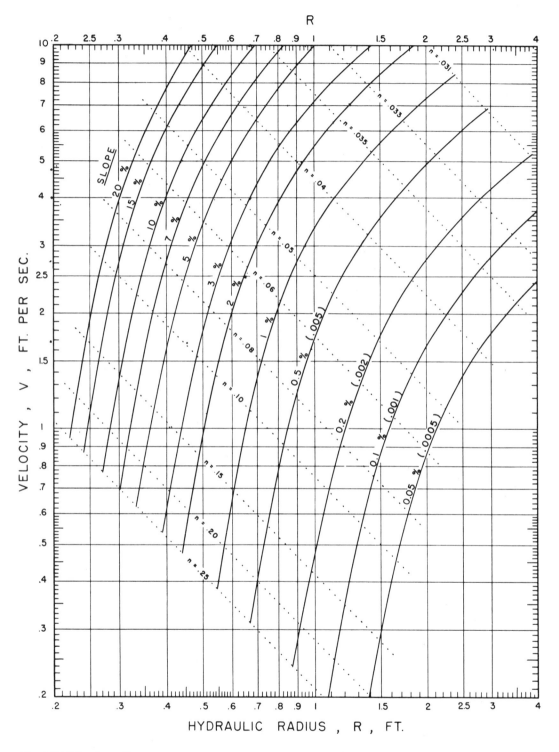

Fig. 6.21 (*Continued*)

b. Retardance C (moderate vegetative retardance)

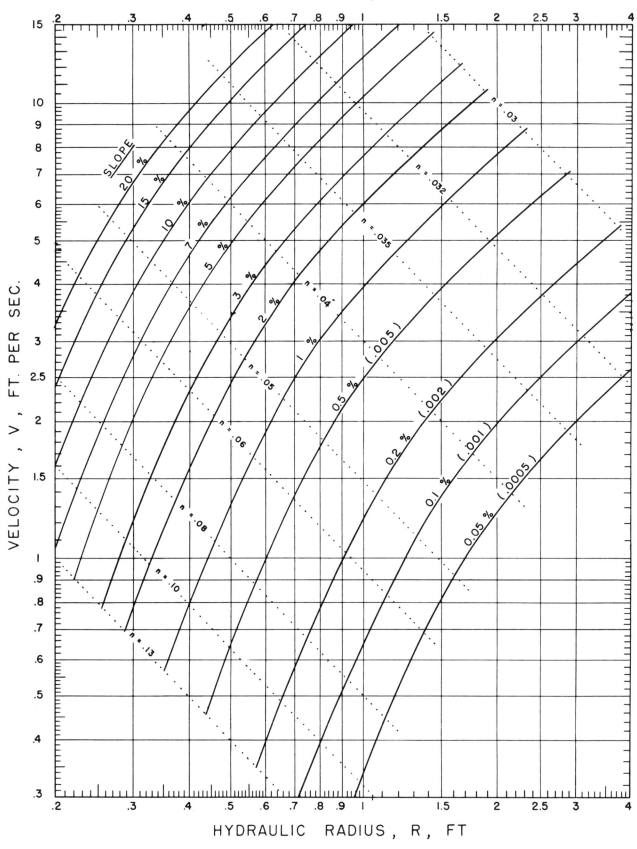

R

VELOCITY , V , FT. PER SEC.

HYDRAULIC RADIUS , R , FT

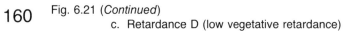

Fig. 6.21 (*Continued*)
   c. Retardance D (low vegetative retardance)

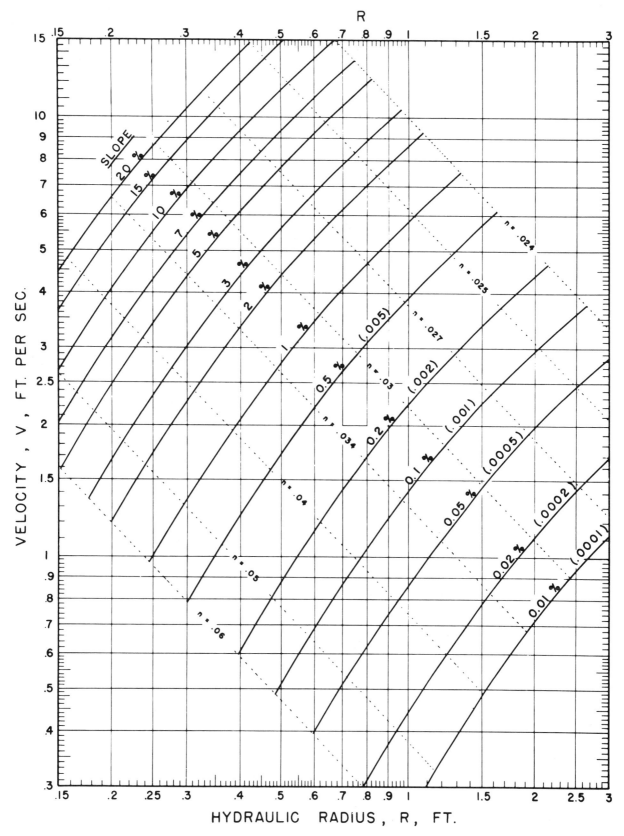

Fig. 6.21 (*Continued*)

d. Retardance E (very low vegetative retardance)

Critical Velocity

To enhance the stability of vegetated waterways by avoiding possible turbulance, some regulatory agencies suggest that design flow velocities be no greater than 90% of the critical velocity. Critical velocity (which occurs at the critical depth) is attained when the specific energy of the flowing water is at the minimum. For a given rate (cfs), flows at less than critical depth (with higher velocities) are called *supercritical* and those at depths greater than critical (with lower velocities) are called *subcritical*. A full discussion of the critical flow phenomenon is beyond the scope of this book, and the reader is referred to texts on fluid mechanics or hydraulics. (Of course, flow velocities should never exceed the allowable velocities stipulated in Table 6.3.)

For parabolic waterways the critical velocity is a function of the flow depth (Fig. 6.22) and can be computed from the equation:

$$V_c = 4.63\, D^{0.5} \tag{6.7}$$

where V_c = critical velocity in fps
D = flow depth of parabolic channel in ft

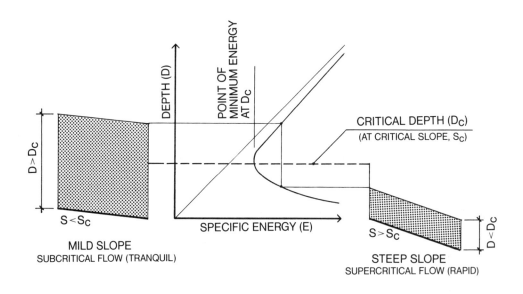

Fig. 6.22. CRITICAL FLOW DEPTH
Critical flow depth, D_c, occurs at the point of minimum energy of the specific energy curve. Above the minimum energy point there are two depths at which flow can occur with the same specific energy for the same Q. One depth is greater than D_c and results in subcritical or tranquil flow, while the other is less than D_c and results in supercritical or rapid flow.

TABLE 6.6.   Critical Velocities and Hydraulic Radii for Parabolic Waterways

Depth (ft)	Critical[a] Velocity (fps)	90% of Crit. Velocity (fps)	Approx. Hydraulic Radius[b] (ft)
0.5	3.27	2.95	0.33
0.6	3.59	3.23	0.40
0.7	3.87	3.49	0.47
0.8	4.14	3.73	0.53
0.9	4.39	3.95	0.60
1.0	4.63	4.17	0.67
1.1	4.86	4.37	0.73
1.2	5.07	4.56	0.80
1.3	5.28	4.75	0.87
1.4	5.48	4.93	0.93
1.5	5.67	5.10	1.00
1.6	5.86	5.27	1.07
1.7	6.04	5.43	1.13
1.8	6.21	5.59	1.20
1.9	6.38	5.74	1.27
2.0	6.55	5.89	1.33
2.1	6.71	6.04	1.40
2.2	6.87	6.18	1.47
2.3	7.02	6.32	1.53
2.4	7.17	6.46	1.60
2.5	7.32	6.59	1.67

[a]Computed from $V_c = 4.63D^{0.5}$
[b]Computed from $R = D/1.5$

Table 6.6 lists values of critical velocities and hydraulic radii for parabolic waterways of various depths. The following examples will illustrate how to design for subcritical flow velocity.

Example 6.8   A grassed waterway with a slope of 4% must carry 50 cfs of runoff. The soil is easily eroded. The vegetative cover will be a good stand of bluegrass sod, which will be kept mowed to a 2.5 in. height. Design a vegetated drainageway with a parabolic cross-section. The regulatory agency limits the design flow velocity to a maximum of 90% of the critical velocity. (Note that, except for the critical velocity requirement, this is the same as Example 6.6.)

   Solution   For a good stand of vegetation, 2.5 in. high, the retardance factor for allowable velocity is determined as D from Table 6.4. The swale design must agree with both Table 6.6 and Fig. 6.21c. From the solution for Example 6.6, it is known that the velocity corresponding to a 0.825 ft depth is 5 fps. According to Table 6.6, this is too great to meet the critical velocity requirement. Therefore, a trial depth of 0.7 ft with 0.90 V_c of 3.49 fps and R of 0.47 is selected. Entering Fig. 6.21c vertically with $R = 0.47$ until the "4% slope line" (between 3 and 5%) is intersected, a horizontal line is extended from the point of intersection to the left and a velocity of about 3.7 fps is obtained. This is more than the 3.49 fps indicated in Table 6.6 as 0.90 V_c for a depth of 0.7 and D and R must be reduced.

A depth of 0.6 with a corresponding R of 0.40 is tried next, resulting in a velocity of about 2.8 fps from Fig. 6.21c. This is less than the 3.23 fps indicated as 0.90 V_c and would meet the velocity restriction. However, by deepening the channel somewhat, the width, which would be required to carry the design flow rate with a depth of 0.6 ft, can be reduced.

For a depth of 0.65, $R = 0.65/1.5 = 0.43$, $V_c = 4.63 \times D^{0.5} = 4.63 \times 0.65^{0.5} = 3.73$, and $0.90\,V_c = 3.36$. (These values could also have been determined from Table 6.6 by interpolation.) From Fig. 6.21c, $V = 3.30$ for $R = 0.43$ at 4% slope. This is less than 90% of the critical velocity. The n-value from the same figure is 0.051.

$$\text{From } Q = AV$$
$$50 = A \times 3.30$$
$$A = \frac{50}{3.30} = 15.2 \text{ ft}^2$$
$$\text{From } A = 2/3\ WD$$
$$15.2 = 2/3\ W \times 0.65$$
$$W = \frac{15.2 \times 3}{0.65 \times 2} = 35.1 \text{ ft}$$

The design dimension are

$$D = 0.65 \text{ ft}$$
$$W = 35.1 \text{ ft}$$

Note that in this case the width necessary to reduce the velocity to subcritical is almost twice that of the previous design for allowable velocity (Example 6.6).

As a check, R, V, and Q should be computed from the design dimensions.

$$R = \frac{W^2 D}{1.5 W^2 + 4 D^2} = \frac{35.1^2 \times 0.65}{1.5 \times 35.1^2 + 4 \times 0.65^2}$$
$$= 0.43$$
$$V = \frac{1.486}{n} R^{0.67} S^{0.5} = \frac{1.486}{0.051} \times 0.43^{0.67} \times 0.04^{0.5}$$
$$= 3.31$$
$$Q = AV = 15.2 \times 3.31 = 50.3 \text{ cfs}$$

Thus, all requirements have been met.

If conditions permit, other methods could be used to reduce flow velocities, such as increasing the retardance factor by letting the vegetation grow to a greater height and/or reducing the gradient. This will be demonstrated in the next example.

Example 6.9 It has been decided that the swale of Example 6.8 requires too great an area, and it will therefore be relocated on the site plan. To decrease the width and cross-sectional area, the flow velocity will be increased to near the permissible velocity of 5 fps while still remaining 90% of critical velocity or less. The vegetation is to remain retardance D. What will be the dimensions and the required slope for this swale?

Solution Table 6.6 indicates that a parabolic swale with a depth of 1.4 ft has a hydraulic radius of about 0.93 ft with 90% of critical velocity 4.93 fps. The intersection of $R = 0.93$ and $V = 4.93$ in Fig. 6.21c indicates a slope of 1.67% and an n-value of 0.036 (by interpolation).

$$Q = AV$$
$$50 = A \times 4.93$$
$$A = \frac{50}{4.93} = 10.1 \text{ ft}^2$$
$$A = 2/3 \ WD$$
$$10.1 = 2/3 \ W \times 1.4$$
$$W = \frac{10.1 \times 3}{1.4 \times 2} = 10.8$$

Thus, the trial design dimensions are

$$D = 1.4 \text{ ft}$$
$$W = 10.8 \text{ ft}$$

and the trial design slope is 1.67%.

When these values are checked by the method shown previously, the resulting velocity slightly exceeds 4.93 fps, which is 90% of the critical velocity. Recalculating with $D = 1.3$ ft (90% $V_c = 4.75$ fps) and checking again leads to values that are within acceptable limits and the final design measurements are

$$D = 1.3 \text{ ft}$$
$$W = 12.1 \text{ ft}$$
$$S = 1.8\%$$

Where it is appropriate, increasing the retardance of the vegetation may be more practical than reducing the slope.

Designing and Sizing Closed (Pipe) Systems

It is often more practical to dispose of excess surface water by means of subsurface piping, or closed systems, rather than by open drainage channels. As previously mentioned, in designing any drainage system the first step is to determine the availability of an adequate outlet. The next step for a closed system is to determine surface slopes and configuration and the location of collection points where the inlet structures will be placed for the piping system. Generally, it is best not to locate these structures near trees, main walks, or buildings, since occasional clogging may cause flooding. The collection points are then connected on the drawing, usually by straight lines, which represent the subsurface pipes. The network should be designed with the minimum adequate amount of pipe for economy. Where two or more pipes join, or where pipes join at different elevations, structures such as manholes, junction boxes, or catch basins should be used. A recommended minimum depth for pipes is 3 ft to protect pipes from being crushed by traffic and, in northern climates, to reduce potential frost problems.

Using the Rational method, the peak rate of runoff Q is calculated for the drainage area collected by each pipe, keeping in mind that the volume is cumulative proceeding downgrade as additional inlets are connected to the system. By selecting a slope for the pipe, a pipe size can be determined by Manning's equation and the continuity equation for the calculated runoff. This process is illustrated in the following example.

Example 6.10   Calculate the pipe size required to carry 10 cfs at a 10% slope. Use vitrified clay pipe with an n-value of 0.015.

Solution   The cross-sectional area of a circular pipe flowing full is πr^2, the area of a circle. The wetted perimeter is equal to the circumference or $2\pi r$. Thus, the hydraulic radius is

$$R = \frac{\pi r^2}{2\pi r} = \frac{r}{2} \qquad (6.8)$$

where R = hydraulic radius in ft
$\qquad r$ = inside radius of pipe section in ft

As from before, Manning's equation is

$$V = \frac{1.486}{n} R^{0.67} S^{0.50}$$

and the continuity equation is $Q = AV$. These two equations can be combined as follows:

$$Q = A \frac{1.486}{n} R^{0.67} S^{0.50}$$

By substituting the known values for the problem, the equation becomes

$$10 = \pi r^2 \frac{1.486}{0.015} (r/2)^{0.67} 0.1^{0.50}$$
$$r^2 r^{0.67} = 0.16$$
$$r^{2.67} = 0.16$$
$$r = 0.16^{1/2.67} = 0.50 \text{ ft}$$

Therefore, a pipe with a 0.50 ft radius, or 1.0 ft diameter, is an adequate size for this problem.

In most cases, several pipes are interconnected to create a closed drainage system. A procedure for sizing pipes for such a system is demonstrated in Examples 6.11 and 6.12. In Example 6.11 a method for determining rates of runoff from various drainage areas that contribute to a piping system is discussed.

Example 6.11 Figure 6.23 schematically illustrates two drainage areas and a proposed drainage system consisting of two catch basins and required piping. The characteristics of the drainage areas are

$$\text{Drainage area } X: \quad A = 1.2 \text{ acres}$$
$$C = 0.3$$
$$T_c = 45 \text{ min}$$
$$\text{Drainage area } Y: \quad A = 0.5 \text{ acres}$$
$$C = 0.7$$
$$T_c = 20 \text{ min}$$

Determine the peak rate of runoff which must be handled by pipes x and y for a 10-year storm frequency.

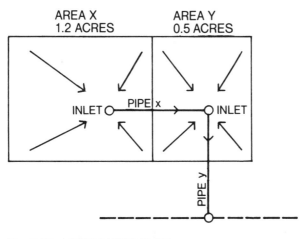

Fig. 6.23. SCHEMATIC PLAN

Solution The first step is to determine the rainfall intensity from Fig. 6.16 for each of the drainage areas. This is 2.5 iph for area X and 4.0 iph for area Y. Using the Rational formula, the rate of runoff for each drainage area can be calculated.

$$Q_X = 0.3 \times 2.5 \times 1.2$$
$$= 0.9 \text{ cfs}$$
$$Q_Y = 0.7 \times 4.0 \times 0.5$$
$$= 1.4 \text{ cfs}$$

Pipe x must handle only the runoff from drainage area X, therefore it can be sized for 0.9 cfs. However, pipe y must handle the runoff from area y plus the water flowing in pipe x. As determined above, the peak rate of flow for area y is 1.4 cfs. This rate is reached in 20 min, but at that time pipe x is still not flowing full, since area X does not peak until 45 min after the beginning of the design storm. If Q_X and Q_Y were simply added, the pipe may be oversized. Thus, a longer time of concentration may be used to determine the rate of runoff from area Y. This time of concentration would be 45 min (T_c for area X) plus the time of flow in the pipe from area X to area Y (for distances less than 300 ft this time is usually negligible). The rate of runoff for the longer time of concentration is

$$Q_Y = 0.7 \times 2.5 \times 0.5$$
$$= 0.88 \text{ cfs}$$

Therefore, the rate of flow which pipe y must handle is $0.9 + 0.88 = 1.78$ cfs or approximately 1.8 cfs. This is above the peak rate of 1.4 cfs that occurs in 20 min for area y but below 2.3 cfs, which would have resulted if the two rates had been added.

However, care must be taken to make sure that pipes are designed to handle peak flow regardless of time of concentration upstream. For instance, assume that all other factors remain the same in this example, except that drainage area y is doubled in size to 1 acre. Using the 45 min time of concentration, the total rate of runoff which pipe y will carry is

$$Q_{TOT} = (0.3 \times 2.5 \times 1.2) + (0.7 \times 2.5 \times 1.0)$$
$$= 2.65 \text{ cfs}$$

The peak runoff for area Y again occurs in 20 min with an intensity of 4.0 iph.

$$Q_Y = (0.7 \times 4.0 \times 1.0)$$
$$= 2.80 \text{ cfs}$$

This rate is *above* the rate determined by the longer time of concentration and therefore would be used in determining the size of pipe y.

Example 6.12 In this problem the site plan for a small office building indicates proposed grades, location of drainage structures, and piping pattern (Fig. 6.24). For this site plan, all parking areas, drives, and streets have 6 in. high curbs, and all areas not paved are lawn with a silt loam soil texture. The off-site drainage area consists of 2 acres of woodland. The longest overland distance for this runoff is 200 ft with an average slope of 4% and, again, a silt loam soil texture that enters the site at the north corner. Use a 10-year storm frequency for the design of the drainage system which is located in New Jersey. Runoff from the building roof must be accommodated in the design.

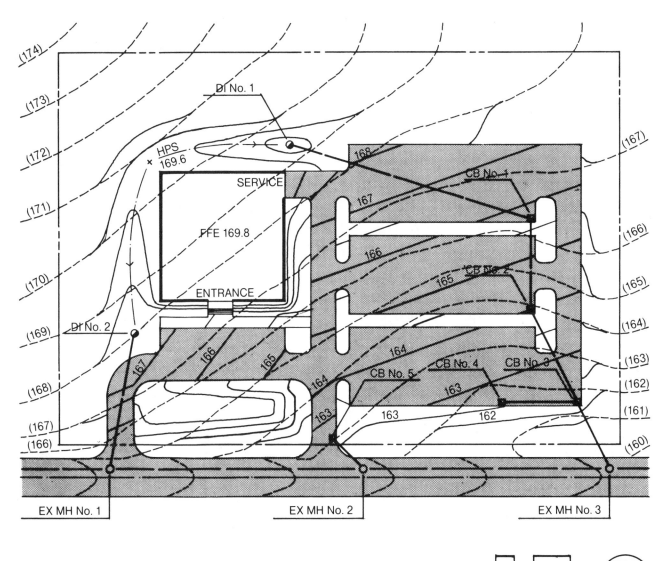

Fig. 6.24.   SITE PLAN

Solution: *Step 1*   The first step is to develop an orderly procedure for recording and organizing all information necessary for sizing and laying out a closed drainage system. This required information is arranged in tabular form as illustrated in Table 6.7.

Step 2   The next step is to determine the extent of the drainage areas, the surface characteristics, and the area of each surface type for each drainage structure. The selected surface coefficients C for each surface type and the respective areas A are recorded in the table. In this problem, the assumption is that one-half of the off-site drainage area (or 1 acre) is directed toward Drain Inlet No. 1 and the other half toward Drain Inlet No. 2 (Fig. 6.25). The same assumption is made for the roof runoff.

Step 3   The third step is to determine the overland flow time (time of concentration) for each of the drainage areas by using the nomograph in Fig. 6.13. An adjusted rainfall intensity value I can then be obtained from the rainfall intensity curves in Fig. 6.16. A 10-year frequency curve for northern New Jersey is used. The information from Steps 2 and 3 can be substituted into the Rational formula, $Q = CIA$, to calculate the peak rate of runoff to be carried in each pipe. Remember that these rates

TABLE 6.7.   Data for Example 6.12

Area	to	c	$T_c{}^a$ (min)	I (iph)	A (acres)	Q_{sub} (cfs)	Q (cfs)	D (in.)	S (ft/ft)	L (ft)	V (fps)	n	INV in	INV out	TF^c
½ Roof	DI No. 1	0.92	37	2.8	0.12	0.31									
DI No. 1	CB No. 1	0.30		2.8	1.45	1.22	1.53	12	0.0024	210	1.9	0.015		156.79	167.60
CB No. 1	CB No. 2	0.30	37	2.8	0.20	0.17									
		0.90		2.8	0.21	0.53	2.23	12	0.0055	75	2.8	0.015	156.29	156.29	165.70
CB No. 2	CB No. 3	0.90	37	2.8	0.30	0.76	2.99	12	0.0095	80	3.7	0.015	155.88	155.88	163.90
CB No. 4	CB No. 3	0.30	10^b	5.8	0.04	0.07									
		0.90		5.8	0.25	1.31	1.38	8	0.018	50	3.9	0.015		156.02	162.60
CB No. 3	MH No. 3	0.30	37	2.8	0.07	0.06									
		0.90		2.8	0.28	0.71	5.14	15	0.0095	55	4.3	0.015	155.12	154.87	162.00
CB No. 5	MH No. 2	0.30	10	5.8	0.12	0.21									
		0.90		5.8	0.18	0.94	1.15	8	0.011	30	3.2	0.015		157.06	162.50
½ Roof	DI No. 2	0.92	40	2.7	0.12	0.30									
DI No. 2	MH No. 1	0.30		2.7	1.36	1.10	1.40	8	0.018	105	3.9	0.015		161.16	167.20

[a]Flow times in pipes between drainage structures have not been included, since the distances between structures are relatively short and the resultant flow times are negligible. However, for longer distances the flow time in pipes must be included in the time of concentration. (To determine the travel time in pipes, the length of the pipe is divided by the flow velocity. For example, the travel time in a 500 ft long pipe with a 2.5 fps flow velocity is 500 ft/2.5 fps = 200 sec or 3.33 min.)

[b]Since it takes several minutes for rain to wet a surface thoroughly, many municipalities permit the use of minimum times of concentration, such as 10 or 15 minutes. This will reduce the intensity used for the computation of the runoff rate and thus the required pipe size.

[c]Top of frame.

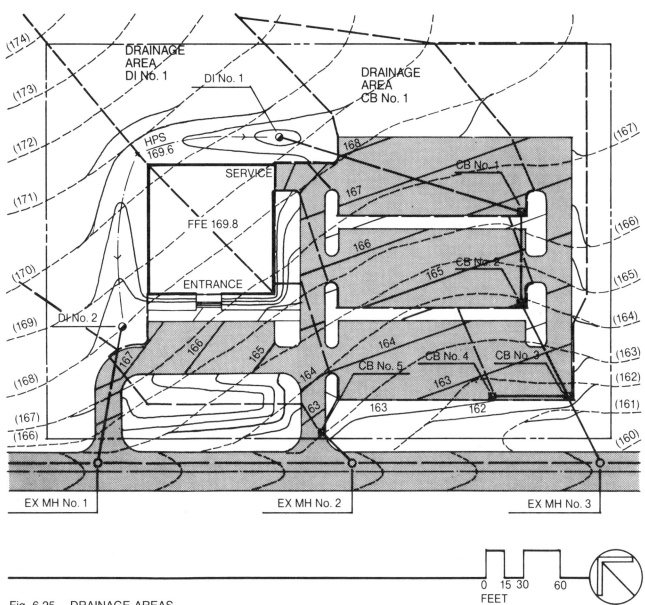

Fig. 6.25.   DRAINAGE AREAS

are additive moving downgrade. For example, the pipe between Catch Basin No. 1 and Catch Basin No. 2 must carry the runoff from the Catch Basin No. 1 drainage area as well as the runoff from the Drainage Inlet No. 1 drainage area and one-half of the roof runoff.

Step 4   At this point the pipes may be sized. However, rather than using equations to calculate the required sizes, the nomograph in Fig. 6.26 is used. There are five components to the nomograph: discharge in

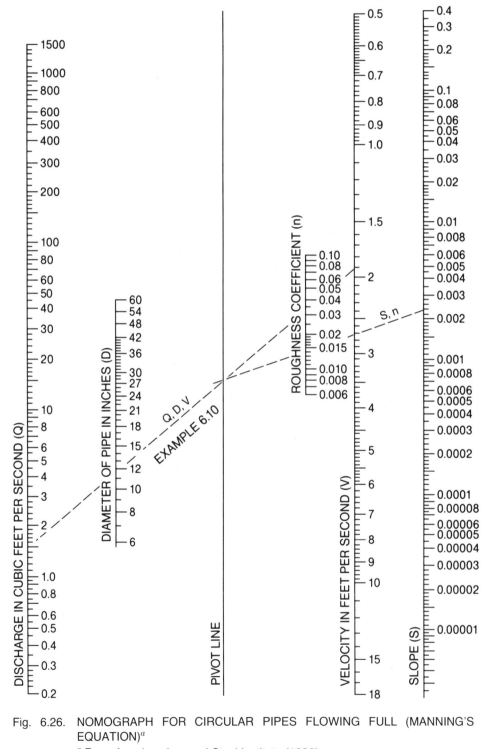

Fig. 6.26.   NOMOGRAPH FOR CIRCULAR PIPES FLOWING FULL (MANNING'S EQUATION)[a]

[a] From American Iron and Steel Institute (1980)

cfs, diameter of pipe in inches, roughness coefficient, velocity in fps, and slope. The figure is actually two nomographs. The first directly relates discharge, diameter of pipe, and velocity. Knowing any two values will allow the determination of the third. The other nomograph relates slope and roughness coefficient to diameter of pipe and discharge. Two values on the *same* side of the pivot line must be known (or selected) in order to determine the other two values. The use of the nomograph is demonstrated by sizing the pipe from Drain Inlet No. 1 to Catch Basin No. 1.

Two issues related to pipe sizing must be discussed before proceeding. The first is the pipe size. To reduce clogging and maintenance problems, a 12 in. diameter pipe is recommended as a minimum size for landscape applications. This minimum does not apply to roof drain and area drain conditions. Also, there are standard pipe sizes for the different pipe materials and manufacturers' catalogs should be consulted. The second issue is velocity. A recommended range for the velocity of water in pipes is 2.5 to 10 fps. A minimum of 2.5 is used to insure self-cleaning, whereas a maximum of 10 is suggested to reduce potential scouring and pipe wear, which may occur above this velocity. Also, from the nomograph, it can be seen that there is an inverse relationship between pipe size and slope and velocity.

Drainage Inlet No. 1 to Catch Basin No. 1   The discharge flowing in the pipe is 1.53 cfs. From experience this is a low rate of flow; therefore, the use of a minimum pipe size is anticipated. In applying the nomograph, the discharge Q is known and a 12 in. diameter pipe size is selected. The procedure for determining the remaining values is as follows:

1. Locate 1.53 cfs on the discharge line.
2. Locate 12 in. on the diameter of pipe line.
3. Draw a straight line through the two points, crossing the pivot line, until it intersects with the velocity line.
4. Read the value of the velocity line at the point of intersection. In this case the velocity is 1.9 fps, somewhat below the recommended minimum. However, rather than reduce the pipe to 8 in. diameter (the next lower standard size for reinforced concrete pipe), the 12 in. diameter is maintained.
5. Next, return to the intersection point of the line drawn in No. 3 above with the pivot line.
6. Locate 0.015 on the roughness coefficient line. This is the selected *n*-value for the piping material (reinforced concrete pipe) used in this problem (see Table 6.5).
7. Draw a straight line from the point on the pivot line through 0.015 on the roughness coefficient line until it intersects with the slope line.
8. Read the value on the slope line at the point of intersection, which is 0.0024.
9. Record all appropriate values in Table 6.7.

The same procedure is applied to the remaining pipes. All data for the problem are recorded in Table 6.7.

Two additional points with regard to the design of pipe systems must be made here. The first is that pipe size should *never decrease* proceeding downgrade. The outlet pipe from a drainage structure should be equal to or larger in diameter than the inlet pipe. Note that the pipe size at Catch Basin No. 4 can be less, since it is a branch line. The second is that, to prevent silting and clogging, it is preferable *not* to decrease pipe flow velocity proceeding downgrade. This is one reason that the 8 in. diameter pipe was not used at Drainage Inlet No. 1. The velocity for an 8 in. pipe would have been over 4 fps, which would have been greater than the subsequent velocities. However, 8 in. diameter reinforced concrete pipe is used for Catch Basins Nos. 4 and 5. The smaller diameter was necessary in order to insure a reasonable velocity due to the very low flow rate.

Step 5   The last step is to determine the invert elevations for the pipes and draw a profile of the system. *Invert elevation* is the elevation of the bottom of the pipe *opening* in a drainage structure as illustrated in Fig. 6.27. The invert elevation of the outlet pipe must be equal to or lower than the invert elevation of the inlet pipe. One technique used to insure this relationship is to match top of pipe elevations.

Fig. 6.27.   INVERT ELEVATION
The invert elevation for a drainage structure is the lowest point of the internal cross-section of the entering and exiting pipes. The invert of the entering pipe is referred to as the invert *in*, while for the exiting pipe it is referred to as the invert *out*. The invert in must not be lower than the invert out. This relationship can be assured by matching the top of pipe elevations.

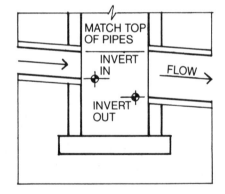

Inlet elevations are determined by proceeding backward from the point at which the proposed system connects to the existing system. The difference in elevation between the existing invert elevations and the proposed invert elevation is calculated by multiplying the pipe slope by the pipe length. To calculate the outlet invert for Catch Basin No. 3, work back from the invert elevation of existing manhole No. 3.

MH No. 3 Inv. Elev. = 154.35 ft
Pipe slope = 0.0095 ft/ft
Pipe length = 55.0 ft
0.0095 × 55.0 = 0.52 ft
154.35 + 0.52 = 154.87 ft outlet invert elevation at CB No. 3

Once this invert elevation is determined, the remaining elevations may be calculated using the same technique.

After all of the invert elevations have been calculated, a profile may be constructed for the entire system. A *profile* is a section with an exaggerated vertical scale often taken at the centerline of a linear project like piping or roads (Fig. 6.28). A profile is a good checking device to evaluate whether pipes slope properly and invert relationships are correct. It also provides an opportunity to analyze whether pipes are placed too deep, thus requiring excessive trenching, or too shallow, thus resulting in insufficient cover and protection for the pipe. If either case exists, the system must be reevaluated and redesigned.

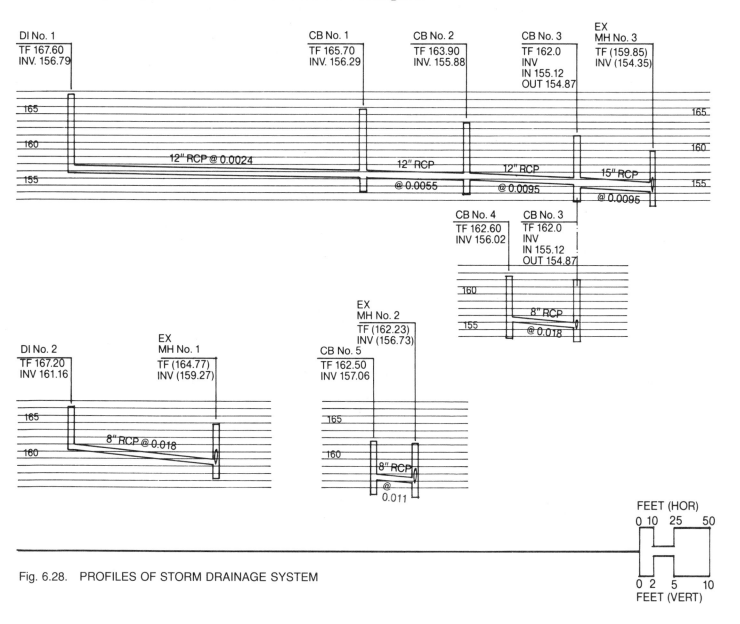

Fig. 6.28.   PROFILES OF STORM DRAINAGE SYSTEM

Delaying Storm Runoff

As a result of urbanization, peak runoff discharges increase because there are more impervious surfaces and usually less vegetative cover. These changes may have significant adverse impact downstream if not properly controlled. To protect downstream areas from potential flood damage, many municipalities have established ordinances that restrict the type of development and the impact of development on a drainage

TABLE 6.8.   Measures for Reducing and Delaying Urban Storm Runoff[a]

Area	Reducing runoff	Delaying runoff

Large flat roof	1. Cistern storage
	2. Rooftop gardens
	3. Pool storage or fountain storage
	4. Sod roof cover
		1. Ponding on roof by constricted downspouts
		2. Increasing roof roughness
		  a. Rippled roof
		  b. Gravelled roof

Parking lots	1. Porous pavement
	  a. Gravel parking lots
	  b. Porous or punctured asphalt
	2. Concrete vaults and cisterns beneath parking lots in high value areas
	3. Vegetated ponding areas around parking lots
	4. Gravel trenches
		1. Grassy strips on parking lots
		2. Grassed waterways draining parking lot
		3. Ponding and detention measures for impervious areas
		  a. Rippled pavement
		  b. Depressions
		  c. Basins

Residential	1. Cisterns for individual homes or groups of homes
	2. Gravel driveways (porous)
	3. Contoured landscape
	4. Ground-water recharge
	  a. Perforated pipe
	  b. Gravel (sand)
	  c. Trench
	  d. Porous pipe
	  e. Dry wells
	5. Vegetated depressions
		1. Reservoir or detention basin
		2. Planting a high delaying grass (high roughness)
		3. Gravel driveways
		4. Grassy gutters or channels
		5. Increased length of travel of runoff by means of gutters, diversions, etc.

General	1. Gravel alleys 2. Porous sidewalks 3. Mulched planters	1. Gravel alleys

[a]From USDA-Soil Conservation Service (1975)

area. One of the primary controls that has been established is the requirement that the rate of discharge from a developed site cannot exceed that of the prior undeveloped site conditions for specified design storm frequencies.

Methods used to control runoff may reduce the volume and/or the rate of flow. The effectiveness of any control method depends on the available storage, the outflow rate, and the inflow rate. Since a variety of methods may be used, the effectiveness of the proposed measure must be evaluated in relationship to the context of the area in which it is used. Measures for reducing and delaying urban storm runoff are listed in Table 6.8 whereas Table 6.9 lists some advantages and disadvantages of each measure.

TABLE 6.9.   Advantages and Disadvantages of Measures for Reducing and Delaying Runoff[a]

Measure	Advantages	Disadvantages
A. Cisterns and covered ponds	1. Water may be used for: 　a. Fire protection 　b. Watering lawns 　c. Industrial processes 　d. Cooling purposes 2. Reduce runoff while only occupying small area 3. Land or space above cistern may be used for other purposes	1. Expensive to install 2. Cost required may be restrictive if the cistern must accept water from large drainage areas 3. Requires slight maintenance 4. Restricted access 5. Reduced available space in basements for other uses
B. Rooftop Gardens	1. Esthetically pleasing 2. Runoff reduction 3. Reduce noise levels 4. Wildlife enhancement	1. Higher structural loadings on roof and building 2. Expensive to install and maintain
C. Surface pond storage (usually residential areas)	1. Controls large drainage areas with low release 2. Esthetically pleasing 3. Possible recreation benefits 　a. Boating 　b. Ice skating 　c. Fishing 　d. Swimming 4. Aquatic life habitat 5. Increases land value of adjoining property	1. Require large areas 2. Possible pollution from storm water and siltation 3. Possible mosquito breeding areas 4. May have adverse algal blooms as a result of eutrophication 5. Possible drowning 6. Maintenance problems

(continued)

TABLE 6.9. *(Continued)*

Measure	Advantages	Disadvantages

D. Ponding on roof by constricted downspouts	1. Runoff delay
	2. Cooling effect for building
	    a. Water on roof
	    b. Circulation through building
	3. Roof ponding provides fire protection for building (roof water may be tapped in case of fire)
		1. Higher structural loadings
		2. Clogging of constricted inlet requiring maintenance
		3. Freezing during winter (expansion)
		4. Waves and wave loading
		5. Leakage of roof water into building (water damage)

E. Increased roof roughness
    a. Rippled roof
    b. Gravel on roof
	1. Runoff delay and some reduction (detention in ripples or gravel)	1. Somewhat higher structural loadings

F. Porous pavement (parking lots and alleys)
    a. Gravel parking lot
    b. Holes in impervious pavements (¼ in. dia.) filled with sand
	1. Runoff reduction (a and b)
	2. Potential groundwater recharge (a and b)
	3. Gravel pavements may be cheaper than asphalt or concrete (a)
		1. Clogging of holes or gravel pores (a and b)
		2. Compaction of earth below pavement or gravel decreases permeability of soil (a and b)
		3. Ground-water pollution from salt in winter (a and b)
		4. Frost heaving for impervious pavement with holes (b)
		5. Difficult to maintain
		6. Grass or weeds could grow in porous pavement (a and b)

G. Grassed channels and vegetated strips	1. Runoff delay
	2. Some runoff reduction (infiltration recharge)
	3. Esthetically pleasing
	    a. Flowers
	    b. Trees
		1. Sacrifice some land area for vegetated strips
		
		2. Grassed areas must be mowed or cut periodically (maintenance costs)

H. Ponding and detention measures on impervious pavement
    a. Rippled pavement
    b. Basins
    c. Constricted inlets
	1. Runoff delay (a, b, and c)
	2. Runoff reduction (a and b)
		1. Somewhat restricted movement of vehicle (a)
		2. Interferes with normal use (b and c)
		3. Damage to ripple pavement during snow removal (a)
		4. Depressions collect dirt and debris (a, b, and c)

TABLE 6.9.   *(Continued)*

Measure	Advantages	Disadvantages

I. Reservoir or detention basin	1. Runoff delay
	2. Recreation benefits
	  a. Ice skating
	  b. Baseball, football etc., if land is provided
	3. Esthetically pleasing
	4. Could control large drainage areas with low release
		1. Considerable amount of land is necessary
		2. Maintenance costs
		  a. Mowing grass
		  b. Herbicides
		  c. Cleaning periodically (silt removal)
		3. Mosquito breeding area
		4. Siltation in basin

J. Converted septic tank for storage and ground water recharge	1. Low installation costs
	2. Runoff reduction (infiltration and storage)
	3. Water may be used for:
	  a. Fire protection
	  b. Watering lawns and gardens
	  c. Ground-water recharge
		1. Requires periodic maintenance (silt removal)
		2. Possible health hazard
		3. Sometimes requires a pump for emptying after storm

K. Ground-water recharge
  a. Perforated pipe or hose
  b. French drain
  c. Porous pipe
  d. Dry well
	1. Runoff reduction (infiltration)
	2. Ground-water recharge with relatively clean water
	3. May supply water to garden or dry areas
	4. Little evaporation loss
		1. Clogging of pores or perforated pipe
		2. Initial expense of installation (materials)

L. High delay grass (high roughness)	1. Runoff delay 2. Increased infiltration	1. More difficult to mow
M. Routing flow over lawn	1. Runoff delay 2. Increased infiltration	1. Possible erosion or scour 2. Standing water on lawn in depressions

[a]From USDA-Soil Conservation Service (1975)

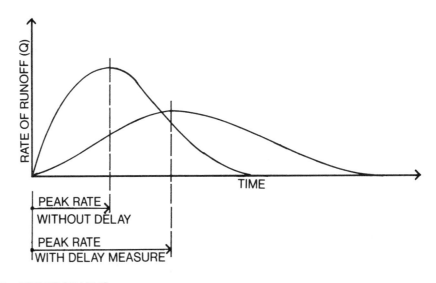

Fig. 6.29. HYDROGRAPHS
Hydrographs plot the relationship of runoff rate to time. Where delay measures are not used, the peak occurs earlier and at a higher rate than if
delay measures are used as qualitatively illustrated in the graph.

Two common methods of detaining runoff are detention and retention
structures if the size and conditions of the site are appropriate. A *detention
structure* or *dry pond* consists of a natural or man-made basin. Runoff
that collects in the basin is released into a drainageway at a controlled
rate. This rate should not exceed the runoff rate that existed prior to the
development of the site (Fig. 6.29). If the volume of runoff exceeds the
storage capacity of the structure, the excess runoff is conducted through
an emergency spillway located at the edge of the structure (see Fig. 6.6).
To be most effective, detention ponds should be located over soils with
high infiltration rates in order to increase ground water recharge and to
prevent standing water. To prevent erosion, the sides and floor of the
basin must be stabilized with water-tolerant vegetation or by the use of
gravel or rip-rap. Sediment must be removed from the basin periodically.
It is recommended that "low flow channels" be installed, to keep detention
basins from becoming muddy.

A *retention structure* is similar to a detention structure. However,
some water is retained permanently in the basin rather than draining
completely after a storm. Because they are permanent water bodies,
retention structures create special opportunities and problems. In addition
to flood control, large-scale impoundment areas may be created for
esthetic and visual purposes as well as to provide the potential for
recreational uses. Whether the impoundment functions at the community
or site scale, it must be designed to maintain a constant water level with
the capacity to store peak flows. As with a detention structure, the excess
runoff is released at the predevelopment rate into the drainageway.

Concern must be given to the water quality of ponds and lakes used for retention and the quality of runoff they collect. To deter algae growth, water temperatures should be kept as cool as possible by maximizing the water depth and minimizing shallow areas. These conditions will also aid in mosquito control. Where shallow areas exist, they should be shaded resulting in cooler water temperatures.

All measures taken to delay runoff must be hydraulically and structurally designed. From a hydraulic standpoint, the storage area and outlet flow must be properly sized, whereas, structurally, the method of containment must be stable, durable, and capable of withstanding the expected loads or pressures. Both of these topics are beyond the scope of this text.

Designing and Sizing Subsurface Systems

Subsurface systems may be laid out either to collect water from poorly drained, wet areas or to drain complete areas. The piping pattern for the former condition is typically random, whereas gridiron or herringbone arrangements are typical for the latter (Fig. 6.30). *Cut-off drains* are

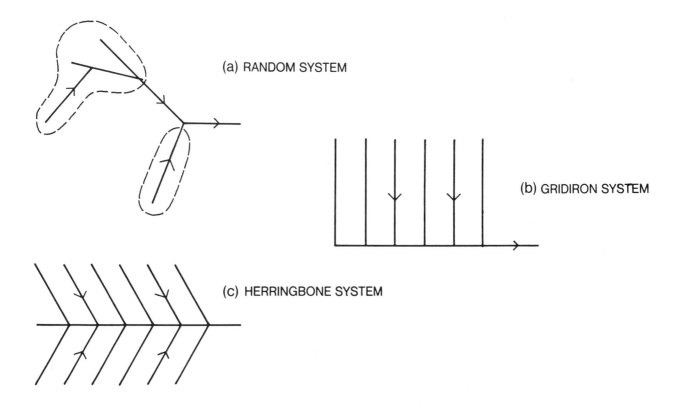

(a) RANDOM SYSTEM

(b) GRIDIRON SYSTEM

(c) HERRINGBONE SYSTEM

Fig. 6.30. PIPING PATTERNS FOR SUBSURFACE DRAINAGE

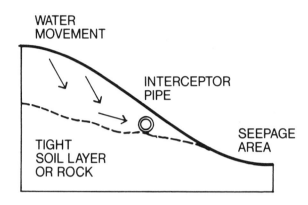

Fig. 6.31. CUT-OFF DRAIN

pipes placed across a slope to intercept water that would otherwise be forced to the surface by an outcropping of an impermeable layer such as a tight subsoil (Fig. 6.31).

The pipe size required to drain a certain acreage depends on the pipe gradient, since an increase in gradient will result in a greater velocity of flow and will permit the pipe to drain a larger area. Pipes are placed at constant gradients, or a variable gradient with the gradient increasing toward the outlet. The gradients should never decrease, since the velocity of flow would decrease and silt would be deposited in the pipe. Typically pipe gradients for lawn areas vary from a minimum of 0.1% to a maximum of 1.0%. Tables 6.10 and 6.11 show the relationship between pipe size, gradient, and maximum acreage drained for smooth clay or concrete drainage lines and corrugated plastic tubing. These tables were computed by Manning's equation and the continuity equation with n-values of 0.011 for the clay and concrete pipe and 0.016 for the corrugated plastic tubing. A drainage coefficient (D.C.) of ⅜ in. (or 0.0312 ft) was used. A drainage coefficient is defined as the depth of water removed over the drainage area in 24 hours. In humid areas of the United States a D.C. of ⅜ in. is normally used for mineral soils. For organic soils, the acreages of the tables should be reduced by one-half. This may also be done for mineral soils if more rapid drainage is desired.

Depth and Spacing   The depth at which drainage lines are installed generally depends on the outlet conditions. However, there should be a *minimum* of 2 ft of cover in mineral soils and 2.5 ft in organic soils. Drainage lines should always be deep enough to prevent possible frost damage.

TABLE 6.10. Maximum Acreage^a Drained by Various Pipe Sizes—Clay or Concrete Pipe. ($n = 0.011$, Drainage coefficient $= \frac{3}{8}$ in./24 hr.)

Pipe size (inches)	Slope (%)									
	0.1	0.2	0.3	0.4	0.5	0.6	0.7	0.8	0.9	1.0
4	4.51	6.38	7.82	9.03	10.1	11.1	11.9	12.8	13.5	14.3
5	8.19	11.6	14.2	16.4	18.3	20.0	21.7	23.2	24.6	25.9
6	13.3	18.8	23.1	26.6	29.8	32.6	35.2	37.6	39.9	42.1
8	28.7	40.5	49.6	57.3	64.1	70.2	75.8	81.1	86.0	90.6
10	52.0	73.5	90.0	104	116	127	138	147	156	164
12	84.5	120	146	169	189	207	224	239	254	267

^{a}Reduce these acreages by one-half for a $\frac{3}{4}$ in. D.C.

TABLE 6.11. Maximum Acreage^a Drained by Various Pipe Sizes—Corrugated Plastic Tubing. ($n = 0.016$, Drainage coefficient $= \frac{3}{8}$ in./24 hr.)

Tubing size (inches)	Slope (%)									
	0.1	0.2	0.3	0.4	0.5	0.6	0.7	0.8	0.9	1.0
4	3.10	4.39	5.38	6.21	6.94	7.60	8.21	8.78	9.31	9.81
5	5.62	7.96	9.75	11.3	12.6	13.8	14.9	15.9	16.9	17.8
6	9.15	12.9	15.8	18.3	20.5	22.4	24.2	25.9	27.5	28.9
8	19.7	27.9	34.1	39.4	44.1	48.3	52.1	55.7	59.1	62.3
10	35.7	50.5	61.9	71.5	79.9	87.5	94.5	101	107	113
12	58.1	82.2	101	116	130	142	154	164	174	184

^{a}Reduce these acreages by one-half for a $\frac{3}{4}$ in. D.C.

The spacing of drainage lines depends on the texture of the soil to be drained. Sandy soils permit more rapid movement of water than do heavy clay soils and therefore lines may be spaced further apart and deeper in sandy soils than in clay soils. If drains are spaced too far apart, the central portion between lines will remain poorly drained. Suggestions for depth and spacing of drainage lines are given in Table 6.12.

To design subsurface drainage systems for some soils, such as organic soils and fine sandy loams, a qualified drainage engineer should be consulted, since special precautions must be taken.

TABLE 6.12. Typical Depths and Spacings of Drainage Lines for Various Soil Textures

Texture	Spacing (ft)	Depth (ft)
Clay, clay loam	30–70	2.5–3.0
Silt loam	60–100	3.0–4.0
Sandy loam	100–300	3.5–4.5
Organic Soils	80–200	3.5–4.5

Drainage Area In order to determine the size of pipe, the acreage that each line has to drain must be known. For a gridiron or herringbone system, the area drained by each line may be computed by multiplying the length of the individual lines by the spacing between the lines. Where surface inlets are connected to the subsurface system, the total area graded toward the inlets must also be included. The following examples demonstrate the procedure for determining drainage areas and pipe sizes.

Example 6.13 A plan for a gridiron drainage system with proposed pipe gradients indicated is illustrated in Fig. 6.32. Determine the pipe sizes for the various parts of the system for a mineral soil and clay pipe. There are no surface inlets.

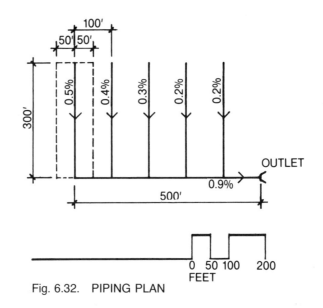

Fig. 6.32. PIPING PLAN

Solution The laterals are 300 ft long and spaced 100 ft apart. This means that each line drains 50 ft on either side. Therefore, the drainage area for each lateral is 300 ft by 100 ft (50 + 50) which equals 30,000 ft², or approximately 0.69 acre. Based on Table 6.10, a 4 in. pipe is sufficient for all laterals. The main line at the outlet must accommodate the flow from the five laterals (or approximately 3.44 acres) plus its own drainage area of 500 ft by 50 ft which equals 25,000 ft², or about 0.57 acres, since it provides drainage on one side. The total drainage area of the system is 4.0 acres (3.44 + 0.57). Table 6.10 shows that a 4 in. pipe is also sufficient for the main line. It might be preferable to increase the pipe size to 5 in., particularly if silting is anticipated.

In certain situations it may be necessary to increase the size of the drainage line, particularly a main line, as it proceeds toward the outlet. This is referred to as a tapered line. Thus it may start as a 5 in. line, increase to 6 in. and perhaps to 8 in. as greater quantities of flow must be accommodated. This condition is illustrated in the following example.

Example 6.14   Figure 6.33 shows a plan for a herringbone system with the spacing indicated. All laterals have a 0.2% gradient and the main slopes at 0.3%. Determine the pipe sizes required for a mineral soil, using clay or concrete pipe.

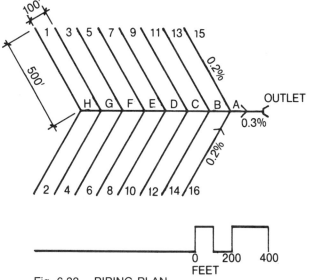

Fig. 6.33.   PIPING PLAN

Solution   There are 16 laterals, each of which drains an area 500 ft by 100 ft or 50,000 ft^2, which is approximately 1.15 acres. Since a 4 in. pipe at 0.2% grade can drain 6.38 acres according to Table 6.10, all laterals may be 4 in. in size.

The main line has a 0.3% grade. From Table 6.10 the maximum acreage that a 4 in. pipe at 0.3% can drain is 7.82 acres. The number of laterals that can be accommodated by a 4 in. main line is determined by dividing the allowable area by the area for each lateral.

7.82 acres ÷ 1.15 acres/lateral = 6 laterals (6.80)

This means that the main line from junction H *to* junction E can be 4 in. pipe. *At* junction E two more laterals are added and the drainage area at this point exceeds 9 acres.

Again from Table 6.10 a 5 in. pipe at 0.3% can drain an area of 14.2 acres. This means that a 5 in. main line can accommodate 12 laterals

$$14.2 \div 1.14 = 12 \text{ laterals } (12.35)$$

From junction E *to* junction B a 5 in. pipe is used, since *at* junction B laterals Nos. 13 and 14 are added that increase the drainage area beyond the allowable 14.2 acres. At a gradient of 0.3%, a 6 in. pipe can drain 23.1 acres, which is more than the entire area of the proposed system. Therefore, a 6 in. pipe may be used from junction B to the outlet. Again, to reduce the potential for problems, it would be preferable to use 5 in. pipe for all laterals and 6 in. pipe for the entire main line. Various types of pipe junctions such as couplings, reducing couplings, tees, reducing tees, end caps, 45° and 90° ells, and "Ys", are available to complete drainage systems.

Example 6.15 If the herringbone system of Example 6.14 is to be installed in an environmentally sensitive area that requires a drainage coefficient of ¾ in., determine the drain sizes, using corrugated plastic tubing.

Solution As previously determined, each lateral drains about 1.15 acres. However, to use the drainage tables with a ¾ in. D.C., all acreages contained therein have to be reduced by one-half. Therefore, 2.30 acres (2 × 1.15), which when reduced one-half will yield 1.15 acres, must be used to obtain the size for each lateral. Table 6.11 shows that 4 in. tubing is sufficient for all laterals, since it can drain up to 4.39 acres with a ⅜ in. D.C. and 2.20 acres with a ¾ in. D.C.

At 0.3% slope, Table 6.11 shows the following maximum acreages for various tubing sizes:

Tubing size	Drainage coefficient	
	⅜ in.	¾ in.
4 in.	5.38	2.69
5 in.	9.75	4.88
6 in.	15.8	7.90
8 in.	34.1	17.1
10 in.	61.9	31.0

The number of laterals that each size can accommodate is

```
 4 in.  2.69/1.15 = 2.3 or 2
 5 in.  4.88/1.15 = 4.2 or 4
 6 in.  7.90/1.15 = 6.9 or 6
 8 in.  17.1/1.15 = 14.9 or 14
10 in.  31.0/1.15 = 26.95 or 26
```

Therefore, the minimum tubing sizes for the design are

Junction	Tubing size
H to G	4 in.
G to F	5 in.
F to E	6 in.
E to A	8 in.
A to outlet	10 in.

The system could be simplified by using 6 in. tubing from H to E.

Outlets Subsurface drainage systems may discharge into open or closed drainage systems, streams, or drainage channels. Where drainage discharges into a stream or channel, a length of solid pipe must be projected beyond the bank to prevent erosion. Preferably, a headwall or drop structure should be installed at the outlet instead of projecting the pipe.

SUMMARY

Various principles regarding drainage system design have been presented in this chapter. However, it must be realized that storm runoff and hydraulics are highly complex subjects. The intent here is to provide some familiarity with the basic principles so that the reader may be conversant with these subjects, since in most cases the handling of storm water runoff will be a collaborative effort between qualified, technically competent engineers and the site designers.

PROBLEMS

6.1 What is the flow velocity of a parabolic grassed swale if the cross-sectional area is 12 ft^2 and the peak rate of runoff is 36 cfs? Is this velocity acceptable for an easily erodible soil?

6.2 A drainage area consists of 8 acres of lawn ($C = 0.36$) and 2 acres of pavement and roofs ($C = 0.90$). Determine the peak rate of runoff for a 10-year storm frequency, to be used for the design of a grassed swale, if the time of concentration is 45 minutes.

6.3 Design a parabolic swale to handle the runoff in problem 6.2 if the grade is 6% and the soil is erosion resistant.

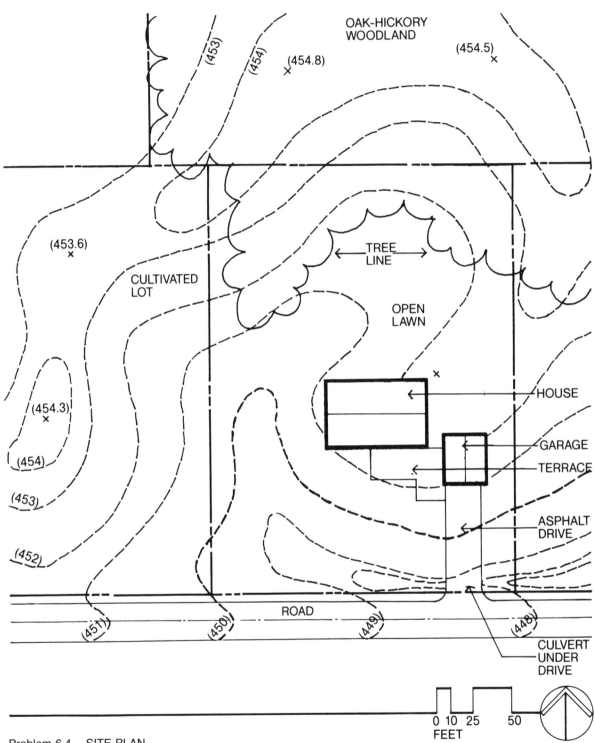

OAK-HICKORY
WOODLAND

(453)
(454)
x (454.8)
(454.5)
x

(453.6)
x

CULTIVATED
LOT

TREE
←   →
LINE

OPEN
LAWN

x

HOUSE

(454.3)
x

GARAGE

(454)

TERRACE

(453)

ASPHALT
DRIVE

(452)

ROAD

(451)
(450)
(449)
(448)

CULVERT
UNDER
DRIVE

0 10 25   50
FEET

Problem 6.4.   SITE PLAN

6.4   Using the Rational method, determine the peak rate of runoff for the drainage area on the site plan illustrated for a 10-year storm frequency. Assume that the site is located in New Jersey and that the soil is a silt loam. Also determine the diameter of a concrete pipe (culvert) which will accommodate the runoff under the driveway.

6.5.   The grading and storm drainage plan for a proposed hotel is illustrated below. Size all the pipes for the storm drainage system based on the following information:

a.   Use a 10-year storm frequency for New Jersey.

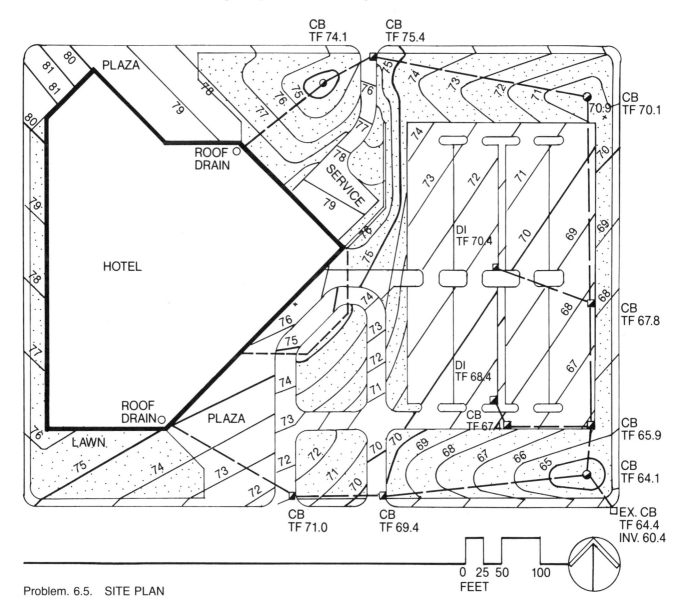

Problem. 6.5.   SITE PLAN

b. Each roof drain collects one-half of the roof runoff. Assume a 10 min time of concentration for this runoff.

c. runoff coefficients are

    roof = 0.95

    drive and parking area = 0.90

    walks = 0.80

    lawn and planting areas = 0.30

d. all pipes shall be reinforced concrete pipe (RCP) with $n = 0.013$

e. all roads, drives, parking areas, and islands in parking areas are edged with 6 in. high curbs.

In addition to pipe size, provide the *slope* for each pipe, the *velocity* in each pipe, and the *invert elevations* for all drainage structures. The proposed system discharges into an existing catch basin in the southeast corner with an invert elevation of 60.4 ft.

Draw a profile (horizontal scale 1 in. = 100 ft, vertical scale 1 in. = 10 ft) of the system indicating top of frame and invert elevations, pipe size, pipe slope, and distance between structures.

6.6a.   Examination of the topographic and land use maps of a drainage area indicates that the flow from the hydraulically most remote point to the point of concentration proceeds as follows:

    300 ft of woodland with a 4% slope

    200 ft of dense grass with a 3% slope

    500 ft of average grass with a 2% slope

    1600 ft of streamflow with a 1% slope

Find the total time of concentration for this area.

6.6b.   If the area of part a contains 125 acres of which 35% is in woodland, 64% is in pasture, and 1% in gravel roads, determine the peak storm runoff rate for a 25-year frequency. All surface slopes of the area are less than 5%.

6.7a.   Design a parabolic waterway for the conditions of Problem 6.3, if the velocity cannot exceed 90% of critical velocity.

6.7b.   Design a parabolic waterway for the conditions of Example 6.7, if the velocity cannot exceed 90% of critical velocity.

6.8a.   Using clay tile, determine the pipe sizes required for the subsurface drainage system illustrated in Fig. 6.32 assuming all distances are doubled.

6.8b.   Using corrugated plastic tubing, determine the pipe sizes required for the subsurface drainage system in Fig. 6.33 assuming all distances are 1.5 times those shown.

CHAPTER 7

Earthwork

This chapter is concerned with the sequence of earthmoving and the calculation of cut and fill volumes. Methods of earthmoving and earthmoving equipment are not discussed, since they are beyond the scope of this text. The following section defines the basic terminology associated with earthwork (Fig. 7.1).

Definitions

Finished Grade.   The final grade after all landscape development has been completed. It is the top surface of lawns, planting beds, pavements, etc., and is normally designated by contours and spot elevations on a grading plan.

Subgrade.   This is the top of the material on which the surface material such as topsoil and pavements (including base material) is placed. Sub-

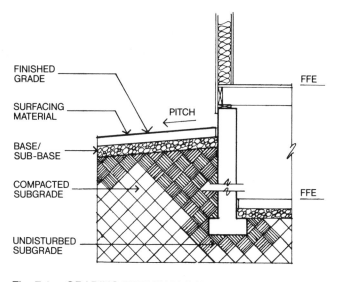

Fig. 7.1.   GRADING TERMINOLOGY

grade is represented by the *top* of a fill situation and the bottom of a cut excavation. *Compacted subgrade* refers to a subgrade that must attain a specified density, whereas *undisturbed subgrade* indicates a soil that has not been excavated or changed in any way.

Base/Sub-base. Imported material (normally coarse or fine aggregate) that is typically placed under pavements.

Finished Floor Elevation. This refers to the elevation of the first floor of a structure, but may be used to designate the elevation of any floor. The relationship of the finished floor elevation to the exterior finished grade depends on the type of construction.

Cut/Cutting. Cutting is the process of removing soil. Proposed contours extend across existing contours in the uphill direction.

Fill/Filling. Filling is the process of adding soil. Proposed contours extend across existing contours in the downhill direction. When the fill material must be imported to the site, it is often referred to as *borrow*. See Fig. 7.2.

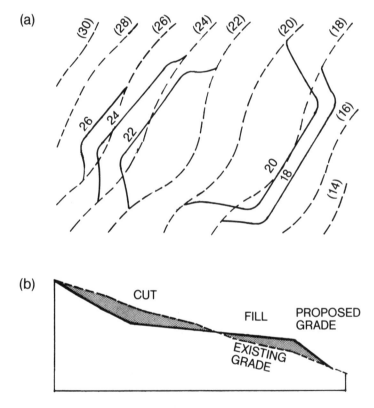

Fig. 7.2. CUT AND FILL
    a. Plan indicating existing and proposed contour lines. Cutting occurs where proposed contours move in the uphill direction, while filling occurs where they move in the downhill direction.
    b. Section showing where there is a change from cut to fill and where proposed grades return to existing grades. Both of these conditions are referred to as no cut−no fill.

Compaction. The densification of soil under controlled conditions, particularly a specified moisture content.

Topsoil. Normally the top layer of a soil profile, which may range in thickness from less than an inch to over a foot. Because of its high organic content, it is subject to decomposition and, therefore, is not an appropriate subgrade material for structures.

CONSTRUCTION SEQUENCE FOR GRADING

Site Preparation

There are four areas of concern in preparing a site for grading: protection of the existing vegetation and structures that are to remain, removal and storage of topsoil, erosion and sediment control, and clearing and demolition. Of course, all four areas are not necessarily applicable to every project.

Protection For the most part, this phase of preparation is self-explanatory. However, as pointed out earlier, any disturbance within the drip line of trees that are to remain should be avoided if possible. This not only refers to cutting and filling, but also to the storage and movement of materials and equipment, since this will result in increased compaction and reduced aeration of the root zone of the trees.

Topsoil Removal The site should be investigated to determine whether the quantity and quality of topsoil justifies storing. The topsoil should be stripped only within the construction area and, if appropriate, stockpiled for reuse on the site. If the topsoil is to be stockpiled for a long period, it should be seeded with an annual grass to reduce loss from erosion.

Erosion and Sediment Control Many states have enacted standards for soil erosion and sediment control, particularly for new construction. Temporary control measures that divert runoff away from disturbed areas, provide surface stabilization, and filter, trap, and collect sediment should be utilized as appropriate. These measures should comply with all governing standards.

Clearing and Demolition Buildings, pavements, and other structures that interfere with the proposed development must be removed prior to

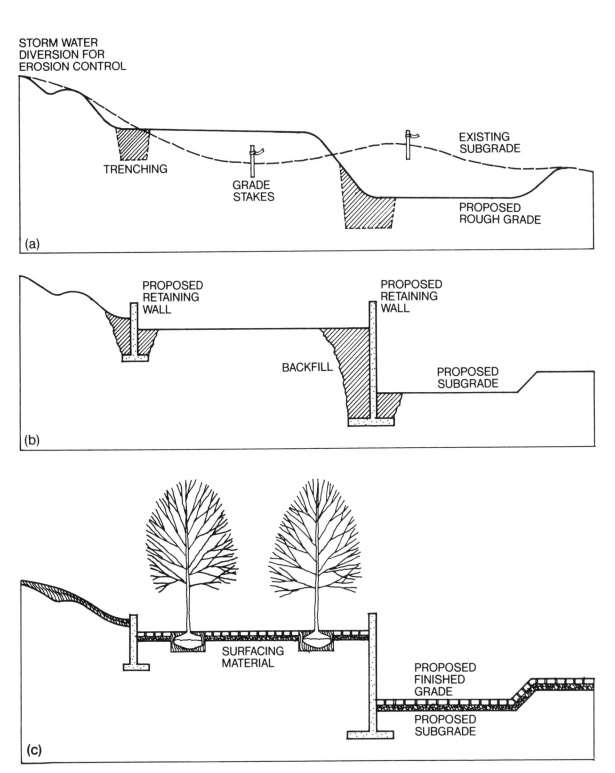

STORM WATER
DIVERSION FOR
EROSION CONTROL

TRENCHING

GRADE
STAKES

EXISTING
SUBGRADE

PROPOSED
ROUGH GRADE

(a)

PROPOSED
RETAINING
WALL

PROPOSED
RETAINING
WALL

BACKFILL

PROPOSED
SUBGRADE

(b)

SURFACING
MATERIAL

PROPOSED
FINISHED
GRADE

PROPOSED
SUBGRADE

(c)

Fig. 7.3. GRADING SEQUENCE
   a. Rough grading is the phase in which major earth shaping and excavation
      occurs.
   b. All utility trenches and structures are backfilled and the subgrade brought
      to the proper elevation during the backfilling and fine grading phases.
   c. Under the finished grading phase all surfacing materials like pavements
      and topsoil are placed.

the start of construction. The same is true for interfering trees and shrubs as well as any debris that may be found on the site.

The last step in preparing a site for excavation is the placement of grade stakes. Grade stakes indicate the amount of cut or fill necessary to achieve the proposed subgrade.

Bulk Excavation

The bulk or rough grading phase is the stage at which major earth moving and shaping take place (Fig. 7.3a). The extent to which bulk excavation is necessary depends on the scale and complexity of a project. Bulk excavation includes shaping of the basic earth form and footing and foundation excavations for all structures.

Backfilling and Fine Grading

Once the rough grade is achieved and structures have been built, finishing work may proceed. This includes backfilling excavations for structures such as retaining walls and building foundations and filling utility trenches for water lines, sewers, etc. All backfills must be properly compacted to minimize future settlement problems and must be executed in a manner that does not damage utilities or structures. The last step is to make sure that the earth forms and surfaces have been properly shaped and that the subgrade has been brought to the correct elevation (Fig. 7.3b).

Surfacing

To complete the project the surfacing material is installed. Usually the hard surfaces (i.e., pavements) are installed first and then the topsoil is placed (Fig. 7.3c). Since topsoil and pavements represent finish material, the final grades of these materials must agree with the proposed finished grades (contours and spot elevations) indicated on the grading plan.

GRADING OPERATIONS

There are two basic ways in which a proposed grading plan may be achieved. The first is to balance the amount of cut and fill required on the site. This may be accomplished by cutting and filling in the same operation; in other words excavating or scraping, moving, and depositing the soil in one operation. An alternative method, which may be necessary depending on the scale and complexity of the project, is to stockpile the cut material and then place it in the fill areas as required. In either case the cut material must be suitable as fill.

The second is to import or export soil to satisfy the cut and fill requirements. This results when cut and fill do not balance on the site or when the cut material is unsuitable as fill material. Obviously, balancing cut and fill on site is the less costly option and normally the most energy efficient.

If it is not possible to balance cut and fill on a site, the issue arises as to which is more desirable: importing fill material (borrow) or exporting cut material. There is no general consensus among professionals, and the answer is somewhat dependent on location, scale of project, and soil conditions. However, the authors feel that it is preferable to export soil for the following reasons.

First, importing soil tends to be more expensive, since it requires the purchase of the material, hauling the material to the site, and then placing and properly compacting the material. Second is the condition that importing material indicates—more of the site is in fill than in cut. A fill condition is generally structurally less stable than a cut condition and is more susceptible to erosion and settlement. To reduce the potential for settlement, costly compaction methods may be necessary, or, in critical situations, special footings may have to be used for structures.

Other factors influencing the cost of grading are size and shape of site, intricacy of grading plan, and types of soil. The size, shape, and scale of a project influence labor and equipment requirements, whereas earth forms and grading tolerances influence the amount of detail and accuracy necessary in executing the design. Soil conditions will also affect the type of equipment that may be used and also the suitability of the of the soil for the proposed uses.

COMPUTING CUT AND FILL VOLUMES

Estimates must be made of cut and fill volumes to establish construction costs and to determine whether the volumes balance or more cut or fill will be required. There are several methods for calculating volumes, three of which are discussed here: the average end area, contour area, and borrow pit (grid) methods. All the methods provide only an *approximation*, since actual cut and fill volumes are rarely the straight-edged geometric solids on which the computations are based. It should also be noted that computer programs exist for each method presented.

Average End Area Method

The average end area method is best suited for lineal construction such as roads, paths, and utility trenching. The formula states that the volume of cut (or fill) between two adjacent cross-sections is the average of the two sections multiplied by the distance between them.

$$V = \frac{A_1 + A_2}{2} \times L \qquad (7.1)$$

where A_1 and A_2 = end sections in ft^2
V = volume in ft^3
L = distance between A_1 and A_2 in ft

To apply the method, cross-sections must be taken at selected or predetermined intervals. The shorter the interval between sections, the more accurate the estimate will be. Each cross-section indicates the existing and proposed grades. Typically, the sections are drawn with the vertical scale exaggerated five to ten times the horizontal scale. The area between the existing and proposed grades is measured, keeping cut separate from fill. Methods for measuring areas include planimeter, digitizer, geometry, and grids. The last step is to average the area of the two adjacent sections and then multiply by the distance between them to determine the volume in cubic feet. To convert to cubic yards—the standard unit of measurement for earthwork volumes—this figure must be divided by 27 ft^3/yd^3. The information is usually organized in tabular form as illustrated in Table 7.1.

TABLE 7.1. Data

Station	Area (ft^2)	Average (ft^2)	Distance (ft)	Volume (ft^3)
2+00	0			
		50.5	50	2525
2+50	101			
		70.5	50	3525
3+00	40			
		20.0	25	500
3+25	0			———
				6550

Example 7.1   A portion of an existing road is to be regraded to accommodate a new inlet as illustrated in Fig. 7.4. Determine the volume of fill required. For the purposes of this problem, stations 2+00 and 3+25 are considered points of no cut or fill.

Solution   The first step is to select an interval between cross-sections and to locate the sections on the plan. An interval of 50 ft is selected for this example and sections are taken at stations 2+50 and 3+00. The sections are drawn indicating the existing and proposed grades with the vertical scale exaggerated five times. Next, the areas of the sections are measured. (Usually areas are measured in square inches and then converted to square feet based on the horizontal and vertical scales of the drawing. In this case 1 in.^{2} = 30 ft $\times$ 6 ft = 180 ft^2. Since there is no cut or fill at station 2+00, the average sectional area between stations 2+00 and 2+50 is

$$\frac{0 + 101 \text{ ft}^2}{2} = 50.5 \text{ ft}^2$$

The volume is now determined by multiplying the average area by the distance between the sections:

$$50.5\text{ft}^2 \times 50 \text{ ft} = 2525 \text{ ft}^3$$

The volume between stations 2+50 and 3+00 is

$$\frac{101 + 40}{2} \times 50 = 3525 \text{ ft}^3$$

The last volume to be calculated is between stations 3+00 and 3+25. Again there is no change in grade at station 3+25.

$$\frac{40 + 0}{2} \times 25 = 500 \text{ ft}^3$$

Notice that the interval between the last two sections is only 25 ft. The data for this example are summarized in Table 7.1.

The result obtained in Example 7.1 significantly overestimates the total volume. This is true because the two end sections are actually conical or pyramidal, for which the volume is $A/3 \times L$, rather than $(A_1 + A_2/2 \times L$. A difference of 50% for the end volumes is caused by the simplification. When the conical (or pyramidal) formula is used, the volumes for Example 7.1 become 1683, 3525, and 333 ft^3 with a total of 5541 ft^3. Note that the previously computed end volumes of 2525 and 500 ft^3 are 1.5 times 1683 and 333 ft^3, respectively.

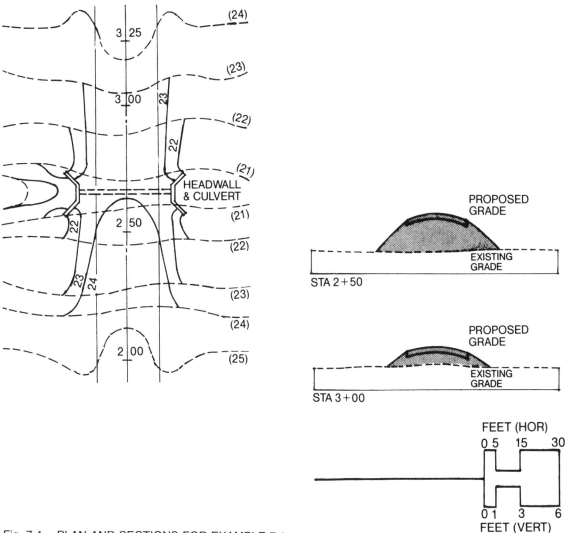

Fig. 7.4. PLAN AND SECTIONS FOR EXAMPLE 7.1.

When a project has many sections, this detail is usually disregarded because of the inherent inaccuracy of volume computations. However, where only a few sections are needed (as in the example), it is advisable to use the conical formula.

Regardless of the formulas used, the average end area method tends to overestimate volumes.

Contour Area Method

This method is appropriate for large, relatively uncomplicated grading plans and may also be used to calculate volumes of water in ponds and lakes. To apply this method the first step is to establish the line of no cut or fill and then to separate the area of cut from the area of fill. The next step is to measure the horizontal area of change for each contour line within the no cut−no fill limit, keeping areas of cut separate from areas of fill. In other words, measure the area bounded by the same numbered existing and proposed contour lines. Finally, the volumes of cut and fill can be calculated by applying the following formula:

$$V = \frac{A_1 h}{3} + \frac{(A_1 + A_2)h}{2} + \ldots \frac{(A_{n-1} + A_n)h}{2} + \frac{A_n h}{3} \qquad (7.2)$$

where A_1, A_2, A_n = area of horizontal change for each contour in ft^2
h = vertical distance between areas in ft

The first and last terms on the right-hand side of the equation are considered as conical or pyramidal solids, as shown by the shaded areas in section in Fig. 7.5. The volume of such a solid $(A/3)\,h$ was given in the preceding example. If the altitude h is equal to the contour interval i the equation can be simplified as follows:

$$V = i(5/6\,A_1 + A_2 + A_3 + \ldots 5/6\,A_n) \qquad (7.3)$$

Because of the approximate nature of computing earthwork, the equation can be further simplified to

$$V = i(A_1 + A_2 + A_3 + \ldots A_n) \qquad (7.4)$$

However, using this final form of the equation will result in overestimated earthwork volumes. For ease of computation the information should be organized as shown in Table 7.2

TABLE 7.2.   Contour Area Measurements

Contour number	Area of cut (ft^2)	Area of fill (ft^2)
67	0	60
68	0	175
69	0	324
70	0	451
71	0	780
72	308	990
73	388	360
74	410	0
75	176	0
Total	1282	3140

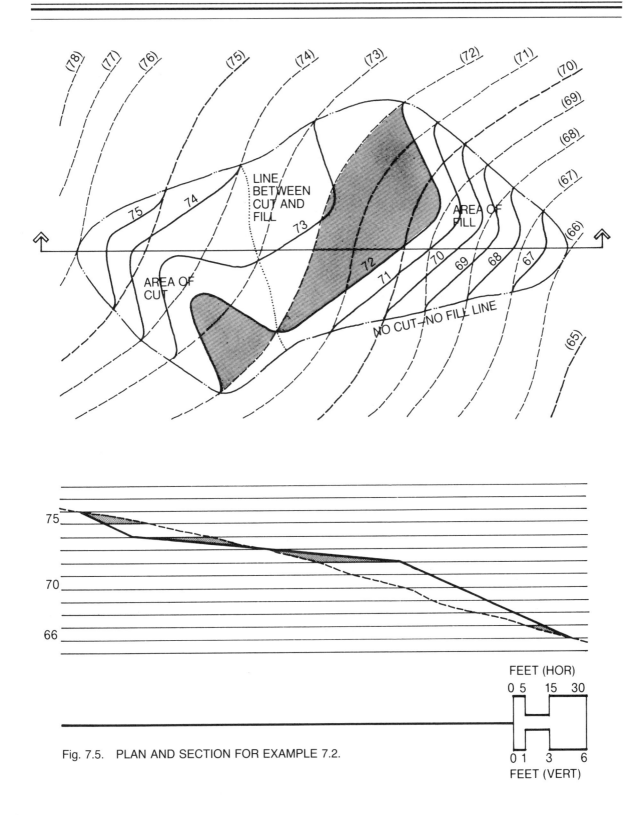

Fig. 7.5. PLAN AND SECTION FOR EXAMPLE 7.2.

Example 7.2. Figure 7.5 illustrates a slope which has been regraded to accommodate a small plateau area. Using the contour area method calculate the volumes of cut and fill required.

Solution As noted, the first step is to delineate the extent of the earthwork by a no cut – no fill line and to separate the area of cut from the area of fill, followed by measuring the area of change for each contour line. This is demonstrated by the shaded areas for the 72 ft contour line. The areas for each contour line are recorded in Table 7.2. The last step is to multiply the total areas by the contour interval, in this case 1 ft, and divided by 27 ft^3/yd^3 to convert the volumes to cubic yards.

$$\frac{1282 \times 1}{27} = 47.48 \text{ yd}^3 \text{ cut}$$

$$\frac{3140 \times 1}{27} = 116.30 \text{ yd}^3 \text{ fill}$$

Borrow Pit Method

The borrow pit method, sometimes referred to as the grid method, is appropriate for complex grading projects and urban conditions. Existing elevations are determined at each grid intersection on the site by "borrow pit leveling" normally done in preparation for contour mapping, as previously described in Chapter 2. If such elevations are not available, but a contour map of the project site has been prepared, a grid is placed over the area to be regraded. Care must be taken in determining the size and location of the grid on the site. The estimate becomes more accurate as the size of the grid decreases, and in some cases it may even be appropriate to break up the area into two or more parts, each with a different size grid. Existing and proposed grades are determined at each grid intersection by interpolation, and the difference between elevations calculated. A notational system should be used to distinguish fill from cut, such as F and C. From this point there are two ways to proceed.

The first approach is to apply the borrow pit method on a cell by cell basis. An average change in elevation is calculated for each cell by determining the difference in elevation for all four corners of each cell, as illustrated in Fig. 7.6, adding all four differences and dividing by 4. The volume is calculated by adding all the averaged values together, keeping cut and fill separate, and multiplying by the area of one grid cell.

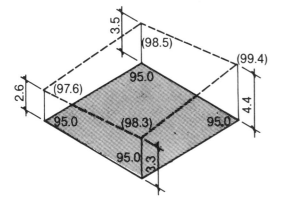

Fig. 7.6. a. EXAMPLE OF SINGLE GRID CELL
FOR BORROW PIT METHOD

b. BORROW PIT LEVELING ON A
PROJECT SITE
Plans for a borrow pit grid are
illustrated in Figs. 2.5 and 7.7

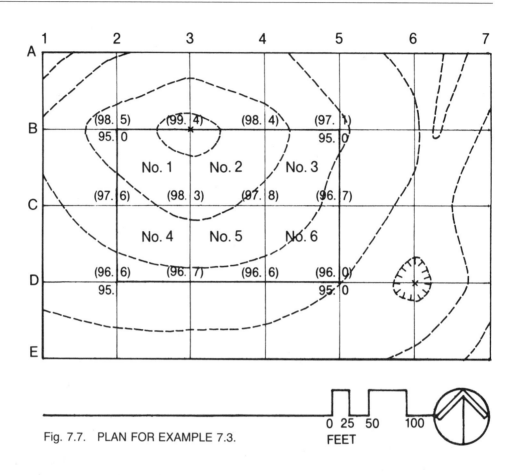

Fig. 7.7. PLAN FOR EXAMPLE 7.3.

0 25 50   100
FEET

Example 7.3 The grid of spot elevations illustrated in Fig. 2.5 is shown in Fig. 7.7 with the resulting contour lines. For this problem a rectangular area bounded by corners B2, B5, D2, and D5 is to be excavated with vertical sides to a finished elevation of 95.0. Calculate the volume of excavation using the borrow pit method. For identification purposes the six cells are numbered in Fig. 7.7.

Solution The first step is to determine the difference in elevation between the existing and proposed grades. This is demonstrated for cell No. 1 as follows (see Fig. 7.6a):

$$\text{Corner:} \quad \begin{array}{lll} \text{B2} & 98.5-95.0 = 3.5 \text{ ft} \\ \text{B3} & 99.4-95.0 = 4.4 \text{ ft} \\ \text{C2} & 97.6-95.0 = 2.6 \text{ ft} \\ \text{C3} & 98.3-95.0 = 3.3 \text{ ft} \end{array}$$

Next the differences are totaled and divided by 4 to calculate the average.

$$\frac{3.5 + 4.4 + 2.6 + 3.3}{4} = \frac{13.8}{4} = 3.45 \text{ ft avg}$$

The same procedure is applied to the remaining five cells with the following results:

Cell No. 2:   3.475 ft avg
No. 3:   2.50   ft avg
No. 4:   2.30   ft avg
No. 5:   2.35   ft avg
No. 6:   1.775 ft avg

The final step is to add up the averages for all the cells and to multiply by the area of one cell (100 ft × 100 ft = 10,000 ft^2).

$$3.45 + 3.475 + 2.50 + 2.30 + 2.35 + 1.775 = 15.85 \text{ ft}$$
$$15.85 \times 10,000 = 158,500 \text{ ft}^3$$
$$\frac{158,500}{27} = 5870.37 \text{ yd}^3$$

Since earthwork computations are only approximate, this may be rounded to 5,900 yd^3.

The second approach is derived by simplifying the equation of the first approach by common factoring. The advantage of this procedure is that it reduces the number of calculations required.

$$V = \frac{A}{4} \times (1h_1 + 2h_2 + 3h_3 + 4h_4) \tag{7.5}$$

where V = volume of cut (or fill) in ft^3

A = area of *one* grid cell in ft^2

h_1 = sum of the cuts (or fills) for all grid corners common to one grid cell

h_2 = sum of the cuts (or fills) for all grid corners common to two grid cells

h_3 = sum of the cuts (or fills) for all grid corners common to three grid cells

h_4 = sum of the cuts (or fills) for all grid corners common to four grid cells

This process is demonstrated in the following example.

Example 7.4   Using Example 7.3, the volume of excavation is now calculated by the simplified equation.

Solution   There are four corners that appear in only *one* grid cell of the area to excavated: B2, B5, D2, and D5. The depth of cut for these corners is obtained by subtracting the proposed finished elevation from the existing elevation, i.e., 98.5 − 95.0 = 3.5 ft for B2. The remaining three cuts are 2.1, 1.6, and 1.0. The sum of h_1 is 3.5 + 2.1 + 1.6 + 1.0, which equals 8.2 ft.

Proceeding clockwise, the corners common to *two* grid cells of the excavated area are B3, B4, C5, D4, D3, and C2. The depth of cut for these corners are 4.4, 3.4, 1.7, 1.6, 1.7 and 2.6, again obtained by subtracting the proposed finished elevation, 95.0 ft, from the existing grades. The sum of h_2 is 15.4 ft.

There are two corners common to *four* grid cells within the area to be graded: C3 and C4. The sum of h_4 is 3.3 + 2.8, which equals 6.1 ft. There are no corners common to three grid cells. Since all twelve corners of the grid have been accounted for, the values may be substituted into the formula. Again each cell measures 100 ft by 100 ft, therefore the area of each cell equals 10,000 ft^2.

$$V = \frac{A}{4}\,(1h_1 + 2h_2 + 3h_3 + 4h_4)$$
$$= \frac{10,000}{4}(1 \times 8.2 + 2 \times 15.4 + 3 \times 0.0 + 4 \times 6.1)$$
$$= 2500\,(8.2 + 30.8 + 0.0 + 24.4)$$
$$= 158,500 \text{ ft}^3$$
$$= \frac{158,500}{27} = 5,870.37 \text{ yd}^3$$

For estimating purposes this may again be rounded upward to 5,900 yd^3.

The method works the same for fill, except that the height of fill required for each corner is determined by *subtracting* the existing elevation from the proposed finished elevation. Where a project consists partially of cut and partially of fill, the cut and fill are determined separately and the net volume of cut or fill can then be computed.

Adjusting Cut and Fill Volumes

Two adjustments must be made in determining cut and fill volumes. The first is concerned with surface materials, while the second involves the compaction and shrinkage of soil volumes.

For estimating purposes, cut and fill volumes are determined between existing and proposed subgrades, *not* between existing and proposed finished grades. However, contour lines and spot elevations on grading plans and topographic surveys usually indicate finished grade conditions. As a result, compensation must be made for both the existing surface material to be removed and proposed surfacing material to be installed. This may be accomplished in a variety of ways, a few of which will be discussed here. It is important, however, to understand the following basic principles.

1. In cut, proposed surfacing material (including pavement and top-soil) *increases* the amount of excavation required.
2. In fill, proposed surfacing material *decreases* the amount of borrow required.
3. In cut, the removal of existing pavement or stripping of topsoil *decreases* the volume of soil to be removed.

4. In fill, the removal of existing pavement or stripping of topsoil *increases* the volume of soil to be placed.

These principles are illustrated in Fig. 7.8. It should be noted that where the depths of the proposed and existing surface materials are the *same*, they are self-compensating and no adjustment is required. With both the average end area and borrow pit methods it is possible to incorporate the adjustment directly into the volume calculations. For the average end area method the cross-sections may be drawn indicating the existing and proposed subgrades rather than finished grades. For the borrow pit method, the spot elevations indicated at the grid corners could be based on the proposed and existing subgrades.

Another alternative is simply to measure the plan area of the surface material, keeping areas within cut separate from areas within fill, and multiply by the depth of the material to calculate the volume. The volume may be added or subtracted to the cut or fill volumes as described in the principles above. This technique is illustrated in Example 7.5.

Example 7.5 Again, using the data from Example 7.3, the volume of excavation is to be adjusted based on the following information. There is an existing 6 in. layer of topsoil that must be stripped before excavation can begin. The proposed 95.0 ft finished elevation is the top of a 6 in. concrete slab with a 4 in. gravel base.

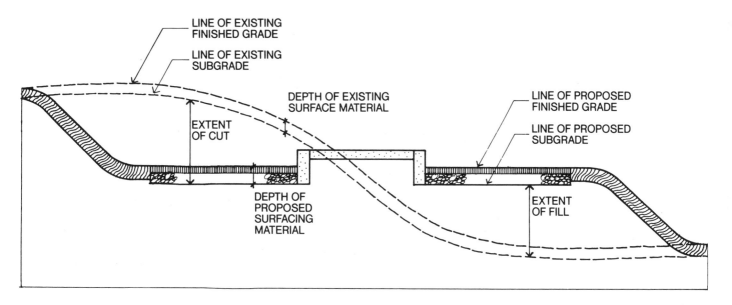

Fig. 7.8.   RELATIONSHIP OF EXISTING AND PROPOSED SURFACING MATERIALS TO CUT AND FILL VOLUMES
Where existing and proposed finished grade elevations, rather than subgrade
elevations, are used to compute volumes make the following adjustments:
Gross Cut Volume − Existing Surfacing Material Volume + Proposed Surfacing
Material Volume = Adjusted Cut Volume
Gross Fill Volume + Existing Surfacing Material Volume − Proposed Surfacing
Material Volume = Adjusted Fill Volume

Solution The topsoil to be stripped reduces the gross volume of excavation. The volume of topsoil is the area (60,000 ft^2) multiplied by the depth (0.5 ft^2).

$$60{,}000 \times 0.5 = 30{,}000 \text{ ft}^3$$
$$\frac{30{,}000}{27} = 1111.11 \text{ yd}^3, \text{ or } 1110 \text{ yd}^3$$

On the other hand, the depth of the excavation must be increased by 10 in. (0.83 ft) to accommodate the concrete slab and base course. The resulting increased cut volume is

$$60{,}000 \times 0.83 = 49{,}800 \text{ ft}^3$$
$$\frac{49{,}800}{27} = 1844.44 \text{ yd}^3, \text{ or } 1840 \text{ yd}^3$$

The final adjusted volume is determined as follows:

5,900 yd^3 (gross cut) + 1,840 yd^3 (proposed surfacing) − 1,110 yd^3 (existing topsoil) = 6,630 yd^3 adjusted volume

The second factor affecting cut and fill volumes is the change in soil volume as a result of compaction and shrinkage. Usually *in-place* volumes of cut, referred to as bank yards, will yield less than their volume in fill by 10 to 20%, depending on soil type and compaction techniques. This means that 100 yd^3 of cut will yield approximately only 80 to 90 yd^3 of fill. Therefore, to balance cut and fill on a site, a 100 yd^3 fill would require approximately 110 to 125 yd^3 of cut. For cost estimating purposes, fill volumes, referred to as compacted yards, should be increased by 10 to 20% depending on the soil to determine the actual quantity of borrow required.

Balancing Cut and Fill Volumes

On some projects it may be desirable, or even required, that all grading be self-contained on the site, i.e., that no soil can be imported to or exported from the site. On such projects, the line of no cut−no fill on the grading plan will result in areas with shapes other than square or rectangular. The borrow pit method described previously can be applied only when all grid cells are identical squares or rectangles. Where the areas of the cells are not equal, the volume for each area must be determined separately.

The basic approximation for computing cut or fill is that the volume is the product of the mapped (horizontal) area multiplied by the average of the cuts (or fills) at each corner of that area. Some of these cuts (or fills) may be zero, but they *must* be included in averaging. Figure 7.9 illustrates the variety of geometrical areas that may occur on a grading plan and formulas for the corresponding volumes.

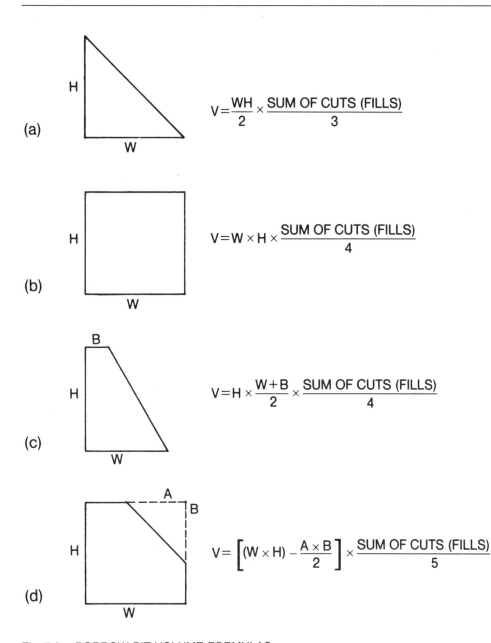

(a) $V = \dfrac{WH}{2} \times \dfrac{\text{SUM OF CUTS (FILLS)}}{3}$

(b) $V = W \times H \times \dfrac{\text{SUM OF CUTS (FILLS)}}{4}$

(c) $V = H \times \dfrac{W+B}{2} \times \dfrac{\text{SUM OF CUTS (FILLS)}}{4}$

(d) $V = \left[(W \times H) - \dfrac{A \times B}{2} \right] \times \dfrac{\text{SUM OF CUTS (FILLS)}}{5}$

Fig. 7.9. BORROW PIT VOLUME FORMULAS
  a. Triangular areas
  b. Square and rectangular areas
  c. Trapezoidal areas
  d. Pentagonal areas

Example 7.6 Figure 7.10 represents a project that will be partially in fill and partially in cut. The number at each corner indicates the height of fill or depth of cut required. Determine the volume of fill and cut for each area and the total volumes of fill and cut. All distances are as shown on the plan.

Solution   Volumes 1, 2, 3, and 4 are in cut and 5, 6, and 7 are in fill. The volumes for each area will be computed separately according to the formulas given in Fig. 7.9.

$$\text{Volume No. 1} = W \times H \times \frac{\text{sum of cuts}}{4}$$
$$= 100 \times 100 \times \frac{4.8 + 3.5 + 0.8 + 4.2}{4}$$
$$= 10{,}000 \times \frac{13.3}{4} = 33{,}250 \text{ ft}^3$$
$$= 33{,}250/27 \text{ ft}^3/\text{yd}^3 = 1231.48 \text{ yd}^3$$
$$\text{Volume No. 2} = H \times \frac{W + B}{2} \times \frac{\text{sum of cuts}}{4}$$
$$= 100 \times \frac{66 + 26}{2} \times \frac{3.5 + 0 + 0 + 0.8}{4}$$
$$= 4600 \times \frac{4.3}{4} = 4945 \text{ ft}^3 = 183.15 \text{ yd}^3$$

Note that the zeros used in the sum of the cuts represent the corners at the no cut–no fill line.

$$\text{Volume No. 3} = [(W \times H) - \frac{A \times B}{2}] \times \frac{\text{sum of cuts}}{5}$$
$$= [(100 \times 100) - \frac{62 \times 31}{2}] \times \frac{4.2 + 0.8 + 0 + 0 + 2.9}{5}$$
$$= 9039 \times \frac{7.9}{5} = 14281.62 \text{ ft}^3 = 528.95 \text{ yd}^3$$
$$\text{Volume No. 4} = \frac{W \times H}{2} \times \frac{\text{sum of cuts}}{3}$$
$$= \frac{26 \times 38}{2} \times \frac{0.8 + 0 + 0}{3}$$
$$= 494 \times \frac{0.8}{3} = 131.73 \text{ ft}^3 = 4.88 \text{ yd}^3$$

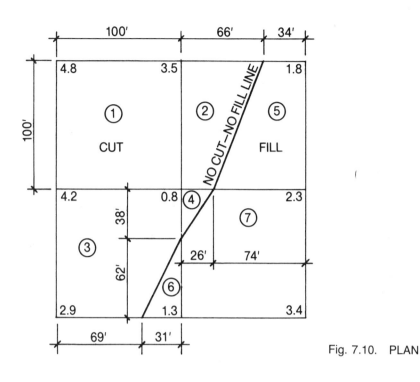

Fig. 7.10. PLAN

Similarly, the volumes of fill are computed as follows:

Volume No. 5 $= 5400 \times \dfrac{4.1}{4} = 5535$ ft^3 $= 205.00$ yd^3

Volume No. 6 $=\ \ 961 \times \dfrac{1.3}{3} = 416.43$ ft^3 $= 15.42$ yd^3

Volume No. 7 $= 9506 \times \dfrac{7.0}{5} = 13308.4$ ft^3 $= 492.90$ yd^3

The total volume of the cut is $1231.48 + 183.15 + 528.95 + 4.88 = 1948.46$ yd^3, which may be rounded to 1950 yd^3. The volume of fill is $205.00 + 15.42 + 492.90 = 713.32$ yd^3, which is approximately 710 yd^3.

It may be noted that the volume of cut is 1950/710 or over 2.7 times the volume of fill, which may also be stated as a cut-to-fill ratio of 2.7. Even considering shrinkage (settling and compaction), it is evident that there will be a considerable amount of extra soil. A ratio of 1.1 to 1.2 ft^3 of cut to each ft^3 of fill required is often used where a balance of volumes is desired. The next example will demonstrate how this may be accomplished.

Example 7.7 Assuming that the desired final grade of the project in Fig. 7.10 is to be level, adjust all cuts and fill heights to achieve a cut to fill ratio of 1.2.

Solution To achieve a 1.2 cut-to-fill ratio requires basically a trial and error procedure. Since there is an excess of cut (or since the proposed grade is too low), the final grade must be raised, resulting in less cut and more fill. As a result, the *area* of cut will decrease while the *area* of fill will increase. Also, for every 0.1 ft that the final grade is raised, 0.1 ft must be subtracted from each cut depth and added to each fill height.

For a preliminary estimate of volumes, it can be assumed that the cut (or fill) occurring on an outside corner is the average cut (or fill) for one-quarter of the area of a grid square. The cuts (or fills) common to two grid squares may be assumed to be the average cuts (or fills) for two-quarters or one-half of the area of a grid square; the cuts (or fills) common to three squares account for three-quarters of a grid square, and cuts (or fills) common to four grid squares may be averaged over four-quarters or the area or one full grid square. This is illustrated in Fig. 7.11. These assumptions make it possible to do preliminary computations with new trial cut depths or fill heights without actually computing volumes, which would be more laborious. Also, as a result of the change in cut and fill *areas*, the actual location of the final no cut–no fill line is not yet known. In the preliminary computations, each cut (or fill) on an outside corner will will have one-quarter weight, each one common to two grid squares will have one-half weight, each one common to three grid squares will have three-quarters weight, while each one common to four grid squares will have one full weight.

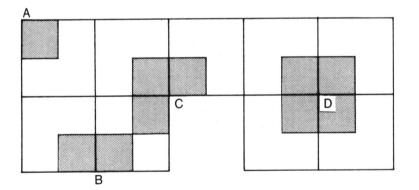

Fig. 7.11. APPROXIMATE AVERAGE CUT AND FILL VALUES
Rather than average the corner values for each grid cell, the cut or fill value at each grid intersection may be assumed to be the average value for the adjacent grid cell area. Thus point A is the average for one-quarter of a cell, B is the average for one-half of a cell, C is the average for three-quarters of a cell, and D is the average for one full cell.

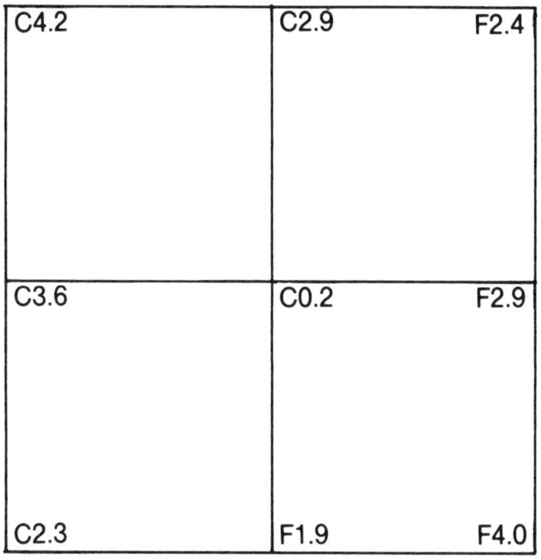

C4.2	C2.9	F2.4
C3.6	C0.2	F2.9
C2.3	F1.9	F4.0

Fig. 7.12. PLAN

For a trial grade the weighted cuts and fills are determined. The sum of the weighted cuts is compared to the sum of the weighted fills. When the ratio of these sums is close to the desired cut-to-fill ratio, actual volumes are computed.

In this example, since there is such a large excess of cut, the first trial will raise the proposed grade 0.6 ft, so that each cut will be 0.6 ft less and each fill 0.6 ft more, as shown in Fig. 7.12. The sum of the weighted cuts is 4.2/4 + 2.9/2 + 3.6/2 + 0.2 + 2.3/4 = 5.075 ft. The sum of the weighted fills is 2.4/4 + 2.9/2 + 1.9/2 + 4.0/4 = 4. Therefore, the trial cut-to-fill ratio is 5.075/4 = 1.27. This is close enough to the desired 1.2 ratio to compute the actual volumes.

To do this, the first step is to locate the no cut−no fill line wherever there is a change from cut to fill. The point at which the no cut−no fill line crosses a grid line can be determined by the following proportion:

$$\frac{d_1}{L} = \frac{C}{C + F} \qquad (7.6)$$

Also

$$d_2 = L - d_1 \qquad (7.7)$$

where d_1=distance to the point of no cut−no fill from the grid corner in cut

L=distance between grid corners (100 ft in this example)

C=depth of cut

F=fill height

d_2=distance to the point of no cut−no fill from the grid corner in fill

The relationship can also be expressed as follows, if it is more convenient to proceed from the grid corner that is in fill:

$$\frac{d_2}{L} = \frac{F}{F + C} \tag{7.8}$$

and

$$d_1 = L - d_2 \tag{7.9}$$

Using these relationships, the distance for the lower left is computed as follows:

$$\frac{d_1}{100} = \frac{2.3}{2.3 + 1.9}$$
$$d_1 = 100 \times 2.3/4.2 = 54.76 \text{ or } 55 \text{ ft}$$
$$d_2 = 100 - 55 = 45 \text{ ft}$$

Similarly, the other distances are determined as follows:

$$d_2 = 100 \times \frac{1.9}{1.9 + 0.2} = 90 \text{ ft } (d_1 = 10 \text{ ft})$$

$$d_1 = 100 \times \frac{0.2}{0.2 + 2.9} = 6 \text{ ft } (d_2 = 94 \text{ ft})$$

$$d_1 = 100 \times \frac{2.9}{2.9 + 2.4} = 55 \text{ ft } (d_2 = 45 \text{ ft})$$

The location of the no cut–no fill line is shown in Fig. 7.13. The line has shifted to the left and, as noted previously, the area of cut has been reduced and the area of fill has increased. The volumes of cut and fill are computed as before with the following results:

Cut

Volume No. 1 $= 100 \times 100 \times \dfrac{10.9}{4} = 27250 \text{ ft}^3 = 1009.26 \text{ yd}^3$

Volume No. 2 $= 100 \times \dfrac{55 + 6}{2} \times \dfrac{3.1}{4} = 2363.75 \text{ ft}^3 = 87.55 \text{ yd}^3$

Volume No. 3 $= \left[(100 \times 100) - \dfrac{90 \times 45}{2} \right] \times \dfrac{6.1}{5} = 9729.5 \text{ ft}^3 = 360.35 \text{ yd}^3$

Volume No. 4 $= \dfrac{6 \times 10}{2} \times \dfrac{0.2}{3} = 2.0 \text{ ft}^3 = 0.07 \text{ yd}^3$

Fill

Volume No. 5 $= 6950 \times \dfrac{5.3}{4} = 9208.75 \text{ ft}^3 = 341.06 \text{ yd}^3$

Volume No. 6 $= 2025 \times \dfrac{1.9}{3} = 1282.5 \text{ ft}^3 = 47.5 \text{ yd}^3$

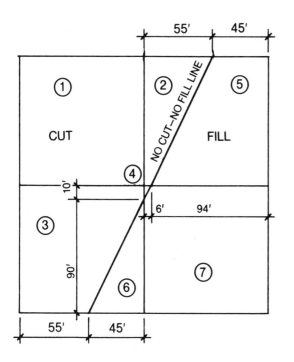

Fig. 7.13.   NO CUT—NO FILL LINE

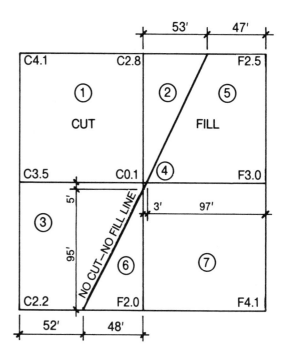

Fig. 7.14.   FINAL PLAN

Volume No. 7 $= 9970 \times \dfrac{8.8}{5} = 17{,}547.2 \text{ ft}^3 = 649.9 \text{ yd}^3$

$\dfrac{\text{Total Volume of Cut}}{\text{Total Volume of Fill}} = \dfrac{1457.23}{1038.46} = 1.4$

This is more than the preliminary ratio of 1.27 and is still too great. The final grade will be raised again by 0.1 ft as shown in Fig. 7.14. The resulting volumes are as follows:

Cut
Volume No. 1 = 972.22 yd^3
Volume No. 2 =   75.19
Volume No. 3 = 331.67
Volume No. 4 = 0.01
    Total Cut = 1379.09 yd^3

Fill
Volume No. 5 = 366.67 yd^3
Volume No. 6 =   56.30
Volume No. 7 = 673.57
    Total Fill = 1096.54 yd^3

The cut-to-fill ratio is now 1.26, which is still a little high. However, raising the final grade another 0.1 ft results in a cut-to-fill ratio of 1.06. Therefore, the 1.26 ratio is accepted, since it is very difficult to grade to tolerances of less than 0.1 ft.

While the desired final surface was to be level in Example 7.7, the method used can be applied to any required final plane surface, level or sloping. The mapped (horizontal) distances should be used to determine the areas for volume computations and to locate the no cut−no fill lines.

Another point that aids in achieving a balance is to understand the relationship of volume to depth and area. Raising or lowering large areas only a few inches may significantly change cut and fill volumes. For instance, if the grade over a 1 acre area is raised or lowered by 4 in., the change in volume is greater than 500 yd^3. Establishing simple area-to-volume relationships for different depths will make the task of balancing cut and fill easier.

PROBLEMS

7.1   Using the average end area method, calculate the volumes of cut and fill for the cross-sections (horizontal and vertical scales as shown) indicated. Adjust the volumes based on the following information.
   a.   depth of existing topsoil: 6 in.
   b.   depth of proposed topsoil: 6 in.
   c.   depth of proposed pavement: 6 in.
Stations 0+00 and 2+35 are points of no cut or fill. Also indicate the approximate volume of *excess topsoil*.

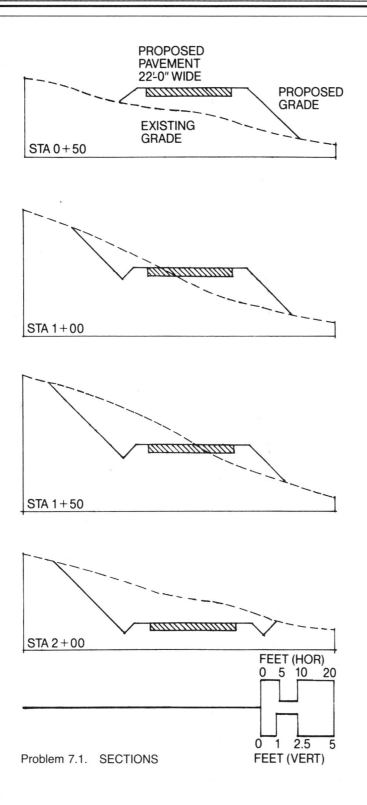

Problem 7.1.   SECTIONS

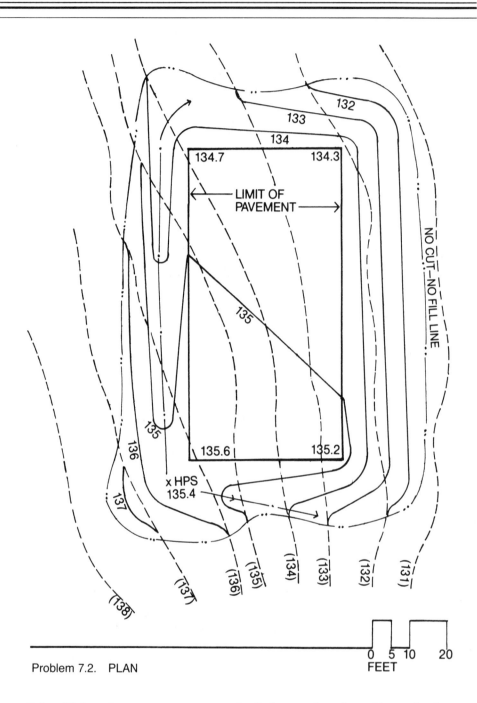

Problem 7.2.   PLAN

7.2.   Using the contour area method, determine the *adjusted* volumes
of cut and fill for the plan above based on the following information:
  a.   depth of existing topsoil: 4 in.
  b.   depth of topsoil replaced in disturbed areas: 8 in.
  c.   depth of proposed pavement: 6 in.
How much soil must be imported or exported from the site?
Also determine the volume of topsoil to be replaced.

7.3. Using the grading plan in Fig. 5.28, construct a grid of 20 ft by 20 ft cells starting at the northeast corner over the entire site. Determine the *existing and proposed subgrades* at each of the grid intersections based on the following:

   a. depth of existing topsoil: 4 in.
   b. depth of proposed topsoil: 6 in.
   c. depth of proposed pavement: 8 in.
   d. subgrade of building 1.0 ft below FFE

Finally, using the borrow pit method compute the volumes of cut and fill for this site.

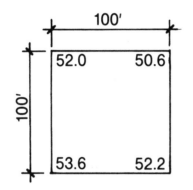

Problem 7.4.   PLAN

7.4. The area illustrated is to be leveled without importing or exporting soil. The desired cut to fill ratio is 1.2. Determine

   a. The final elevation.
   b. The volume of cut.
   c. The volume of fill.
   d. The final cut-to-fill ratio.
   e. Show the location of the no cut−no fill line.

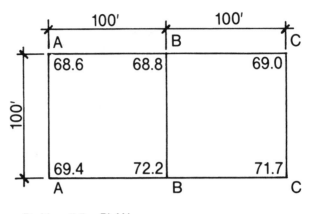

Problem 7.5. PLAN

7.5.   The existing elevations at the grid corners of a 100 ft × 200 ft area are given. The site plan for the project requires that line B-B be level and that there be a 2% slope downward from B-B toward A-A and toward C-C. Also, the cut-to-fill ratio is to be as close as possible to 1.2. No soil is to be brought to or taken from the site. Draw the final grading plan, showing the elevation at each grid corner. Show the no cut−no fill line with all distances indicated. Determine the volumes of cut and fill and the final cut-to-fill ratio.

CHAPTER 8

Horizontal Road Alignment

Generally, landscape architects and site designers are involved with the design of low speed residential and park roads, entry and service drives, and parking areas. Involvement with high speed roads is limited to corridor or route selection but, for the most part, is not concerned with highway engineering. The purpose of the next two chapters is to present the basic engineering necessary to lay out roads and drives in the landscape. Visual, experiential, and environmental issues, traffic engineering, and traffic management techniques are not addressed, since they are beyond the scope of this text.

In order to create safe, enjoyable, and easily maneuverable vehicular circulation, roads must be engineered in both the horizontal and vertical planes. The horizontal plane is concerned with the alignment of roads *through* the landscape, referred to as *horizontal alignment*. The vertical plane is concerned with the alignment of roads *over* the landscape, which is accommodated by vertical curves (for further discussion see Chapter 9).

TYPES OF HORIZONTAL CURVES

In the horizontal plane, road alignment consists of two basic geometric components: the straight line, or *tangent*, and the *curve*. The tangent is the most common element of road alignment. It represents the shortest distance between two points, and it is easy to lay out. In flat or featureless terrain or in urban grid situations its use may be appropriate. However, due to its predictability and limiting view point, a straight line in the landscape may become esthetically and experientially uninteresting. To create interest and respond to natural features like topography and vegetation, tangents may change direction. Two basic types of curves are used to accommodate this change in direction.

Circular Curves

As the name implies, these are circular arcs with a constant radius. They are easy to calculate and lay out and may be used in four basic configurations (Fig. 8.1).

Simple Curve.   This is a curve with a single radius and is the most common configuration for low speed roads.

Compound Curve.   This is a curve consisting of two or more radii in the same direction. For continuity and ease of handling, the difference in length of the radii should not be greater than 50%.

Reverse Curve.   This curve consists of two arcs in *opposite* directions. Usually a tangent is required between the two arcs, the length of which is determined by the design speed of the road.

Broken-back Curve.   This consists of two curves in the *same* direction connected by a tangent. Where the tangent distance is relatively short, these curves may be uncomfortable to maneuver and visually disjointing. Therefore, if possible, this condition should be avoided by using one larger curve.

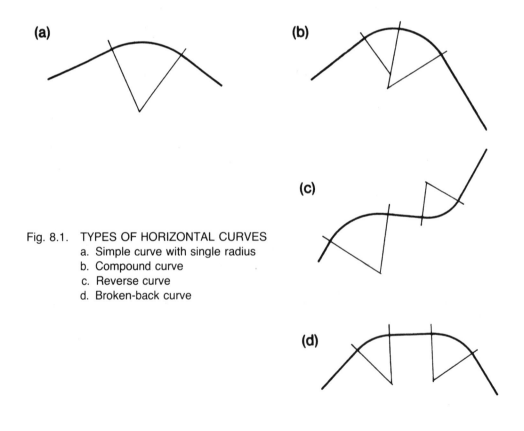

Fig. 8.1.   TYPES OF HORIZONTAL CURVES
      a. Simple curve with single radius
      b. Compound curve
      c. Reverse curve
      d. Broken-back curve

Spiral Transitional Curves

The normal path through a curve at high speeds is not circular, but through a series of curves with a constantly changing radius. This phenomenon is reflected in road alignment design by the use of spiral curves. The major disadvantage of this type of curve is that it is more difficult to calculate and lay out. For the design speeds and scale of roads in which landscape architects are involved, circular curves are sufficient. Therefore, spiral curves will not be discussed here.

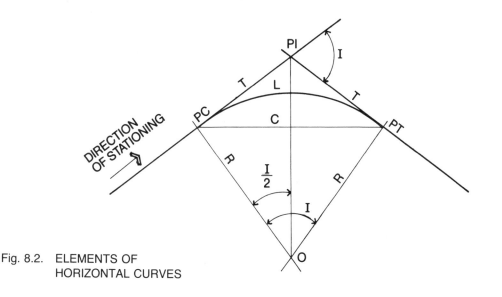

Fig. 8.2. ELEMENTS OF
HORIZONTAL CURVES

CIRCULAR CURVE ELEMENTS

Figure 8.2 illustrates the elements of circular curves which are defined as follows.

Point of Curvature (PC). This point marks the beginning of the curve at which the road alignment diverges from the tangent line in the direction of stationing.

Point of Tangency (PT). This point marks the end of the curve at which the road alignment returns to the tangent line in the direction of stationing.

Point of Intersection (PI). The point at which the two tangent lines intersect.

Included Angle (I). This is the central angle of the curve which is *equal to the deflection angle between the tangents.*

Tangent Distance (T). This is the distance from the PI to the either the PC or PT. These distances are *always* equal for simple circular curves.

Radius (R). This is the radius of the curve.

Length of Curve (L). This is the length of the arc from PC to PT.

Chord (C). This is the distance from PC to PT measured along a straight line.

Center of Curve (0). This is the point about which the included angle I is turned.

CIRCULAR CURVE FORMULAS

Using basic trigonometric and geometric relationships in conjunction with the preceding definitions, the following formulas may be derived for circular curves:

$$T = R \tan \frac{I}{2} \tag{8.1}$$

$$C = 2R \sin \frac{I}{2} \tag{8.2}$$

Note that the radius is always perpendicular to the tangent line at PC and PT. The two relationships can be derived from Fig. 8.2. The arc length L can be computed as part of the total circumference of a circle by proportion as follows:

$$\frac{L \text{ (length of curve)}}{2\pi R \text{ (circumference of circle)}} = \frac{I \text{ (included angle)}}{360° \text{ (total degrees in circle)}}$$

$$L = \frac{(2\pi R) \times I}{360} \tag{8.3}$$

Example 8.1 Two tangent lines intersect at point B as illustrated in Fig. 8.3. The bearing of tangent line AB is N76°30′E, while the bearing of tangent line CB is N15°20′W. A circular curve with a 100 ft radius is to be constructed to connect the two tangent lines. Find the included angle, the tangent distance (the distance from point B to the beginning or to the end of the curve), the length of the curve (arc), and the chord distance.

Solution With the aid of Fig. 8.4, the deflection angle between the tangent lines is determined to be 88°10′. As previously noted, the deflection angle and the included angle are equal; therefore, the included angle for this circular curve is 88°10′.

The formula for calculating the tangent distance is

$$T = R \tan \frac{I}{2}$$

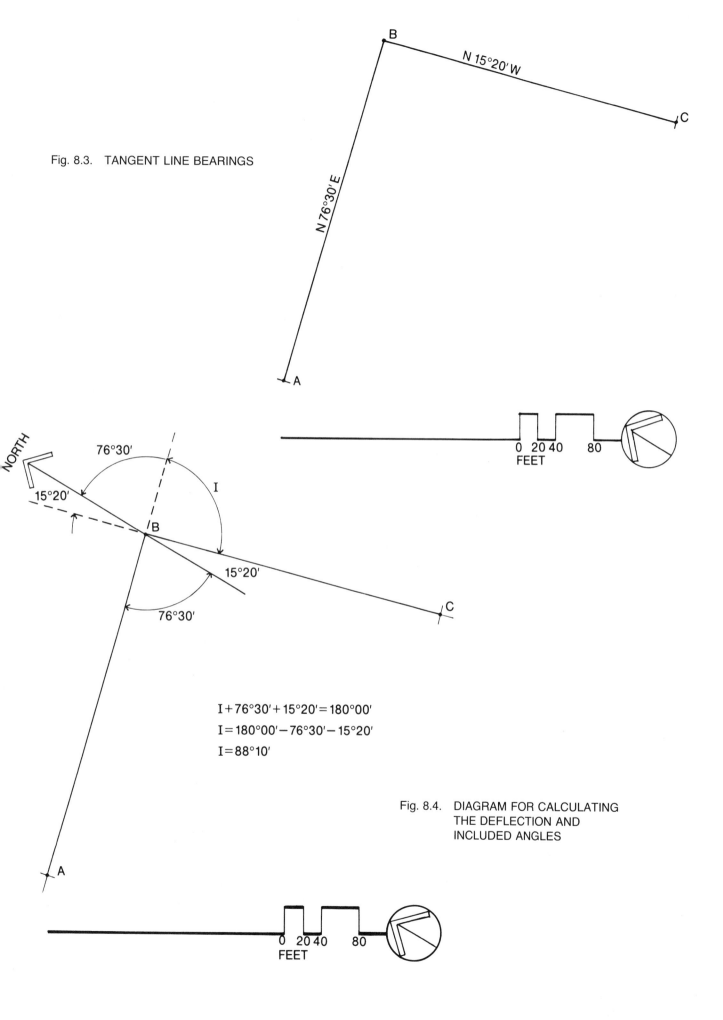

Fig. 8.3.   TANGENT LINE BEARINGS

NORTH

76°30'

15°20'

I

B

15°20'

76°30'

C

A

$I + 76°30' + 15°20' = 180°00'$

$I = 180°00' - 76°30' - 15°20'$

$I = 88°10'$

Fig. 8.4.   DIAGRAM FOR CALCULATING
THE DEFLECTION AND
INCLUDED ANGLES

0 20 40   80
FEET

0 20 40   80
FEET

N 76°30' E

N 15°20' W

By substituting the known values the equation becomes

$$T = 100 \tan \frac{88°10'}{2}$$
$$= 100 \tan 44°5'$$
$$= 100 \times 0.9685$$
$$= 96.85 \text{ ft}$$

The length of the curve is determined by substituting the known radius into the following proportion.

$$\frac{L}{2\pi R} = \frac{I}{360°}$$
$$\frac{L}{2\pi 100} = \frac{88°10'}{360°}$$
$$L = \frac{2\pi 100 \times 88.167°}{360}$$
$$= 153.88 \text{ ft}$$

Note that the minutes (and seconds if applicable) of the included angle are converted to decimals of degrees before using them in multiplication or division.

Finally the chord length is determined by the following equation:

$$C = 2R \sin\frac{I}{2}$$
$$= 2 \times 100 \sin 44°5'$$
$$= 2 \times 100 \times 0.6957$$
$$= 139.14 \text{ ft}$$

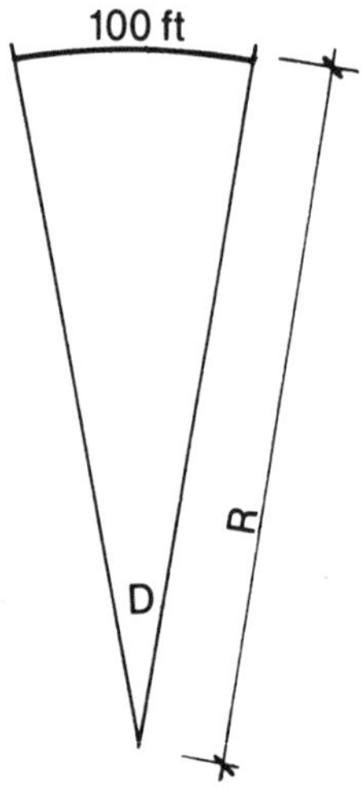

Fig. 8.5. DEGREE OF CURVE

DEGREE OF CURVE

Some organizations such as highway departments simplify their computations for curve layouts and establish minimum curve standards by using the designation *degree of curve*. There are two definitions for degree of curve. The *chord definition* defines it as the angle subtending a 100 ft chord while the *arc definition* defines it as the angle subtending a 100 ft arc. This discussion will be limited to the latter definition, since it is the one most commonly used today.

From the relationship illustrated in Fig. 8.5, the following proportion may be established (the same proportion as that used to determine length of curve):

$$\frac{100}{D°} = \frac{2\pi R}{360°}$$

where $D° =$ subtended angle (degree of curve)

$R =$ radius of curve

thus

$$R = \frac{100 \times 360°}{2\pi D°}$$

$$R = \frac{5729.578}{D} \approx \frac{5730}{D}$$

Therefore degree of curve D is inversely proportional to the radius. This relationship is illustrated by the following example: A curve with a radius of 2865 ft would have a degree of curvature of 2°, while a curve with a radius of 286.5 ft would have a degree of curvature of 20°.

Example 8.2 Determine the radius, tangent distance, length of curve, and chord length for a 10° curve with an included angle of 60°00′.

Solution The radius is calculated from the following proportion:

$$R = \frac{5729.578}{D} = \frac{5729.578}{10}$$
$$= 572.96 \text{ ft}$$

The remaining information is calculated using the formulas applied in Example 8.1.

Tangent distance:

$$T = R \tan \frac{I}{2}$$
$$= 572.96 \tan\frac{60°}{2}$$
$$= 572.96 \tan 30°$$
$$= 572.96 \times 0.57735 = 330.80 \text{ ft}$$

Length of curve:

$$\frac{L}{2\pi R} = \frac{I}{360°}$$
$$= \frac{2\pi R \times I}{360}$$
$$= \frac{2\pi(572.96) \times 60}{360}$$
$$= 600.00 \text{ ft}$$

It should be noted that the following proportion, based on degree of curve, may also be used to calculate the length of arc:

$$\frac{L}{100} = \frac{I}{D}$$

$$L = \frac{100 \times 60}{10}$$

$$= 600 \text{ ft}$$

Chord distance:

$$C = 2R \sin\frac{I}{2}$$

$$= 2 \times 572.96 \sin\frac{60°}{2}$$

$$= 2 \times 572.96 \sin 30°$$

$$= 2 \times 572.96 \times 0.5000$$

$$= 572.96 \text{ ft}$$

Example 8.3   Determine the degree of curve for Example 8.1.

Solution   The degree of curve is calculated from the proportion:

$$R = \frac{5729.578}{D}$$

The proportion may be arranged as follows:

$$D = \frac{5729.578}{R}$$

As given in the problem, R equals 100 ft; therefore,

$$D = \frac{5729.578}{100}$$

$$= 57.29578°$$

$$= 57°17'45'', \text{ or about } 57°18'$$

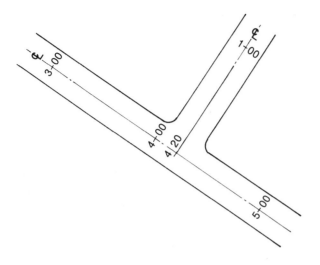

Fig. 8.6. TYPICAL CENTERLINE STATIONING

STATIONING

Stationing is a measurement convention applied to route surveying for streets, power lines, sanitary and storm sewers, etc. Stationing is marked out continuously along a route centerline, usually at 100 ft intervals, from a starting point designated as station 0 + 00. In addition, critical points like high and low points, street intersections, and beginnings and ends of curves are located by station points. The typical manner for noting station points is illustrated in Fig. 8.6. As shown in the figure, a separate stationing system is used for each road.

Example 8.4   This example illustrates the procedure for stationing roads that contain horizontal circular curves. Using Example 8.1, locate the 100 ft stations, the stations for PC and PT, and the station at the end of the road.

Solution. *Step 1*   The first step in the process is to determine the bearings and lengths of the tangent lines. In addition to the bearings that were previously established in Example 8.1, lengths have now been assigned to tangent line *AB* (372.25 ft) and tangent line *BC* (326.90 ft). This information is summarized in Fig. 8.7. Note that point *A* is the beginning of the road and point *C* is the end of the road.

Step 2   The next step is to establish the horizontal curves and calculate all necessary horizontal curve data (*R*, *T*, *L*, and *I*). As previously calculated, this information is as follows:

$$I = 88°10'$$
$$R = 100.00 \text{ ft}$$
$$T = 96.85 \text{ ft}$$
$$L = 153.88 \text{ ft}$$

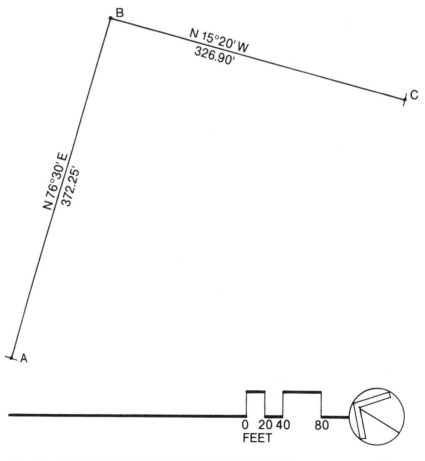

Fig. 8.7.   TANGENT LINE LENGTHS AND BEARINGS

Step 3   The third step is to calculate the station points for PC and PT (Fig. 8.8). PC is located by subtracting the horizontal curve tangent length T from the total length of tangent line AB.

$$372.25 \text{ ft}$$
$$- \underline{96.85 \text{ ft } (T)}$$
$$275.40 \text{ ft} = \text{station } 2+75.40 \text{ PC}$$

The station at PT is determined by adding the length of the arc L to the previously determined station of PC.

$$275.40 \text{ ft}$$
$$+\underline{153.88 \text{ ft } (L)}$$
$$429.28 \text{ ft} = \text{station } 4+29.28 \text{ PT}$$

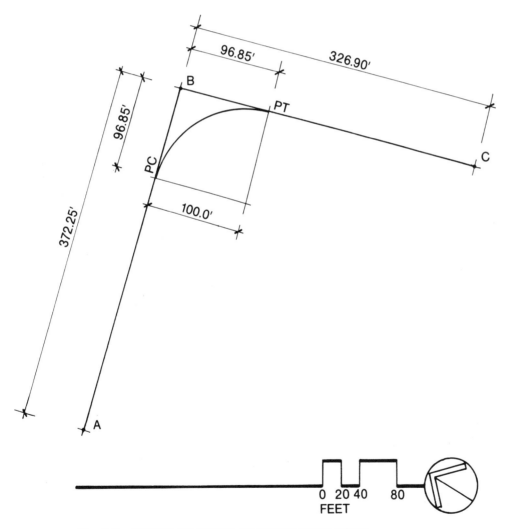

Fig. 8.8.   CIRCULAR CURVE TANGENT DISTANCES

Step 4 The last step is to station the tangents and circular curves completely, including 100 ft station intervals and the station at the end of the road (Fig. 8.9). The distance along tangent line *AB* to PC is 275.40 ft; therefore stations 1+00 and 2+00 must occur along this length. Since the station at PT is 4 + 29.28, stations 3+00 and 4+00 must occur along the arc. These stations can be located by using the proportion

$$\frac{L}{2\pi R} = \frac{I}{360}$$

to determine the angle formed by the known length of the arc. To locate station 3+00, the length of arc from PC (station 2+75.40) is determined.

$$
\begin{array}{r}
3{+}00 \\
-2{+}75.40 \\
\hline
L = \quad 24.60 \text{ ft}
\end{array}
$$

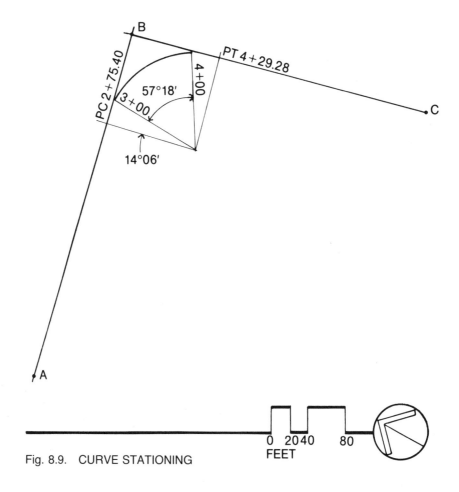

Fig. 8.9. CURVE STATIONING

The angle subtending this length can now be calculated by substituting L into the proportion.

$$\frac{I}{360} = \frac{24.60}{2\pi 100}$$
$$I = \frac{24.60}{2\pi 100} \times 360$$
$$= 14.095$$
$$= 14°5'\,41'' \text{ (or approximately } 14°06')$$

Marking off an angle of 14°06′ at the center of the curve from PC will locate station 3+00.

To locate station 4+00, substitute 100 ft for L, since stations 3+00 and 4+00 are 100 ft apart.

$$\frac{I}{360} = \frac{100}{2\pi 100}$$
$$I = \frac{100}{2\pi 100} \times 360$$
$$= 57.30$$
$$= 57°18'$$

Marking off an angle of 57°18′ the center of the curve from station 3+00 will locate station 4+00. Note that, consistent with the degree of curve definition, the included angle for the 100 ft arc agrees with the degree of curve previously calculated in Example 8.3.

Finally, the end of road station is calculated by determining the length of the tangent line from PT to point C. This distance can be determined by subtracting the horizontal curve tangent length T from the total length of tangent line BC.

$$
\begin{array}{r}
326.90 \\
-\ 96.85\ (T) \\
\hline
230.05
\end{array}
$$

This distance is then added to the station at PT.

$$
\begin{array}{l}
429.28 \text{ ft} \\
\underline{230.05 \text{ ft}} \\
659.33 \text{ ft} = \text{station } 6+59.33 \text{ (end of road)}
\end{array}
$$

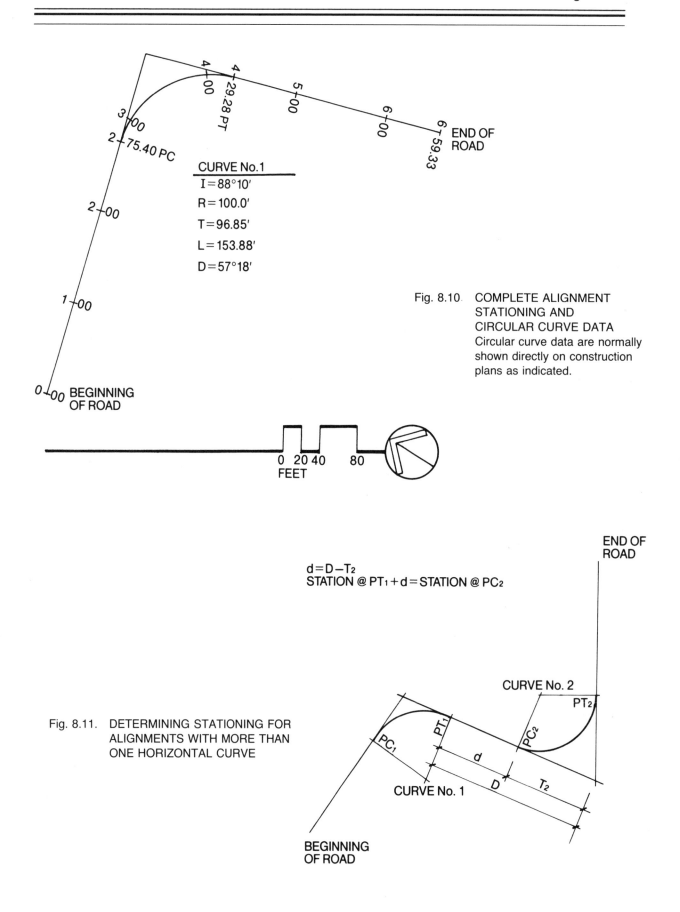

CURVE No.1

I = 88°10'
R = 100.0'
T = 96.85'
L = 153.88'
D = 57°18'

Fig. 8.10 COMPLETE ALIGNMENT
STATIONING AND
CIRCULAR CURVE DATA
Circular curve data are normally
shown directly on construction
plans as indicated.

$d = D - T_2$
STATION @ $PT_1 + d$ = STATION @ PC_2

Fig. 8.11. DETERMINING STATIONING FOR
ALIGNMENTS WITH MORE THAN
ONE HORIZONTAL CURVE

Thus the total length of this road is 659.33 ft (Fig. 8.10).

For alignments containing more than one horizontal curve, the procedure is the same as outlined above. However, once the stations have been determined for the first curve, the next step is to determine the tangent distance from the PT of the first curve to the PC of the second curve (Fig. 8.11). This distance is then added to the station of the first PT to determine the station at the second PC. This process is applied to each successive curve.

It must be emphasized that stationing and curve data are usually determined for the centerline of a route alignment.

HORIZONTAL SIGHT DISTANCE

A visual obstruction close to the inside edge of a horizontal curve restricts the driver's view of the road ahead, as illustrated in Fig. 8.12. Preferably, the forward sight distance should not be less than the safe stopping distance for the design speed of the curve, thus providing the driver sufficient time to stop once an object has been spotted in the roadway. If the curve is drawn to scale and the obstruction properly located, the sight distance can be obtained by scaling. Sight distances may also be determined analytically by equation, but this is not within the scope of this text.

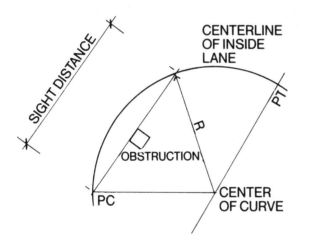

Fig. 8.12.   HORIZONTAL SIGHT DISTANCE

CONSTRUCTION DRAWING GRAPHICS

For identification purposes, horizontal curves are usually assigned numbers on construction drawings. The information presented on drawings includes the following:

1. included angle (I)
2. radius (R)
3. tangent distance (T)
4. length of curve (L)
5. degree of curve (D) (optional)
6. station points for PC and PT
7. centerline stationing
8. bearings for tangent lines
9. length and bearing of chord (C) (optional)

The presentation of the information may be arranged in a variety of formats. One typical format is illustrated in Fig. 8.10. Where the scale or complexity of the drawing makes this format difficult, the curve data may be summarized in separate charts or tables.

HORIZONTAL ALIGNMENT PROCEDURE

To this point the problems presented in this chapter have been structured, since specific circular curve data have been predetermined. However, there has been no discussion as to the initial procedures involved in establishing the horizontal alignment for a road or path.

Step 1

The first step in the process is to establish freehand *desire lines* on the site plan based on an analysis of natural and cultural conditions as well as the criteria to be used for the road design. Desire lines indicate the optimum path of travel according to the analysis of the site and function of the road and are typically drawn as tangent lines (Fig. 8.13). As mentioned at the beginning of the chapter, an in-depth discussion of these considerations is beyond the intent of this book. However, a brief list of the items of information usually required is presented here for awareness and reference purposes.

Natural site conditions including topography, soils, vegetation, drainage patterns, wildlife habitats, etc., should be inventoried and analyzed. In addition, cultural considerations including neighborhood context, existing traffic patterns, views both to and from the proposed alignment,

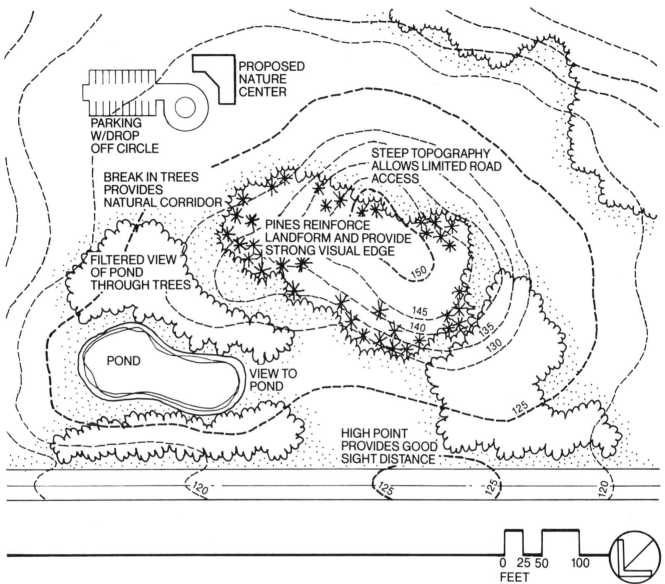

Fig. 8.13. HORIZONTAL ALIGNMENT PROCEDURE
  a. Conduct site analysis to determine best location for proposed road or drive.

safety, potential air and noise pollution, etc., should also be analyzed. In order to establish physical design standards such as minimum horizontal curve radius, maximum slopes, sight and stopping distances, number of traffic lanes, and cross-sectional design, a profile of the type of use that the proposed alignment will receive must be developed. This includes design speed, type of vehicles, estimated traffic volumes, direction of flow, timing of flow both hourly and seasonally, etc. An additional consideration for any proposed alignment is cost.

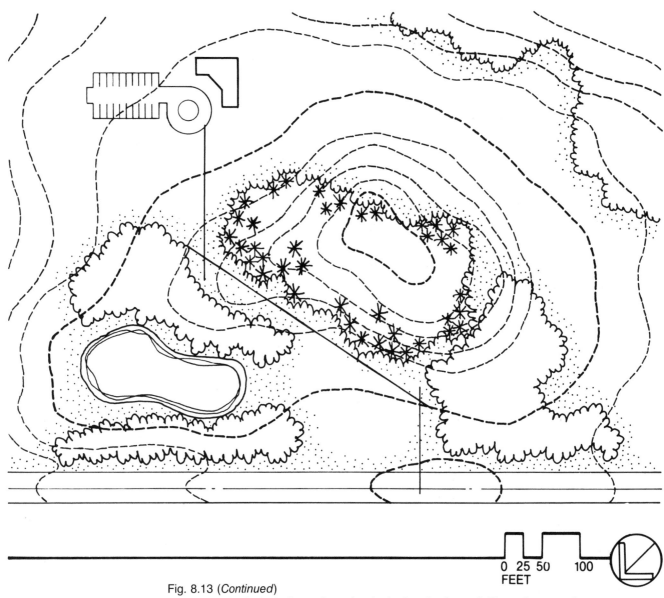

0 25 50   100
FEET

Fig. 8.13 (*Continued*)

b. Draw in lines along the desired path of travel. These become the tangent lines for the proposed alignment.

Step 2

The next step is to transform the freehand drawing into a preliminary alignment for the road centerline. This is done by mechanically drafting the tangents and horizontal curves.

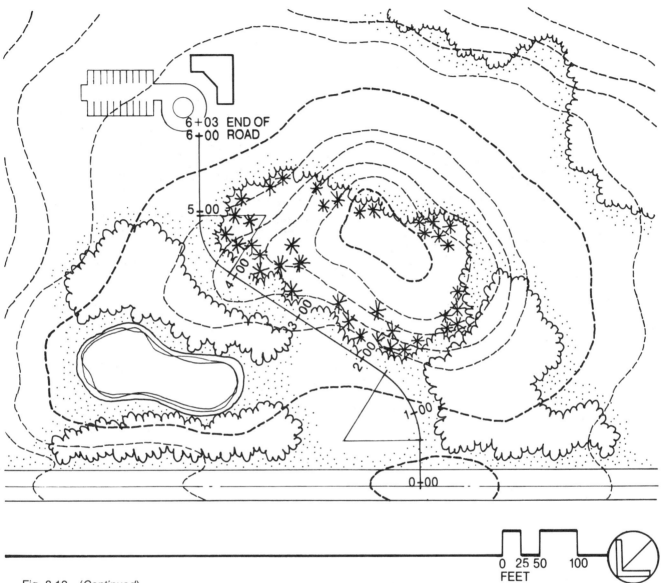

Fig. 8.13 (*Continued*)

    c. Draw in curves and station the road or drive. Usually the curves will
       first be drawn freehand and then circular curves will be designed to
       approximate the desired curves.

Step 3

Once the centerline has been drafted, horizontal curve data can be
computed. In order to do the calculations, however, two values of the
circular curve equation must be known. Typically, the deflection angle is
measured or determined by bearings if possible. Then *either* the tangent
distance or radius is determined by scaling the drawing (or lengths are
assigned). *The deflection angle and the tangent length or radius are the
only two quantities that are predetermined or measured*; all other information must be calculated.

Fig. 8.13 (*Continued*)
   d. The roads have been terraced to provide access to the different levels of the
      parking garage.

Step 4

The last step is to check the horizontal curve calculations against the design criteria and review the entire alignment with regard to the site analysis. Where problems arise, the alignment should be reworked. Finally, the horizontal alignment should be completely stationed.

It should be noted that the formulas and procedures described in this chapter for circular road curves can also be applied to laying out any other circular site feature such as paths, walls, fences, etc.

TABLE 8.1. Alignment Standards in Relation to Design Speed[a]

Design speed (mph)	Minimum radius of horizontal curves (ft)	Maximum percentage of grade	Minimum length of vertical curve for each 1% of algebraic difference (ft)
20	100	12	10
30	250	10	20
40	450	8	35
50	750	7	70
60	1100	5	150
70	1600	4	200

[a]Adapted from Lynch (1971)

SUPERELEVATION

When a vehicle travels around a curve, a centrifugal force acts on it. To partially counteract this force, road surfaces are usually banked or tilted inward toward the center of the curve. The banking of horizontal curves is called *superelevation* and is generally accomplished by rotating the road surface about its centerline or, in cut situations, preferably about its inside edge (Fig. 8.14).

Superelevation does not occur abruptly at the PC or PT, but rather there is a gradual change as the curve is approached along the tangent lines. The length over which this gradual change occurs is referred to as the *runoff distance*, which is sometimes computed by adding the rate of crown of the road in in./ft to the rate of superelevation in in./ft and multiplying the sum by 160.

Superelevation can be determined by the formula

$$S = 0.067 \frac{V^2}{R}$$

where S = superelevation in ft/ft of pavement width
V = design speed in mph
R = radius of curve in ft

Where snow and ice are a consideration, S should not exceed 1 in./ft or 0.083 ft/ft. If snow and ice are not a problem, a preferred maximum value is 1.50 in./ft or 0.125 ft/ft.

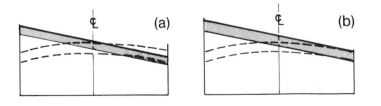

Fig. 8.14. SUPERELEVATION
a. Rotated about the centerline
b. Rotated about the inside edge

Example 8.5 Determine the superelevation and runoff distances for a 400 ft radius curve on a road with a 30 mph design speed in a snowy climate. The road has a crown of 0.25 in./ft.

   Solution The superelevation is calculated by substituting into the equation:

$$S = 0.067\frac{V^2}{R}$$
$$= 0.067\frac{30^2}{400}$$
$$= 0.15 \text{ ft/ft of width of } 1.8 \text{ in./ft of width}$$

This value exceeds the recommended maximum of 1.0 in./ft, therefore, the proposed superelevation for this curve is 1.0 in./ft or 0.083 ft/ft.

   The runoff distance is calculated by adding the crown rate (0.25 in./ft) and the superelevation rate (1 in./ft) and multiplying by the constant (160).

$$(0.25 + 1.0) \times 160 = 200 \text{ ft}$$

This means that the banking of the road begins at a gradual rate 200 ft before the PC and PT. A technique for handling the transition from the total crown cross-section to the total superelevation cross-section is illustrated in Fig. 8.15. The full rate of superelevation occurs at the PC and PT and is maintained through the entire curve. As a safety factor, roads are usually widened on the inside of horizontal curves.

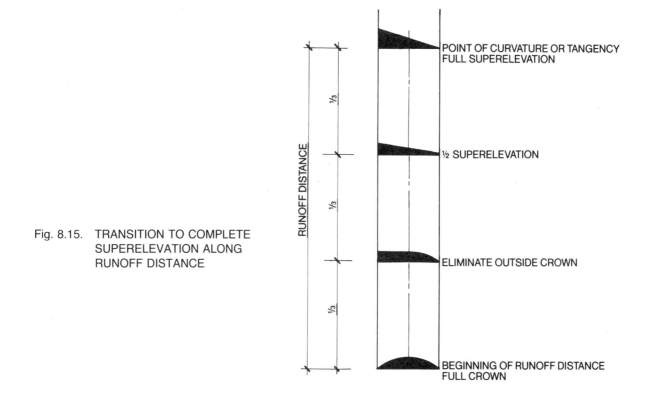

Fig. 8.15.   TRANSITION TO COMPLETE
            SUPERELEVATION ALONG
            RUNOFF DISTANCE

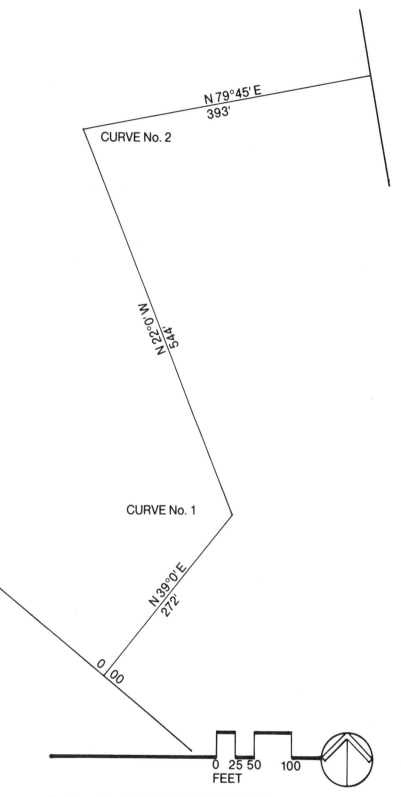

CURVE No. 2

N 79°45' E
393'

N 22°0' W
544'

CURVE No. 1

N 39°0' E
272'

0 | 00

0 25 50   100
FEET

Problem 8.2.   TANGENT BEARINGS AND LENGTHS

PROBLEMS

8.1. The center line of a proposed road runs on a direction of N15°00′W to a point *A* and then changes direction to N58°40′E. A circular curve with a radius of 500.0 ft is to be designed to accommodate the change in direction. Calculate the included angle, tangent distance, curve length and degree of curve.

8.2. Bearings and tangent lengths for a proposed road alignment are given. Design curve No. 1 with $T = 190$ ft and curve No. 2 with $R = 130$ ft. Provide all horizontal curve data for each curve including radius, tangent distance, included angle, curve length, degree of curve, and chord length. Station the road completely with 100 ft stations, at points of curvature and tangency, and at the end of the road.

8.3. Compute the superelevation and runoff distances for a 450 ft radius curve for a road with a 25 mph design speed. The road crown is ⅛ in./ft.

8.4. For an 8° curve with an included angle of 50°, determine the radius, tangent distance, length of curve, and length of chord.

CHAPTER 9

Vertical Road Alignment

Vertical curves are used to ease the transition whenever there is a vertical change in direction (slope). Such transitions eliminate awkward bumps along the vehicular path, allow for proper sight distances, and prevent scraping of cars and trucks on the pavement at steep service drives and driveway entrances. Generally, vertical curves are required for low speed roads and drives when the vertical change exceeds 1%. This vertical change is computed by determining the algebraic difference between the tangent gradients, with tangents in the uphill direction assigned positive values and those in the downhill direction negative values. Thus, the vertical change for a +2.0% gradient intersecting with a −2.0% gradient is 4.0% [+2.0−(−2.0) = 4.0].

There are six possible variations for grade alignment changes. The first is the *peak curve* in which the entering tangent gradient is positive and the exiting tangent gradient is negative in the direction of stationing. The resultant curve profile is convex. The second is the *sag curve* with the entering gradient negative and the exiting gradient positive. The resultant curve profile is concave. The four remaining variations are *intermediate peak or sag curves* in which the change in slope occurs in the same direction (i.e., both values either positive or negative) as illustrated in Fig. 9.1.

It is important to note that the computation of horizontal and vertical alignments for roads are *separate* procedures; thus horizontal and vertical curves may partially or completely overlap or may not overlap at all. There are certain relationships between the two curves that affect safety and perception of motion. For example, sharp horizontal curves should be avoided at the apex of peak vertical curves. A more thorough discussion of these relationships should be pursued in other texts (see Bibliography at end of volume). Also, do not become confused by the similarity in terminology between horizontal and vertical curves. Realize that tangent lines for horizontal curves are *direction* lines in the horizontal plane (*through* the landscape), while tangent lines for vertical curves are *slope* lines in the vertical plane (*over* the landscape).

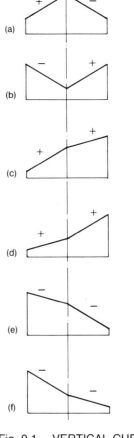

Fig. 9.1. VERTICAL CURVE
          TANGENT VARIATIONS
   a. Peak curve
   b. Sag curve
   c. Intermediate peak curve
   d. Intermediate sag curve
   e. Intermediate peak curve
   f. Intermediate sag curve

245

VERTICAL CURVE FORMULA

Generally parabolas are used for vertical curves, since they lend themselves to simple computation and leveling procedures. For parabolas, the offset distances from the tangent line to the curve vary as the square of the distances from either end of the curve (see Fig. 9.2).

The components of vertical curves are illustrated in Fig. 9.2. Note that the illustration depicts a peak curve. There are two types of vertical curves: equal tangent curves and unequal tangent curves. For *equal tangent curves*, also referred to as symmetrical, the horizontal distance from the beginning of curve (BVC) to the point of vertical intersection (PVI) *equals* the horizontal distance from the PVI to the end of curve (EVC). For *unequal tangent curves*, also called asymmetrical, the horizontal distance from BVC to PVI does *not* equal the horizontal distance from PVI to EVC.

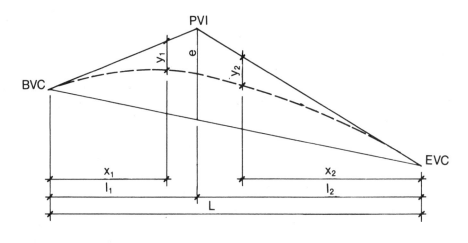

Fig. 9.2. ELEMENTS OF ASYMMETRICAL VERTICAL CURVES

UNEQUAL TANGENT CURVES

The formulas for computing asymmetrial vertical curves are

$$ e = \frac{l_1 l_2}{200(l_1 + l_2)} A \tag{9.1} $$

where e = tangent offset at PVI, in ft
  l_1 = horizontal distance from BVC to PVI, in ft
  l_2 = horizontal distance from EVC to PVI, in ft
  A = algebraic differences between tangent gradients, in %

and

$$y_1 = e\left(\frac{x_1}{l_1}\right)^2; \quad y_2 = e\left(\frac{x_2}{l_2}\right)^2 \qquad (9.2)$$

where y_1 = vertical distance from entering tangent line to the curve (tangent offset), in ft

x_1 = horizontal distance from BVC to point on the curve, in ft

y_2 = vertical distance from exiting tangent line to the curve (tangent offset), in ft

x_2 = horizontal distance from EVC to point on the curve, in ft

l_1, l_2, and e have previously been defined.

Example 9.1 For the preliminary profile for a road center line, a +2.0% grade intersects a −3.0% grade at station 35 + 40. The elevation at the PVI is 261.40 ft. The horizontal length of the entering tangent is 200 ft, while the length of the exiting tangent is 300 ft. Calculate the elevations of the curve at all 100 ft stations (Fig. 9.3).

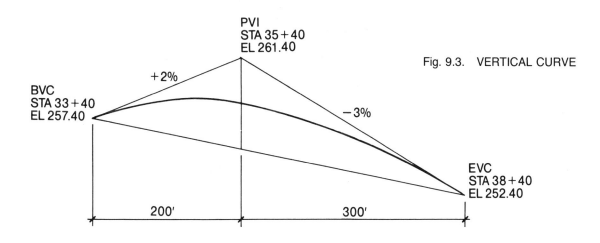

Fig. 9.3. VERTICAL CURVE

Solution First the tangent offset at the PVI must be calculated.

$$e = \frac{l_1 \times l_2}{200(l_1 + l_2)}A$$

$$= \frac{200 \times 300}{200(200+300)} \times 5$$

$$= \frac{60,000}{100,000} \times 5$$

$$= \frac{300,000}{100,000} = 3$$

Next, the elevations of the 100 ft stations along the tangent lines and at the BVC and EVC are calculated.

Station 33+40 (BVC): $261.40 - (200 \times .02) = 257.40$
33+40 (BVC): $261.40 - (200 \times .02) = 257.40$
34+00 $261.40 - (140 \times .02) = 258.60$
35+00 $261.40 - (40 \times .02) = 260.60$
35+40 (PVI) $= 261.40$
36+00 $261.40 - (60 \times .03) = 259.60$
37+00 $261.40 - (160 \times .03) = 256.60$
38+00 $261.40 - (260 \times .03) = 253.60$
38+40 (EVC): $261.40 - (300 \times .03) = 252.40$

The tangent offset distances are then calculated for the entering tangent and exiting tangent based on the horizontal distance from BVC and EVC, respectively.

Entering tangent:

$$y = e\left(\frac{x_1}{l_1}\right)^2 \tag{9.3}$$

$$\text{Station } 34 + 00: \quad y = 3\left(\frac{60}{200}\right)^2 = 0.27 \text{ ft}$$

$$35 + 00: \quad y = 3\left(\frac{160}{200}\right)^2 = 1.92 \text{ ft}$$

Exiting tangent:

$$36 + 00: \quad y = 3\left(\frac{240}{300}\right)^2 = 1.92 \text{ ft}$$

$$37 + 00: \quad y = 3\left(\frac{140}{300}\right)^2 = 0.65 \text{ ft}$$

$$38 + 00: \quad y = 3\left(\frac{40}{300}\right)^2 = 0.05 \text{ ft}$$

Finally, the tangent offset distances are *subtracted* from the tangent elevations to determine the curve elevations, since this is a peak curve. Table 9.1 illustrates a typical form used to record vertical curve data.

EQUAL TANGENT CURVES

Most vertical curves are designed as equal tangent or symmetrical curves. This simplifies the calculations, since l_1 equals l_2. Thus the previous equations can be simplified to one generalized equation:

$$y = e\left(\frac{x}{l}\right)^2 \tag{9.4}$$

TABLE 9.1. Vertical Curve Data

Station	Point	Tangent elevation	Tangent offset	Curve elevation
33+40	BVC	257.40	0.00	257.40
34+00		258.60	0.27	258.33
35+00		260.60	1.92	258.68
35+40	PVI	261.40	3.00	258.40
36+00		259.60	1.92	257.68
37+00		256.60	0.65	255.95
38+00		253.60	0.05	253.55
38+40	BVC	252.40	0.00	252.40

where y = tangent offset distance, in ft

x = horizontal distance from BVC (*or* EVC) to point on the curve, in ft

l = one-half the length of curve, in ft

e = tangent offset at PVI, in ft

Points located at the same horizontal distance from the BVC and EVC will have the same tangent offset distance, but not necessarily the same curve elevation. This is demonstrated in the following example.

Example 9.2 On a preliminary profile of the center line of a road, a −2.0% grade intersects a + 1.5% grade at station 79 + 00.

The elevation at the PVI is 123.50 ft. A vertical curve with $L = 800$ ft is desired. Calculate the elevations of the curve at all 100 ft stations (Fig. 9.4).

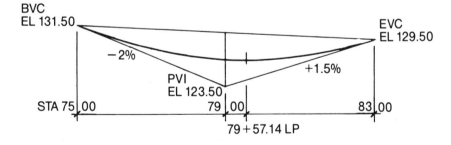

Fig. 9.4. VERTICAL CURVE

Solution The first step is to calculate the elevations at BVC and EVC and at 100 ft intervals along both tangent lines. Since the curve is symmetrical about the PVI, the station at BVC is 75 + 00 and the station at EVC is 83 + 00. Elevations at these points can now be determined by applying the slope formula.

$$(400 \times 0.02) \ +123.50 = 131.50 \text{ elevation at BVC}$$
$$(400 \times 0.015) + 123.50 = 129.50 \text{ elevation at EVC}$$

The elevations at 100 ft intervals along the tangent lines are easily determined, since, for the entering tangent, a -2.0% gradient results in a 2.0 ft drop in elevation for every 100 ft of distance from the BVC. For the exiting tangent, the change in elevation is 1.5 ft for every 100 ft. The tangent elevations at the 100 ft stations are summarized in Table 9.2.

The next step is to determine the height of the middle offset. From the previous equation simplified the height is computed as follows:

$$e = \frac{l^2}{200 \times 2 \times l} \times A$$
$$= \frac{400^2}{200 \times 2 \times 400} \times 3.5$$
$$= 3.50 \text{ ft}$$

The elevation of the curve at the PVI station 79+00 is $123.50 + 3.50 = 127.0$ ft.

With e known, the tangent offsets can be calculated for the desired 100 ft intervals.

$$\text{Station } 75 + 00: \ y_0 = 3.5 \left(\frac{0}{400} \right)^2 = 0.00 \text{ ft}$$

$$76 + 00: \ y_1 = 3.5 \left(\frac{100}{400} \right)^2 = 0.22 \text{ ft}$$

$$77 + 00: \ y_2 = 3.5 \left(\frac{200}{400} \right)^2 = 0.88 \text{ ft}$$

$$78 + 00: \ y_3 = 3.5 \left(\frac{300}{400} \right)^2 = 1.97 \text{ ft}$$

$$79 + 00: \ y_4 = 3.5 \left(\frac{400}{400} \right)^2 = 3.50 \text{ ft}$$

Station 79 + 00 is the center of the curve.

Since both tangent lines are the same horizontal length from the ends of the curve to the PVI, the tangent offsets are symmetrical about the PVI, and do not have to be computed again for the curve from PVI to EVC.

Since this is a sag curve, the tangent offset distances are added to the corresponding tangent elevations to determine the elevations of the curve. The resultant vertical curve is plotted in Fig. 9.5. For peak curves, the tangent offset distances would be subtracted from the tangent eleva-

TABLE 9.2.   Vertical Curve Data

Station	Point	Tangent elevation	Curve elevation	Tangent offset	First difference	Second difference
75+00	BVC	131.50	131.50	0.00		
76+00		129.50	129.72	0.22	0.22	0.44
77+00		127.50	128.38	0.88	0.66	0.43[a]
78+00		125.50	127.47	1.97	1.09	0.44
79+00	PVI	123.50	127.00	3.50	1.53	
79+57.14	LP	124.36	126.93	2.57		
80+00		125.00	126.97	1.97		
81+00		126.50	127.38	0.88		
82+00		128.00	128.22	0.22		
83+00	EVC	129.50	129.50	0.00		

[a]Discrepancy due to rounding.

tions. The data for the curve are summarized in Table 9.2. Table 9.2 also demonstrates a convenient check for vertical curve computations. The *second differences* of the tangent offsets at *equal horizontal intervals* are constant. (The discrepancy between 0.44 and 0.43 occurs due to rounding.)

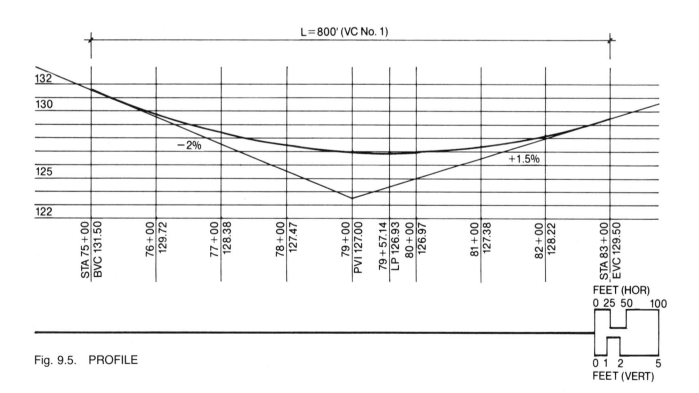

Fig. 9.5.   PROFILE

CALCULATING THE LOCATIONS OF HIGH AND LOW POINTS

The locations of low points are needed to position drainage structures, while those of high points may be required to determine sight distances. Both high and low points may be necessary to determine critical clearances under structures such as bridges.

The high or low point of a vertical curve coincides with the midpoint of an equal tangent curve only when the gradients of the tangent lines are equal. In all other cases, the high or low point is located on the side of the PVI *opposite* the steepest gradient.

The formula for locating the high or low point of a vertical curve is

$$d = \frac{Lg_1}{g_1 - g_2} \tag{9.5}$$

where d = distance from BVC to HP or LP, in ft
      L = total length of curve, in ft
      g_1 = gradient from BVC to PVI
      g_2 = gradient from PVI to EVC

Example 9.3   A drain outlet is to be installed at the low point of the curve in the previous example. Find its location and elevation.

Solution   To determine the distance from BVC, substitute the known values into the equation.

$$d = \frac{800 \times (-0.02)}{-0.02 - (+0.015)}$$
$$= \frac{-16.0}{-0.035} = 457.14 \text{ ft}$$

Thus, the low point occurs 457.14 ft from BVC, which is station 79 + 57.14.

Next, compute the tangent elevation at station 79 + 57.14. This location is 57.14 ft past the PVI, therefore the tangent elevation is 123.50 + (57.14 × 0.015) = 124.36 ft. The distance from EVC is 400.00 − 57.14 = 342.86 ft and the tangent offset is determined as

$$y_{\text{lp}} = 3.5 \left(\frac{342.86}{400} \right)^2 = 2.57 \text{ ft}$$

The elevation of the low point on the curve is 124.36 + 2.57 = 126.93 ft. Note that this elevation is for the centerline of the road. If the drain inlet is located at the edge of the road, an adjustment based on the road cross-section would be necessary to determine the top of frame elevation. For example, if the crown height of the proposed road is 0.25 ft., then the elevation for the drain is 126.93 − 0.25 = 126.68 ft.

CONSTRUCTION DRAWING GRAPHICS

Unlike horizontal curves for which all data are presented on the layout plan, vertical curve data are presented on a profile of the road centerline. The presentation format for the curve in Example 9.2 is shown in Fig. 9.5. Information provided on profiles includes

1. Vertical curve number (for identification purposes)
2. Total length of curve L
3. Stationing at BVC, PVI, EVC, HP or LP, and 100 ft intervals
4. Curve elevations for all stations in No. 3 above.
5. Tangent gradients

Figure 9.5 indicates the profile of only one curve. However, the entire road from station 0+00 to the end would normally be profiled. Also the profile of the edge of the road may be indicated by a dashed line on the same drawing.

It should be noted that the *horizontal* alignment must be calculated before the profile can be constructed, since stationing occurs along the centerline of horizontal curves. A profile is then constructed from the beginning to the end of the road and represents the total length along the curved as well as straight portions.

VERTICAL SIGHT DISTANCES

There are two types of sight distance. The first is safe stopping sight distance; in other words the distance required to react, brake, and stop a vehicle at a given speed. The second is safe passing sight distance. Both of these are a concern on peak curves, since the convex profile shortens the line of sight. For low speed roads in which landscape architects are involved, passing will most likely be prohibited; therefore safe stopping distance is of greater concern. Roads requiring safe passing sight distances should be designed by qualified highway engineers.

In determining safe stopping sight distance, generally an eye height of 3.75 ft and object height of 0.50 ft are used. Although formulas may be used to calculate the minimum length of vertical curve necessary to maintain a safe stopping distance at a given speed, sight distances for vertical curves can be determined to a certain degree by measuring from

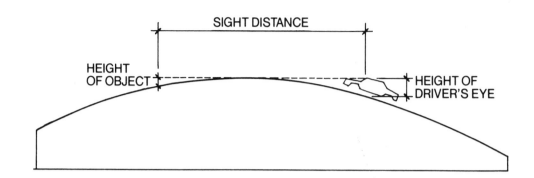

Fig. 9.6.   SIGHT DISTANCE FOR PEAK CURVES

the height of the eye to the height of the object on the profile as shown in Fig. 9.6. Where the measured distance is less than the safe stopping sight distance, the vertical curve must be redesigned. Again, a highway engineer should be consulted if sight distances are a critical concern.

ROAD ALIGNMENT PROCEDURE

The following outline is a systematic procedure which may be used to ease the task of laying out both horizontal and vertical alignment for roads, drives, paths, etc.

Step 1

As discussed briefly in Chapter 8, the first step is to develop design criteria and constraints for both horizontal and vertical curves and to conduct a site analysis to determine the best route or corridor location (see Fig. 8.13a).

Step 2

Once Step 1 has been completed, desire lines can be established *through* the landscape. Desire lines represent movement along the horizontal plane; therefore, it is necessary to design horizontal curves to make this movement or flow as smooth as possible. During this step, then, horizontal curves should be preliminarily designed, all necessary data calculated, and the centerline of the road or path completely stationed (Figs. 8.13b and c).

Step 3

Next, a profile of the *existing* grades along the *proposed* centerline is constructed (Fig. 9.7).

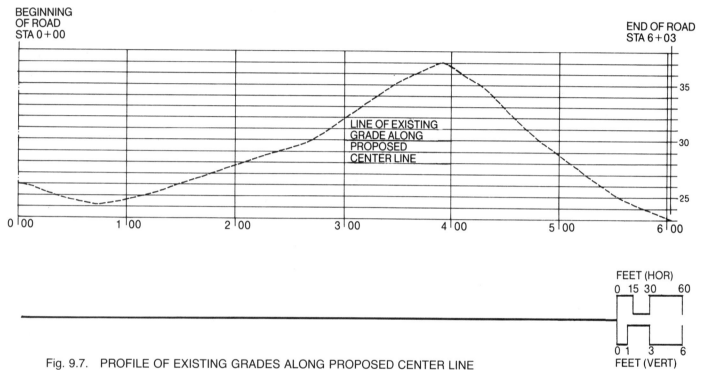

Fig. 9.7.   PROFILE OF EXISTING GRADES ALONG PROPOSED CENTER LINE

Step 4

At this point the alignment *over* the landscape can be designed. To begin, the *proposed* vertical curve tangent lines are placed on the profile of existing grades. The actual placement of these tangent lines is influenced by many factors including balancing cut and fill, design speed, roughness of topography, horizontal curve placement, etc. (Fig. 9.8).

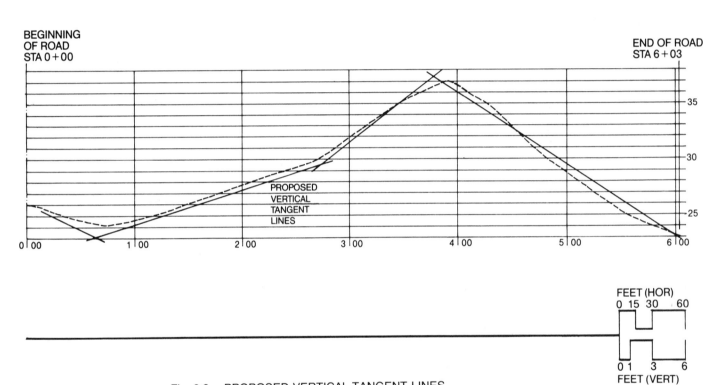

Fig. 9.8.   PROPOSED VERTICAL TANGENT LINES

Step 5

From the profile, station points and elevations for the intersections of the proposed vertical curve tangent lines are established (Fig. 9.9). The differences in elevation between intersection points can now be determined. Since the distances between the intersection points can be calculated from the stationing, the slopes of the tangent lines can be computed.

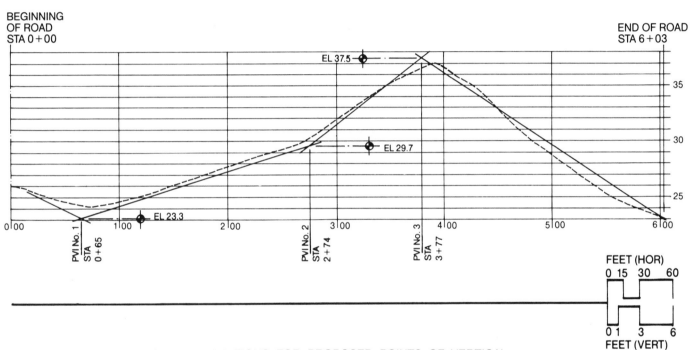

Fig. 9.9.   STATIONS AND ELEVATIONS FOR PROPOSED POINTS OF VERTICAL INTERSECTION

Step 6

The next step is to determine the lengths of vertical curves required. This depends on such factors as design speed, topography, esthetics, and sight distances. Vertical curves may be designed as equal tangent (symmetrical about the PVI) or unequal tangent (asymmetrical about the PVI) curves (Fig. 9.10).

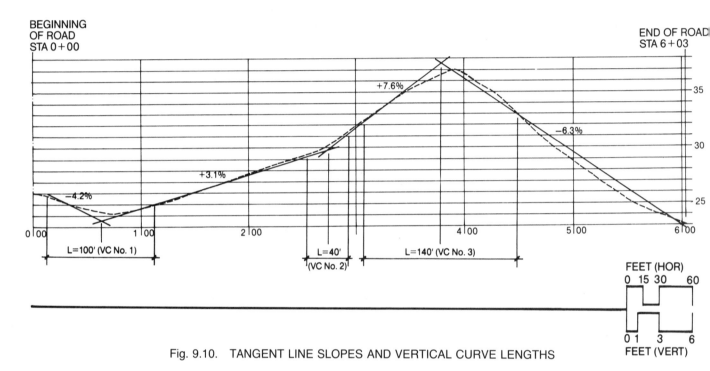

Fig. 9.10.   TANGENT LINE SLOPES AND VERTICAL CURVE LENGTHS

Step 7

At this point the slope of the tangents, lengths of curves, elevations at points of vertical intersection, and the stations for all BVCs, PVIs, and EVCs are known. Therefore all data necessary to calculate the vertical curves are available and the profile can be completed.

Step 8

Once the profile has been completed, the *proposed* grades are transferred from the profile to the centerline of the horizontal alignment on the plan. The road (path, etc.) is graded according to the proposed cross-section design and the proposed contour lines are appropriately connected

Fig. 9.11.
REVERSE HORIZONTAL CURVE
WITH SAG VERTICAL CURVE

to the existing contour lines. The proposed grading plan is now analyzed for problem areas like steep slopes, excessive cuts or fills, drainage, and removal of vegetation. Where problems arise, either the vertical alignment (profile) or horizontal alignment (plan) or both must be restudied and the profile and plan must be adjusted accordingly.

PROBLEMS

9.1. A proposed park road, straight in plan view, crosses a small stream where a vertical sag curve is required. One of the tangents slopes toward the east with a −2.0% grade through station 14+00, which is at elevation 110.0 ft. The other tangent slopes west with a −5.0% grade through station 23+00, at elevation 120.0 ft. Find the location and elevation of the point of intersection of the tangents. Once the PVI has been determined, design a symmetrical curve with a total length of 400 ft. Determine the elevations of the curve at BVC, EVC, 100 ft stations, and the low point.

9.2. From the information given, calculate the curve elevations for an equal tangent curve at each 50 ft station (e.g., 0+00, 0+50, etc.) and determine the station points for BVC, EVC, and high point.
   a. slope of entering tangent: +3.2%
   b. slope of exiting tangent: −4.4%
   c. tangents intersect at station 6+00
   d. elevation at PVI: 25.9 ft
   c. total length of curve: 400 ft
Draw a profile of the curve using a horizontal scale of 1 in. = 50 ft and vertical scale of 1 in. = 5 ft.

9.3.   From the information given, calculate the curve elevations for an equal tangent curve at each 50 ft station and determine the station points for BVC, EVC, and low point.

a. slope of entering tangent: −6.0%

b. slope of exiting tangent: +3.8%

c. tangents intersect at station 5+30

d. elevation at PVI: 29.2 ft

e. total length of curve: 300 ft

Again draw a profile of the curve, using the same scales as in Problem 9.2.

9.4   The plan of a proposed road alignment is shown below. Construct a profile of the existing topography along the proposed centerline with a horizontal scale of 1 in. = 50 ft and a vertical scale of 1 in. = 5 ft. Design a vertical alignment that works well with the existing topography assuming a design speed of 20 mph. Transfer the proposed grades from the profile to the plan, grade the road with a 4 in. crown, and connect the proposed to the existing contour lines in an appropriate manner.

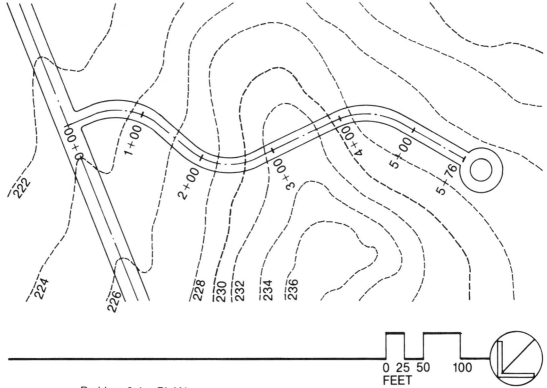

Problem 9.4.   PLAN

Glossary

Abrasion   Wearing away by friction.

Alignment   The course along which the center line of a roadway or channel is located.

Angle of repose   The angle which the sloping face of a bank of loose earth or gravel or other material makes with the horizontal.

Backfill   Earth or other material used to replace material removed during construction, such as in pipeline and culvert trenches and behind retaining walls.

Base (Course)   A layer of specified or selected material of planned thickness, constructed on the subbase or on the natural subgrade to distribute the load and provide drainage, or on which a wearing surface or a drainage structure is placed.

Blading   Planing or smoothing the ground surface.

Borrow area   A source of earth fill materials used in the construction of embankments or other earth fill structures.

Catch basin   A receptable, with a sediment bowl or sump, for diverting surface water to a subsurface pipe.

Center line   The survey line in the center of a road, ditch, or similar project.

Channel   A natural stream, or a ditch or swale constructed to convey water.

Compaction   The densification of a soil by a mechanical process.

Contour line   An imaginary line, or its representation on a map, following all points at the same elevation above or below a given datum.

Critical depth   The depth of flow in an open channel at which critical flow occurs. For a given flow rate, depths greater than critical result in subcritical, or tranquil, flow. Those smaller than critical result in supercritical, or rapid, flow.

Critical flow   An unstable flow condition in open channels for which the specific energy is at the minimum for a given rate of flow.

Critical velocity   The velocity of flow in an open channel which occurs at critical depth.

Crown   The rise or difference in elevation between the edge and the center line of a roadway.

Culvert   Any structure, not classified as a bridge, which provides a waterway or other opening under a road.

Cut section (or cut)   That part of the ground surface which, when graded, is lower than the original ground.

Datum   A horizontal reference plane used as a basis for computing elevations.

Discharge Q   Flow rate in a culvert, pipe, or channel.

Diversion   A channel, with or without a supporting ridge on the lower side, constructed across a slope to intercept surface runoff.

Drainage   Interception and removal of ground water or surface water by artificial or natural means.

Drainage area   The area drained by a channel or a subsurface drain.

Edaphology   The study of the soil from the standpoint of higher plants and crop production.

Elevation   (a) The altitude relative to a given datum. (b) A scale drawing of the upright parts of a structure.

Glossary Continued

Embankment   A bank of earth, rock, or other material constructed above the natural ground surface.

Emergency spillway   A vegetated earth channel for safely conveying flood discharges exceeding the capacity of the principal spillway of a detention or retention pond.

Erosion   Detachment and movement of soil or rock fragments by water, wind, ice and gravity.

Excavation   (a) The act of taking out materials. (b) The hollow or depression after the materials have been removed.

Fill section (or fill)   That part of the ground surface which, when graded, is higher than the original ground.

Fine grade   Preparation of the subgrade preceding placement of surfacing materials.

Foundation   The portion of a structure (usually below ground level) that distributes the pressure to the soil or to artificial supports.

Free water   Soil water that moves by gravity, in contrast to capillary and hygroscopic water.

French drain   A trench filled with coarse aggregate (with or without a pipe) for intercepting and conveying ground water.

Grade   **Finished Grade**   The completed surfaces of lawns, walks, and roads brought to grades as designed.

   Natural Grade   The undisturbed natural surface of the ground.

   Subgrade   The grade established in preparation for top surfacing of roads, lawns, etc.

Gradient   The degree of inclination of a surface, road, or pipe, usually expressed in percent.

Grading   Modification of the ground surface by cuts and/or fills. Fine or finish grading is light or thin grading to finish a prepared earth surface.

Grassed waterway   A natural or constructed channel usually broad and shallow, covered with erosion resistant vegetation, used to conduct surface runoff.

Gravel   Aggregate composed of hard and durable stones or pebbles, crushed or uncrushed, often mixed with sand.

Ground water   Free subsurface water, the top of which is the water table.

Gutter   An artificially surfaced and generally shallow waterway, usually provided at the sides of a roadway for carrying surface drainage.

Headwall   A vertical wall at the end of a culvert to support the pipe and prevent earth from spilling into the channel.

Hydraulic radius   The cross-sectional area of flow of a pipe or channel divided by the wetted perimeter.

Hydrograph   A graph showing, for a given point on a channel, the discharge, stage, velocity, or other property of water with respect to time.

Imperviousness   The property of a material through which water will not flow under ordinary hydrostatic pressure.

Inlet   An arrangement for conveying surface water to an underdrain.

Intercepting ditch An open drain to prevent surface water from flowing down a slope by conducting it around the slope.

Interpolation (Topographic) The process of determining the location of elevations from the plotted locations of known elevations.

Invert The lowest point of the internal cross-section of a pipe or of a channel.

Low flow channel A small ditch, constructed in flat bottoms of larger ditches or detention basins, to facilitate their drainage during periods of low flow.

Manhole A structure, covered with a lid, which allows a person to enter a space below ground level.

Moisture content The percentage, by weight, of water contained in soil or other material, usually based on dry weight.

Monument A boundary stone or other permanent marker locating a property line or corner.

Outlet Point of water disposal from a stream, river, lake, tidewater, or artificial drain.

Peak discharge The maximum instantaneous flow rate resulting from a given storm condition at a specific location.

Percolation Movement of soil water toward the water table.

Pervious The property of a material which permits movement of water through it under ordinary hydrostatic pressure.

pH A measure of alkalinity or acidity, with pH 7 being neutral and pH 6.5 being a desirable degree of soil acidity.

Porous Having many small openings through which liquids may pass.

Principal spillway A component of retention or detention ponds, generally constructed of permanent materials. It is designed to regulate the normal water level, provide flood protection and/or reduce the frequency of operation of the emergency spillway.

Pedology The study of the soil as a natural body, including its origin, characteristics, classification, and description.

Ramp An inclined plane serving as a way between two different levels.

Retaining wall A wall built to support a bank of earth.

Right of way The entire strip of land dedicated for highway purposes.

Riprap Stones or other material placed on a slope to prevent erosion by water.

Rough grade Stage of grading operation in which the desired landform is approximately attained.

Roughness coefficient (*n*) A factor in the Manning formula representing the effect of channel or conduit roughness on energy losses in the flowing water.

Runoff That part of precipitation carried off from the area on which it falls. Also, the rate of surface discharge of the above. (The ratio of runoff to precipitation is a coefficient, expressed as a decimal.)

Sediment Solid material, both mineral and organic, in suspension, being transported, or having been moved from its original site by air, water, gravity, or ice.

Sediment basin A depression formed by the construction of a barrier or dam built at a suitable location to retain rock, sand, gravel, silt, or other material.

Glossary Continued

Shoulder   The portion of roadway between the edge of the hardened wearing course and the ditch or embankment.

Sight distance   The distance between approaching vehicles when first visible to one another on a horizontal or vertical curve.

Slide   Movement of soil on a slope resulting in a reduced angle of repose usually occurring as a result of rainfall, high water, or thaw.

Slope   The face of an embankment or cut section. Any ground whose surface makes an angle with the horizontal plane.

Splash block   A masonry block with its top close to the ground surface, which receives roof drainage and prevents erosion below the spout.

Storm sewer   A conduit used for conveyance of rain water.

Structure   Anything constructed that requires a permanent location on the ground or is attached to something having a permanent location on the ground.

Subdrain   A pervious backfilled trench containing a pipe with perforations or open joints for the purpose of intercepting ground water or seepage.

Superelevation   The rise of the outer edge of the pavement relative to the inner edge at a curve in the highway, expressed in feet per foot, intended to overcome the tendency of speeding vehicles to overturn when rounding a curve.

Tangent   A straight road segment connecting two curves.

Terrace   An essentially level and defined area, usually raised, either paved or planted, forming part of a garden or building setting.

Watershed   Region or area contributing to the supply of a stream or lake. (Also drainage basin or catchment area.)

Water table   The level below which the ground is saturated.

Waterway   A natural course, or a constructed channel, for the flow of water.

Weephole   A small hole, as in a retaining wall, to drain water to the outside.

Weir   An opening in the crest of a dam or an embankment to discharge excess water; also used for measuring the rate of discharge.

Wetted perimeter   The length of the wetted contact between the water and the containing conduit, measured along a plane that is perpendicular to the conduit.

Bibliography

AMERICAN CONCRETE PIPE ASSOCIATION. 1980. Concrete Pipe Design Manual. American Concrete Pipe Assoc., Vienna, VA

AMERICAN IRON AND STEEL INSTITUTE. 1980. Modern Sewer Design. American Iron and Steel Institute, Washington, DC.

BARFIELD, B. J., WARNER, R. C., AND HAAN, C. T. 1981. Applied Hydrology and Sedimentology for Disturbed Areas. Oklahoma Technical Press, Stillwater, OK

DAY, G. E., AND CRAFTON, C. S. 1978. Site and Community Design Guidelines for Stormwater Management. College of Agriculture and Urban Studies, Virginia Polytechnic Institute and State University, Blacksburg, VA

GRAY, D. H., AND LEISER, A. T. 1982. Biotechnical Slope Protection and Erosion Control. Van Nostrand-Reinhold Company, New York

LYNCH, K. 1971. Site Planning, Second Edition. MIT Press, Cambridge, MA

MUNSON, A. E. 1974. Construction Design for Landscape Architects. McGraw-Hill Book Co., Inc., New York

NATHAN, K. 1975. Basic Site Engineering for Landscape Designers. MSS Information Corp., New York

NEW JERSEY ASSOCIATION OF CONSERVATION DISTRICTS. 1982. Standards for Soil Erosion and Sediment Control in New Jersey. New Jersey Department of Agriculture, Trenton, NJ

PARKER, H., AND MACGUIRE, J. W. 1954. Simplified Site Engineering for Architects and Builders. John Wiley & Sons, Inc., New York

PIRA, E. S., AND HUBLER, M. J. n.d. Tile Drainage Systems, University of Massachusetts, Amherst, MA

SCHROEDER, W. L. 1975. Soils in Construction. John Wiley & Sons, Inc., New York

SCHWAB, G. O., FREVERT, R. K., BARNES, K. K., AND EDMINSTER, T. W. 1971. Elementary Soil and Water Engineering. John Wiley & Sons, Inc., New York

SCHWAB, G. O., FREVERT, R. K., EDMINSTER, T. W., AND BARNES, K. K. 1981. Soil and Water Conservation Engineering. John Wiley & Sons, Inc., New York

SEELYE, E. E. 1968. Data Book for Civil Engineers: Design, Third Edition. John Wiley & Sons, Inc., New York

SNOW, B. Editor. 1959. The Highway and the Landscape. Rutgers University Press, New Brunswick, NJ

STEELE, F. 1981. The Sense of Place. CBI Publishing Co., Inc., Boston, MA

SUE, J., AND PATILLO, C. 1976. Landscape grading design, in Handbook of Landscape Architectural Construction, J. D. Carpenter (editor). The Landscape Architecture Foundation, Inc., McLean, VA

UNTERMANN, R. K. 1978. Principles and Practices of Grading, Drainage and Road Alignment: An Ecologic Approach. Reston Publishing Co., Inc., Reston, VA

USDA-SOIL CONSERVATION SERVICE. 1975. Urban Hydrology for Small Watersheds (Technical Release Number 55). National Technical Information Service, Springfield, VA

YOUNG, D., AND LESLIE, D. 1974. Grading Design Approach. Landscape Architectural Construction Series. The Landscape Architecture Foundation, Inc., McLean, VA

ZOLOMIJ, R. 1976. Vehicular circulation, in Handbook of Landscape Architectural Construction. J. D. Carpenter (editor). The Landscape Architecture Foundation, Inc., McLean, VA

Index

The Sea Traders

The Emergence of Man

The Sea Traders

by Maitland A. Edey
and the Editors
Of TIME-LIFE BOOKS

TIME-LIFE BOOKS
New York

THE EMERGENCE OF MAN

SERIES EDITOR: Dale M. Brown
Editorial Staff for The Sea Traders:
Picture Editor: Jean I. Tennant
Designer: Albert Sherman
Assistant Designer: Elaine Zeitsoff
Chief Researcher: Peggy Bushong
Researchers: Josephine G. Burke,
Kumait Jawdat, Joann W. McQuiston
Design Assistant: Jean Held

Editorial Production
Production Editor: Douglas B. Graham
Assistant: Gennaro C. Esposito
Quality Director: Robert L. Young
Assistant: James J. Cox
Copy Staff: Rosalind Stubenberg (chief),
Nancy Houghtaling, Elaine Pearlmutter,
Florence Keith
Picture Department: Dolores A. Littles,
Marianne Dowell

Valuable assistance was given by the following departments
and individuals of Time Inc.: Editorial Production,
Norman Airey; Library, Benjamin Lightman; Picture Collection,
Doris O'Neil; Photographic Laboratory, George Karas;
TIME-LIFE News Service, Murray J. Gart; Correspondents
Ann Natanson (Rome), Margot Hapgood and Dorothy Bacon
(London), Maria Vincenza Aloisi, Josephine du Brusle
and Michele Berge (Paris), Joe Fitchett (Beirut),
Helga Kohl (Athens), Elisabeth Kraemer (Bonn), Traudl
Lessing (Vienna), John Shaw (Moscow), Lucretia Marmon
and Marlin Levin (Jerusalem), Tanya Mathews (Tunis).

The Author: MAITLAND A. EDEY is the former Editor of TIME-LIFE BOOKS. His interest in the Phoenician sea traders comes naturally to him. He has sailed small boats all his life and crossed the Atlantic in 1957 as a working crew member of the Mayflower II, a replica of the original vessel. While researching this book, Edey traveled to sites of the ancient sea traders' ports in Lebanon, North Africa and Sicily. He is also the author of The Northeast Coast in The American Wilderness series, The Missing Link in The Emergence of Man series and The Cats of Africa.

The Consultants: A distinguished authority on the ancient Near East, JAMES BENNET PRITCHARD is the Associate Director of the University Museum at the University of Pennsylvania and President of the Archaeological Institute of America. He has led, or taken part in, six archeological expeditions to lands adjacent to the eastern Mediterranean and has been the author or editor of numerous publications in his field, including the definitive Ancient Near Eastern Texts Relating to the Old Testament. STANLEY GEVIRTZ, long a faculty member of the University of Chicago's Department of Near Eastern Languages and Civilizations, is now serving as Professor of Bible and Near Eastern Civilization at the Hebrew Union College-Jewish Institute of Religion in Los Angeles. His studies of Semitic languages, biblical literature and the cultures of the ancient Near East have appeared in scholarly journals.

Editorial Associate: SALLY DORST, formerly a researcher on the staff of TIME-LIFE BOOKS, worked closely with the author in all phases of the preparation of his text.

The Cover: A square-sailed Phoenician trading vessel prepares to head for the distant shore, where it will put in for the night. Such tubby boats—called "black ships" by the Greek poet Homer because of their protective coating of pitch—plied the Mediterranean on trading missions, ranging all the way from present-day Lebanon to Morocco.

Contents

Introduction

Of the three peoples—the Israelites, the Philistines and the Phoenicians—who played parts in the ascendant history that was being made about 1200 B.C. on the eastern coast of the Mediterranean, the Phoenicians are perhaps the least well known. The entry of the Israelites into Canaan is celebrated in the heroic sagas of the Bible. The Philistines, too, have been immortalized in the same source, although pictured in such an unfavorable light that their very name has come to signify uncouth barbarians—which they were far from being. But the Phoenicians escaped real attention. Except for the tradition that they invented the alphabet and a process for dyeing wool to a deep royal purple, their achievements as sea traders and colonizers have not been widely heralded.

The reasons for the oblivion into which the Phoenicians fell are many—and they are fascinatingly discussed in this book. Fortunately, their story can now be pieced together. Phoenician ships anchored at sheltered coves in Cyprus, Sicily, Sardinia, North Africa, Spain and on the western shores of Morocco. Recent evidence, uncovered not only at their home ports but at these ports of call around the rim of the Mediterranean and beyond, has provided many new insights into their pattern of behavior and shed much new light on their accomplishments. As the sailors went ashore to trade, and later to establish trading posts and colonies, they left traces whose full meaning we have only lately been able to comprehend.

Now archeologists, working at dozens of sites around the shore of what once was known as the Great Sea, are busy excavating the Phoenician past.

I, for one, have spent several years picking my way through the buried ruins of one of the Phoenician cities on the coast of Lebanon, trying to uncover its history and perchance to catch the spirit of the seafarers who set sail from its port. Even now it is clear that the city, then called Sarepta, was a center for craftsmen: metalworkers, potters, dyers, weavers —all played their part in the lucrative trade for which the Phoenicians were famous.

Standing in Sarepta's ruins one can but wonder what induced men to set sail from Lebanon for unknown parts at the end of the Second Millennium B.C.; at the time their fathers had been content to live for centuries in a few city-states that were nurtured by a narrow strip of land between a massive range of mountains and the sea (map, pages 12-13). That they did set sail is a tribute to their courage and their skill as seafarers. But more important is the fact that in doing so they became the first to provide a link between the culture of the ancient Near East and that of the uncharted world of the West. They brought with them skills from their homeland that were quickly mastered within the colonies. Further, their approach to these ventures represented something new. They went not for conquest, as the Babylonians and Assyrians did, but for trade. Profit rather than plunder was their policy. In their peaceful penetration of new markets the Phoenicians became the first Easterners to discover the Atlantic and to bear with them a useful invention, the alphabet. Had they not done so, the story of Western man might have taken quite another turn.

Professor James B. Pritchard
Associate Director
The University Museum
University of Pennsylvania

Chapter One: Who Were the Phoenicians?

One day, about 3,200 years ago, a small trading vessel was poking its way along the southern coast of what is now Turkey. There is no way of telling whether it was headed east or west when it got into trouble, in what season of the year it was traveling or what port it hailed from. But trouble did strike. It sank just off Cape Gelidonya in about 100 feet of water.

In 1960 two young Americans who have since become experts in the study of ancient wrecks, George Bass and Peter Throckmorton, decided to investigate the Cape Gelidonya wreck, whose existence had been reported to them by local sponge fishermen. They found that it had landed on a hard, rocky bottom where there had been little or no deposition of sand or mud to cover and preserve it. Therefore nearly all of the hull of the little ship had long since been eaten away by marine worms. All that was left of it was its cargo and, underneath that, some bits of its bottom planking, along with a layer of coarse twigs and branches. This stuff is known as dunnage and has been widely used down through marine history as packing to prevent cargo from bumping and banging during rough passages at sea. By carbon dating, these remaining bits of dunnage helped confirm the age of the vessel—an age that had already been given it after the divers had a chance to study its cargo.

For marine archeologists the Gelidonya wreck is a critically important one. With the possible exception of one other, located in shallow water near Marsala

Coasting along the rocky Mediterranean shore, a high-bowed Phoenician cargo vessel carries a load of fir and cedar logs, oxhide-shaped copper ingots, some covered bales of mixed cargo and two shipments of clay amphorae filled with olive oil and wine. On the starboard side a man—wearing a typically Phoenician cap—is taking a sounding with a lead line.

off the coast of Sicily, the Gelidonya wreck is the only known fragment of a ship that is believed to have been built by the Phoenicians.

Common knowledge about the Phoenicians is as skimpy as the remains of their vessels. Most people, if they have heard of the Phoenicians at all, know only two things about them: they were great seafarers and traders, and they invented the alphabet. The first of these statements is true; the second is not (Chapter 4). What else is known about the Phoenicians is quickly told.

They were indeed the greatest sea traders of the ancient world. They had their start in the eastern Mediterranean in what is now part of Lebanon. They began to appear on the historical scene around 1200 B.C. and became an important influence in the commerce, the culture and the history of their world for nearly a thousand years. Over that long span they spread westward throughout the Mediterranean, and so, for convenience's sake, it has been customary to speak of the cities that occupied the Lebanese coast as Phoenicia East, and the scattered settlements in the western Mediterranean as Phoenicia West. But, having so identified Phoenicia East and Phoenicia West, one must quickly say that there never was a country or an empire called "Phoenicia," only a collection of independent cities more interested in trade than in the development of an empire.

Furthermore, as traders they were their own worst competitors and were extremely jealous of one another, with the result that, though they spoke a common language and worshiped the same gods, they never did coalesce into a country. They spoke of themselves as Tyrians, Sidonians, Byblians, Carthaginians, Motyans and so on. The very word "Phoenician" was unknown to them; the label probably was pasted on them by the Greeks and preserved by the accident that the Greek language and its literature, and not the Phoenician, have been passed down to us. The Phoenician scholar Donald Harden notes that the word "phoenix" first crops up in Homer, where it means a dark red or purplish-brown color. Since the Phoenicians were dyers of great skill, renowned for their purple cloth, it is not hard to see how the name stuck. (Their name has nothing to do with the mythical bird phoenix, although both are derived from the same Greek root.)

The Phoenicians have occupied a curious place in history for a long time. Through many references to them by others—in the Bible, in ancient literature and in the works of classical historians—they earned their reputation as the outstanding seafarers, traders, traveling artisans, explorers and shipwrights of their day. They went everywhere. They swapped goods with Egyptians, Greeks, Assyrians, Babylonians, Africans and Spanish tribesmen. The entire Mediterranean world was their bazaar. They even went beyond it, out into the Atlantic, far down the African coast and possibly north to Brittany and the British Isles. And yet, until comparatively recently, almost nothing directly was known about them because they appeared to say so little about themselves.

In this respect they were quite different from their better-known neighbors, who have left behind myths, stories, detailed historical accounts and marvelously intimate glimpses into their daily lives. The Babylonians and Assyrians speak to us from literally hundreds of thousands of clay tablets and from inscriptions on monuments. The Egyptians speak from papyri, from a stunning collection of household ob-

A Phoenician Chronology

1200-1100 B.C.
Coastal Canaanites become known as Phoenicians.
1000-700 B.C.
Phoenicia East establishes trading routes and settlements in Mediterranean.
c.880 B.C.
Assyrians embark on 250 years of harassing Phoenicians.
c.814 B.C.
Tyre founds Carthage.
735-728 B.C.
Greeks begin to settle Sicily.
c.700 B.C.
Carthage founds Motya, in western Sicily.
c.600 B.C.
Carthaginians begin alliance with Etruscans against Greeks.
585-572 B.C.
Nebuchadnezzar II of Babylon besieges and captures Tyre.
567-559 B.C.
Tyre under Babylonian control; judges rule city.
c.550 B.C.
Carthaginian general Mago campaigns successfully against Greeks in Sicily and establishes 150-year Magonid Dynasty.
494 B.C.
Phoenicia begins naval aid to Persia in 14-year campaign against the Greeks.
480 B.C.
Battle of Salamis. Greeks conquer Persians, who were fighting with Phoenician naval aid. Carthaginian army also routed by Greeks at Himera, Sicily.
397 B.C.
Motya falls to Greeks.
336 B.C.
Alexander the Great sets out to conquer the East.
333 B.C.
Byblos and Sidon surrender to Alexander the Great.
332 B.C.
Tyre besieged by Alexander. End of Phoenicia East.
264-241 B.C.
First Punic War between Rome and Carthage.
c.237 B.C.
Hamilcar Barca of Carthage develops power base in Spain; establishes Barcid Dynasty.
229 B.C.
Hamilcar Barca dies in battle; Hasdrubal, his son-in-law, succeeds him and founds New Carthage in Spain.
221 B.C.
Hasdrubal assassinated; succeeded by Hamilcar Barca's son Hannibal, known as Hannibal the Great.
218 B.C.
Second Punic War begins. Hannibal successfully crosses Alps to fight Romans.
202 B.C.
Hannibal recalled to Africa and defeated by Roman Scipio. Second Punic War ends.
146 B.C.
Third Punic War ends. Carthage falls. End of Phoenicia West.

jects and works of art, from long messages carved on temples and tombs. We know an enormous amount about the Hebrews from the Bible, about the ancient Greeks from Homer, Herodotus and Thucydides —from many other poets, dramatists and historians. The Phoenicians, by comparison, are strangely mute.

It is from others—from people who in talking about themselves talk about the Phoenicians—that much of our knowledge has come. Wall carvings from Egypt and Mesopotamia give us better pictures of Phoenician ships and cities than any Phoenician source does. Only two significant collections of clay tablets that scholars are willing to ascribe to Phoenicians or their immediate ancestors have ever been discovered. One devotes itself to politics, the other to religion. Neither says anything about Phoenician daily life. No Phoenician tale has ever been found, no song. The soul of a people is revealed by the songs they sing, the jokes they crack. On the record the Phoenicians never cracked a single joke. I cannot believe they didn't. But there is no Phoenician Aristophanes to memorialize their humor, just as there is no Aeschylus to preserve their sense of tragedy, no Homer to talk about good food, good ships, good fighting, fine weapons and beautiful women. The Phoenicians were familiar figures in the ports of the Mediterranean when Homer wrote the *Iliad*. Surely they were as passionate about ships, the sea, war and women as the Greeks. But what they thought about them and what they said we simply do not know.

No country, no civic records, no historians, no poets, no songs, no jokes. Who, then, were the Phoenicians? And if they were so well known to their contemporaries in the ancient world, how is it that they faded into such obscurity later on?

Fair questions. The Phoenicians faded because of the special circumstances they found themselves in, both geographical and historical—a particular climate, neighbors of a certain bent—and because of the particular kind of life they were able to work out for themselves in those circumstances. It is possible to write about them because, while their ships are still more or less a mystery, there has been recovered a growing collection of the trade objects that the Phoenicians carried about, assembled over the years by archeologists working throughout the Mediterranean. Some of these were of Phoenician manufacture, some the goods of others for whom they were acting as middlemen—all of them widely scattered throughout the ancient world, thus proving the classical presumption that the Phoenicians were extremely busy traders and travelers.

Then there are the Phoenician sites, many of them the merest traces of abandoned trading posts stretching ever westward like a string of beads along the African coast. An archeologist, finding one and knowing how far a trading vessel could be expected to travel in a day (about 30 miles), can quite accurately forecast the next likely spot where the trader might have been tempted to put in for the night. A number of sites have been located in this way. Finally there were the settlements and trading posts that eventually became cities. The location of some of these places and their identity as Phoenician have been well known throughout history. Others were lost and had to be rediscovered. One, Sarepta, only eight miles from Sidon, was turned up as a rich archeological site as recently as 1970. Today, though battered down by Greek and Roman, and by many an Arab and Crusader as well, the roots of those Phoenician towns

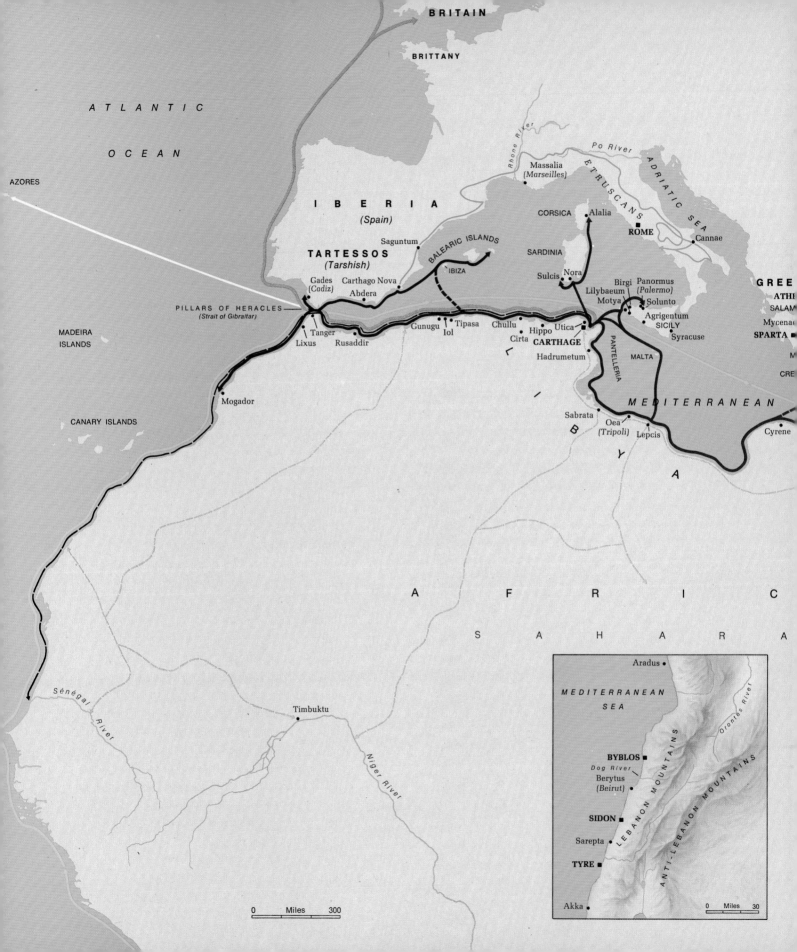

ATLANTIC

OCEAN

AZORES

MADEIRA
ISLANDS

CANARY ISLANDS

BRITAIN

BRITTANY

IBERIA
(Spain)

Rhone River   Po River

Massalia
(Marseilles)   ETRUSCANS   ADRIATIC SEA

Saguntum   BALEARIC ISLANDS   CORSICA   Alalia   ROME

TARTESSOS
(Tarshish)   IBIZA   SARDINIA   Cannae

Carthago Nova   Sulcis Nora   GRE
Gades   Birgi Panormus   ATHI
(Cadiz)   Abdera   Lilybaeum   (Palermo)   SALAM
                                Motya Solunto   Mycena
PILLARS OF HERACLES   Agrigentum   SPARTA
(Strait of Gibraltar)   Gunugu   Tipasa   Chullu   Utica   SICILY
Tanger   Iol   Hippo   CARTHAGE   Syracuse   CRE
Lixus   Rusaddir   Cirta   Hadrumetum   PANTELLERIA
                                                        MALTA
                                                        MEDITERRANEAN
Mogador   Sabrata
                                                Oea
                                                (Tripoli) Lepcis   Cyrene
                                        B
                                        Y
                                        A
AFRIC
SAHARA

Sénégal River   Timbuktu

Niger River

0   Miles   300

MEDITERRANEAN
SEA

Aradus

BYBLOS
Dog River
Berytus
(Beirut)

SIDON

Sarepta

TYRE

Akka

LEBANON MOUNTAINS   Orontes River   ANTI-LEBANON MOUNTAINS

0   Miles   30

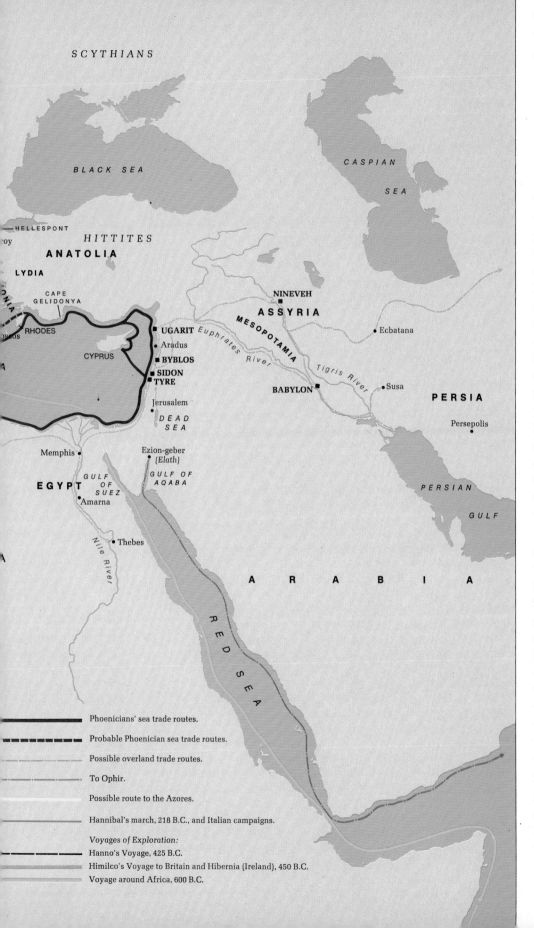

SCYTHIANS

BLACK SEA

CASPIAN
SEA

HELLESPONT
Troy

HITTITES
ANATOLIA

LYDIA

CAPE
GELIDONYA

RHODES

IONIA

Nossos

CYPRUS

NINEVEH

ASSYRIA

MESOPOTAMIA

Euphrates River

Tigris River

Ecbatana

UGARIT
Aradus

BYBLOS
SIDON
TYRE

BABYLON

Susa

PERSIA

Jerusalem

DEAD
SEA

Persepolis

Memphis

Ezion-geber
(Elath)

GULF OF
AQABA

GULF
OF
SUEZ

EGYPT

Amarna

PERSIAN

GULF

Nile River

Thebes

A R A B I A

R E D   S E A

Phoenicians' sea trade routes.

Probable Phoenician sea trade routes.

Possible overland trade routes.

To Ophir.

Possible route to the Azores.

Hannibal's march, 218 B.C., and Italian campaigns.

Voyages of Exploration:
Hanno's Voyage, 425 B.C.
Himilco's Voyage to Britain and Hibernia (Ireland), 450 B.C.
Voyage around Africa, 600 B.C.

The Far-flung World Penetrated by the Sea Traders

The boldness of the Phoenicians as traders and explorers can be gleaned from this map. Before 1000 B.C. they were a huddle of small cities crowded along the very eastern edge of the Mediterranean. Anything lying west of Greece or Egypt was dangerously far from home; anything farther west —beyond Sicily—loomed as a fearsome waste of unknown geography, strange winds, currents, tides, whirlpools, ocean storms and savage people. The Phoenicians braved them all. Every town marked on the African coast—save Cyrene, a Greek colony —was settled by Phoenicians, with Carthage their western capital. So were towns in Malta, Sicily, Sardinia, the Balearic Islands and Spain.

The inset map shows why the eyes of the Canaanite coastal traders were turned seaward; they were hemmed in on land by the mountain ranges behind them. The key at left shows trade and exploration routes—though those shown running across the Sahara are largely conjectural. They touched at oases long since dried up and were used more by natives bringing things to the coast than by the Carthaginian traders themselves.

The period covered in the map extends from about 1300 B.C. to 140 B.C. in order to include and locate such peoples as the Hittites, whose empire collapsed soon after 1200 B.C., and the Etruscans, whose power began to wane after 500 B.C.

Lebanon's coast is rocky. Many of its reefs and ledges provide good harbors; others are lethal to ships blown ashore in storms.

still survive in the form of old walls, stairways, cisterns, temple foundations, tomb shafts and even paved dockyards for ships. The ghosts of the traders can still be heard whispering in those places, mingled with a hum of commerce and the creak of cordage, the clink of metals and the admiring sighs of people who came from far away to barter for rich purple cloth and shiny new toys.

How remote those old Phoenician cities are, their names disappearing into time like echoes struck from gongs: Oea, Utica, Hippo—all of them located in Mediterranean Africa. Motya, Lilybaeum (Marsala) and Panormus (Palermo) in Sicily. Sulcis in Sardinia. Alalia in Corsica. Abdera and Gades (Cadiz) in Spain. Finally, Mogador, vanishingly remote, a dream flickering far down the coast of Morocco, but no dream because recognizable Phoenician roots are still there. These are only a few of the scores of settlements, large and small, with which the Phoenicians dotted

their world and, in so doing, left us with the wherewithal to begin answering some of the questions about who the Phoenicians were and what they did.

As to the question of "who": the Phoenicians were Canaanites, one group of a large number of Semitic-speaking peoples who had been spreading through the Near East for some thousands of years. Where they all came from is difficult to say, but many scholars believe that they represent successive waves of tribal expansion by semidesert herders, who over the centuries moved out from the enormous semiarid expanses of northern Arabia eastward into the more fertile Tigris-Euphrates valley, and westward toward the Mediterranean into an area that now comprises Syria, Lebanon, Jordan and Israel. Thus, most of the people who walked the pages of early Near Eastern history were Semites: the Babylonians, the Assyrians, the Israelites, the Canaanites, the Moabites, the

Cedars of Lebanon down the centuries supplied Byblos, Tyre and other Phoenician cities with an immensely valuable export.

Amorites, the Ammonites, the Amalekites and others whose identities are not even known today. They were the beneficiaries of two immensely important human "inventions": agriculture (the domestication of wild plants) and husbandry (the domestication of wild animals); both are believed to have had their start in the Near East some 10,000 years ago. These inventions helped change man from a hunter-gatherer —dependent wholly on the natural seasonal bounty of fruits, seeds and wild game—to one who could settle down as a farmer or one who wandered only to secure food and water for his animals. With the establishment of towns and cities, societies became more complex, and eventually powerful empires evolved. In the narrower, upcountry valleys there was not that incentive to get together; the terrain tended to keep people apart. Thus small city-states, rather than empires, emerged, each with its own king.

As far as can be learned, it was in about 5000 or 4000 B.C. that one group of Semitic people began trickling into what is now Lebanon and Israel, nearly 300 miles of seacoast along the eastern edge of the Mediterranean, with mountains and upland valleys behind it. This area, particularly its inland sections, should be well known to readers of the Bible as the Land of Canaan. Along the shore are excellent harbors. There is also good coastal farmland, but not much of it because a range of mountains marches parallel to the sea only a few miles inland. The original Canaanite invaders who got as far as the seacoast settled down there, either displacing or mingling with some aboriginal inhabitants who lived by a combination of farming and fishing. The Canaanites established towns, learned to build boats and go to sea, began trading up and down the coast with their neighbors. It was these people who became known to others as the Phoenicians.

Having identified and located them, it is now ap-

From their earliest days the ancestors
of the Phoenicians were forced by a
range of mountains that ran down the
Canaanite coast behind them to look
toward the sea. Centuries of logging
denuded the mountains of their dense
stands of cedar and fir, and finally of
their topsoil. Though little grows there
now, the Lebanese government hopes
to improve the slopes by reforestation.

propriate to turn to the second question: Why for so long has so little been known about the Phoenicians? One reason is the climate. Coastal Lebanon is fairly damp. Anything written on papyrus quickly disappears; wood rots; clay tablets, unless safely buried in the ground, crumble. Even stone monuments or inscriptions, if exposed long enough to the weathering of wind, rain and frost, become blurred and eventually indecipherable. Therefore, while the Phoenicians over a period of about a thousand years undoubtedly were very busy making things, saving things and writing things down, the elements were equally busy destroying them.

A second reason has to do with the geographical position of the Canaanite coastal towns. They were not only strategically located with respect to trade, but also with respect to invasion. The most powerful forces of the day were the Assyrian and Babylonian empires to the east of Lebanon, the Egyptian empire to the south and the Hittite empire on the Turkish —or Anatolian—plateau to the north. All three were land powers with large armies but no fleets. They were separated from one another by rugged, dry terrain, much of it true desert. The only way they could get at one another was by established caravan routes through a few mountain passes—or by moving along the Canaanite coast. Thus, control of the Canaanite ports became of enormous strategic importance to the imperial dreams of Babylonian or Egyptian conquerors. As a result, those ports, each a separate little trading kingdom trying to get along on its own, were fought over constantly, sacked, knocked down, built up again—their contents trampled, crunched, burned, carted away—reused over and over again.

And it did not stop with the Babylonians and the

Egyptians. The center of the Levant became a cockpit for the Persians, the Greeks, the Romans, the Byzantine emperors, the Saracens, the Crusaders, the Turks, and in more recent times the British, the Germans and the French. It is scarcely surprising that by the beginning of the 19th Century, when archeologists first began to concern themselves with those elusive people, the Phoenicians, there seemed to be almost nothing Phoenician lying about for anyone to study. But as scholars began poking into the ground they found that they had reason to do so.

The five principal eastern Phoenician cities were Aradus, Byblos, Berytus (Beirut), Tyre and Sidon. All are still inhabited today, and in the underground rubble around the edges of the modern towns archeologists not much more than a hundred years ago began the slow rediscovery of the Phoenician past. And here is a dreadfully frustrating circumstance. Though the Phoenicians did their traveling and trading in ships, during more than a century of archeological research not one ship was turned up in the mud of a Phoenician harbor or in the wreckage of a dockyard. No Phoenician carving or drawing of a ship was ever found. As far as the Phoenicians' own record was concerned, the extraordinary mercantile operation that these clever people conducted could well have been launched on tin trays. It was in that near vacuum of direct evidence of Phoenician ships that the two marine archeologists Bass and Throckmorton swam down to a wreck at Cape Gelidonya in 1960 and began to examine it (pages 27-31).

They did not know, of course, when they first went down what they had found. Following a rule that is observed in all conscientious archeological work today—whether digging in prehistoric caves, ruined cities or deep in the sea—the first step Bass and Throckmorton took was to map the wreck site noting the exact position of every object in it. Scholars now recognize that the precise position of a find often is as important as the object itself. In this wreck the distribution of things on the bottom gave a clear clue to the size of the ship. Although the hull had almost completely vanished, its contents were still lying where they had originally settled, making it possible to estimate that the ship had been about 60 feet long. Their mapping done, Bass and Throckmorton, together with members of a 20-man underwater archeological team they had assembled, then proceeded to remove the cargo and the remaining bits of hull piece by piece. Everything was almost totally encrusted with a thick, rock-hard layer that had slowly been deposited on it by marine organisms over the centuries, making it impossible for the divers to identify much of the material until it had been pried free in chunks and brought to the surface, where the encrustation could be chipped away.

In the course of their chipping and cleaning Bass and Throckmorton quickly realized that what they had found was the ship of a traveling smith or tinker and his crew. Most of the cargo consisted of ingots of copper and tin—the raw material for making bronze—plus some pieces of scrap bronze that the smith obviously had been saving for use in fashioning whatever metal objects might be in demand at the ports he put into.

Along with the raw materials of a smith were the tools of his trade: a large, flat stone anvil, two stone hammers, a whetstone, several polishing stones for buffing up a fine finish on metal articles and a special block of bronze with holes used for making wire. These tools and the ingots were recognizable both by their shape and markings as having come from the nearby island of Cyprus. Bass's first thought was that this was a Cypriot ship, but it turned out not to be. When he and Throckmorton had brought more to the surface, they found that they were beginning to assemble a small, pathetic collection of personal belongings. They were clearly Phoenician: several carved scarabs, a cylinder seal (for signing clay tablets), some stone mortars and hammers, plus a number of graduated weights for a balance-pan scale —all of them of Canaanite origin.

From these homely bits and pieces a glimpse of the life of a Canaanite trader-craftsman is revealed. Since both raw materials and the wherewithal for making things were on board, it seems clear that this was a traveling workshop, either owned or leased by a seagoing artisan, and that perhaps his entire stock of worldly goods was carried with him. Whether he had partners or how big his crew was cannot be guessed. All we know is that he ate olives; deep in the wreckage was found a small heap of them, the meat gone but the hard little pits still there. When did he eat those olives? About 1200 B.C.; carbon dating and the style of the objects found aboard both point to that date.

In terms of Phoenician history this is an extremely awkward date. It is just about this time in history that scholars are willing to recognize the metamorphosis of coastal Canaanite into Phoenician. No race, no people, no culture, no way of life suddenly appears on the historical stage fully formed and neatly labeled. For example, the way of life practiced by colonial settlers on this continent was not "American"

The earlier tradition out of which
Phoenician art and culture emerged can
be traced in this bronze head of a
man found in 1936 at Ugarit, a proto-
Phoenician city. Once a prosperous
trading center with commercial ties to
Greece and Crete, Ugarit was sacked
in 1234 B.C. The owner of this head was
probably a metalsmith or dealer
who used it as a balance-pan weight.

the day after the Declaration of Independence was signed and "un-American" the day before.

Similarly with the cities of the Lebanese coast. That part of their history that was played out prior to about 1100 or 1200 B.C. scholars properly identify as Canaanite. After this time scholars are willing to identify the Canaanite coastal peoples as Phoenicians. The event that made the name change appropriate was actually a whole series of events that did not take place in Canaan at all but in Egypt, in the Aegean world of the Bronze Age Greeks and on the upland plateau of Anatolia. In all these places great political upheavals were taking place. Rulers rose and fell and empires were collapsing.

The Canaanites, heretofore confined more or less to their own doorsteps by more powerful neighbors, suddenly found this constraint removed. They began flowing outward, cautiously at first, then with increasing boldness and rapidity into the vacuum left by their prostrate neighbors. Within a remarkably short period they had changed from local coastal traders to far-ranging seagoing merchant venturers with a network of trading posts throughout the Mediterranean. The existence of that trading network is the key to the identification of the Phoenicians as a recognizable people, though it should be emphasized again that they did not see themselves that way. That is why the Gelidonya wreck is so interesting. It is a small piece of positive evidence about the seagoing and mercantile habits of somebody from down the coast just at the moment when he was beginning to earn the label "Phoenician." By 1000 B.C. there would be no question whatsoever as to who a Phoenician was. The relatives and descendants of the Gelidonyan tinsmith had spread far. They had worked their way south, leapfrogging across the Nile Delta past Egypt, and established settlements along the North African coast. Within a few hundred years they were all over the place. Carthage was founded, toeholds were secured in Malta, Sicily, Sardinia, Corsica, the Balearic Isles and Spain. Expeditions were even made into the Atlantic.

The point of changeover from coastal Canaanite to Phoenician is critically important to an understanding of Phoenician history. Unfortunately, there is no agreement among experts as to its exact timing. Some think the name "Phoenician" can be applied by 1200 B.C. or even earlier. Others would put the changeover as late as 1000 B.C. and will not concede that the Gelidonya wreck is Phoenician. I accept the older date—and thus that the wreck is indeed Phoenician—on the logic that the Canaanite merchant seamen had already begun a significant outreach in trading and that the Gelidonya wreck proves it. It is highly unlikely that the only or the farthest excursion of a Canaanite trader should have ended in disaster and that the results of that single disaster should have been preserved for discovery today. In other words, Gelidonya seems symptomatic of a considerably larger activity already underway and probably already going in a number of directions.

Be that as it may, there is absolutely no question that the opportunities open to a Canaanite trader after about 1100 B.C. were entirely different from those open to him prior to about 1200 B.C. An early merchant from Byblos, gazing out to sea and scratching his head over how to develop a profitable two-way line of trade, had rather limited options. He could look south toward Egypt and deal on Egyptian terms. Or he could look west to another rich market: the is-

land world of the Aegean, where superb trade goods —notably pottery and inlaid metalwork—were being manufactured and distributed by two peoples, the Minoans and the Mycenaean Greeks. What more could a little coastal trader hope for than to expand into that world of islands, with its multitude of fine harbors, local produce, fresh water—with scarcely more than a day's good sailing needed to carry a ship from one sheltering shore to another?

Unfortunately for the dreams of the Canaanite trader, that world was rather effectively closed to him. Crete, an island nearly 200 miles long, lay like a bar across the foot of the Aegean. Crete was the central home base of the architects of the first true maritime power in history. The entire Aegean was their private lake. Its people, the Minoans, controlled commerce with the cities of the Ionian coast and with all the Aegean Islands. They dealt with the ancestors of Agamemnon and Nestor in Greece. They went to Troy and beyond. They probed the bottleneck of the Black Sea, which opened up eastward like a cornucopia, for trade with horsemen from the Russian steppes, with Scythians, with Parthians and with unnumbered, unnamed people surging over a vast land that stretched to no one knew where.

Mighty people, the Minoans. If a Canaanite trader so much as put his nose into the Minoan lake, he did it on sufferance. More likely he had to accept Minoan trading concessions in his own home port. This could have discouraged him from anything more ambitious than local coastal trading, turning him into little better than a transfer agent of goods, which he sent on to Egypt or loaded for the long cross-country journey over the Lebanon Mountains and dusty plateaus to arrive eventually at Babylon or Nineveh.

That was the early pattern of trade for places like Byblos for a good many hundreds of years: south to Egypt, east to Mesopotamia. Then, beginning about 1400 B.C., there occurred a series of political upheavals that shook this relatively stable trading world to its roots. Somehow the Mycenaean Greeks got control of Crete and the Minoan sea empire vanished, leaving only scorched palaces and a glow of past glories behind. The Greek occupation lasted about 200 years and then in its turn collapsed. The Greek cities on the mainland were sacked one by one.

How this happened is not entirely clear. Some historians believe that the upheaval was internally generated and that Mycenaean civilization was self-destructive. Others believe that it became the victim of waves of invasion by a Greek-related people known as the Dorians, pouring in from the north. In either case the Bronze Age was ending, and it went out in a series of convulsions whose shock waves were felt throughout the entire Mediterranean world. "Sea Peoples" from the north, from Crete and from the other islands flooded ashore in Ionia and may even have overrun the Hittite Empire. They also appeared on the Lebanese and Syrian coasts—some in panicky flight, others as invaders looking for a new place to take over and settle.

In all the confusion during the years around 1200 B.C. piracy became a way of life for many peoples. Once the Minoan control was broken brigands multiplied like cockroaches in every coastal cranny. They took to looting coastal towns, and as their successes grew so did their ambitions. They joined forces. Their sinister fleets grew bigger and went after bigger game. Some authorities believe that the siege of Troy was nothing more than a giant piratical expedition of

Bronze Age Greeks reacting to increasingly chaotic conditions in the Aegean. In 1200 B.C. the palaces of Crete were ravaged for the second time and were never rebuilt. Shore people crept away to place their citadels inland on safer crags.

In this world of chaotic change the Canaanite traders began to emerge as Phoenician. Their ports quite suddenly showed a marked increase in vigor and enterprise, and two of them—Sidon and Tyre—would have long and bright histories. This coastal blooming came at a moment of power vacuum everywhere else. The pirate fleets shrank to local nuisances. Mycenaean and Minoan sea power was completely unraveled. The Hittite Empire lay smoking. Egypt slid into a long decline and lost its hegemony over the Canaanites forever; instead of exacting large annual tribute in the form of timber from Byblos, as it had in the good old days, Egypt was reduced to buying timber at increasingly stiff prices.

The difference to Byblos—and, by extension, to all the other ports and their rulers—was remarkable.

There is hardly a better way of looking at this phenomenon than by making the acquaintance of two kings of Byblos: Rib-Addi (who ruled in about 1375 B.C.) and Zakar-Baal (who ruled in about 1075 B.C.) —the former unmistakably a coastal Canaanite king, the latter just as unmistakably a Phoenician.

Rib-Addi's world, like his own thinking, was dominated by Egypt and had been for a long time. Through various ups and downs extending back a thousand years or more, Egypt had been the mightiest power of the ancient world. Though it was never much of a naval power, it went through several periods of great military expansion on land, gaining

control of the whole Canaanite coast and exacting tribute from the Canaanite ports. For centuries Egypt used them as sources of supply and as bases for its campaigns eastward against the Mesopotamian empires of Assyria and Babylon. In return it offered the Canaanite ports security against invasion by others.

In this long relationship the longest and closest ties were between Egypt and Byblos. Byblos was Egypt's principal supplier of prime timber—chiefly cedars of Lebanon—which grew in dense groves on the flanks of the mountains back of Byblos. They were consumed in such quantities by the Egyptians—for furniture, room paneling and especially river barges used for ceremonial purposes—that the ships sent up from the Nile to collect this wood were known as Byblos ships. The Egyptians paid well for Byblos' cedarwood, courted its kings with gifts of carved boxes and stone portrait busts inscribed with the personal seal of the pharaoh. In return, the Bybli-

an kings were outstandingly loyal to the Egyptians.

However, the Canaanite-Egypt axis suffered an inherent problem: when Egypt was strong, there could be little threat of invasion; when it was weak and the threats rose, it could not help its allies. The struggling little Canaanite seaports had to deal with local disturbances as best they could. They were constantly under the predatory eye of the Hittites, a powerful and warlike people glowering down at them from the heights of Anatolia to the north. Later they would be assaulted again and again by Assyrians and Babylonians from the east. It was Rib-Addi's bad luck to be seated on the throne of Byblos during a period of Egyptian weakness. The ruling pharaoh at the time was Amenhotep III, followed by his son, a religious zealot named Akhenaton. The latter resolved to impose the concept of one god, Aton, on an Egyptian society that had a long tradition of many gods. This caused a convulsion in Egypt and brought Akhena-

The lumber trade, on which so much of Phoenicia's wealth was floated, is illustrated in this Assyrian carving— on alabaster—of three high-ended Phoenician cargo vessels. Large logs are being wrestled aboard and towed.

ton into such conflict with a well-entrenched priestly class that for a number of years he had little or no time for foreign affairs. Egyptian control of the Canaanite coast loosened. Large bands of wandering roughnecks began hiring themselves out as soldiers in an eruption of simmering intercity conflicts that had formerly been kept under fairly good control by the Egyptian presence. Worse, the Hittites were fomenting these quarrels with the long-term aim of taking over the entire Levant themselves.

It was in this disturbing climate that Rib-Addi sat down one day to dictate a letter that was duly inscribed on a clay tablet and sent off to Egypt. We know this because his letter has been miraculously preserved. It was found in Egypt in 1887 at a place called Amarna, along with 63 others from Rib-Addi and about 300 more by other writers. This cache of clay tablets turned out to be a portion of the royal files of Akhenaton and his father. An extraordinary collection, it contains correspondence from the kings of Assyria and Babylon on matters of state, as well as from the Hittites and the smaller vassal Canaanite kingdoms. But of all the letter writers, none was more importunate than Rib-Addi.

He had reason to be. A couple of neighboring Amorite princes, Abdi-Ashirta and later his son Aziru, had taken up with the local mercenary gangs and were openly plotting with the Hittites while continuing to profess allegiance to Egypt. From the point of view of one like Rib-Addi, whose fortunes were closely tied to those of Egypt, this was treachery of the rankest sort. It was also a source of danger to him, for if it succeeded he would be out on the end of a limb of an essentially Egyptian tree, with nobody to catch him if he slipped. Accordingly, he fired

off a series of letters to Egypt, at first warning about the treacherous Amorites, later—when their treachery began to pay off in towns captured and local rulers deposed—pleading for help. He asked for soldiers, for horses and, when the perfidious Aziru was strong enough to besiege the city of Byblos itself, for food. Nothing came.

Next a faction of traitors sprouted within the city walls. "My gates have taken copper [bribes]," wrote Rib-Addi in a panicky letter, explaining that if he did not get help immediately, he might have to flee Byblos entirely. No word came back from Egypt, so he sent his sister and her children south to Tyre for safety. But eventually Tyre went over to the other side and they were all murdered.

By this time Rib-Addi's stubborn loyalty had placed him in extreme peril. Desperate, he dropped a shrewd hint to the pharaoh that he was about to throw in the sponge; his wife and all his courtiers were advising him to go over to Aziru. When even this elicited no helpful response, Rib-Addi as a last resort went to neighboring Berytus to rally support. Returning to Byblos, he discovered that his own brother had defected and taken over the city; its gates were now barred to him.

Rib-Addi's final letter to Akhenaton informs him that now he has nowhere to turn, that his enemies are about to persuade the king of Berytus to hand him over to Aziru.

Presumably this happened, for Rib-Addi vanished, never to be heard from again. We can deduce that Aziru caught him and killed him since another letter from the Amarna cache, written by a prominent citizen of Byblos, informs the pharaoh that Aziru is a horrible rascal who has the murder of several kings on his hands, among them a king of Byblos.

The Amarna correspondence is one of the most interesting and revealing—and painful—in the whole legacy of material dealing with the Phoenicians and their forbears. It brings home, with a snarl that jumps from those innocent-looking clay tablets, how slippery the footing must have been for the insecure Canaanite king who wrote them. Grim, too, for unremembered others like him who were forced to make similar choices and who also may have guessed wrong as they were constantly faced with decisions about whether to dicker or fight. They had to trim sail frantically—not only to the large Egyptian wind that blew from the south and the Hittite wind from the north but to all the gritty little dust squalls that set neighbor against neighbor time and again.

But jump ahead some 300 years and a different Byblos is encountered. Once-potent Egypt has slid still further. Subservient Canaanite princes like Rib-Addi have been replaced by independent Phoenician kings, the change vividly revealed in another fascinating document. This is an Egyptian papyrus dating from about 1100 B.C. and describing the adventures of an envoy who was sent up from Thebes to dicker with King Zakar-Baal of Byblos for cedarwood the pharaoh needed in order to build a ceremonial barge for the god Amon. In former days, when the little Canaanite princes had to hustle to keep in the good graces of the Egyptians, we may be sure that the arrival of an Egyptian purchasing agent caused a great stir. How the local timber dealers, and perhaps the local king too, must have bowed and scraped to him.

How different now was the experience of the Egyptian agent whose name was Wen-Amon. The old visits, full of pomp and fine compliments, had washed out with the tide. There was not even an Egyptian ship of state to bring Wen-Amon; he had to make his own passage in a Syrian vessel, and thieves stole most of his money during the voyage. When he stepped ashore at Byblos there was nobody at all to welcome him. On the contrary, not only did the king, Zakar-Baal, refuse to see him, he ordered Wen-Amon to leave. For 29 days in a row the king sent curt messages down to the harbor telling Wen-Amon to get out immediately. The only reason Wen-Amon did not go was that he could not find a ship to sail in.

Zakar-Baal may have been expressing a heady new sense of Phoenician independence or, on a more practical level, he may have heard that Wen-Amon had been robbed on his journey and had scarcely any money left with which to buy timber, let alone any kind of gift for the king.

Whatever the reason, Wen-Amon was still wringing his hands down at the harbor, wondering what to do next, when a young courtier of Zakar-Baal's conveniently fell down in some kind of religious fit, during which a voice spoke to him saying that the king should see the Egyptian purchasing agent. So Wen-Amon had his audience with Zakar-Baal, whom he found in an upstairs room in his palace "with his back turned to a window so that the waves of the great Syrian sea broke against the back of his head."

This revealing passage tells us that palaces in the early Phoenician towns were more than one story, that they had windows and that they were built very close to the water. The ruins of ancient Byblos tend to confirm this. They lie in a jumble of old walls and foundations on a point of land jutting into the sea. The shoreline is abrupt and rocky, the old fortifica-

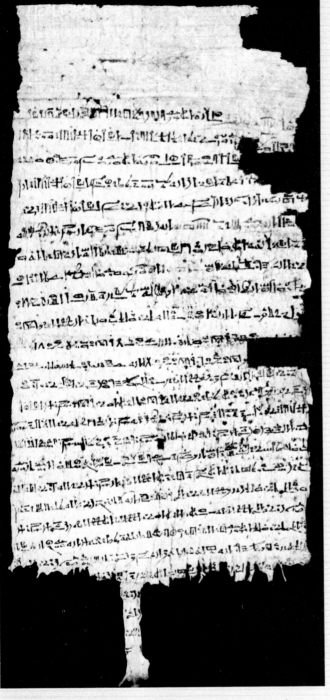

The adventures of Wen-Amon, a luckless agent sent up from Egypt to buy timber from King Zakar-Baal of Byblos, are described in this papyrus, which dates from the 11th Century B.C. Found in Egypt, it was bought and published by a Russian Egyptologist named Vladamir Golenischeff in 1899—at a time when Egypt's archeological treasures were being gobbled up by collectors. It is now in the Museum of Fine Arts in Moscow.

tions are right next to the water, and it is possible that the palace of a king interested in marine commerce could have been erected just within the walls, possibly overlooking a small snug harbor that still lies alongside. In bad weather a storm urged on by strong west winds would have sent the surf surging against those rocks. The spray could easily have flown a couple of stories high, to glisten in the sun behind the head of a king seated with his back to the light—the more easily to stare down a petitioner.

The king's reception of Wen-Amon was chilly. It boiled down to: "I'll sell you wood if you want, but you had jolly well better pay for it, and it doesn't look to me as if you can." He then hauled out some scrolls that recorded previous timber transactions. This reference also is revealing: it indicates that Byblian records were being kept on papyrus and not on clay tablets. It also confirms that Egypt had already been buying timber (not taking it in tribute) for a number of years—and at prices that made poor Wen-Amon, his pocketbook thin to begin with and now almost flattened by theft, wince.

Wen-Amon tried to remind Zakar-Baal of the long and close relationship between the two countries and of the importance of the great god Amon. None of this impressed Zakar-Baal in the slightest. He finally agreed to load as much wood as Wen-Amon had money for, not one stick more, then fixed the Egyptian agent with a cold kingly eye and said: "See, the commissions [substantial timber deliveries] that my fathers carried out formerly, I have carried out, even though you have not done for me what your fathers would have done for me [in gifts and payments]. . . . I did not even do to you what was done to the messengers of Ka-em Waset when they spent seventeen years in this land. They died [and were buried here]."

He offered to show Wen-Amon the tombs of the unfortunate messengers and began talking of other Egyptian agents whom he had detained until they too had died. Wen-Amon, thoroughly cowed, begged not to be shown the tombs and sent back a message to the pharaoh for more funds. In due course he got several jars of gold and silver, 10 bolts of Egyptian linen, 500 rolls of papyrus, 10 pieces of fine royal linen clothing, as well as 500 cowhides, 500 ropes, 20 sacks of lentils and five baskets of fish. He even got some lentils and fish for himself. With these he was able to complete his purchase of timber. His tale goes on to tell of the difficulties he had in getting away from Byblos—capture by pirates, shipwreck on Cyprus. Whatever became of the luckless Wen-Amon we do not know: the final parts of the papyrus that complete his story have never been found.

It is worth pausing a moment to compare Rib-Addi to Zakar-Baal. What a contrast there is between those two Byblian kings, separated by only 300 years in time. But for the emerging Phoenicians those 300 years measured the difference between dependence and independence. Rib-Addi is a petitioner, a leaner. For all his enterprise and his scurrying about, he knows that the real power lies elsewhere and that unless he has support he will go under. His letters are sprinkled with "My Lord, this" and "My Lord, that": "Let my Lord know that I would die for him. When I am in the city I will protect it for my Lord, and my heart is fixed on the King, my Lord."

Zakar-Baal stands squarely on his own feet. He will deal with the Egyptians if it suits him; if it doesn't, he won't—and the Egyptian envoy can rot in a dungeon forever, for all he cares. Zakar-Baal and the other Phoenician princes now emerging as heads of the various coastal cities are the survivors—the wiliest, most long-headed, the most accommodating and the most overbearing people in their societies. These traits have brought them to the top. They have survived 10 generations of turmoil. Power radiates from them. They have earned it and they know how to use it. And they will use it for nearly a thousand years.

Recoveries from the Earliest Known Shipwreck

The only known Phoenician trading vessel—and the oldest wreck of any kind yet discovered in the Mediterranean—was found and explored in 1960 by two Americans, George Bass and Peter Throckmorton. Their studies of this wreck reveal clearly that it was the ship of a traveling metalworker who probably was headed west in about 1200 B.C. with a cargo of copper ingots and pieces of bronze and tin. His ship apparently hit some rocks in a storm just off the Turkish coast near Cape Gelidonya, then filled with water and sank. However, it did not turn over and spill out its cargo. Rather, it slid down a steep underwater slope with all its trade goods still inside and came to rest in about 90 feet of water. To retrieve the cargo, divers had to work in swift currents at a depth that limited their time underwater.

The 1960 expedition's main surface vessel was a Turkish sponge dragger. It had a powerful winch, shown here bringing up copper ingots cemented together by marine deposits from the 3,200-year-old ship lying below.

Problems in Recognition and Recovery

The Gelidonya wreck was deeply encrusted with a coating of marine deposits. At first only a few of the bonded lumps lying on the bottom were recognized as man-made. But as the divers became more familiar with their discovery, they realized that many of the "rocks" lying about in the bluish light were in fact artifacts.

The archeologists had to devise new ways of mapping each piece of their find, then of getting the large, heavy chunks up to the surface. Once ashore, the finds were carefully broken into smaller pieces and the rocklike covering chipped away to expose what was inside. This painstaking process revealed such articles as ingots, a seal, a lamp, beads, weights and measures, anvils, metal tools, broken pottery—and pieces of the ship itself.

Raising heavy chunks of material from the sea bottom posed serious problems: first, coping with great weight under water; and then the hazard that a load might slip and fall, crushing other artifacts. One solution: a balloon that helped float loads to the surface.

A detailed drawing to mark the exact location of every object in the wreck was made before each find was brought to the surface. Here a draftsman sketches the positions of sticks that had been packed between items of cargo in the ship's hold to ease chafing.

One of the expedition's divers sets down his hammer to collect small objects that had been hidden beneath a pile of ingots. The bicolored ruled bar, at left under his flippers, was used to facilitate painstakingly accurate mapping of every single item found.

Putting the Pieces Together Again on a Rocky Shore

The difficulties encountered underwater at Cape Gelidonya were matched by those at the shore camp. Temperatures on the narrow beach soared into the 100s. Flies bit unmercifully, requiring the scientists to crouch under nettings while they worked. By the end of summer, storms rose, flooding the beach and leaving big drifts of sand. Rocks fell intermittently from the cliffs overhead, and there was a threat of rain-induced avalanches. For all this, the entire cargo was raised, cleaned and identified. The biggest single category was 34 copper "oxhide" ingots, so called because of their shape. Some were intact. Others—because they were lying next to bars of tin—were partly eaten away by electrolysis: the result of salt-water action on the two metals.

Several ingots, welded by encrustation into a single chunk, lie on the deck of the surface vessel. An automobile jack was used to pry pieces loose from the rocky bottom, with great care taken not to crack the ingots themselves.

George Bass (above left) and Peter Throckmorton examine some of the 34 copper ingots. Their oxhide shape was common in the Bronze Age for ease in handling, not—as some think—because each ingot was worth one ox.

Artifacts already chipped clean are laid out on the beach for study. The woman (foreground) is sifting through bottom debris in search of such small objects as carved scarabs. At rear: the expedition's mess table and kitchen.

Fossil ships (to use the term very loosely), like fossil humans, are extremely rare. Wood disintegrates as readily as bone and, like bone, requires the protection of something to preserve it: the still water of a bog where plant growth can be deposited to form peat; the quieting arm of a harbor or bay, preferably one at the mouth of a river whose steady freight of silt will gradually cover the harbor bottom; a spot along the coast where a combination of ocean currents and storms can move large quantities of sand.

Amateur underwater prospecting has been going on in the Mediterranean for a long time. In recent years, with the development of scuba equipment, it has vastly accelerated. As a result, all the best-known and most accessible hulks from the classical world have been disturbed and looted so that they are virtually worthless for archeological study. Understandably, there is no greater thrill for the amateur diver than to find a cluster of encrusted wine jars lying in a nest of half-buried timbers, and no greater temptation than to pry a couple of jars or beams loose to be carried off, perhaps to a different continent, for display on a mantelpiece.

Nonetheless, such pilfering destroys a much greater treasure. The wine jar, beautiful and interesting as it may be, or the worm-eaten timber—despite the fantasies it may conjure up—retains its true value only in the context of all the objects and ship parts surrounding it. By itself it is simply a curiosity.

Good pictures of Phoenician ships are very rare. This one of a warship is among the best. From an Assyrian wall relief carved about 700 B.C., it shows a bireme (i.e., a ship propelled by two banks of oars) with a shield-lined upper deck, or catwalk, on which archers and soldiers stood. Projecting from its bow is a long, pointed beak for ramming enemy vessels.

That is why the emergence of one end of a ship in 1971, as a result of sand-dredging in the shallow water near Marsala at the western tip of Sicily, has caused such a stir among marine archeologists, particularly those interested in Phoenician naval history. For there is a strong possibility that this hulk may be Carthaginian. Furthermore, its study from the very start has been under the protection and direction of a team of professional underwater archeologists headed by an Englishwoman, Honor Frost (page 35).

Frost is an experienced diver who has worked in the Mediterranean for a number of years. She has an exclusive contract with the Italian government to investigate the Isola Lunga wreck—so-called because of its proximity to an island of that name. And while it will take years before the Frost team can fully interpret its findings, the evidence so far holds out the promise of new insights into late Phoenician ship construction and use.

To begin with, there is the possibility that the Isola Lunga hulk, which dates from the Third Century B.C., may be a warship—nothing like the Gelidonya wreck described in Chapter 1, which is a cargo vessel. The latter comes from the east, from Byblos or Tyre perhaps; it is relatively small and dates from about 1200 B.C. The former comes from Phoenicia West, is perhaps three times as large and may be as much as a thousand years younger.

As the Isola Lunga wreck is cleared of its mantle of sand, one by one its parts are being meticulously plotted, numbered, raised and then put in fresh-water tanks in the Palermo Museum. There they will be soaked for three years to remove all traces of salt before being impregnated with a chemical to preserve them. After that, an attempt will be made to reassemble the pieces of the wreck for museum display.

Accurate reconstruction of ancient hulks is next to impossible. When a wooden ship sinks it eventually spreads and comes apart as a result of gradual rotting, water movement and the weight of its own cargo or ballast. It ends up flattened out on the sea bottom, its original contours and dimensions hard to recapture. This problem has been made especially acute for classical wrecks by the total absence of ships' ends. Why bows and sterns are more prone to disintegration than amidships parts I do not know; it may only be because they stick up farther from the protective sand. But the fact remains that neither bow nor stern of a classical wreck, among the hundreds that dot the Mediterranean floor, had ever been recovered—until Isola Lunga.

Here is a well-preserved ship's end, with pieces of protective lead sheathing still attached to it, along with bits of the original cloth padding that was packed under the lead, the whole held in place by copper tacks still embedded in the wood. Frost believes it to be a stern, but she cannot be sure until she uncovers the rest of the vessel. Whichever it turns out to be, it is an invaluable find, for its shape should provide sufficient clues to show the rate at which the hull widens. Once this is known and related to the overall length of the hull (in this case probably 90 feet), some pretty shrewd estimates can be made of its beam and its cross-section curves. Therefore, when the true shape of the Isola Lunga wreck is worked out, Frost thinks it will be possible to establish with fair certainty that it was indeed a warship, assuming that its hull turns out to be long and slender. This would prove that the ship was designed for speed—by propulsion from many oars.

In addition to yielding up one of its ends, the Isola Lunga hulk has provided some bits of superstructure (another first for classical wrecks) and a large number of frames and planks, the latter with neat mortise-and-tenon joints that show how the planking was held together. Frost hopes that further recoveries will include some sections of decking, more planking and —given extraordinary fortune—a few of the rowers' benches. If this particular material can be found and coherently fitted together, Frost may succeed in solving a riddle that has plagued marine archeologists ever since they started thinking about it: How were ancient warships with more than one bank of oars rowed? How were the oarsmen seated?

The standard warship of the Third Century B.C. was a trireme, a "three-banker." By that time every naval power had triremes in their fleets. Occasional pictures of them show up in wall paintings and in frescoes. They have even been found on pottery and in carved relief on temples.

But their details, particularly their inner workings, are nowhere clearly illustrated. Consequently nobody knows for certain how the rowers of those three banks of oars were fitted into the ship. If Frost's studies enable her to throw some light on the "trireme problem" it will be a great achievement.

She may also be able to establish beyond doubt that the ship is indeed Carthaginian and not Roman, as some scholars suspect. Her strongest case here would seem to lie in the discovery of a series of carpenters' marks, apparently based on the Phoenician alphabet, painted on some of the ship's timbers. The marks were easily seen by the divers, and although they have since faded they were copied while still fresh by an expert who is studying them. So far, more

A Rare Find in Sicilian Waters

The only known relic of a ship suspected of being a Carthaginian war vessel is buried in sand beneath eight feet of water at Isola Lunga in western Sicily. A team of archeologists headed by the English scuba diver Honor Frost has been working on the hulk since it was exposed by sand dredgers in 1971. Unlike other ancient hulks, it has not been vandalized; from it, in the years to come, the team hopes to learn much more than is presently known about ships with multiple banks of oars. They also may be able to figure out where this vessel was first launched by identifying the native rocks that served as its ballast and that still lie piled around it, and by identifying the dunnage—sticks, leaves and twigs of various kinds collected at the launch site and used to protect the hull from being chafed by the rock ballast. Although the wood of the ship itself has already been determined—oak, maple and pine—that knowledge does not help in establishing the launch site; the wood probably was imported in bulk by the shipwright from other places.

Sand removal around the Isola Lunga hulk has already revealed part of its keel, a couple of dozen ribs and sections of its planking (top picture). The black-and-white metal pipes have been put down on the sea bottom to form a grid for precise location of the ship's parts before they are brought ashore. The vessel's apparent sternpost (bottom picture), projecting from the sand, led to the hulk's discovery. It is the only ancient ship's end ever found. Lead sheathing and the copper nails that held it are still in place.

From Log Raft to True Boat

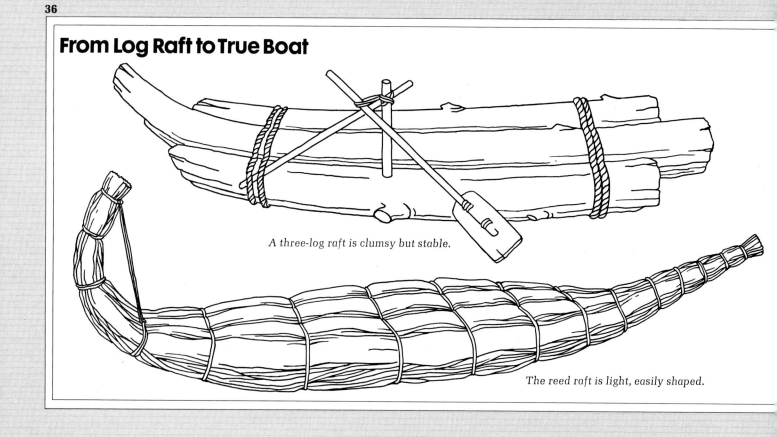

A three-log raft is clumsy but stable.

The reed raft is light, easily shaped.

than 100 of these carpenters' marks have been discovered, covering 10 of the 22 letters of the Phoenician alphabet. For Frost, this makes the Carthaginian origin of the ship unmistakable. Others are not so sure, nor are they sure she has found a warship. The naval historian Lionel Casson points out that ballast was seldom carried in naval vessels; it would have made the warships unnecessarily heavy and would not have been needed for stability in craft designed with a low center of gravity. He also points out that lead sheathing is characteristic of cargo vessels. But Frost is sticking to her guns. She believes that the shape of the ship will bear her out. If she is right, it will.

Meanwhile Frost reasons that the markings indicate some kind of mass-production activity. It is known that the Carthaginians often built large fleets in a very short time to meet political emergencies. The quickest and most sensible way to do this, of course, would have been to build ships of a standard size and to keep a large prefabricated warehouse

stock of plank "A," plank "B," frame "C" and so on.

Speculation about where the Isola Lunga ship was built is also possible. The clues here are the stones used for ballast and the dunnage placed under those stones to keep them from gouging the wood in the hull bottom. The ballast, which is being studied by a geologist, seems to consist of volcanic rock from Pantelleria, a Carthaginian-held island near Sicily. The dunnage turns out to be a highly interesting mixture of wood chips, the shells of nuts and a quantity of twigs and leaves from such diverse trees as oak, maple, pistachio and olive—10 or more varieties in all. If a place can be found where all these grew in abundance and where there also is a good supply of the right kind of stone, it logically could be assumed that the Isola Lunga ship was built and launched there.

The reason is that this ship seems to have been a brand-new one whose caulking was still not entirely dry when it was launched, and whose dunnage was also fresh—green stuff that had just been gathered. If the vessel had been old, the possibility of pinpoint-

A dugout is dry but extremely heavy.

Best: The coracle, a frame boat with a "skin."

The earliest form of watercraft undoubtedly was the log; seen floating on rivers, its buoyancy was quickly recognized. Lashing several logs together to carry a load was a natural development. In the Nile, bundles of papyrus were shaped for the same purpose. The hollowed log, which offered protection and extra buoyancy, came later. But digging out a log was a backbreaking job and, of course, was not possible where logs themselves were absent. At some point skins or small planks were attached to a wood frame, and the boat was born.

ing its origin would not be nearly as good, because dunnage is replaced from time to time and there would be no telling where it came from.

How did ships themselves come into being? Man is not a seagoing creature. Unlike almost all other mammals, he does not swim naturally. A man who has not learned how and who falls into the water will probably drown. And yet in all societies that have developed near water man has learned to venture out on it in boats of every conceivable type.

The oldest boat so far discovered dates from about 6000 B.C.: the remains of a wooden dugout exhumed from a bog in Holland. The oldest-known picture of a boat is much younger. It dates from about 3400 B.C. and is a drawing of a fairly sophisticated Egyptian river craft with several oars or paddles on each side. By 3000 B.C. bits of pottery from the Aegean Islands begin to show up; on them are scratched drawings of a long, low boat with many oars. Quite an ambitious craft, it was surely able to go from island to island.

Both the Holland dugout and the Mediterranean picture are obviously products of a long evolution from more primitive forms. Here is one of the tantalizing problems that arise when one tries to unravel the misty origins of one of man's inventions. The first evidence of it—hard evidence that a fact-respecting scientist can put his thumb on—is usually that of a rather sophisticated device. What took place before that is pure guesswork. Nevertheless, a considerable prior history must be assumed.

The simplest water vehicle of all is the log. And the raft is a fairly simple extension of that idea. Several logs lashed together will provide a more stable, drier platform than a single log can—something a man can sit on instead of merely clinging to.

A hollowed log, or dugout, is a far more sophisticated device than a raft. Whereas the latter relies on its own instantly apparent buoyancy (It floats! It will support me!), the dugout must be crafted into a dish that displaces water and relies on that displacement for its ability to float and carry things. It can be either a log hollowed out as thin and light as crude technology permits, or it can be a watertight skin stretched over a framework of bent branches; the principle is the same. But it is a far more advanced notion than that of a raft. Nevertheless, both dugout and raft are capable of considerable development. Both forms evolved in the Mediterranean, and threads of that evolution can be traced.

The story is clearest in Egypt where, thanks to the extreme dryness of the climate, a great number of tomb paintings, papyri, wall sculptures and actual models of a wide variety of boats have been preserved. The Nile was Egypt's source of life as well as her thoroughfare, and her boats took an evolutionary course most suitable to river conditions. The earliest river craft of the Egyptians were rafts. They came in all sizes and were made of bundles of papyrus reed, since good wood was in short supply. Later, when a demand for larger and more durable craft developed —particularly for the movement up and down river of heavy loads of building stone—the Egyptians did develop true boats, some of considerable size, almost all of them made of local acacia wood.

Acacia wood is poor stuff. It is hard enough, but the trees tend to be small and crooked and can yield only short, narrow boards. Consequently, a typical Egyptian river boat of any size must have looked something like a floating jigsaw puzzle, with its quantity of small planks all neatly fastened together—the butts joined by wooden dowels and the sides held together by hourglass-shaped pegs, somewhat like the dovetail construction of a bureau drawer.

This method of building, while ingenious, is extremely fussy and inherently weak—suitable for protected river waters but not for putting out to sea.

It is interesting to note that when the Egyptians got around to exploring rougher waters they had to strengthen their boats.

One problem they had to contend with was "hogging," the tendency of a long overhanging bow or stern to droop down. The surge of ocean waves will exploit this weakness, even to the point of breaking the back of the vessel and sending it to the bottom. Since Egyptian river craft did have long raised bows to facilitate running up on river banks, this problem was serious. It was dealt with in an extremely clever way that is clearly pictured in numerous Egyptian wall carvings. A heavy, multistranded rope was fastened to the bow and stern; in between, it passed over a couple of crutchlike posts that stuck up six or eight feet from the deck. By inserting a bar through the rope's strands and twisting it, a ship's captain could tighten the rope like a tourniquet and hold up the bow and stern to whatever extent was needed. This tourniquet, known as a truss, also increased the overall rigidity of the hull.

It is certain that the coastal Canaanites, whom the Egyptians had begun visiting as early as 3000 B.C. to get timber, had numerous opportunities to examine at their leisure Egyptian trussed ships and to note whatever useful refinements in hull construction or rig the visitors had devised. We have no evidence at all that the Canaanites had developed a maritime capability of their own at this early date. But their proximity to the sea makes it probable that they had. If so, it is most likely that they did not copy Egyptian models, for they were also being exposed to a different, and better, method of ship construction.

By the time the Egyptians were going up to Byblos in their patchwork trussed ships, other peoples—Minoans and Mycenaean Greeks—were coming down to Byblos from the northwest in long, narrow, better-made vessels that were essentially large dugout canoes whose sides were built up to increase capacity. As this type of vessel evolved, the dugout log —which originally had been the basic boat—was reduced in size and function to a long rigid keel to which built-up sides of the vessel were attached.

Thus the citizens of a place like Byblos were confronted very early with two basically different concepts of ship construction. The Egyptians first built a shell of many small pieces and later added ribs and thwarts—and possibly a strengthening member along the bottom. Northerners laid down that strengthening member—the keel—first and anchored the planking to that. This latter method of ship construction is far superior to the Egyptian method and has been followed right up to modern times. What made it possible, of course, was the availability of large trees, which were lacking in Egypt. Since the coastal Canaanites had an abundance of excellent timber for the strong keels that seagoing ships need, it is overwhelmingly logical that they followed the Aegean rather than the Egyptian tradition.

Logical it may be, but in the present state of knowledge it cannot be certain. The early Aegean legacy is far skimpier than the Egyptian. Nothing survives from around 3000 B.C. beyond those cryptic little scratched drawings on broken bits of pottery, and they are so crudely done that it is impossible to tell anything about the ships they represent except that they had oars and extremely high stemposts as their bows. Or is it sterns? Experts are not entirely sure, although they suspect they are bows because some have figureheads in the form of fish pointing in a for-

ward direction. Better documented vessels of later periods commonly had carved objects of one sort or another in their bows: birds, fish, the heads of animals. Many had large eyes painted on each side of the bow. The purpose of all such ornaments was to help the vessel see its course or speed it on its way.

Not until about 2000 B.C. did pictures of vessels definitely known as Minoan begin to appear. Then, rather suddenly, there were a good many of them. The Minoans were superb potters, and many of their jars and vases are decorated with paintings of ships. They also carved enormous numbers of small personal seals. These were the "signatures," or identifying emblems, of individual men and were widely used for the signing of clay tablets.

Seldom more than an inch or two long, Minoan seals were exquisitely carved on very hard stone. It is possible to make sharp impressions from many of them even today. Those that depict ships show a vessel of a characteristic type. It had a sensible rounded hull, turned up at either end for seaworthiness. It had a mast amidships and ropes of some material for raising and trimming a sail. Vessels of this general type would, in the following centuries, make their way throughout the Mediterranean. They are the most logical model for the proto-Phoenician seagoing trader to have copied. In fact, the first-known picture of a Phoenician ship (page 32), carved on the wall of an Assyrian palace in about 700 B.C., bears a close resemblance to the Minoan designs that were approximately a thousand years older.

Summarizing this admittedly sketchy skein of evidence: the most likely prototype for the Phoenician ship was a vessel with a rounded hull and a strong keel derived from Aegean models. By 2000 B.C., per-

haps even earlier, the ancestors of the Phoenicians in Lebanon were putting it to local coastal use. Certainly it was in wide use by 1500 B.C. It was driven by sails or by oars, or by both—the former being the principal propulsive agent for cargo vessels, the latter for warships.

Where did oars and sails come from? This is another very elusive and tantalizing question. The oar was surely preceded by the paddle, and paddling is probably about as old as boats themselves. The first men to use log rafts to cross lakes or rivers undoubtedly learned rather quickly that they could propel them better with broad, flattened sticks than they could with their hands. Very early—on the evidence of wall art and actual models—the Egyptians were using well-shaped paddles with broad blades.

In due course, some genius invented the oar. This does not seem like a very momentous discovery, but it was. The oar is far superior to the paddle in power because the rower is using a fulcrum—an oarlock, a loop of rope, a thole pin or simply a hole in the side of the boat—as a brace against which he exerts his strength efficiently by pulling on one end of the oar as the other bites the water. A rower does not have to lift the weight of his oar for every stroke as a paddler does: the oar is supported by the side of the boat. Therefore, an oar can be much longer and heavier than a paddle—with multiple advantages. The most obvious is that an oar can be used in a larger boat from a higher position above the water. A paddler sitting in such a position would have to have such a long, heavy paddle simply to reach the water that he would quickly become exhausted by the mere effort of lifting it for successive strokes. Paddles are useful only in long narrow craft where the user can sit close to the water and close to the edge of the boat, as he does in a canoe. For anything significantly higher or wider, oars are superior.

Furthermore, two men cannot operate one paddle, but they can sit side by side on a seat to pull on one oar from positions quite far inboard from the side of the boat. This has important implications for the multiple use of oars in warships.

The Egyptians were using paddles from time immemorial for their reed rafts and small river boats. By 3000 B.C. they had shifted to oars for their larger craft. But by that time Aegean ships were oar-driven too. One may have learned from the other, or the improvement may have come about independently in both places. Whichever the case, the oar as a familiar and superior device for seagoing vessels was widely known by the time the ancestors of the Phoenicians began going to sea.

The invention of the sail, like that of the oar, was momentous. It provided man with a power supply far stronger and more enduring than his own muscles and transformed the waterways of the world from barriers into highways. Like boats themselves, sails probably were first developed in the relatively safe confines of lakes and rivers: the Nile, the Tigris and Euphrates, the great rivers of India and China. Sailing craft emerged in all those places, each with individual styles that would persist down through the centuries. But in all places the primitive sail was essentially the same.

It was the simplest kind of device imaginable and reflected man's dawning realization that if he hung up a piece of cloth or a mat where the wind could catch it he would be blown along. For this he needed a pole (a mast) to hold up the sail and a cross-piece (a boom or yard) to spread it out so that it could fill with wind. These needs produced a single square sail almost identical with the kind that boys still put on toy boats whittled from shingles. Shingle boats have their masts up near the bow, since they are designed to be blown before the wind and go straightest with their masts so situated. The earliest river boats probably did the same. The oldest-known picture of a sailboat—once again Egyptian and dating from about 2900 B.C.—shows the mast and sail up near the bow.

The Egyptians conceivably could have been the first people anywhere to use sails. They were extremely inventive, and the peculiar conditions of the Nile could have beckoned them in that direction with an almost overwhelming persuasiveness. The Nile lies in a north-south direction. The current flows steadily north and the wind blows just as steadily south. This meant that a boat with a sail could be wafted upstream against the current without any effort beyond that of steering. Coming back downstream, the boatman could lower his sail and drift with the current. Oars could have been used either way to increase speed or improve steerage.

Early Egyptian masts were tall and often were "bipods"—i.e., double masts running up from the sides of the boat and coming together at the top. The reason for this design seems to have been that reed rafts were too flimsy to support the entire weight of a single mast at one spot in the center of a boat; a bipod distributed the weight better.

Conditions on the open sea are quite different from the predictable, protected ones on the Nile. It is often extremely rough at sea. Currents are variable, often depending on the direction of the wind. The winds themselves vary with the seasons, even with the days or hours. Sometimes they do not blow at all. It is those conditions that produced the useful little vessels shown on Minoan seals, vessels which—in the opinion of many experts, an opinion I share —were ancestral to the trading vessels of the Phoenicians. The differences in design between them and Egyptian ships clearly reflect the differences in the conditions under which they operated.

The Phoenician cargo vessel probably ranged between 30 and 80 feet in length. Although it may have had oars for getting in and out of crowded anchorages and for progress in calms and against headwinds, its principal propulsive agent was its sail, whose design represented a considerable improvement over the tall early Egyptian version. The Phoenician mast was short, probably set in a mast step or slot in the bottom of the ship. Since the Phoenician hull had a very strong backbone in the heavy wooden beam that served as its keel, the butt of the mast could rest in its step with little danger of being driven through the bottom of the hull. A short mast promised good hull stability during squalls and gales, and reduced strains aloft.

Even a short mast will give trouble if it is not set tight in its step and held firm aloft by stays. This makes lowering the mast a nuisance. While it could be done in ancient vessels, particularly warships, it probably was seldom resorted to in cargo vessels —which presented the Phoenicians with the problem of how to shorten sail. They could not simply lower it. The wooden boom, or yard, from which it hung was heavy; it had taken a great deal of sweating to haul it up the mast in the first place. Once up, no sensible ship's master would have lowered the yard unless he had to, particularly since pulleys with revolving sheaves were unknown in ancient times, and ropes were thick, unevenly made and unreliable. Without proper pulleys, even a modern rope will chafe through quite quickly. Frequent raising and lowering of a heavy yard would have worn out in no time the inferior hoisting halyards of the past. So, once up, a yard stayed up, and the problem remained: How did one furl a square sail without lowering it?

The Phoenicians, or some Greek or Minoan predecessor, solved the problem very neatly. They attached ropes, called brails, to the bottom edge of the sail, half a dozen or more of them, and ran them vertically up the sail's front side, fastening them at intervals to the sailcloth. The brails were then led over the top of the sail and down to the deck. Crew members standing on the deck and hauling on the brails could draw up the sail like a Venetian blind, bunching it in loose folds against the bottom of the yard.

Another basic improvement incorporated into the Phoenician trading ship was a better positioning of the mast. A simple river craft going before the wind up the Nile could sail straight upstream with its mast forward. But for a seagoing vessel expected to move in a number of directions under a variety of wind conditions, the Phoenicians needed something more versatile. With the mast amidships, and with ropes called braces leading from the outermost tips of the yard all the way down to the deck, it was possible to swing the yard so that the sail—instead of lying at right angles to the direction of the ship—could be set almost parallel to it. This innovation allowed the vessel to take advantage of winds coming from the side and still roll speedily along in the direction the captain wished, instead of being able to utilize only those winds that came from directly astern.

Since much of the voyaging the Phoenicians engaged in on the Mediterranean was in a general east-west direction, that meant that the winds that often blow from north and south there—and heretofore useless a good deal of the time—could now be used for travel in either direction virtually all of the time. As the traders became more and more familiar with wind patterns in their great inland sea, they surely exploited them seasonally, hugging one coast on the way west to take advantage of the breezes that blow favorably there in spring, but following a different course and different breezes in summer and fall. Along the African coast, for example, the prevailing winds are easterly from May to October, and westerly from October to May.

But no Phoenician ship could "go to windward" —that is, sail at better than a right angle to the breeze, zigzagging back and forth, gaining a little each time

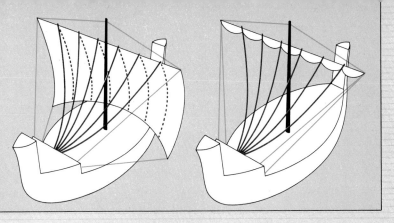

and gradually working its way upwind. If a trader's course lay directly into the eye of the wind, there was nothing to do but furl sail, grit teeth and start rowing—or wait for the wind to shift.

Steering the Phoenician coastal trader was no great problem, although the true rudder—one that hangs amidships from the stern—would not be invented for another couple of thousand years. All ancient sailing ships were controlled by steering oars, hanging down from each side of the ship near the stern.

What living conditions were like aboard Phoenician traders is a mystery. No drawings, models or carvings exist to show the interiors of any ancient vessels, except for some of the specialized Egyptian river craft. Since we also do not know how large a ship's crew was—whether its members doubled as sail handlers, boatswains, riggers, loaders and un-loaders when the ship was beached for trading—life aboard can only be surmised.

Somewhere on the vessel there may have been a platform with a sand base in which a fire could be lit for cooking. Otherwise there probably were no ame-nities whatsoever, for traders of that time preferred to travel only during the day. At night they beached their boats and went ashore.

If it rained they probably went back aboard and sprawled on the rowers' benches below decks or tried to find comfortable places in the cargo. Decking, with hatches to give access below, can be assumed. It has multiple advantages: it is a hull strengthener and a protector of cargo that might be spoiled by rain or salt spray; it guards against instant swamping if a huge sea should come aboard; and it provides a plat-form for cargo, whether livestock or lumber, that does not suffer from a wetting.

So much for the Phoenician merchant vessels, the unobtrusive but persistent work horses of the Med-iterranean, showing up wherever there was business to be done—beamy, rounded, durable, efficient and known in the waterfront slang of whatever port they put into as "tubs."

How different was the warship. Originally, all sea-going ships of the Greek and Minoan strain probably were pretty much alike. Naval warfare had not yet evolved as a special way of fighting and therefore commanders did not need specially designed fighting craft. They used ships primarily as troop transports and supply carriers. But inevitably there were shrewd tacticians who began to realize that it was easier to destroy enemy troops at sea by drowning than it was to kill them in hand-to-hand combat on the beach. Somewhere along the line vessels designed to fight other vessels began to evolve.

The fighting ship had to be fast and maneuverable, able to carry a large number of fighting men. It had to provide places for these men to stand and from which they could shoot arrows, wield pikes or—at an instant's notice—jump over the side and wade di-rectly into battle if the action was on the beach or, if at sea, force their way aboard an enemy vessel and engage that enemy on his own deck.

The vessel that these needs produced was long and low and narrow, and propelled by oars. It had a sail used only to get from place to place, never in com-bat. Winds were too fickle and in summer sometimes entirely absent. Smart commanders therefore left their masts and sails ashore before big sea battles so as not to clutter up their decks during the fighting. In consequence, most of the great naval engagements of classical times were fought very close to shore, sometimes in narrow bays or harbors, sometimes only a mile or so off the coast.

They often took place under the gaze of people whose lives were riding on the outcome. Crowds of Greeks and Persians stood on different bluffs and headlands surrounding the Strait of Salamis to watch a Greek fleet meet and destroy a larger Persian one (pages 49-55). Among the Persians was their monarch, Xerxes, who sat on a throne that had been carried a thousand miles from Persepolis for just this purpose. Doing by far the best fighting for his side was a squadron of Phoenician mercenary ships. When they were finally beaten along with the others and Persian hopes for conquering Greece sunk with the wreckage of Xerxes' fleet, Xerxes summoned the Phoenician captains and according to legend had them all murdered.

Salamis was fought in 480 B.C. By that time both the Greek and the Phoenician war galleys had evolved into highly specialized and remarkably similar war machines, culminating almost two thousand years of development. A war galley is essentially a long rowboat: long so there will be room for a large crew of oarsmen to move it fast; narrow to make it as light as possible and also so that it will slip smoothly and easily through the water. But narrowness produces a serious problem that is best illustrated by a quick look at a modern eight-oared racing shell.

The racing shell is needle narrow, barely wide enough to accommodate the hips of the oarsmen, who sit one in back of another. If a racing shell's oarlock (the fulcrum against which the oar is pulled) is placed on the gunwale, or edge, of the boat, the rower will have to use either a ridiculously short and inefficient oar or one of sensible length but with a handle so close to the fulcrum that he cannot exert enough leverage to pull it. The solution, of course, is not to pivot the oar on the gunwale but on an outrigger that projects about three feet from the side of the boat. This way the oarsman gets all the leverage he needs to pull an oar that may be twice as long as he is.

According to a tentative reconstruction offered by the naval archeologist Bjorn Landstrom, the early galleys used in the Aegean, dating back to about 3000 B.C., were large dugouts made of tree trunks, with outriggers slanting out from each gunwale and running the length of the boat. The oars, maybe a dozen to a side, rested on the outriggers, giving the rowers plenty of pulling leverage. With the addition of small platforms or decks in the bow and stern to hold fighting men and helmsmen, this interpretation produces a hull that must have been about 65 feet long and four feet wide, not counting the outriggers—light enough and slender enough to be driven fairly fast by its two dozen oarsmen.

A larger, more powerful dugout with, say, 50 rowers could have overtaken and destroyed a 24-oared ship if it could have caught it offshore. The hitch was in the catching. A 50-oared ship would necessarily have been nearly twice as long and therefore handicapped by a much larger turning radius. Its more nimble adversary, always able to make tighter turns, probably could have kept away from a large ship almost indefinitely and in the process totally exhausted the oarsmen of the heavier pursuing vessel. In actual combat, of course, such simple matchups seldom occurred. As noted before, naval battles often took place where maneuverability was limited, and engagements almost always involved fleets of considerable size: dozens, sometimes scores, even hundreds

The Phoenician Cargo Vessel

Phoenician trading ships came in a variety of sizes, but all were built very much to the pattern shown here: tubby vessels about three or four times as long as they were wide, with high bows and sterns. Their planking was completely covered with pitch (not shown here) to make them watertight, which explains Homer's phrase for them: "black ships." Each had a single mast stepped approximately amidships, with one square sail hanging from a long wooden pole, or yard, and controlled by two ropes—braces—running from the yard ends to the deck. The other seven ropes—brails —leading down from the yard were for furling the sail (page 43). The sail was trimmed by ropes attached to its lower corners. Steering was managed by means of two oars controlled by a single helmsman. He stood between them and turned the oar blades in the water by pushing or pulling the two short, horizontal tillers.

of ships on a side. A fleet of big galleys moving up abreast could surround little ones, unless the little ones had big ones of their own for protection.

Naval warfare, despite the relative simplicity of ancient ships, has itself never been simple. A fleet had to have vessels of various types if it expected to succeed in battle. Maneuvers and strategy were as intricate as they are today.

The better fleet was, almost by definition, the one with the better rowers. It was as simple as that, which is why slaves were not used in fighting ships; their reliability was too uncertain. A war galley had to have highly trained, patriotic citizens willing to pull their hearts out. If the ability of the rowers made a ship faster and more maneuverable than an enemy ship, the enemy was doomed. Sooner or later the faster vessel would get the other into a position where it could not avoid being rammed broadside or in its unprotected stern by a sharp beak that stuck out from every warship's prow just below the water line.

Some authorities give credit to the Phoenicians for developing the ram, which apparently was invented around 1000 B.C., just about the time the eastern ports were emerging as trading powers in their own right and building up their war fleets. If the Phoenicians did not invent the ram, they were quick to adopt it; for it was a revolutionary development that would affect naval strategy for centuries. A good smash from a ram and a skillful backing away by the rammer's oarsmen would leave the other vessel in a helpless condition with a huge hole stove in her side. The rammer could then depart to seek out another enemy vessel or lie fairly close by while her archers methodically picked off the enemy soldiers and oarsmen struggling in the water.

Since speed was so decisive, and since the only way to achieve speed in galleys was with human muscles, ancient warships began to grow in size in order to accommodate more power. But growth carries a penalty. Long thin ships are slow turners and, if made too long and thin, fatally fragile amidships; they cannot withstand the shocks of bumping or ramming. What then does one do to accommodate more rowers and still keep one's ship fairly short? One solution is to put several men on the same oar and give them a bigger oar to tug on. But to do that the ship must be made wider so that there is room on each bench for four or five men sitting abreast. This is not a very good solution. For one thing, a wide ship tends to be heavy and sluggish. For another, since an oar enters the boat at an angle, the longer the oar is, the higher above the rowers' bench it will be at its inboard end —too high perhaps for the inmost rower to pull on it unless he stands up at the beginning of each stroke and sits down again at the end of it. Because rowing, particularly combat rowing, is exhausting work to begin with, all that extra sitting and standing will wear out a crew just that much faster. A better solution is to have two banks of oars, one above the other.

Again, the Phoenicians may have had a hand in developing the two-banked ship, or bireme. The vessels shown on the Assyrian wall carving at Nineveh are two-bankers. However, paintings of biremes also begin to show up on Greek vases of about the same date. Naval historian Lionel Casson says that with the present evidence it is impossible to decide which of the two was the inventor. "Whichever it was," Casson goes on, "the other quickly followed suit." Like the ram, it was a stunning invention and, like all truly original ideas, very simple.

It would be nice to imagine some now-forgotten genius sitting down at his drawing board and saying: "Let me see; we have ships of 12 oars to a side.

"I've been ordered to design a ship with 24 oars to a side. If I design it the old way, the ship will come out looking like this:

"That is much too long and unwieldy. But suppose I make my ship higher and build another row of benches over the first one. Then I can stagger the oars like this:

"That does it. I've doubled the rowing power, with a ship that is very little longer than the original."

Unfortunately, it probably did not happen that way. Just how and when that upper row of oarsmen became a permanent feature of the fighting galley and turned it into a bireme is not known. Some Greek vase paintings of this period show two banks of rowers at work, some show only one. But in those that show only one, it is often the upper bank that is doing the rowing. Empty slots for the lower oars and tholepins for fastening them are carefully drawn. Experts conclude that while cruising the lower position was not apt to be used.

This makes sense. From the rower's point of view, the lower banks of those old galleys were uncomfortably close to the water. Clearing an oar after a stroke must have been a hard job in rough seas, particularly in a narrow hull that was rolling badly and dipping alternate sides. Catching crabs (being unable to get one's oar out of the water in time to keep up with the other rowers) would have been commonplace—with all the bruising of ribs and smashing of knuckles that resulted, not to mention the broken rhythm of the stroke. In bad weather, therefore, and when not absolutely necessary because of fighting, the lowest bank in a multibanked vessel probably was not used. In combat, however, the lower position probably was preferred during close-in fighting; it protected the rowers and left the upper deck clear for the soldiers. It was only a step from there to the use of both banks and to the design of ships that made that practical.

In calm water and during battle, what a tremendous improvement the bireme was. Scarcely longer than a one-banked vessel, it packed nearly double the muscle. In time, the Phoenicians and the Greeks would develop three-bankers—called triremes—and these would become the standard big warships of their respective fleets. By 500 B.C. they were common in the Mediterranean.

With the trireme perfected, an ancient war fleet was a formidable weapon. The Carthaginians became superb naval fighters. They were masters at the maneuver of attack at full speed, in line, abreast. They would row right through the enemy ships, whirl quickly around and attack them from the rear. If the enemy bunched tight to prevent this, the Carthaginians would execute end runs and again attack from behind against ships that were so tightly packed they were getting in one another's way. They also perfected a technique of near-head-on collisions, sliding by an enemy so close that the oncoming hull of the Carthaginian vessel would shear off the oars on one side of the opposing ship and leave it helpless.

The confusion of a major naval engagement waged between two large, evenly matched fleets must have been overwhelming: such a gasping of straining men and a thrashing of oars, ships moving in slow-motion patterns, the crunching and splintering of wood, yells and curses, boardings, poking with pikes, flights of arrows, capsizings, swampings, drownings and half-drownings, men clinging to floating wreckage, some hiding in it and pretending to be dead, others swimming for a shore which, if it belonged to an enemy, could only offer slavery.

The Phoenicians knew this world well and lived in it for hundreds of years. They undoubtedly engaged their coastal neighbors, fought it out with sea raiders from the Aegean, with endless generations of pirates, and after about 700 B.C. more and more with the Greeks. The latter were as much at home in the wa-ter as the Phoenicians—as hardy, as venturesome, as determined, as good shipbuilders and sailors as they. Their aims, however, were somewhat different. The Greeks wished to establish colonies to relieve land shortages and overflowing populations at home; the Phoenicians wanted trading strongholds and markets. The objectives, though different, took both peoples to the same places, and inevitably to hundreds of years of seesaw conflict.

They were fatally well matched, particularly in the technology of their ships. A Phoenician would have been instantly at home in a Greek vessel and vice versa. In fact, one of the dividends of a naval victory was the ships captured from the enemy. They were towed home or sailed home with prize crews, refitted and added to the fleets of the victors. Thus, it was almost impossible for one side to get any significant technological jump on the other. If Greek or Phoenician had been able to gain such an advantage, the conflict would not have gone on for so long.

The Great War against the Greeks

The bridge of ships ordered by Xerxes was built at Abydos, where the Hellespont is a mile wide. The vessels were lashed side to side, their bows pointed upstream so that they would be exposed to a minimum of strain from the currents flowing out of the Black Sea and from winds blowing in from the Aegean. A total of 674 ships was used. When the bridge was done, Xerxes crossed it in a chariot drawn by matched Nisaean horses.

By 500 B.C. the Phoenicians found themselves under the relatively benign umbrella of Persia, which had replaced those old Phoenician enemies, Assyria and Babylon. The only cloud on the horizon was the increasing aggressiveness of the Greeks, who were establishing colonies throughout the Mediterranean, interfering with Phoenician trade and becoming increasingly annoying to the Persians.

In 484 B.C. the Persian king Xerxes decided to crush the Greeks. He recruited a huge army of nearly 200,000 men and in 480 B.C. aimed them north around the top of the Aegean, planning to fall on the Greek cities one by one. But to do this he had not only to supply his army but also to protect it from Greek naval activity and—eventually—to engage and destroy the Greek fleet. Most important, the Persian king had to get across the Hellespont, the narrow strait that separates the continent of Europe from Asia.

These needs were met in large measure by the Phoenicians, who supplied Xerxes with 300 warships, plus fleet-support vessels and invaluable know-how. The latter was put to use in building a double bridge of ships strung across the Hellespont. When sections of this bridge, secured by cables woven of flax and papyrus, blew away in a storm, their architects were beheaded. Phoenician workmen helped repair the bridge and strengthened it by using extra-heavy anchors and beefing up the cables, which, according to Herodotus, weighed 50 pounds a foot. The bridge of ships, thus solidly fixed in position, was then floored with planks, which were covered with earth to calm skittish cavalry. And then Xerxes' mighty army rumbled over it. Herodotus says that their number was so great that the crossing took seven days.

The Battle of Salamis: A Debacle for Xerxes

Xerxes' army pushed south, crushing Greek resistance as it went. It finally captured Athens, whose government fled to a nearby island, Salamis, there to be protected by a combined Greek fleet. The Greek cities, hopelessly at odds with one another, agreed to stand at Salamis largely because of the persuasiveness of the Athenian admiral Themistocles, who managed to convince most of them that their only chance of turning back Persia was by beating the enemy fleet in the Strait of Salamis. There, the narrowness of the sea would enable the Greeks to engage only a few of the Persian ships at a time, thus neutralizing the Persian numerical superiority. The location would also prevent a battle involving open-sea maneuvers, at which the Phoenicians—the elite of the Persian fleet—were so adept.

Pretending indecision, the Greeks lured the Persians into the strait. The scene that unfolds on these pages shows the Phoenician spearhead, with gilded sterns and guardian statues of gods on board, bearing down on the Greek line, which is waiting at right and across the bottom of the picture. The bulk of the Persian fleet is still trying to crowd through the narrow strait at top left. When enough ships have squeezed in, the Greeks will surround them from the right and crush them.

A number of vessels from independent Greek cities had joined the Persian fleet. One was commanded by a woman, the imperious Queen Artemisia of Halicarnassos. Shrewd enough to realize that the Persians were falling into a trap, she quickly rammed a Persian vessel (top center) in the hope of deluding the Greeks. She did—and escaped. In the end, the Phoenician contingent was chewed to bits and the Persians fled, losing 200 ships to the Greeks' 40. Repulsed, Xerxes returned to Persia.

Pressed from behind by friendly ships crowding to get into action, the Phoenicians attack the Greek line and immediately get into trouble. One ship (lower left) has been rammed and is sinking. Another (center) is being hit by a Greek ship that has swung out of line. The Phoenician ships behind them are having trouble keeping position because a wind has risen.

An Artist's Attempt at a Trireme that Works

The painting of the Battle of Salamis on the preceding pages was made by Fred Freeman, who did a prodigious amount of research to prepare himself for it. Presented here are just two pages from his sketchbook, the near one an attempt to reconstruct how a Phoenician trireme may have been rowed, the far one devoted to a Greek trireme.

Freeman first did some studies of oars and their proportions (*top left*), then attempted to fit three banks into a ship without outriggers (1, 2, 3, 4), remembering that he was dealing with a time period between 500 and 300 B.C., when many authorities think Phoenician triremes were completely decked over. He found a possible solution by assuming oars of different lengths, but this raised another problem: short-oar men can row a much faster stroke than long-oar men. Figure 5 is a bow view of a Phoenician ship, and below it a stern view. Figure 6 shows a side view of the whole vessel; below it, a top view. A close look at the side view will reveal that the uprights next to each rower in the top bank are placed in such a way that the rower cannot complete his stroke. In later sketches Freeman had to change that.

The Greek trireme is conceived of as a ship with outriggers, and oars that are all the same length. The combination makes for easier stockpiling of oars, as well as better rowing. The Phoenician system may have been more like the Greek than the one Freeman originally sketched. He got a clue to the Greek arrangement from a piece of Greek sculpture (9) and used it to satisfy himself with vertical and horizontal studies (10, 11) that his placement of men would work through a full stroke, using oars about 14 feet long (8). Figure 12 is a side view of a Greek trireme and shows the triple beak that those vessels are known to have had. Why such a prow was preferred is not known; later the Greeks went back to the single spike used by the Phoenicians (6). Figure 13 is a top view that experiments—again unsuccessfully—with oars of different lengths. The unnumbered sketches are bow and stern views of the Greek trireme—the former showing the *oculi,* or eyes, that were commonly painted on the bows of ancient vessels, presumably to help them find their way.

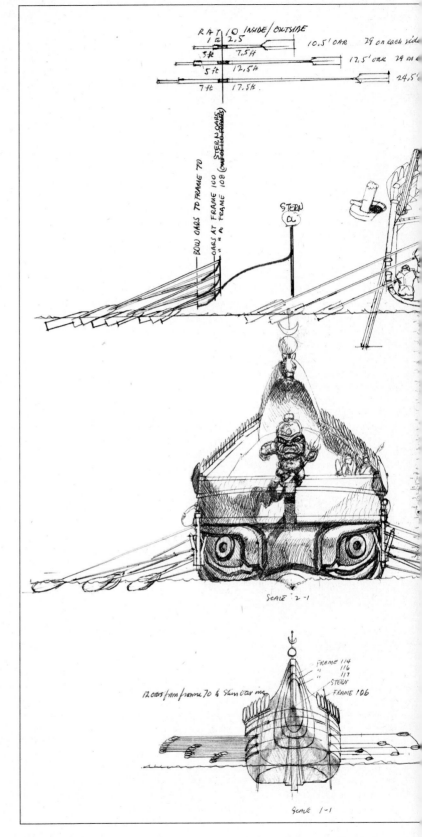

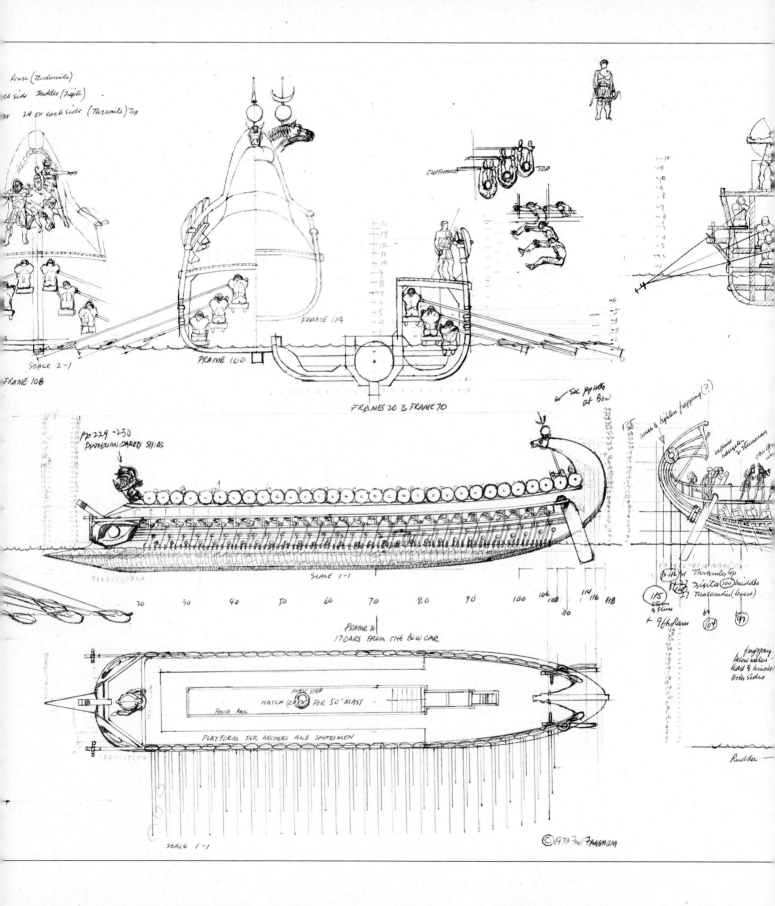

house (Thalamila)
ch side Thalilie (Zigite) .
w 24 on each side (Thranite) Top

SCALE 2-1
FRAME 108

FRAME 100

FRAME 114

FRAMES 20 & FRAME 70

OUTBOARD   TOP

pp 229 - 230
PHOENICIAN OARED SHIPS

SCALE 1-1

20   30   40   50   60   70   80   90   100 106 114 116 118
                                                      108 110

FRAME 70
17 OARS FROM THE BOW OAR

MAST STEP
HATCH (OPEN) FOR 50' MAST
FENCE RAIL
PLATFORM FOR ARCHERS AND SPORTSMEN

SCALE 1-1

© 1978 Paul Freeman

Thranite Top
Zigite (100) Middle
Thalamites (Lower)

Rudder

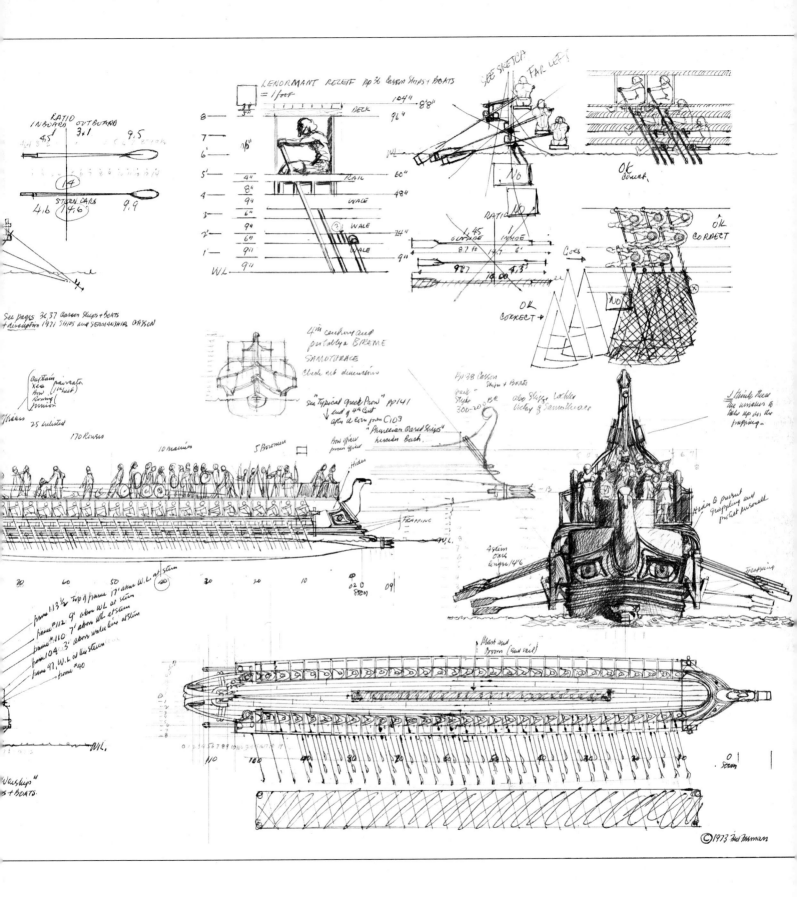

For many living in a backwater of the then-civilized world, the Phoenician trader who came ashore might be the only stranger encountered in their entire lives. In more cosmopolitan spots where strangers were common there was still something special that set the Phoenician apart. He had been to places other men had only heard about.

This reputation grew quickly after 1000 B.C. reflecting the speed and energy with which the coastal traders began flowing outward at about that time and, in so doing, metamorphosed themselves from Canaanites into Phoenicians. That energy cannot be accounted for simply by calling the Phoenicians superenergetic. Energetic they were, but there were other ingredients in their situation that might almost have foretold their important role as an exploring and sea-trading people.

First and foremost was their location. They stood literally at the center of the ancient world. Much of that world's trade wound up traveling in Phoenician bottoms or was stored in Phoenician warehouses. If the Tigris-Euphrates people wished to communicate with the west, they did so by overland caravan routes that came out on the Lebanese coast.

Halfway between Byblos and Beirut is a river gorge that winds down out of the mountains to the sea. Known as the Dog River, it has been both a trade route and an invasion corridor for several thousand years. During that time many invaders have passed

that way and left memorial plaques carved in the rock to record their passage.

The oldest of these monuments are so weathered now as to be indecipherable. But they are still there (page 59), staring impassively at a sea that winks as blue as it did when poor Rib-Addi was scurrying up and down the coast, past this very spot, scheming how to keep Byblos—and himself—intact.

More than three thousand years of plaques marking invasion and military conquest make clear the unique strategic importance of Lebanon. When an Egyptian pharaoh aimed his eye and his regiments eastward toward Assyria or Babylon, he first had to take a hard squint at the Lebanese ports to make sure they were secure to him. Similarly, when Assyrian or Babylonian armies pressed westward, there could be no descent on Egypt without some kind of accommodation—agreed or forced—between the invader and the kings of Tyre and Sidon.

No less important than its strategic value was the actual value of the region itself. The Phoenician ports grew enormously wealthy, and they attracted Assyrian invaders as a honey pot attracts wasps. As a result, even though the Assyrians often had no real geopolitical excuse for coming, they came anyway. During their predatory prowls they sometimes intimidated the Phoenicians into giving them tribute, sometimes they extracted it by force. Sometimes they simply marched back home afterward, sometimes they left garrisons or imperial agents behind to ensure that the tribute kept coming.

For the most part, the Phoenician merchant princes apparently found it prudent to pay; their long trading experience told them that if they were patient a good deal of the wealth being taken from them by

Cyprus was a major source of copper for Phoenician traders, and the decorative element of this Cypriot stand for an incense burner tells that story clearly. The man, wearing one of the long robes favored by Phoenicians, is carrying off a copper ingot in the shape of an oxhide. Such odd-shaped ingots were common in the Mediterranean world at that time.

Cut into the rock of the Dog River gorge in Lebanon is the plaque believed to commemorate an invasion by the Assyrian king Shalmaneser III in 858 B.C. It is one of 19 plaques that were scattered along the gorge in eight different languages. The oldest one is Egyptian, going back to 1297 B.C. The most recent is Lebanese, celebrating the expulsion of the French in 1946.

force would return in more peaceful ways later. The recuperative powers of the Phoenician cities were remarkable, and it is not wholly unfair to speculate that they regarded intermittent invasion as a sort of disagreeable excess-profits tax that they had to pay from time to time in order to stay in business.

One reason the Phoenician cities recuperated so fast was their great political flexibility. Each city was a separate entity, free to act in its own best interest, to bargain independently, alert to any business advantage that might arise, ready to join a neighbor in a commercial or political enterprise one year if it seemed attractive, just as ready to stab him in the back the next year.

Just how much stabbing went on is hard to judge, although the scant records that do survive tend to show that the coastal towns were unreliable allies, made more so by Assyrian pressures. Balancing off that tendency toward mutual squabbling was the larger and more important reason for rapid recuperation: tremendous commercial opportunity. The Mesopotamian world of the Tigris and Euphrates rivers was only one of three important markets that were joined at the Phoenicians' doorstep. A second was Egypt to the south. A third was Cyprus, Crete and the whole Mediterranean world to the west. If the Babylonian king Nebuchadnezzar wanted some fine Greek pottery, he could get it most easily from the Phoenicians. If some northern or western Mediterranean people wanted Egyptian papyrus—they, too, found it most convenient to get it from the Phoenicians. And so on.

Thus, though the Phoenicians were by no means the only traders in the Mediterranean world, they were the most centrally situated. And, thanks to their enterprise in establishing their unique network of trading posts, they could offer the greatest variety in merchandise. Finally, being mariners, they could penetrate markets inaccessible to nonmaritime peoples. In sum, they were the hub around which a great deal of the early Mediterranean and Near Eastern trade revolved. But they were not content to be merely a hub, clipping commissions from whatever passed through their hands. They had other assets also: two natural ones and a third that they had to work up themselves over the centuries.

The natural assets were timber and purple dye. Byblos was long a lumber center, well known for its cedar and fir. Tyre and Sidon were dyeing centers, famous for their purple cloth, which depended on Phoenicia's second natural asset, the murex, a kind of snail that was abundant in the coastal waters. Someone—perhaps a fisherman—discovered that if the soft body of a murex was removed from its shell and exposed to the sun in a shallow pan of salt water, it would start to rot and liquid from a gland in the snail's body would separate out. This liquid was used to dye cloth. Depending on how long the rotting process was allowed to go on and how concentrated the extract was, the color that resulted could vary anywhere from a pale pink through various shades of red to a deep violet. This latter hue was the royal Tyrian purple (pages 60-61), known and admired throughout the ancient world and in some countries worn only by kings.

The third asset the Phoenicians used to propel themselves into commercial preeminence was knowhow. Placed as they were at the trading hub of the world, they had a chance to familiarize themselves with a wide variety of materials, as well as manu-

facturing techniques and artistic styles. They sucked up all this information like sponges and put it to their own use. From being traders in ivory, they became expert workers of ivory. They got the secret of glassmaking from Egypt and exploited it. They became great fabricators of jewelry. They learned *repoussé* and enamel work, and applied both those techniques to the decoration of ornaments and jewelry made of fine gold and silver. Although a few scholars detect elements of a "Phoenician" style in this work, the artists leaned primarily on the designs of others for their inspiration. Similarly with metal containers, silver basins and copper and bronze bowls. Some of these utensils are beautifully made, but with designs that clearly derive from Mesopotamia, from Egypt or from the Aegean world.

This is not to say that the Phoenicians lacked originality. More probably they permitted themselves to be influenced by market conditions. "If Egyptian necklaces with scarab designs are good sellers," one can almost hear a Phoenician craftsman saying to himself, "I'll copy them. No need to buy from Egypt; I'll save by making them myself." Furthermore, as items for export tended more and more to be produced in larger volume, the skills and the originality of the artist-artisan tended to be suppressed in the demand for objects that could be turned out as rapidly and as cheaply as possible.

Having a fine source of wood close at hand, the Phoenicians were known from the outset as excellent carpenters and cabinetmakers. Apparently they did not use much wood in actual house building —they used stone or brick for that—but they did use it extensively in decoration and in furniture. In all, their familiarity with metal, wood and stone put them much in demand as traveling craftsmen. One who sought the advantage of these skills was the Israelite king David. Having consolidated the kingdom of Israel in about 1000 B.C., David wanted an outlet to the sea and timber for "an house" for himself. He called on his neighbor Hiram, who was then king of Tyre, for craftsmen, and a mutually profitable trading alliance resulted.

From the Old Testament we know that Hiram was a great man—probably the most powerful on the entire coast. A strong ruler with a trader's instinct for expansion wherever profit lay, he recognized the value of the Israelite connection. Having done well with one Israelite king, Hiram was delighted to continue with another, David's son Solomon.

Solomon's needs were more ambitious than David's. First, he wanted to erect a temple more splendid than any the Hebrews had ever known. So Hiram sent an entire work force over the mountains to Israel to design and build from scratch a temple. In return, Hiram got a yearly supply of oil and wheat. The latter, we can imagine, was much needed by the burgeoning population of Tyre, whose own farmlands were narrow as a result of the nearness of the mountains to the sea. The second of Solomon's aims was to expand his trade south and east via the Red Sea and the Indian Ocean—specifically to Ophir, where gold was produced. Down the course of history the exact location of Ophir has been lost, but many experts think it was probably somewhere in southern Arabia. Wherever it was, Solomon saw a chance to get to it by using an outlet he had in the Gulf of Aqaba at the head of the Red Sea—if only he had ships. But he was a landsman, as were all his people, sons of nomadic herders.

Again Hiram alertly stepped forward. According

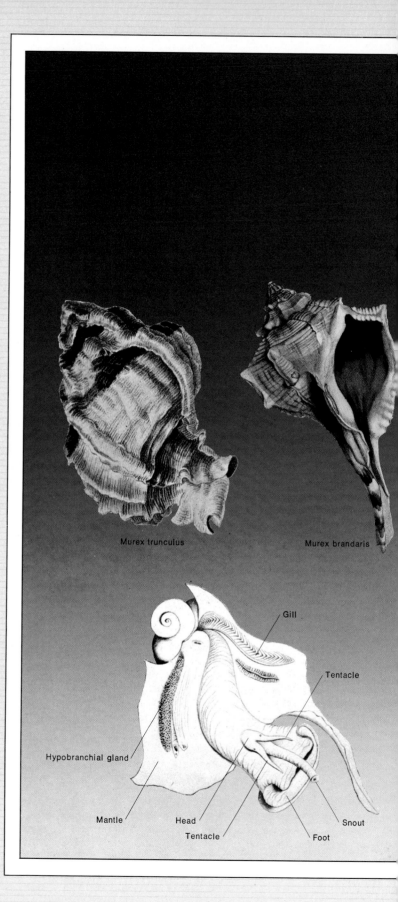

Murex trunculus

Murex brandaris

Gill

Tentacle

Hypobranchial gland

Mantle   Head

Tentacle

Snout

Foot

The Royal Purple—and How It Was Manufactured

According to legend, the Tyrian god Melqart was strolling by the seashore one day with his beloved, a nymph named Tyrus, when a dog that was accompanying them picked up a murex snail and bit it in two. Immediately the dog's mouth became deeply crimsoned, and Tyrus, admiring the beautiful color, announced to Melqart that she would not accept him as her lover until he had provided her with a gown of the same hue. Whereupon Melqart gathered up a large quantity of shells—and the Tyrian dyeing industry was born.

A delightful legend, and based perhaps on the fact that early dyers learned where to obtain their colors by noticing the tinted mouths of people who ate murexes. At any rate, by 1000 B.C. Tyre and Sidon had become the centers for dyed wool and silk of a quality unsurpassed throughout the ancient world.

The dye came from a small gland in the body of the murex, which had to be removed from a living snail if the brightest hues were to develop properly. Each gland yielded only a drop or two of a yellowish liquid that darkened when it was exposed to sun and air. Processing required constant slow simmering in an outdoor pan for almost two weeks, during which time the precious liquid boiled down to about one sixteenth of its original volume. At this rate, it took the glands of some 60,000 snails to produce only one pound of dye, which explains why the essence was so fantastically expensive. One expert has calculated that a single pound of fine quality silk dyed according to the highest Tyrian standards could have fetched as much as $28,000 in modern currency.

The best dyers did all their processing in lead or tin pans, knowing that brass or iron would discolor the essence. Mainly they used two species of murex (left). Brandaris alone produced a heavy dark tint in cloth, and needed just the right admixture of trunculus plus a carefully controlled double-soaking with added dye from a third snail—not a murex at all—to achieve the lustrous royal purple that was so avidly sought. Other tints —shading down to a pale pink, shown in the graduated background opposite —were achieved by varying the mixture and the amount of exposure to light. All Tyrian purple dyes were colorfast—that is, they did not fade, which contributed as much to their value as their beauty did.

There was a time, as Rome's power and prestige began to grow, when any rich citizen could "wear the purple," a narrow band on his toga. Later this privilege was reserved for senators and, finally, for the emperor alone. Antony and Cleopatra are reputed to have had a warship notorious for its ostentation; its mainsail was colored with Tyrian purple dye.

Murex dyeing was practiced in several places in the Mediterranean area, including the islands of Malta and Motya, but nowhere was it done with a skill that matched that of Tyrian and Sidonian dyers. Their immense productivity is attested to by the mounds of shells—literally millions of them —that still lie piled around the ruins of the old dye works. In both Tyre and Sidon the works were located to the south, just out of town and downwind, because of the dreadful stench that emanated from the rotting bodies of the mollusks.

Throughout many ups and downs the dyeing industry continued, surviving even the fall of Tyre and struggling on to 800 A.D., when Charlemagne was importing Tyrian-dyed cloth. It languished thereafter because of its prohibitive cost. Cheap, colorfast aniline dyes ensure that it will never again be revived.

Both murex trunculus and murex brandaris (left, above) were abundant in the eastern Mediterranean. A diagram of the latter (left, below) indicates its parts. The hypobranchial gland produced the essence sought by dyers.

to reports, he sent a team of shipwrights, sailmakers and riggers to construct a fleet of merchantmen for Solomon at Ezion-geber, near the modern Israeli port of Elath. After the fleet was built it was manned by Phoenician sailors, and Hiram apparently got his cut of the gold and precious stones that were brought back from the mysterious Ophir. Of gold alone brought from Ophir the Bible gives a figure of 420 talents. With a talent weighing slightly more than 75 pounds and at today's inflated price of gold, this—if the Biblical figure can be believed—works out to just under $50 million.

Gold from Ophir. Copper from Cyprus. Silver from Ethiopia. Tin from Spain. More and more the trade of the Mediterranean world was coming to be governed by the demand for metals. The Phoenicians were in the thick of it all. Tin was sought because it could be mixed with copper to make bronze, a far harder metal than copper. Many scholars believe that it was the lure of rich tin deposits in Spain that first drew the Phoenicians westward, and from there perhaps to Brittany and the British Isles, where tin was also produced. Meanwhile, the secret of smelting iron had been worked out in Asia Minor, and the Phoenicians quickly added that skill to their repertoire of talents. By about 1000 B.C. they were uniquely equipped for the role that would establish them as the mariner-traders par excellence of their day. And with a thorough knowledge of metals, with trade goods of all kinds, with a whole arsenal of industrial techniques, with a fine knowledge of ships and the sea, the Phoenicians were ready to go almost anywhere. And they did. They flowed westward, establishing small trading posts at strategic points as they went. Eventually they reached the western limits of the Mediterranean itself: the Pillars of Heracles (known as Hercules to the Romans, and as the Strait of Gibraltar in modern times), the gateway to the Atlantic. Still they did not stop.

Some of the trips they took are literally astounding. In about 600 B.C. their reputation as dependable voyagers to far places was so great that they were asked by the Egyptian pharaoh Necho to undertake a voyage of exploration. In those days all of Africa was known as Libya—a vague term for all the unexplored sandy wastes that made up the Sahara and lay to the south of a much better-known strip of fertile coastline along the Mediterranean. How big ancient Libya was nobody knew. Faint caravan tracks linked by oases wandered off into the desert. Strange black people lived somewhere at the far ends of those trails. That was known because trade goods—gold, ivory and black slaves—came back via those trade routes. But how far Libya extended or what shape it was remained utterly unknown. Necho must have believed it was an island because his instruction to the Phoenician venturers was to sail south out of the Red Sea and return from the west via the Pillars of Heracles —in short, to sail around Africa. Astonishingly enough, that is what the Phoenicians appear to have done. No one would sail around Africa again for another 2,000 years.

It took the Phoenician sailors three years. The Greek historian Herodotus describes how they did it. When fall came wherever they happened to be, they went ashore, cleared some land, planted it with corn and waited for it to ripen. When it did, they harvested it and continued on their way. No other word survives of what else they did, whom they met or

what they saw—save one interesting fact. Reporting to Necho, the sailors insisted that as they rounded the southern end of Libya and headed west the sun had been on their right hand. Herodotus, one of the most charming tale-tellers who ever lived—but also one of the most skeptical—conscientiously reported this odd bit of news, but declared that he did not believe it. Of course, it is just that observation that gives weight to the claim that the Phoenicians had indeed gotten down into the southern hemisphere and for a while had the sun on their right hand—i.e., rising and setting slightly to the north of them.

Another, more reliably documented African trip was taken by the Carthaginian admiral Hanno in about 425 B.C. Hanno was not trying to sail around Africa. Rather, he was interested in solidifying African trade. He kept a log, a Greek translation of which still survives. By following it, one can recognize some of the landmarks he saw and locate the places at which he stopped to found cities or trading posts. Virtually all experts agree that one large river he crossed was the Senegal. But south of that his account becomes increasingly fuzzy. It is hard to say whether it was Sierra Leone he reached before turning back because of a shortage of supplies or, as some think, the Cameroons, nearly 1,500 miles farther down. In either case he had some strange adventures. He saw great herds of elephants in riverine reed beds, also enormous numbers of crocodiles and hippos in what seems to have been an arm of the Senegal. At one place, trying to land, he was attacked by a swarm of skin-clad savages, standing on cliffs overhead, who threw so many rocks down on his party that it was forced to sail on. At another place he encountered some hairy-bodied inhabitants whom an African interpreter accompanying him identified as a people named gorillas. The "men" got away by climbing straight up a cliff, but Hanno's party did manage to catch a few of the "women," who bit and mangled their captors so fiercely that it was necessary to kill them. Hanno brought the skins of three of them back to be displayed in Carthage.

Prior to Hanno's relatively well-documented voyage, another trip may have been made by Himilco, also a Carthaginian admiral and possibly Hanno's brother. Records of Himilco's trip, as well as the relationship of the two men, are practically nonexistent. However, most historians report that Himilco's expedition went north out of the Pillars of Heracles instead of south. This voyage tends to confirm that the Phoenicians were involved with the metal trade in Britain. Accounts unfortunately are vague, written long after the fact, and may mix more than one voyage. But they do supposedly describe how Himilco sailed up the coast, around the peninsula of Brittany and on to the British Isles. There is no direct Phoenician archeological evidence to prove the story, but it is certain that somebody was going there from Spain during the Iron Age; traces of such visitations have turned up in Cornwall. Whether the visitors were Himilco and his party, other Phoenicians or Celts trading up and down the coast on their own is impossible to determine. These three Phoenician voyages, two in Africa and one to Britain, took place over a period of about 200 years. During that time there were surely many others of which no written record or archeological trace survives. Tradition has it that the Phoenicians reached the Canary Islands, Madeira and the Azores. Accidental discovery

The Nora stone, from Nora, Sardinia, has an inscription written in Phoenician characters. It is the oldest evidence yet known of Phoenician penetration of the western Mediterranean. Dating from the Ninth Century B.C., it may well predate the founding of Carthage. The message, though fragmentary, appears to spell out the crimes for which a man could be banished from Sardinia for a year.

of all these islands by vessels blown to sea by storms is a distinct possibility. A prudent captain, caught in a real howler, would have battened down his ship and ridden out the gale, hoping to be able to sail or row back to land again once the storm subsided. The nearest of the Canary Islands is only 65 miles from the coast of southern Morocco. Since traders were going up and down that coast continually, it is hard to imagine that during several centuries of coastal traffic somebody was not blown to the Canaries. Madeira is farther out to sea, the Azores farther yet—at least a thousand miles to the west of Gades (Cadiz). But it is in the Azores, of all places, that eight Carthaginian coins have been found. It cannot be proved that Carthaginians brought them there, but the likelihood that somebody else did is remote.

Great seamen the Phoenicians. What is most impressive about their recorded voyages is that nothing like them was attempted by any of their contemporaries. No one else, it seems, had the energy, the daring and the skills to pull them off. The Phoenicians combined these qualities, and on top of that they certainly must have been tough—hard, pragmatic men who vanished over the horizon not for romance but because there was gold or ivory there, or because the elements took them. Others, writing about them, emphasize their daring. But they also emphasize their hardness as traders, their trickiness. They are described as dishonest when they could get away with it, and not above murder and enslavement.

In fact, they had a bad reputation as slavers. A stock character in Greek and Roman comedies is somebody who has been carried off by Phoenicians as a child and sold into slavery. Homer's *Odyssey* tells how the infant Eumaeus of Syria was kidnaped by the Phoenicians—"famed for their ships, greedy knaves bringing countless trinkets in their black ship"—who connived with Eumaeus' Phoenician nurse to seize them both. What Homer failed to mention was that the nurse may well have been a slave herself, victim of a Greek kidnaping or sacked city years before—and only too glad to find an opportunity to get a little of her own back while making her way home to Phoenicia.

In defense of the Phoenicians, it must be remembered that it is their enemies who are doing the talking, and also that they were living in a rough world where everybody grabbed his when others were not looking.

Finally, we can turn to Herodotus again for some evidence that the Phoenicians were more honorable as traders than they were painted. Since they traveled as far as they did, they were constantly in contact with less civilized peoples whose languages they could not speak and of whose customs they were largely ignorant. This was particularly true of the African coast beyond the Pillars of Heracles. There, trade—if it was to be conducted at all and if the traders had any expectation of coming back—had to be built on some sort of mutual trust. According to the account of Herodotus:

"They [the traders] no sooner arrive—they unload their wares. Having arranged them in an orderly fashion along the beach, leave them and returning aboard their ships, raise a great smoke. The natives, when they see the smoke, come down to the shore—lay out as much gold as they think the goods are worth, then withdraw to a distance. The Carthaginians then come ashore and look. If they think the gold enough, they take it and go their way. If it does not seem sufficient, they go aboard ship once more and wait patiently. Then the natives approach and add to their gold until the Carthaginians are content. Neither party deals unfairly by the other: For the Carthaginians never touch the gold until it comes up to the worth of their goods, nor do the natives ever carry off the goods until the gold is taken away."

A nice story and—measuring the Phoenicians as practical, long-headed traders—probably a true one.

Dramatic as the great voyages of discovery may have been, it was the slow day-to-day poking about the Mediterranean that kept the Phoenician mercantile enterprise ticking, its "tubs" a common sight in almost every civilized port—and some not so civilized. An exception was the Aegean. The Phoenicians had an early try at penetrating that sea. They were already well established at several places in Cyprus, and they went on from there to set up trading stations in Rhodes and even in Crete. But their toeholds were quickly trampled on by the Greeks, and any hope of a real presence in the Aegean had to be abandoned for the time being.

The Mediterranean, by contrast, was wide open to them, with its pot of Spanish metallic treasure beckoning at the end of a 2,300-mile watery trail to the west. It is quite possible to follow the westward movements of the Phoenicians by keeping an alert eye for the kinds of places along the coast that their captains might have chosen as good overnight anchorages, each one just about 30 miles beyond the last. The French archeologist Pierre Cintas has refined this research tool by urging that the exploratory eye concentrate on finding "a 'landscape,' a certain kind of landscape—a 'Punic landscape.' "

What does Cintas mean? "Punic" is the Latin word for western Phoenician, and Cintas means simply that the Phoenicians had well-known preferences in their choice of where to set up trading posts that might eventually grow to cities; and if an archeologist keeps those preferences in mind while prospecting, the chances of locating additional Phoenician sites are greatly enhanced.

The "Punic landscape" involved either an easily defended promontory sticking out into the sea or a small island close to the shore. A good source of fresh water was important, as was a good stone quarry to be drawn upon for fortifications and buildings. Another requirement: a good anchorage, preferably two —one for summer weather and one on the opposite side of the island or promontory for the different winds that blew in winter. A final and very important need was land for agriculture available nearby. The Phoenicians have been so fixed in the minds of everybody as mariners supreme that one tends to forget they also were extremely good farmers. Living in cities—and in what for the time were densely concentrated and rather large populations—they needed dependable sources of food. They ensured these by annexing farmland around their cities and cultivating it intensively.

The result of this practice was a pattern of little spots of "Phoenicia" sprinkled widely over the Mediterranean, each surrounded by a much larger population of local people who were less advanced culturally and commercially. Much of the Phoenicians' success as traders grew from that cultural difference. Their neighbors were either unable or unwilling to make many of the trinkets and ornaments that the Phoenicians dealt in, and they innocently traded off spices, ivory, gold or other metals for much less than those raw materials would bring elsewhere. That was the Phoenician trading margin, and it was a big one. It enabled flourishing cities to spring up wherever there were good hinterland markets to support them, or wherever strategic necessity dictated the planting of an outpost.

One strategic spot was the bottleneck between Sicily and North Africa, a narrowing of the Mediterranean that served to separate the western half of that great inland sea from its eastern half.

The Phoenicians took every precaution to ensure control of the bottleneck by establishing strong settlements in three places: on the island of Malta, which commanded the eastern approaches to the bottleneck; at Carthage, where the African coastline juts out close to Sicily; and at the nearest Sicilian point opposite, specifically at a small fortified island named Motya at Sicily's western tip. So entrenched, the Phoenicians could keep the Greeks, their chief competitors, out of the western Mediterranean and reserve the Spanish metal trade for themselves.

We now come to a most perplexing and difficult matter: Exactly when did all this happen?

There can be no "exactly," but there is beginning to be a "probably," and it raises the second of the two major problems that plague Phoenician study. The first is the already much-mentioned matter of when Phoenicia East can properly be given the name Phoenicia. The second has to do with the timing and the dynamics of the development of Phoenicia West —particularly in Sicily, where a long struggle with the Greeks was to take place. What has been said here so far about the second matter has followed traditional historical thought, much of it based on the writings of dozens of classical historians, poets, chroniclers, travelers and occasional myth-sayers. All this material has been sifted by later scholars and, taken with the necessary grains of salt, fitted together into a chain of events whose links—through time —hold together remarkably well.

It is this traditional historical view that suggests a Phoenician settlement of Spain as early as 1100 B.C., of Utica on the North African coast at about the same time, of Carthage prior to 800 B.C. and the establishment of outposts throughout much of Sicily shortly thereafter. The picture that this develops is one of established Phoenician presence in Sicily well before the Greeks came to contest it. Awkwardly, the most recent archeological evidence, backed up by new methods of interpretation, suggests that the tradition may be wrong.

What is wrong is that nobody has been able to find in any western Phoenician site—Carthage, Sicily or elsewhere—any object that can be reliably dated earlier than about 735 B.C. Since it is almost literally impossible for permanent settlements of any size to conceal their age from the most sophisticated modern analysis, this means that the ideas that scholars, both ancient and modern, had about the role of Greeks and Phoenicians in the west may have to be seriously revised.

The trouble, oddly enough, seems to go back to one of the most scrupulous and reliable historians who ever lived, the Greek writer Thucydides. In describing the rapid colonial expansion of many Greek cities in response to land shortages and social turbulence at home, Thucydides duly records the settlement of southern Italy and then of Sicily by these early Greek colonists, who began arriving in numbers in the west after about 735 B.C. He goes on to say that the Phoenicians who had been living in Sicily slowly retreated once this Greek invasion began until they were confined to three cities at the far western end of the island.

This statement has had the weight of gospel ever since it was written, but it is suspect. Colonization is difficult under the best of circumstances. The arriving Greeks carried fierce mutual jealousies with them and did considerable fighting among themselves. To assume that they could have settled their internal squabbles and at the same time find the energy to dislodge a network of well-entrenched Phoenician settlements strains credulity.

Why, then, did Thucydides make this claim? According to Rhys Carpenter, a specialist in classical archeology and Greek history who has written an absorbing study of this entire matter, Thucydides was probably led astray by the poet Homer. For a sober historian to be deluded by a poet requires explaining. To begin with, something must be understood of the exceptional position Homer occupied in the minds of the Greeks: he was believed to be the fountainhead of practically all the knowledge they had of a big slice of their own past and even their origins. His right to the respect that Greeks and later Romans accorded him has also been acknowledged in modern times—albeit in a less literal, more interpretive manner.

Excluding the myths and miraculous events that interlard his epics, he turns out to be—the deeper one delves into his work—a wonderfully accurate portrayer of the Greek Bronze Age. The *Iliad,* which deals with events that took place in about 1200 B.C.

—some 400 years before Homer himself supposedly lived—re-creates that time and that world in such detail as to make the jaw drop at the accuracy and perception of it all. The more sophisticated one's knowledge of Homer is, the more respect one has for him as a chronicler of life in Mycenaean Greece.

No wonder Thucydides leaned heavily on him. Unfortunately, in doing so he made one simple but bad mistake. He assumed that both the *Iliad* and the *Odyssey* were written at about the same time by the same man and that they both dealt with events of 1200 B.C. That, according to the best modern scholarship, is not so and brings us to the prickly question of the identity of Homer.

The Greeks themselves did not know exactly who Homer was, where he lived or when. We do not know today. We cannot even be sure that such a man existed at all. We do know that at the time he is supposed to have lived there were professional bards who often sang at the courts of princes. If Homer did indeed exist, he was one of those, drawing for his inspiration on a long background of spoken legend woven into song by a succession of unknown men and passed down by word of mouth from generation to generation. Exhaustive study of Homer's two great epics, the *Iliad* and the *Odyssey,* suggests that he was an Ionian who lived on the island of Chios in about 800 B.C. How much of the *Iliad* or the *Odyssey* he composed himself, how it was passed down—verbally or in written form—is also unknown. But analysis of both epics makes it increasingly clear that parts of the *Odyssey* are very probably not by Homer but were interpolated later by one or more other poets whose identities are now lost. What is important to the matter at hand is that the entire *Odyssey* seems

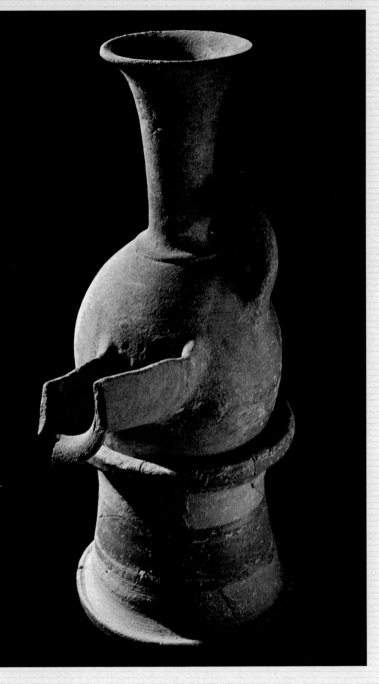

An Eighth Century B.C. Sidonian pitcher, with a set of sievelike holes at the base of its spout, suggests that the Phoenicians may have been tea drinkers—not of true Oriental tea but some local infusion like camomile.

to have been composed a good many years after the *Iliad,* perhaps half a century or a century later. References to the Phoenicians in both works reinforce this view, since they inadvertently reveal how the Greek attitude toward the Phoenicians had changed in the one hundred years between 800 and 700 B.C.

When the *Iliad* was written, the Aegean dark age had ended and the Greeks were just beginning to fan out again as traders and colonists. Their arts were not yet as highly developed as they later would be, and as they moved through the Aegean eastward to mercantile contacts with Phoenicia East, they were unfailingly impressed by the sophistication of the products they found there. As a result, the Phoenicians appear in the *Iliad* as master craftsmen and nothing more. That was the Eighth Century Greek view of them; and that is the view reflected in the *Iliad,* even though it professes to talk of events that took place 400 years earlier.

The view in the *Odyssey* is quite different. By this time Greek art had developed greatly, as had Greece's outward colonial thrust. Greek was bumping into Phoenician everywhere, no longer as friendly trader but as bitter rival. The former now looked on the latter as a nasty, crafty, thieving, child-snatching, woman-seducing, ocean-roving pest who was more a purveyor of trumpery wares than a master craftsman. That is the Phoenician of the *Odyssey*—the actual Seventh Century Greek view.

Thucydides, who did not understand these nuances, particularly the time-gap between the creation of the *Iliad* and the *Odyssey,* spliced the two epics together in the belief that they depicted real events that took place within a decade or two of each other. This left him with an awkward problem. Somehow or other he had to fit the time of the Trojan War as described in the *Iliad* (and which he correctly estimated to have taken place shortly before 1200 B.C.) with the movements and behavior of the Phoenicians as described in the *Odyssey*. The best assumption he could make was that the Phoenicians had been at their nasty, crafty, far-ranging business for a long time. As a result, when he came to writing an account of the colonization of Sicily by the Greeks in 700 B.C., Thucydides had to explain the failure of those aggressive Phoenicians to prevent it. He did so by merely stating that they withdrew westward. Deluded by the *Odyssey,* it never occurred to him that they might not have been there at all.

Why has Thucydides' statement gone unchallenged for more than 2,000 years? The reasons are many. For one, his own care and accuracy and skepticism gave whatever he said enormous weight. For another, the fact that Phoenician records about their own activities have never been found makes it necessary to rely on the records of others. For a third, and deriving from the second, the Phoenicians had always been a mysterious, elusive people. For a long time almost nothing was known about them except for their reputation as supreme seamen and long-distance travelers. When archeological evidence about them finally did begin to turn up, it tended to confirm this view since their settlements were widely scattered throughout the west. Finally, and perhaps most important, the archeological finds made at those places were not always systematically analyzed.

This brings us to the specialized subject of pots. The clay pot was the container of the ancient world; almost everybody made pots. Those who couldn't traded for them. They were in daily use as pitchers, drinking vessels and tableware. They were used to hold and store wine, water, oil—all liquids. They also held grain and such valuables as gold dust, not to mention the cremated ashes of the dead. Since pots were such universally employed objects, they also provided a good outlet for the artistic impulses among peoples, who made them in every conceivable shape and decorated them with all kinds of patterns. Later, after glazes became common, potterymaking became an art of great beauty and subtlety.

Pots break fairly easily. When broken they are thrown away. Their pieces, however, are very durable. As a result, the most common bits of human detritus found in every archeological site through the Mediterranean and Near Eastern world are bits of pottery. Since certain styles are easily attributable to certain peoples, and since the evolution of a single style over a period of years can be worked out, experts realized very early in the archeological game that pottery was the best way to analyze the different levels in the sites they were investigating—not only to determine the age of the pots but also to determine just who had lived there at a given time and with whom they had been trading.

The trouble with the pottery of the Phoenicians, particularly that found in Carthage and other western Mediterranean sites, was that it did not at first seem to show all that much variety. Their major output was a so-called red-slip burnished pot—an object of a brick-red hue, sometimes veering toward pale orange, and with a shiny interior surface. Designs were conservative. Decoration was minimal or entirely absent. Apparently the practical Phoenicians regarded their own pottery as utilitarian stuff.

Accustomed to trafficking in more exotic and valuable items like jewelry, scarabs and ornaments, and accustomed to dealing with the wares of others if they could find a market for them, they did not develop their own pottery designs much, but depended rather on trading in Greek and other wares. Nevertheless, all types of Phoenician pots inevitably traveled throughout the Mediterranean and, of course, exist in fragments, sometimes in great numbers, in all major sites that were occupied by Phoenicians for any length of time.

Despite their ubiquity, Punic pots were, in Rhys Carpenter's words, "long dismissed as a dreary sequence of undistinguishable uniformity," and hence not worth the archeologist's time to sort—"so devoid of character that they cannot be interpolated into any chronological system and hence are archeologically worthless for historical inferences."

Not so, says Carpenter; and he goes on to cite the work of Cintas, who after many painstaking years has given the pottery of Carthage and other western Phoenician sites a vitally needed and dependable sequence. Now for the first time it is possible to evaluate some of the material from sites in southern Italy, Sicily, Sardinia, North Africa, even Spain, to learn who was actually first in the west, the Phoenicians or the Greeks.

Answer: the Greeks.

An astonishing conclusion. Carpenter comes to it only after an exhaustive review of many Punic sites and an analysis that goes beyond pots to works of art, inscriptions and even includes a new way of dating pots themselves by laboratory analysis of the magnetic particles in the clay. All this analysis is beyond the scope of this book, but its cumulative weight is formidably impressive. Furthermore, it tends to un-

derscore doubts that other Phoenician experts have expressed about the accuracy of those very old traditional dates. Particularly it validates an argument advanced 80 years ago by J. Beloch, the German classical scholar. Beloch had the same ideas Carpenter advances now, but he was ahead of his time. He did not have the pottery analysis of Cintas to back him up; historical tradition was too strong, and he was laughed out of court.

So, how are tradition and the new archeological ideas to be reconciled? I would like to suggest something like this:

In the power vacuum that followed the collapse of Mycenaean Greece, the Phoenicians in the east did begin to reach out. They touched Cyprus, Rhodes, Crete, other Aegean Islands, even Greece itself. They also went south to Egypt and west from there. But they went as traders, not as settlers, and as a result left behind in the towns they visited little record of their early presence other than the goods in which they traded. As for the uninhabited harbors or beach fronts where they may have dropped anchor and gone ashore for only a night or so on their travels, they left little trace at all.

This pattern of activity began to develop around 1100 or 1000 B.C. It steadily expanded and, by the Ninth Century, had established the Phoenician ports as centers of great maritime and trading capability. Beginning then and continuing for the next 150 years were series of invasions by Assyrians from the east. At some point during this period these assaults had become so burdensome as to suggest to the Phoenicians—particularly the Tyrians, who were the only ones to stand up consistently against the Assyrians—that it might be prudent to establish a colony in the west, out of the reach of those avaricious invaders. Not only would this be good for the long-term outlook of Tyre, it would help with the exploitation of metals in Spain, a business opportunity that was by this time known to the Phoenicians. Ironically, even in Spain they may not have been first. Though they are generally credited with having been the first through the Pillars of Heracles, the Greeks appear to have beaten them there too. Phoenician pottery and other archeological material in Spain follow the dating pattern just described, whereas two Greek war helmets of an earlier period have been recovered from the bottom of a river that runs down to the Atlantic Ocean at Gades.

The Greeks, for reasons we do not know, did not follow up this early penetration and did not manage to develop any kind of regular trade with the far west. The Phoenicians did. By 750 B.C., perhaps earlier, they were going there regularly. It was only when increasing numbers of Greek colonists began popping up in southern Italy and Sicily that the Phoenician trade route to the west became threatened. Only then did the traders from Phoenicia occupy Sicily, and by that time the only part they could occupy was the western end, which the Greeks had not yet taken themselves. The first Phoenician toehold in Sicily seems to have been located on the island of Motya, which probably was first settled and fortified in about 700 B.C. The establishers of Motya were most likely the Carthaginians.

Exactly how Carthage itself fits into this picture is far from clear. The accepted date for the founding of Carthage is 814 B.C., when a group of dissident aristocrats went there from Tyre. The problem this date poses is that nothing quite that old has ever been found at Carthage. The earliest objects so far recovered date from a good 75 years later. The oldest parts of the original settlement have now been identified to the satisfaction of experts most familiar with the place. Nothing older, they say, will ever be found; only bedrock lies beneath. What the Carthagininans did during those first 75 years—if indeed they actually were there—remains a mystery.

Nevertheless, Carthage was founded and it grew rapidly. Although it initially kept ties with Tyre and sent representatives there for religious observances, it was far enough away to be completely independent and to develop a style and thrust all its own. To counter the rising Greek presence, Carthage abandoned the traditional Phoenician policy of sticking strictly to trade and to the management of its own city. It expanded its own hinterland, subdued the local tribes, developed a mercenary army and a large war fleet and began to speak for all the western Phoenician towns. It turned itself into a power with control over the western Mediterranean and developed an aggressive foreign policy. It began wars and defended itself vigorously in wars that were forced on it. Carthage grew into something quite unlike its mother city, Tyre.

In weighing all these matters it may not be too much to say that the Greeks made Carthage by giving it the incentive to become what it did. It is surely wrong to say that Carthage—or Phoenicia—was already settled throughout the west, or an important power, when the Greeks arrived. It is the persistence of that second and essentially romantic idea of a history extending mistily back for hundreds of years that continues to confuse the overall picture of the actual Phoenician enterprise.

What the Peddlers Peddled

Made of terra cotta, this bowl was found in a grave at Motya. Originally it had an unbroken ring of seven cups, each for a different liquid and all connecting to a ram's head from which the resulting blend was drunk.

For a thousand years it was impossible to move through the Mediterranean world without encountering Phoenician goods. Much of what was sold there—the jewelry, the glass, the carved ivory, the decorated metal bowls—was Phoenician. These came in a bewildering variety of designs, which resourceful artisans borrowed from other cultures to satisfy their customers' varied tastes.

In the beginning, the Phoenicians probably acted more as dealers, as middlemen, only too glad to handle Minoan pottery or Egyptian scarabs superior to any they could make. But their skills grew rapidly; in time they made most of the decorative objects in which they dealt.

One curious aspect of all this peddling is that most of what survives comes from other countries, which reflects the way Phoenician merchants flooded their markets. But it does make difficult the unraveling of what in fact was "Phoenician" in style and what was something else.

Generally speaking, the Phoenicians drew on two major style sources: Egyptian and Mesopotamian—the latter predictably, since Canaanites and Mesopotamians had a common cultural heritage.

Exquisitely Carved Ivory Miniatures

Although they made figurines, ornamental plaques and such useful objects as combs and hairpins from ivory, the Phoenicians' most notable ivory output was decorative panels for furniture. The Assyrians were great connoisseurs of Phoenician furniture and amassed tons of it in tribute and booty. The furniture itself has long since disappeared, but occasionally a piece of ivory inlay shows up —like the panel below, thrown into a well during the sack of the Assyrian city of Nimrud in about 700 B.C. and not recovered until 1951. Phoenician ivory came from the tusks of both Indian and African elephants. The Carthaginians, in fact, raised elephants on farms.

An ivory furniture panel shows a jeweled lion seizing a gilded slave's throat. The floral background: carnelians and blue enamel.

From Megiddo comes this crowned female nude, her hair elaborately braided. The figure's front is missing.

An ivory spool for spinning or weaving was found in the Carthaginian town of Lilybaeum in Sicily, near Motya.

The "Mona Lisa of Nimrud," about six inches high, was found in the same Assyrian well as the panel opposite.

Highly Wrought Gold Trinkets

However enormous their output of what today would be called "junk" or costume jewelry—assembly-line items of copper and bronze—the Phoenicians were also the quality jewelers of their world. They got their designs from Egypt and from the Aegean, and turned out exquisite ornaments of gold and silver. Most of the latter have oxidized and disappeared, but Phoenician gold endures. Much of it is "granulated"—its surface covered by minute beads of gold that were created by snipping small slivers from a thin gold wire. Heated, the slivers turned into globules. The process was lost for many centuries and baffled jewelers until its rediscovery in the 1920s.

A pendant earring of granulated gold links a crescent, a hawk and an acorn, all derived from Egyptian models.

One end of the hoop on this Minoan-style, whorled earring can be loosened, placed in a pierced ear and fastened.

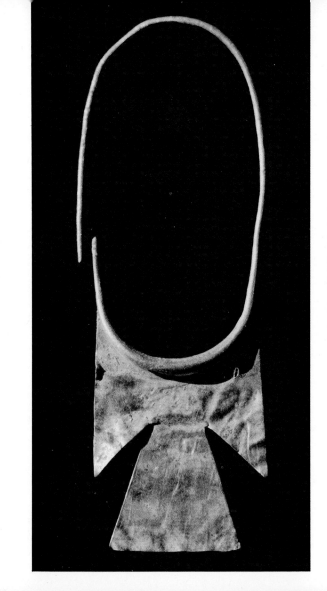

Snakes and a sun god adorn a pendant whose small size underscores the delicacy of Phoenician craftsmanship.

This crude earring has a beaten gold ornament that resembles an ankh, a good-luck symbol common in Egypt.

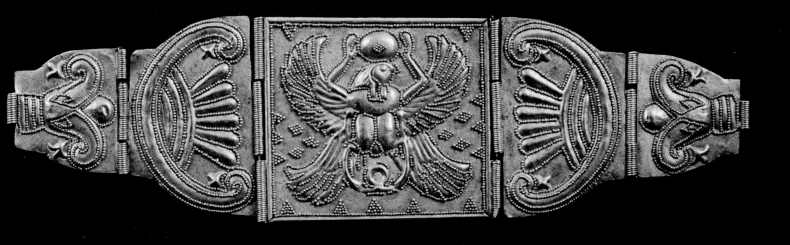

A superb hinged bracelet has its Egyptian motifs of lotus buds and a winged sun god picked out in tiny granules.

Beads and Bottles of Colored Glass

Inheriting a tradition of glassmaking from Egypt and Mesopotamia, the Phoenicians rapidly developed great skill in the manufacture of beads and ornamental objects. They also made small incense bottles and other containers, relying—according to tradition—on high-quality sand from a beach near Tyre. The Phoenicians used a paste of fine-ground sand combined with soda. Under high temperatures, and with pigments added, the mixture became colored glass. Since glass blowing was not yet known, containers either had to be hollowed out of solid glass blocks or molded around clay cores, which could be removed after the paste outside had been fused into glass by great heat.

Five necklace beads from a tomb in Sardinia typify the huge Phoenician traffic in small, molded-glass objects.

This jug was molded from blue paste. The colored decorations were added directly to the surface.

The vial at right and jug above are under five inches tall; the clay-core method yielded only small objects.

A Blend of Styles in Fine Metals

As silversmiths and as workers in figurative bronze, the Phoenicians achieved skills that made them almost without peer. Even the Greeks recognized the fact. Both the *Iliad* and the *Odyssey* admiringly describe Sidonian silver bowls, whose fame undoubtedly derived from specimens like the two shown here. But, once again, the best examples were not found in Phoenicia. The one opposite comes from a tomb near Rome. The one below, at left, is from Assyria. While both are unquestionably Phoenician, they represent a melange of Egyptian and Mesopotamian motifs that only those masters of stylistic cannibalizing—the Phoenicians—could possibly have dreamed up.

A lion hunt is the motif on this bronze bowl, one of a hoard amassed by Assyria's King Ashurnasirpal.

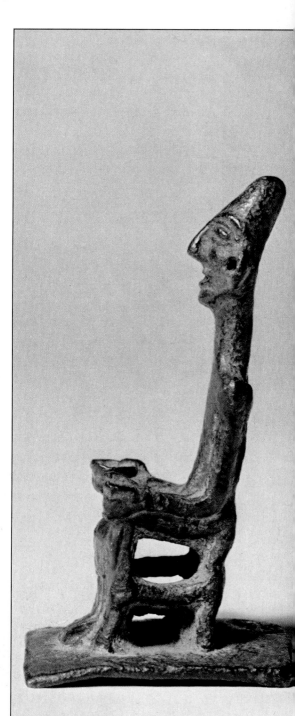

Far cruder than the bowls is this cast-bronze figurine, mass-produced by the shipload for dedication to a god.

A superb gilt silver cup combines an Assyrian castle and chariots (top) with unmistakably Egyptian figures (center).

What was it like to be a Phoenician living in one of the major ports? What did people wear? What kinds of houses did they have? How did they run their businesses, keep their records? What kind of a writing system did they use? How did they govern themselves? What kinds of taxes did they pay? How did they deal with their ferocious neighbors, the Assyrians? Above all, what did a Phoenician town *look* like? Answers to any of these questions are not exactly easy to come by.

As far as appearance goes, the best single bit of evidence is a handsome carved wall relief *(page 82)* from the royal palace of Sennacherib at Nineveh. It shows in detail the looting of a Phoenician city by Assyrian soldiers. Whoever the artist was, he certainly had a vivid idea of his subject. The principal impression it seems to have left on him was one of lushness and opulence. For an invader who has trudged across hundreds of miles of dusty plains and scaled iron-hard mountains, this is not surprising. A Phoenician port must have seemed green and rich beyond imagining. Water flows through the center of this relief —either the edge of the sea or a river. It teems with fish. There are fruit-bearing trees and grapevines. Palm trees sprout everywhere, some with plump pigeons flying through them and even a nest full of fledglings on one branch.

The city itself is a splendid one, ringed with turreted walls. Its houses are tall, with high narrow

Assyrian soldiers carry loot from a Phoenician city in this drawing of a relief found at Nineveh. The town—possibly Tyre—is strongly defended. It has high walls with towers. The houses rise two or three stories. Their upper windows have small rows of columns almost identical with those in the ivory on page 98—clearly a popular Phoenician architectural motif.

doors, colonnaded windows on the second stories and peculiar roofs that appear to reflect the artist's attempt to depict tiled domes, or else high bushes growing on roof gardens. Out of the city march the looters, loaded down with bundles of captured weapons and unidentifiable rods of some sort. Others are carrying furniture, handsome chairs or tables of Egyptian pattern with carved animal heads. In the background other soldiers are measuring trees and cutting them down; for the timber-hungry Assyrians, even the wood in a Phoenician city apparently was worth taking back home with them.

What city is this, so lovingly preserved in Sennacherib's palace? No one knows. But it could be Tyre, which is known to have been the target of Sennacherib's wrath in about 700 B.C. Whatever place it describes, this relief gives a unique picture of the external appearance of a Phoenician city. Only one other such representation is known, a much cruder relief scratched on a tomb at Cape Bon, in Africa —so crude as to nearly disqualify itself as a useful bit of evidence about what Phoenician towns really looked like. All it has in common with the stunning relief from Nineveh is the suggestion that its houses, too, had strange rounded shapes—domes or bushes —projecting from the tops of their roofs.

Of the interior of a Phoenician town, or what life was like therein, no reliefs or pictures survive at all, no written description of any sort. For that one must rely on inference drawn from contemporary cultures and religions, from the hints that those cultures drop in their own literature, from a few Phoenician inscriptions. Finally, and most important, one must rely on archeology—on what is turned up by the spade as it digs through layer after layer of cultural debris hidden in the earth. Unfortunately for the archeologist, all the major Eastern Phoenician port cities—Byblos, Berytus, Tyre and Sidon—are still occupied, their ancient quarters now buried beneath larger modern towns. It is impossible to get at the old Phoenician dwellings and temples except by the occasional accident of an excavation being made for a new hotel or business building.

The visitor to this area of the world does not at first realize what the true situation is. There are ruins all about him at the major sites, most of them Greek or Roman: single temple columns standing here and there, open-air theaters, paved avenues, baths, storage vaults, tiled drains and the foundations of numberless small buildings—none of them Phoenician. Where archeologists have been able to excavate at Byblos they have turned up a part of the city that dates from the pre-Phoenician Bronze Age, from Rib-Addi's time or earlier. The Phoenicia with which this book deals, the coastal ports of 1200 B.C. or later, has nowhere yet been properly revealed.

This extraordinary situation may be on the verge of a dramatic change, thanks to work now being done by James B. Pritchard of the University of Pennsylvania. In 1970 Pritchard and a team of coworkers started excavating a site eight miles south of Sidon that he had identified as the old Phoenician town of Sarepta. Never in quite the same class of importance as Sidon, perhaps because its harbor was smaller and poorer, Sarepta was nevertheless a thriving place as early as 1600 B.C. It ultimately covered several hundred acres and contained a good many thousand people. Now it is a wheat field, its surface uninhabited, and thus a prize that has heretofore not been available to archeologists: a Phoenician port site with no people presently living on top of it to bar proper scientific study of its ruins.

Where to start work on a large site is always something of a problem. Pritchard began with a straight narrow test trench that, with luck, led right into the old potterymaking quarter of Sarepta. His team has found 19 kilns and masses of broken and blistered pots that were ruined in firing and thrown away by their makers. Already half a million bits of pottery have been laboriously catalogued and cross-indexed as to their shape and their position at the site. All together, the gradually changing styles of these shards cover about 1,000 years of continuous production. Their absolute age has not yet been fixed, but Pritchard hopes to be able to do that when he has had a chance to broaden the excavating. If and when hard dates are found for this sequence of pottery, it should solve many riddles about Phoenician life and history, one of the most vexing of which is the already-mentioned problem of dating the founding of the Carthaginian colony.

Pritchard's first probe has already revealed that this one Phoenician town—and presumably others—had its various trades and industries concentrated in separate quarters. The pattern still prevails in many Near Eastern cities, but heretofore proof that it was followed in any Phoenician town has been lacking. A second Sarepta probe by Pritchard's team, so far very limited, promises to be as interesting as the first. Work there already has uncovered the location of a shrine (Chapter 5).

Also unknown as yet is the nature of Sarepta's defenses. All major Phoenician cities were walled towns located with a wary eye against assault, but Sarepta seems to violate this rule. It is not on an island, not on a hilly promontory, which raises the question of whether it was able to resist attacks on its own or whether it had to depend on neighboring Sidon for help in emergencies. There is some evidence that Sarepta was under the political domination of Sidon during much of its history. It may conceivably have been a sort of Sidonian suburb, a bit of ancient industrial urban sprawl without any of its own defenses. Further digging may answer that question.

Something similar did exist 15 miles farther down the coast at Tyre. Tyre, built on an island, is a perfect example of the kind of site the Phoenicians picked over and over again during their history. The island lay less than half a mile offshore. It was surrounded by low reefs and ledges that could be extended to form breakwaters for "summer" and "winter" harbors on the north and south sides of the island. Close at hand, along the coast, lay a flat expanse of extremely fertile land. This became the shoreside extension of Tyre, was intensively farmed and bore the name of Uzu. Since it was difficult to fortify, Uzu was overrun time and again when invaders appeared. The island citadel of Tyre itself, however, was a tougher nut to crack. From about 1000 B.C., and for some 700 years thereafter, Tyre would be a city famous for its defenses, immune to land assault because of its island situation, safe from invading fleets because of the strength of its own navy. It withstood many sieges and really succumbed only three times during its long history as a Phoenician city.

One probable reason for this long success is that for several hundred years fortified towns had been developing an increasing ability to resist sieges through the use of slaked lime as a waterproof plaster. This material was introduced in about 1400 B.C.,

and by the time Tyre had become a prominent city slaked lime was widely used for the construction of underground cisterns—applied either to rock or brick. Before the introduction of slaked lime the only possible large underground water container that a town could hope to have was one hewn out of solid rock. Cutting a reservoir big enough to supply the water needs of an entire town for months, or even years, was a huge task, and there was never any guarantee that it would not have cracks in it. Now, with slaked lime as a sealer, reliable cisterns could be made, and in places where solid rock did not exist. Since thirst had always been a problem in besieged towns without springs within their walls, the development of the cisterns was a great boon to island fortresses like Tyre.

The matter of defense was a perennial preoccupation of the Phoenician towns. Not only were they constantly squabbling with each other, they were prey to a far greater menace: periodic assaults by Assyrian armies from Mesopotamia. Assyria was only one of three ponderous invaders—the other two being Babylonia and Persia—that came trundling out of the east to harry the coastal cities. Of the three, the Assyrians were by far the worst. They hung like a black cloud over the area and for hundreds of years affected the politics of the coast and the fate of its cities and its kings. For a while, Tyre, Sidon, Byblos and other smaller towns were shielded by geography, by buffer states like Syria and Israel, which had to be subdued first before the Assyrians could reach the coast. The Bible is full of the agony and convulsions of those years. The prophet Isaiah wrote vividly about them, his stern warnings about desolation and darkness on the earth uttered against a background of pillaging Assyrian armies that assaulted the inland cities and crushed them one by one, scattering their people far and wide.

"Their arrows are sharp," said Isaiah of the Assyrians, "their bows bent, their horses' hoofs are as hard as flint, and their wheels like the whirlwind. Their roaring is like a lion, like young lions, yea, they roar. They growl and seize their prey; they carry it off and none can rescue it."

In due course the Assyrians reached the coast. For a time things were not too bad. The invaders had made it plain during their savage campaigns up in the stony plateaus that cities that resisted would be dealt with mercilessly—and they were. For those who acknowledged the preeminence of the Assyrian king, treatment would be much milder. In fact, one early invader, Ashurnasirpal II, took the trouble around 880 B.C. to summon 69,574 officials, ambassadors, assorted other bigwigs and just plain hostages from a number of different states, including Tyre and Sidon, to a huge levee, where for 10 days he "provided them with the means to clean and anoint themselves. I did them due honors and sent them back, healthy and happy to their own countries."

Since this was a bombastic ruler talking, carving out his exploits in stone to be remembered for all posterity, the quality of his entertainment—even the willingness of the guests to experience it—must be regarded with a good deal of suspicion. Whether the Tyrian and Sidonian representatives felt any happiness is doubtful. Certainly they were respectful, and very probably they carried gifts with them, carefully measured out so that they would be pleasing but not so munificent as to inflame Ashurnasirpal's cupidity.

What drew the Assyrians was the wealth of the Phoenician towns, which could not really be concealed. They came back again and again, sometimes to quell "revolts," which actually were refusals to pay crushing tribute, sometimes for no excuse at all. To a man they were braggarts. They set up inscriptions to immortalize themselves and their deeds. Of his first visit to the coast around 840 B.C. the Assyrian king Shalmaneser III wrote: "I marched as far as the mountains of Hauran destroying, tearing down and burning innumerable towns, carrying booty away from them which was beyond counting. . . . I received the tribute from the inhabitants of Tyre, Sidon . . ." A few years later he wrote: "I marched against the towns of Hazel of Damascus. Four of his larger urban settlements I conquered. I received tribute from the inhabitants of the countries of Tyre, Sidon and Byblos." It is worth noting that he did not claim to have burned Tyre or Sidon. They may have been too strong for him; more likely they bought him off.

Over many years of Assyrian harassment the relationship that seems to have been worked out was peace at the price of reasonable tribute. Terrible turmoil continued inland for a century or more, but the Phoenician traders apparently managed to purchase the kind of relative stability that a mercantile society must have to prosper. Unfortunately, this did not last. The descendants of Shalmaneser became greedier and more power-hungry than he had been. Tribute no longer sufficed; conquest was the aim. During the Eighth Century B.C. some smaller coastal towns were actually annexed to the Assyrian realm, with Assyrian governors running them. By the end of the century the noose had begun to tighten around the neck of Tyre, possibly the strongest of the Phoenician towns,

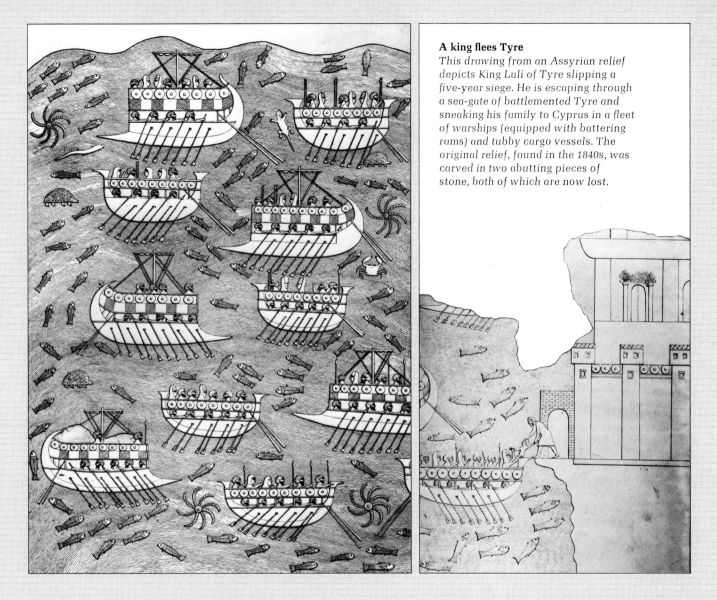

A king flees Tyre
This drawing from an Assyrian relief depicts King Luli of Tyre slipping a five-year siege. He is escaping through a sea-gate of battlemented Tyre and sneaking his family to Cyprus in a fleet of warships (equipped with battering rams) and tubby cargo vessels. The original relief, found in the 1840s, was carved in two abutting pieces of stone, both of which are now lost.

ruled at the time by a notably stubborn and independent king named Luli.

Secure on his fortified island, Luli, who was also king of Sidon, in the past had watched the Assyrians come and go and had withstood at least one siege. Now he decided to risk another, calculating that he could hold out indefinitely against the Assyrian invader Sennacherib. He was mistaken. According to one account, Sennacherib turned the whole coast against Tyre, seized a fleet of 60 Sidonian ships and blockaded Tyre by land and sea. Luli held out for five years on Tyre but finally gave up. The wall carving shown on this page seems to show Luli slipping the blockade and escaping to the nearby island of Cy-

prus. There is no way of telling for sure whether the reported cooperation of the other Phoenician cities against Tyre was a prudent, neck-saving course forced on them by Sennacherib or whether it was inspired by bitter intercity hatreds.

Sennacherib was followed by Esarhaddon and then by an equally bloodthirsty Assyrian ruler, Ashurbanipal, who went at the Phoenicians again. This time the roles of the two principal coastal cities may have been reversed. Sidon was knocked flat, getting no help from the Tyrians, who concentrated on holding their own until a deal could be worked out. Apparently one was. "I marched against Baal, king of Tyre," wrote Ashurbanipal. "I surrounded him . . . seized

Buying off the Assyrians

Tribute from Tyre (the seagirt citadel represented at right) has been placed aboard loot-laden boats that are being hauled upon the beach by ropes. There, Phoenician porters carry the booty to the Assyrian king Shalmaneser III, who commissioned this memorial bronze about 830 B.C.

his [approaches] by sea and land. I intercepted and made scarce their food supply and forced them to submit to my yoke." For all this boasting, Ashurbanipal does not claim to have breached Tyre. A compromise was worked out in which King Baal agreed to hand over a daughter and several of his nieces as concubines, all with large dowries.

A good solution for King Baal. Not so good for the young princesses, who were shipped to Assyria and disappeared from history. Worst of all for the "approaches" mentioned by Ashurbanipal. Those approaches were the ill-defended farmlands and town settlements of Uzu and nearby Akka on the mainland. Some idea of how warfare was conducted in those days may be gleaned from a carved statement written by Ashurbanipal when he departed the coast: "I killed those inhabitants of Uzu who did not obey their governors by refusing to deliver tribute which they had to pay annually. I took to task those among them who were not submissive. Their images and their surviving people I led as booty to Assyria. I killed those inhabitants of Akka who were not submissive, hanging their corpses on poles which I placed around the city."

All in all, the Assyrian presence on the Phoenician coast seems to have had three phases measured by an increasing escalation in violence and cruelty. The first consisted of sporadic raids and conquests, with the Assyrians content to depart after sweating as much tribute as they could out of the Phoenician cities. The second established the principle of a continuing Assyrian presence, with resident Assyrian governors or agents, or even puppet kings under control of the Assyrians to ensure that tribute would be forthcoming on a regular basis. The third, stemming from Assyria's inability to prevent revolts and refusals to pay tribute, led to the destruction of cities and to the slaughter or deportation of entire populations. A gruesome lot, the Assyrians.

It is ironic that what little we know about who was who in the Phoenician cities during the period of their maximum harassment by the Assyrians is from the Assyrians themselves, and results from their unquenchable desire to record their exploits in stone. If it were not for the boasts of Sennacherib, for example, we would not even know of the existence of King Luli. With so little information about the rulers themselves, it becomes even harder to work out the nature of their rule and the extent of their powers.

That they were kings in the proper sense of the word—that their office was hereditary—we can be sure; monarchy was the familiar model for rule in all the old Semitic states. The word for king—*mlk*—is nearly the same in Hebrew and Phoenician. It was a potent word. Recognition as king gave a man special powers and the reverence and awe of his subjects. He stood in a closer relationship to the gods than

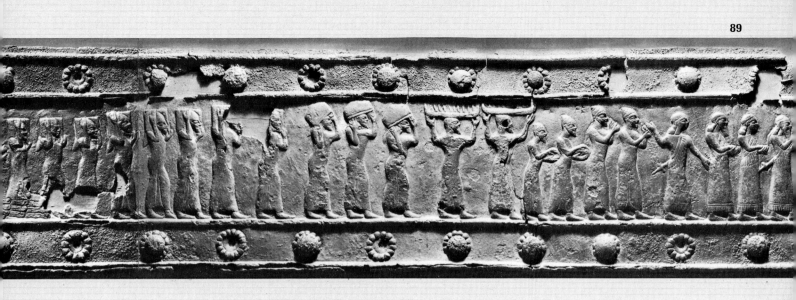

they. In fact, some Phoenician monarchs appear to have arrogated to themselves certain priestly as well as secular powers. One Tyrian high priest, Ithobaal, seized the throne after a series of palace murders. There is no record of his having given up his powerful priestly authority and perquisites after he became king.

Although kings and high priests undoubtedly came out of the same top drawer in Phoenician society, the latter had a different kind of authority. The Phoenicians' relations with their gods were propitiatory; that is to say, they felt obliged to make sacrifices to them in order to keep in their good graces and forestall calamities. Being fearful of their gods, they were equally fearful of the priests who represented the gods. The priests, after all, were the experts in dealing with the gods, in interpreting the gods' wishes, in blunting the gods' anger, in correctly carrying out the complicated rituals that were necessary to prevent evil from falling on an entire city, in knowing just how to accept the sacrifices needed to make the gods smile on the people. And if the priests could affect cities because of their special relationship with the gods, how much easier to affect the fortunes of one being.

That is why in all ancient societies spiritual authority carried such an immense weight. While not backed up by the threat of instant mutilation or imprisonment or death that a king could mete out by a wave of his hand, a priest was backed up by some-

thing equally intimidating: the whim of the deity, which could be used to cripple or destroy men—and even their descendants for generations—more terribly and more finally than could any king. This situation must have produced a very interesting tension between king and priest. How the two balanced out their respective powers is not known, although there may well have been considerable inherent overlap, resulting from the close blood ties that would have existed among individuals at the very top of Phoenician society.

One thing they almost certainly would have to have had was wealth. The connection between power and wealth, close in all societies, was extraordinarily close in the mercantile societies of Phoenicia. An aristocracy based on wealth ran each city. To the extent that the rich traders and merchants could hold on to their wealth, dynasties of noble families appeared in all cities and constituted a ruling class, with priestly and other perquisites—either earned, bought or grabbed—gradually accrediting to them. Once acquired, those perquisites, together with the power and wealth that they conferred, were clung to as "rights." It is those rights, legitimatized by law or custom, that perpetuate a ruling class.

In some such fashion a stratified society, all of whose layers were preoccupied with business, consolidated itself. Below the Phoenician nobility were lesser businessmen, *arrivistes,* a whole host of craftsmen, dealers, shopkeepers and entrepreneurs of all sorts. Below them were the still smaller scramblers and scufflers that any mercantile society supports. Below them were slaves.

Just how widespread the use of slaves in Phoenicia was is difficult to measure. Written references to them are almost entirely lacking, and what little survives is made obscure by the fact that the word for slave could also be used to define the relationship between a man and his god or a man and his king. Nevertheless, slavery as an institution was commonplace throughout the Near East; its existence in coastal Lebanon can be assumed. Clay tablets of a slightly earlier period from Ugarit and other places contain interesting references to slavery. From them we learn that manumission—a slave's right to buy his freedom if he could save up the money—was possible. We also learn that adjoining states had agreements for the return of runaway slaves. From a different source, Homer, we learn that the Phoenicians were slave traders. The main source of supply probably was prisoners of war, although there apparently was a steady drifting into slavery of some Phoenician citizens who sold themselves because they could not survive economically as free men.

All other Phoenicians, of course, were free men, citizens of their respective towns. The French historians Gilbert and Colette Charles-Picard make the important point that the Phoenician political unit, like the Greek, was a city-state. If that is so, it explains in yet another way why "Phoenicia" as a country never emerged, each city being too preoccupied with its own affairs and its own individuality, and too jealous of its own hegemony to endure being merged into a kingdom that embraced a large territory and a num-

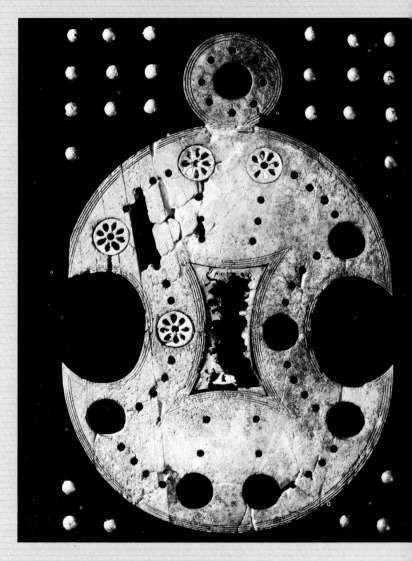

This 12th Century B.C. ivory game board was found at Megiddo, southeast of Tyre. The gold balls probably were heads of pins that were moved from hole to hole according to rules now unknown.

ber of cities. In a city-state, citizenship is a valuable asset. And citizenship means, in theory at least, that all citizens will have a say in how things are run. A good deal is known about how the Greeks, through much social turmoil over a century or two, managed to evolve from highly authoritarian little city-states run by single rulers or small groups of autocrats into societies where lower-ranking citizens did have a vote and did exercise it.

There is almost no information about how—and to what extent—this took place in either Phoenicia East or Phoenicia West, but clues exist. One clue comes from Tyre. There, by about 800 B.C., the common citizens apparently had some muscle. They were strong enough to give one of their kings, Pygmalion, the backing he needed for control of the throne in a palace struggle with his sister Elissa, who was backed by a faction of rich aristocrats. Her husband (a high priest, incidentally) was murdered by Pygmalion, and Elissa with her friends fled west to Africa to found the city of Carthage.

Somewhat later in Tyrian history, in about 600 B.C., civic control is known to have rested in the hands of a panel of suffetes, administrators with some judicial authority. It is true that suffetes ran Tyre for only a few years and that they were imposed on the city at a time when it was subjugated by the Babylonians. But the very fact that there could be recourse to suffetes suggests that the office already existed and had some powers to offset the authority of the king. Furthermore, Carthage, founded by Tyrian refugees, had suffetes even earlier than 600 B.C. The office presumably was brought from Tyre, since the flow of influence in that direction is more likely than from colony back to mother city. Finally, in Car-

thage itself there is a good possibility that there never was a king in the traditional sense. Certainly by about 550 B.C. the Carthaginian leader—typically a general —was answerable to a council as well as a senate of 300 members and was not called king.

From these shreds of evidence we can guess that some kind of social progress through the dilution of kingly power must have taken place throughout Phoenicia. But undoubtedly it was slowed down along the Phoenician coast by a special circumstance. By the time ideas of suffrage and democracy were beginning to penetrate Greece and Rome, Assyria had succumbed to the Babylonians. The Phoenician cities fell increasingly under the thrall of Babylonian rulers and, in turn, of their conquerors, the Persians. The Babylonian and Persian potentates were absolutists of the most absolute. Nebuchadnezzar II or Darius the Great would have been dumbfounded at the thought that anybody could tell him what to do. The Phoenicians dealt with those awesome men as best they could. Badly with the Babylonian Nebuchadnezzar, a ruler of appalling cruelty, who in 572 B.C. finally succeeded in winning the second of the three great sieges lost by Tyre (this one lasted 13 years). Better against the Persian Darius, who was more enlightened, and who gave the Phoenician kings considerable autonomy. Still, the Phoenician thrones, in the face of batterings from the east, tended increasingly to become a kind of extension of the administrative arm of whatever eastern ruler was exacting tribute. He had his own representative there at the Phoenician king's elbow, and his job was to observe and report. Once, the Assyrian king Esarhaddon went so far as to instruct King Baal of Tyre: "You are not to open [any] letter which I send you without the royal deputy. If the royal deputy is absent, wait for him and then open it."

But this overview was for the purpose of top-level control and to keep tribute flowing. How the Phoenicians regulated their day-to-day affairs was probably of little interest to the imperial agent, and their details are unknown today. The king had a Council of Ancients to advise him and a "governor," actually an administrative deputy, to see to the running of the city and the court. Beyond that, information is meager. We do not know what sort of judicial system a Phoenician city had, how the city administration was set up, what the titles and duties of the officials were (other than those of the governor), how civic order was maintained or even who paid for it and how. In addition to the tribute levied by Mesopotamia, there must have been local taxes. Evidence for that comes from Ugarit, whose clay tablets list various kinds of taxes, and also—shades of today—tax loopholes.

We can be fairly sure of two things. First, since business was the business of the Phoenicians, society was certainly shaped to deal efficiently with it. There must have been a rather sophisticated expertise in contracts and agreements and an equally sophisticated machinery, based on a code of civil law, to handle the misunderstandings and arguments that flower in all mercantile environments. We can assume that the Phoenicians had a court system that was well adapted to the handling of civil cases and that the court calendars were flooded with them.

Second, we can assume that the tilt of power, privilege, favoritism—whatever word is chosen—was strongly in the direction of the mercantile upper class. There are continued references to nobles and aristocrats. Where titles exist, privileges follow; the laws undoubtedly were written to favor the nobility. It would be nice to be able to trace the emergence of some sort of egalitarianism in an evolving Phoenician city. But aside from the few hints already mentioned, the evidence just is not there.

And yet the concept of a city-state—where citizenship is both a privilege and a responsibility—requires an egalitarianism of sorts. Phoenician cities must have had it. Therefore, the question becomes: How widely in society did it spread? To all citizens most probably, but considerably diluted as one went down the scale of wealth. The saving grace of a mercantile aristocracy is that it is fluid. Anyone—any citizen, that is—can work his way into it simply by becoming a rich man.

In that kind of society, with rich and poor alike engaged in manufacturing, banking, shipping or barter, something of the hum of daily Phoenician activity begins to be heard. Life for most of the citizens of Sidon or Tyre or Sarepta cannot have been very different from the bazaar-flavored life of eastern Mediterranean cities today—with their family-owned glass shops, potteries, metal shops, woodworking shops, jewelry shops, all huddled cheek by jowl in their respective quarters (as the pottery concentrations at Sarepta suggest). The stocks of merchandise would have been displayed in crowded booths, with a great deal of haggling and bargaining going on constantly, much of it in the streets. Streets were surely narrow (as they were in an earlier Byblos) and buildings rather modest. Limited space on islands like Tyre, and the desire for the most easily defended stone walls ringing the mainland cities, would have tended to keep all buildings and activities jammed together.

Sidon did not get around to minting coins until nearly 400 B.C., and then only under the influence of the Persians, who had done it for some time. This Sidonian silver half shekel shows a war galley with shields and a high stern lying by a walled city —presumably Sidon. The reverse side is imprinted with the head of the Persian king and attests to the close Persia-Sidon ties at that time. Sidon was Persia's principal naval base. Sailors probably were paid off there in these coins, which may have been minted under the direction of a Persian governor.

Warehousing, shipbuilding and repair, ship chandlery and such specialized occupations as rope working and lumber storing were important ingredients of Phoenician trade. Much of this activity undoubtedly spilled out beyond the city wall. At Tyre, with all its mercantile and manufacturing ferment taking place on the tiny island citadel itself and probably on a larger scale on the mainland, there must have been a tremendous bustle of small-boat service between the two. The dye works, for example, were located ashore. But considering the vulnerability of shore-side warehousing, the finished products—being extremely valuable—were more likely stored on the island, where they could be easily guarded.

Then there was the problem of delivery of food from the mainland. The Tyrians ate a great deal of fish, but their vegetable garden was a strip of coastal plain that the city controlled. It was intensively planted in cereals, grapes, olives, figs and dates. Some or all of these things could have been grown on the island too, but probably not in quantities large enough to support Tyre's population; the overriding need was for "office" space on a small island given over almost entirely to temples, palaces, government buildings, private housing and the demands of trade.

With all this buzz of business, there had to be a great deal of paperwork. It may seem strange that absolutely nothing of Phoenicia's files has survived in Phoenicia itself. The reason is simple. Paper—papyrus—has a short life in a climate like that of Phoenicia East. So has parchment. The sun-dried clay tablet lasts longer, but even it disappears in time unless it is artificially hardened by firing. Furthermore, Phoenician businessmen, being up-and-coming, probably used clay tablets very little and kept most of their rec-

Aids to Elegance

The Phoenicians dealt extensively in pretty boudoir items, always taking care to see that the decorative elements satisfied their customers. For example, the Carthaginian bronze razor at left has incised on it a figure in keeping with a demand for things Greek; the mirror has a lotus handle, reflecting an earlier taste that demanded Egyptian motifs.

Bronze razor, Carthage, c. 250 B.C.

Ivory comb, Megiddo, c. 1250 B.C.

Silver mirror, Byblos, c. 1250 B.C.

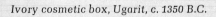

Ivory cosmetic box, Ugarit, c. 1350 B.C.

ords on the more conveniently handled and more conveniently stored—but more perishable—papyrus that was a major trade item with Egypt.

A switch from one writing material to another usually requires a switch in writing method. Long before the Phoenicians came on the scene, the method that had been worked out in Mesopotamia, where papyrus was hard to obtain but clay very abundant, was well suited to the latter material. A clay tablet is soft. Scratching thin curved lines on its surface is difficult, but it is easy to press small straight indentations into it. Mesopotamian scribes used a special writing tool for this purpose, and the impressions that it left were wedge-shaped. It is these wedge-shaped indentations, arranged in various patterns to form a large number of signs, that gave Mesopotamian writing the name cuneiform, a word that derives from the Latin cuneus, or wedge.

Cuneiform signs, though ideal for clay tablets, are something less than ideal for quick, easy writing on a paper surface because of their complexity. Therefore, as the Phoenicians (and presumably their most immediate ancestors) began using an entirely new writing material, they also began using a different set of simpler signs that could be set down more efficiently on that new material. This new set of signs led to the modern alphabet—one of man's greatest cultural achievements and widely credited to the Phoenicians. The story, however, is not that simple. The Phoenicians did not "invent" the alphabet, but they did have a large hand in developing it.

As far as experts can determine, writing starts with crudely drawn pictures: a man, a cow, a spear. In time a picture becomes so simplified or stylized that it no longer looks like a man but still means "man" to anybody who can recognize the symbol—i.e., "read" the writing. A later development comes when those stylized signs no longer stand for objects but for sounds. At that point the sound-sign for "man" can do multiple duty: it can be used with other sound-signs to make entirely new words. For example, combined with three other sound-signs—"ip," "yew" and "late"—"man" makes a new word: "manipulate." Or combined with the sound-sign "snow," it makes another: "snowman," and so forth.

By 2500 B.C. Mesopotamian cuneiform, generally conceded to be the oldest-known form of writing, had already reached a point where it was based on abstract patterns of wedge-shaped sound-signs, two or three thousand of them. To the uninitiated they look like the letters of some strange alphabet. But alphabets are made up of individual letters—single sounds that cannot be simplified or reduced further. Mesopotamian signs had not reached that stage. Some of them represented entire words, some of them represented syllables, none of them represented individual letters. Therefore, a list of Mesopotamian signs can be called a syllabary, but not an alphabet.

As time passed, the number of word-signs in the Mesopotamian syllabary shrank considerably, while the proportion of those that represented syllables grew. By Babylonian and Assyrian times the cuneiform syllabary was down to six or seven hundred signs, of which about 150 were syllables: sounds like "we" or "wa," "mu" or "mo," "rid" or "red." These, of course, could be combined with other syllables to make literally thousands of words.

Cuneiform spread widely through the Near East and was taken up by many tongues. By 1500 B.C. the inhabitants of Ugarit were using it on their clay tab-

The oldest Phoenician sarcophagus found, dating from about 1200 B.C., is that of Ahiram, King of Byblos. It presents a puzzle because the inscription (detail on opposite page) that identifies it as Ahiram's apparently was added 300 years after it was made. Its original occupant is unknown. The sides of the coffin itself are carved with friezes of figures and with decorative motifs derived from Egyptian and Syrian styles.

lets. In their hands cuneiform became so streamlined that it was reduced to only about 25 or 30 characters of their own design. Superficially, they looked like the old Mesopotamian syllables, but their inner purpose was quite different. They had been stripped down and simplified until—with a couple of exceptions—they had become single consonants.

The Ugaritians, like the Israelites and later the Phoenicians, were Semitic peoples who spoke variations of a single mother tongue: northwest Semitic. In writing the various dialects of northwest Semitic it is possible to get along without vowels, and so the Phoenicians and their neighbors eliminated them. In doing so they seem to have followed the example of the Egyptians, who also wrote without vowels and who may have transported that idea to places like Ugarit and Byblos, with whom they had long contacts. But the Phoenician coastal towns apparently were clever enough to take the Egyptian idea without the Egyptian signs. Egypt was mired in a complex system of pictorial hieroglyphics whose signs took time to draw and numbered in the hundreds. Only about 25 of them were true sound-syllabic signs. Here the Phoenicians appear to have stepped in with their epochal contribution to writing. According to the language expert Ignace Gelb, they lifted from the Egyptian system only the small number of flexible

sound-syllabic signs that it contained and produced from them an "alphabet." What is more, the Phoenicians did not bother with the elaborate Egyptian signs: pictures of birds and human figures and drinking vessels. Instead they substituted much simpler signs they seem to have invented themselves: circles, crosses, slanting lines—things that look like modern letters, things that could be scribbled quickly on papyrus by busy bookkeepers.

I have put the word alphabet in the preceding paragraph in quotes because the Phoenician model contained no vowels—just 22 consonants. A true alphabet requires vowels, and if we are to be precise we should give credit to the Greeks for developing one, since it was they who took over the Phoenician letters and simply added some symbols of their own to stand for vowels. That, at last, was an alphabet.

Though their contribution to writing was enormous, the written heritage the Phoenicians have left us is disappointingly small, for all the reasons already discussed. The earliest-known text in Phoenician characters that is more than a few words long is an inscription carved on a large stone sarcophagus found at Byblos. The sarcophagus was subsequently determined to be the tomb of King Ahiram (not to be confused with Hiram of Tyre), who reigned in Byb-

los early in the 10th Century. When deciphered, the inscription turned out to be a warning to others, calling down a curse on them if the tomb was opened. Whatever else of Phoenician writing that has survived is also largely inscriptions, most of them carved on steles, or small stone monuments. They consist of short dedications to a god or goddess, and are monotonously alike. Beyond informing that the Phoenicians were devoted to erecting such monuments to their gods and giving us the names of a good many individual Phoenicians, they tell little else. The rich store of clay tablets from Ugarit, it is true, says a great deal about the Phoenician religion. But it should be emphasized again that Ugarit, in the opinion of many, lies just outside the time scale of Phoenicia. Also this is not "Phoenician" writing; it is in Ugaritian and other dialects, all of them written in cuneiform. This proto-Phoenician city was apparently destroyed before papyrus could replace the clay tablet there and, hence, the old Mesopotamian method of writing was retained. The kind of Phoenician documents that *would* inform: business accounts, stories, codes of law, historical writings, royal archives—all presumably written on papyrus—are completely nonexistent in Phoenicia.

So we are left still wondering what kind of breakfasts people ate, where they gathered to gossip and what the gossip was about. Even what they wore is vague. True, there are careful pictures by Assyrians and Egyptians depicting Phoenicians, but they usually portray important persons: trading emissaries, tribute-bearers, high-ranking captives. All wore long, dresslike garments, thickly embroidered and usually secured by wide belts. Their affinity to the formal attire of other Near Eastern people is close, but it says nothing about what a carpenter wore to work every day. A comparable vagueness appertains to women's dress. Although museums contain a considerable number of small female statuettes, clay models and ivory carvings made by Phoenicians, most are believed to depict goddesses.

In any event, we can surmise that Phoenician men were bearded. They wore their hair long and rather elaborately curled. Jewelry was abundant; the Phoenicians made and dealt in it in enormous quantities and certainly were connoisseurs of it for their own use. The jewelry included finger rings, bracelets, earrings, necklaces both beaded and made of metal links, and pendants of all sorts, including the flat, circular or oval plates known as plastrons. Displayed on the breast, plastrons were supported by fine necklace chains and decorated with enamel, jewels or delicately incised designs.

In any speculation about Phoenician dress three

*The "woman in the window" is a familiar
motif in small Phoenician ivory
carvings, although who she was—goddess,
priestess or private citizen—is
not clear. What is clear is that she is
looking out of an upper-story window;
the same row of small columns
underneath the sill crops up in Assyrian
pictures of Phoenician towns.*

things should be kept in mind. First, as noted, their own representations of clothed figures are more often than not of gods and goddesses and may not be reliable evidence for ordinary dress. Second, they were not only borrowers but deliberate borrowers, seeking to satisfy the stylistic demands of their customers. Thus, though there may be a strong Egyptian or Mesopotamian cast to many Phoenician-made objects that depict clothing and even hair styles, it is impossible to state conclusively that the Phoenicians themselves dressed like the models they were copying. Third, the world changed during the course of Phoenician history. Early Phoenicia was oriental in its overall flavor; late Phoenicia became Hellenized as Greece rose. Greek manners and Greek styles turned out to be extraordinarily seductive throughout the Mediterranean. Late Phoenician and Carthaginian sites show that their own cultural traditions were no match for the Hellenism that began to blaze through the Mediterranean world after about 400 B.C. Sarcophagi begin to show the influence of Greek art. So does other statuary. Greek clothing styles begin to creep in. Greek and Phoenician gods begin to get confused with each other and are no longer easily sorted out. Even Greek mosaics have been found in the floors of Phoenician houses.

But all this was very late. During their heyday, and before they were ground down by the Babylonians, the Phoenician ports glowed with a special refulgence of their own—particularly Tyre. Tyre might be called the Paris of the ancient world. It was a center of luxury, a place where the best of everything had been collected, where the finest Phoenician artists and craftsmen worked. The Biblical prophet Ezekiel, in a furious denunciation of this rich, pulsing city, gives a stunning description of it, listing the extraordinary variety of its merchandise and its no-less extraordinary web of mercantile connections. Here are some excerpts from Ezekiel's tirade:

"Oh Tyre, you said, 'I am perfect in beauty.' Your frontiers are on the high seas, your builders made your beauty perfect; they fashioned all your timbers of pine from Senir; they took a cedar from Lebanon to raise up a mast over you. They made your oars of oaks from Bashan; they made your deck strong with box-wood from the coasts of Kittim. Your canvas was linen, patterned linen from Egypt to make your sails; your awnings were violet and purple from the coasts of Elishah. Men of Sidon and Arvad became your oarsmen; you had skilled men within you, Oh Tyre, who served as your helmsmen. You had skilled veterans from Gebal caulking your seams. You had all sea-going ships and their sailors to market your wares; men of Pharas, Lud and Punt served as warriors in your army; they hung shield and helmet around you. . . . Men of Arvad and Cilicia manned your walls, men . . . were posted in your towers.

"Tarshish was a source of your commerce . . . offering silver and iron, tin and lead. Javan, Tubal, and Meshech dealt with you, offering slaves and vessels of bronze. . . . Men from Togarman offered horses, mares, and mules. Rhodians dealt with you, great islands were a source of your commerce, paying what was due to you in ivory and ebony. Edom . . . offered purple garnets, brocade and fine linen, black coral and red jasper. Judah and Israel dealt with you, offering wheat from Minnith, and meal, syrup, oil, and balsam, as your imports. Damascus was a source of your commerce . . . offering wine of Helbon and wool of Suhar, and casks of wine from Izalia . . .

A Medieval View of Alexander at Tyre

The exploits of Alexander the Great have fascinated people ever since he lived. Shown here are sections of a 14th Century illuminated manuscript —its pictures a blend of Byzantine, Moslem and European styles—telling of Alexander's siege of Tyre in 332 B.C. Unfortunately, the artist knew nothing of actual events. He was even unaware that Tyre was an island and that Alexander built a causeway to it. All the artist got right was that Tyre was strongly fortified and desperately defended. When Alexander actually took the city, he crucified 2,000 surviving males and sold the women and children into slavery.

wrought iron, cassia, and sweet cane. Dedan dealt with you in coarse woollens for saddle cloths.

"Arabia and all the chiefs of Kedar were the source of your commerce in lambs, rams, and he-goats. Dealers from Sheba and Raamah dealt with you, offering the choicest spices, every kind of precious stone and gold as your staple wares. Harran, Kanneh, and Eden, dealers from Asshur and all Media, dealt with you; they were your dealers in gorgeous stuffs, violet cloths and brocades, in stores of coloured fabric rolled up and tied with cord."

This is Phoenicia at its very peak—its vividness intensified by Ezekiel's dire prophecy: the subjugation of the citizens of Tyre by the Babylonians, which indeed came to pass in 572 B.C.

That assault by Babylon represents a watershed in Phoenician history. Tyre had a ghastly time at the hands of Nebuchadnezzar II and recovered slowly from the terrible 13-year siege he laid down. It would never again be the premiere city of the Phoenician world. For one thing, Tyre's colony Carthage, far to the west and beyond the reach of Assyrian or Babylonian destroyer, was at the time nearly 250 years old and had become larger and more powerful than Tyre itself. From now on, Phoenicia West, growing increasingly away from the homeland in style, in politics and in its trading activities, would spin out a separate history of its own. More and more it would overshadow Phoenicia East in the Mediterranean.

But the old trading ports were far from done. Resiliency and accommodation had always been their long suit. They gritted their teeth and endured the Babylonians. Then in 539 B.C. Babylon itself fell to Persia—a miracle—and the cities of Phoenicia quickly addressed themselves to accommodating the new conqueror. To their vast relief, the Persians turned out to be relatively reasonable people with good ideas about running an empire. Persia continued to exact tribute, even made Phoenicia a part of one of its satrapies, or provinces. But Persia also shrewdly recognized the strategic importance of the area in its larger plans and permitted the Phoenician kings to di-

*The illuminations start with an attempt by Alexander
(wearing crown far left) to storm Tyre. Repulsed by arrows,
he rides off. He then has a dream (above) warning him not
to enter Tyre in order to parley. In truth, Alexander dickered
with the Tyrians for an open city so that he might secure his
rear while campaigning elsewhere. Refused, he attacked.*

rect their own states. The monarchs were, in fact, elevated almost to the status of allies. They were happy to provide the Persians with war fleets, first for campaigns against the Egyptians, later against the Greeks.

Persian dominance of the Near East was a stabilizing influence and helped Phoenicia in three ways. First, Persia established an internal message service —a kind of pony express with horse changes at regular stops along the way—that greatly speeded communication. Second, coinage, recently adopted by the Greeks and the Lydians, was taken up by the Persians shortly after their conquest of Lydia. They struck their own coins and made them the standard of exchange throughout their huge empire. For a trading people like the Phoenicians, access to such a standard was a godsend. Third, Aramaic, a Semitic dialect written in Phoenician characters, was adapted as the lingua franca from one end of the Persian empire to the other, from the Aegean Sea to India. It meant that all the bartering and record-keeping that the Phoenician traders had been engaging in could

now be conducted in a language that was almost identical with their own, and written in a script that they themselves had invented.

All in all, though the Phoenician ports were once again confronted with the problem of dealing with an immensely powerful empire from the east, Persian control was relatively benign and they prospered under it. They were even feisty enough to talk back. According to Herodotus, when the Persian king Cambyses conquered Egypt in 525 B.C. with the help of a Phoenician fleet commanded by Phoenician admirals, he then proposed to continue west and conquer Carthage as well. But the Tyrians objected strenuously, pointing out that Carthage was a colony of Tyre. That would be parents attacking their own children, they said, and declared that if this plan were pursued they would withdraw their fleet entirely. Cambyses quietly abandoned the project.

When the Persian kings Darius and Xerxes began cranking up plans for conquering Greece, all the major Phoenician cities jumped at the chance to help in

The reason for the dream-warning on the previous page is now made clear. Two of Alexander's ambassadors go to parley (above) and are crucified (right). The Greeks wrote that Alexander tried to enter Tyre by asking permission to make a sacrifice to Heracles at a temple inside the city; but the Tyrians, suspicious of his intent, would not let him in.

that venture. Greece had become their enemy too, interfering more and more with their trading activities in the Mediterranean. They therefore joined energetically in the plan to march a ponderous Persian army, supported by a Phoenician fleet, north around the Aegean Sea. This army would cross the Hellespont on a bridge of ships' hulls held together by cables, and then pour down into Greece, annihilating the Greek city-states one by one.

Unfortunately for the Phoenicians, they picked the losing side, although the loss was not their fault; they did their own and more. They helped with the bridge across the Hellespont, repairing and strengthening its cables and anchors when it was carried away by a storm. When Xerxes' other engineers were balked by constant cave-ins during their efforts to cut a canal through a peninsula in Thrace in order to get a more protected route, the Phoenicians showed how the cut could be successfully made by digging a wide "V." They provided a fleet of war vessels, troop carriers and cargo ships for the great Persian army as it rum-

bled south. They fought a gallant naval engagement in the Strait of Salamis (pages 49-55). But for all this help, the Persians were defeated in 480 B.C., and the Eastern Phoenicians lost their chance to eliminate the Greeks as trading rivals. In this period the Phoenicians also lost out in the west. The Carthaginians had been involved for years in a struggle with the Greeks in Sicily for control of that island. With eastern Greek cities faced by overwhelming Persian might, a faction in Carthage persuaded the government that now was the time to strike in Sicily, when the city-states back in Greece were too preoccupied with saving their own skins to send reinforcements to Sicily. Accordingly, a Carthaginian army landed in western Sicily in 480 B.C. but surprisingly suffered a catastrophic defeat at Himera.

As a result of those twin setbacks in east and west the Greek presence began to be felt with increasing strength everywhere: in Sicily in the west, throughout the Aegean and in Ionia in the east. The Mediterranean was becoming colored by Hellenic

Alexander has another go at Tyre (left), this time successful, and rides off (above). His siege actually took seven months, during which the Tyrians protected their walls against battering rams by cushioning them, using skins stuffed with seaweed. As the outer walls crumbled, the Tyrians built others inside them, meanwhile raining red-hot sand on Greek troops.

ideas and traditions, rather than by Asiatic ones.

This coloration, strangely enough, took place during a near century of recklessly self-destructive wars among the Greeks themselves. Athens and Sparta were the chief protagonists, but their rivalry drew in virtually every one of the several dozen Greek city-states. When it was all over by 380 B.C., Greece was so enfeebled that it was no match for some rude country cousins from the north, the Macedonians. For the first time in its history the Greek peninsula was consolidated under the rule of one man, King Philip II of Macedon. And it was his son Alexander the Great who really set the stamp of Hellenism on the eastern Mediterranean by deciding to conquer Persia.

With an expeditionary force of tough Macedonian cavalry, Alexander destroyed the Persian armies in a couple of quick battles: at the Granicus River in 334 B.C. and at Issus in 333 B.C. Like all campaigners in the area, he instantly recognized that the Phoenician ports would have to be secure to him before he could strike south into Egypt or east into Persia. Ever prac-

tical, the Phoenician cities abandoned their erstwhile Persian friends, hauled in their canvas and prepared to dicker with the new conqueror—all the cities, that is, but Tyre. Safe on their island behind battlements that were stronger than ever before, siege-hardened and with a large fleet, the Tyrians were confident that they could stare down and eventually discourage this madly impatient Macedonian. Impatient he may have been, but he was also implacable. He set every able-bodied man on the coast to hauling stone and earth, dragging tree trunks down from the mountains, and built a causeway from the mainland to the island. Tyre fell in a last, furious, smoking siege. All its men were killed, 2,000 of them crucified. The women and children were sold into slavery.

Of all the men who went against Tyre, Alexander is the only one whose handiwork still shows. His causeway remains. Swept by the tides, a steady deposition of sand gradually accumulated. Today the causeway is a quarter of a mile wide, supporting houses and a highway. Tyre is an island no longer.

Ugarit, that ancient Canaanite city up the coast from Byblos, was sacked and leveled by invading sea people or by pirates in about 1234 B.C., probably within a few decades of the fall of Troy. It could even be called an unsung Troy because Ugarit had neither a Homer nor a later history; it was never reoccupied or rebuilt. Rich as it was, it might never have been remembered at all except as a mound of earth-covered rubble had it not been excavated by the archeologist Claude Schaeffer in 1929.

What Schaeffer found at Ugarit was by far the largest collection yet discovered of proto-Phoenician clay tablets dealing with religion and myths. Scholars argue over whether the Ugaritic texts properly can be called Phoenician. They do not argue over the many insights these valuable texts gave into what the Phoenicians believed.

An important fact that the Ugaritic texts help confirm is the connection between many of the religions of that time and that part of the world. Whether Canaanite, Assyrian, Babylonian or primitive Greek, the general structure of the pantheon was the same, although the names of the gods and goddesses—and some of their specific attributes—changed from place to place. Thus, though it cannot be established for certain that the cults that emerged in the various Phoenician cities are descended directly from those described in the Ugaritic texts, it is clear that the cults are closely related. It can be assumed that they had a common Canaanite origin and diverged increasingly through the passage of time. With this model in mind, the Phoenician pantheon can be described.

Its head was a male deity called El in Ugarit. His name meant simply "god," and he seems to have incorporated within himself the widest aspects of a universal deity. He was called "the father of the gods," "the creator of creators." For all this, he seems to have been a rather passive deity who continued to exist as a shadowy father figure for the other gods and goddesses in the later pantheons of the many Phoenician cities.

The active role was taken by Baal, the god of storms. It is Baal's identification with strength, violence, youth, dynamism that characterizes his position as the leading male god throughout Phoenicia. Baal has come down to us as *the* Phoenician god, the one who personified for the Hebrew prophets a faith that was all too competitive with their own. The Bible is full of thunderous declamations against the evils of Baal. He represents, by extension, the entire non-Hebrew Semitic pantheon, with all its trappings of multigods, infant sacrifice, idol worship and so on.

Actually there was a great deal more to the Phoenician religion than Baal. It had a basic structure similar to those of a number of contemporary faiths, based on a very old myth that attempted to explain the mystery of the cycle of the seasons. El had a consort, the mother goddess, Asherah-of-the-Sea, whose son died each year to symbolize the cutting of the harvest and the drying up of the land. The son was then reborn to signal the return of spring and a new crop.

Elaborations on this myth are varied and interesting. In the Ugaritic texts Baal, who is associated with rain and life-bringing water, is the young god who

This ivory plaque, scarcely five inches in height, was found near Ugarit and shows a goddess flanked by two goats. It dates from the 13th Century B.C., a time just before the collapse of the Bronze Age culture of the Aegean. The Canaanite cities were still being influenced by Aegean styles, as the bare breasts and flounced skirt of the goddess show.

dies. He disappears underground. There Baal's sister Anat comes to his rescue, finds his body and retrieves it. In another text, cited by the Canaanite scholar J. Gray, Baal himself fights with Mot:

They glare at each other like glowing coals:
Mot is strong, Baal is strong:
They thrust at each other like wild oxen;
Mot is strong, Baal is strong;
They bite like serpents;
Mot is strong, Baal is strong;
They kick like stallions;
Mot is down, Baal is down on top of him.

The symbolism of the text is clear. The earth has managed to survive death and drought. The young god will appear, alive and healthy, at the time of the sprouting of the new crop in the spring.

In addition to these gods and goddesses, the Phoenician pantheon had a large number of others, some in charge of specific activities, like the Sidonian Eshmun, whose particular province was healing. Another, Dagon, was associated with wheat; still another, Reshef, with plague, and so on. To complicate matters further, identities were not stable. El and Baal, for example, assumed different names and somewhat different characteristics from city to city. In Tyre Baal became Melqart, and as such was duly exported to Carthage. The name derives from "mlk," meaning king, and "qrt," meaning city. But the god inside the new name was the same old Baal, active lord of storms, the presiding deity in most Phoenician cities. The leading female deity was the fertility goddess Astarte. Her name varies from country to country, even from one Phoenician city to another. In the Bible she is known as Ashtoret; in Babylon, Ishtar; in ancient Greece, Aphrodite. But in Byblos she was known as Baalat, or simply "lady," clearly the feminine form of Baal, which means "lord."

An important characteristic the Phoenician faith had in common with others of its day was sacrifice. The ceremonies had two purposes. The simpler and more direct intention was to appease the god, make him think well of you, smile on your hopes, temper his wrath. The second purpose of the rites was the strengthening of the god himself. Giving up something to him, particularly something that was extremely valuable to you, enhanced his own worth and ultimately his power. Failure to honor the god regularly and properly not only weakened his desire to do well by you but also weakened his ability to do so.

The Phoenicians—it must be admitted of them—practiced the ultimate in sacrifice: human lives. Other faiths succeeded in getting away from human sacrifice, as did the Phoenicians eventually. But they were late to do so. The Hebrews knew they practiced it and were revolted. Even after Phoenicia East apparently abandoned human sacrifice, it continued in Carthage—and revolted the Romans.

For evidence of human sacrifice in Phoenicia East we have only a couple of references in the Old Testament. For Phoenicia West the evidence is irrefutable: hard evidence dug out of the earth. There is an old burial ground in Carthage from which thousands of small clay pots containing the remains of babies and young children have been recovered. Mixed with these urns are others containing the remains of young animals: kids, lambs, kittens, puppies. Clearly the Carthaginians had been making infant sacrifices but were also using substitutes in the form of those young animals. But—and here is the interesting and com-

An infant about to be sacrificed is held in the arm of a Carthaginian priest. This carving was made on a limestone obelisk that was found in the precinct of the goddess Tanit at Carthage, and dates from the Fourth Century B.C.

pelling part—the substitutes were deemed ineffective. As late as about 320 B.C. noble families who had fallen into the habit of substituting young slaves, or perhaps animals, for their own children were blamed for a military disaster that had overtaken them. Since they had slighted the gods, they were forced to make restitution, and 500 infants from the best families were offered up.

By that time religious sacrifice in Carthage had been going on for about 400 years. Infants were brought to the Tophet, a sacred place containing an idol or a very old and holy stone, and killed there. As in the case of other contemporary faiths, sacrifice of flesh was accompanied by burning. This accounts for the many references to fiery furnaces, to "passing through the flames." Apparently the tiny child was brought to the idol, calmed by a priest and its throat cut. It was then placed in the arms of a bronze statue that had a furnace or grate beneath it. There are hints that the arms of the god may have been operated mechanically in such a way as to drop the dead infant into the flames.

Certainly devices of one kind or another were used to heighten the awe of the worshipers and their belief that the deity was responding to acts of piety. In the case of a hollow statue of one goddess (page *128*), holes were bored in her breasts, then plugged with wax. At an appropriate point in the rite, the wax would melt under the influence of heat, and milk, which had previously been poured into the statue, would then begin to flow miraculously from the holes.

In a harsh faith, interpreted to fearful people only by priests, the priestly power was obviously very great. Priests were numerous and divided into a hierarchy, with a high priest in charge of each temple

UGARIT: BAAL, C. 1500 B.C.

Graven Images from the Phoenician Pantheon

Two problems plague the identification of the "graven images" that the Phoenicians and their neighbors made of their gods. First, nearly all the peoples of the area had similar faiths and similar gods, though the names and attributes varied somewhat from country to country. Second, since most of the religious wall carvings and statues survive unnamed, it is necessary to infer from what the god is doing or carrying who he is. At left, for example, the message is pretty clear. The deity—from Ugarit—is Baal, the god of storms, of energy, of action. He stands before a tree of symbolic lightning, holding a spear in one hand and brandishing a club with the other. Opposite him could be another lightning-wielding Baal, this time from Syria. The next image—depicted in a long tight robe and a tall headdress—poses a puzzle. Could this be Astarte, goddess of fertility? No one knows. Beyond her is an Ugaritic figure of Baal, but with an Egyptian crown. And, finally, there is an unidentifiable Phoenician goddess with an elaborate Egyptian-style headdress and wearing a clinging Egyptian gown.

SYRIA: BAAL, C. 725 B.C.

LEBANON: ASTARTE, C. 1400 B.C.   UGARIT: BAAL, C. 1350 B.C.   LEBANON: DEITY UNKNOWN, C. 900 B.C.

and other subordinate priests under him. In addition the temples had scribes, butchers for cutting up sacrificial animals, lamp-tenders, barbers whose job it was to shave the heads of high priests, plus great numbers of general workers, temple assistants, gardeners, craftsmen and slaves.

The preoccupation of the Phoenicians with their faith was enormous. As a result, the priesthood had great financial as well as political and religious clout. Offerings were served up constantly: wine, perfume, incense, animals and sometimes simply fruits or vegetables. (Humans were reserved for special occasions or dire calamities.) The priests maintained lists of the tariffs imposed for each type of sacrifice. They prescribed the proper offering to expunge a particular offense, also the fee that went to the priest for accepting the offering and for performing the ritual that went with it. One such listing provided that for every ox sacrificed the priest would get a fee of 10 pieces of silver, and if the sacrifice were being made to relieve a sin (rather than being a mere expression of devotion to the god) a portion of the ox would also go to the priest. By such customs both temples and priests became wealthy, and the office of high priest became a plum jealously secured by certain noble families.

The size of the priestly hierarchy and its varied duties suggest that temples were large and elaborate places. This is not necessarily so. Indeed there is evidence that much Phoenician worship took place at small open-air shrines, which very often were simply designed. A rock or altar or small enclosure located in some exposed "high place" served very well. "Place" was important since divine powers were attributed to specific waters (springs or rivers), groves of trees and stones. The oldest-known shrine

at Carthage is a small square space cut into a rock. Devoted to the goddess Tanit, the shrine is scarcely a yard wide. Like many another Phoenician holy place, it drew its strength from its age and quite possibly from the sacred objects on or near the site. It may be, of course, that the unusually small size of this shrine reflects only the extreme poverty of those who first settled in Carthage.

A slightly larger shrine, recently discovered by James Pritchard at his exciting new dig at Sarepta, is in the form of a small oblong building with a raised altar at the back. Running around the inside perimeter of this building is a stone bench or platform with a plastered top. It juts from the wall like a low counter on which worshipers set out their offerings to the god. In addition to the foods and incenses that they regularly put down, the Sareptans also left a great number of small clay statuettes. Such little figurines have been found in a number of Phoenician sites, and were undoubtedly votive offerings of some kind. Whether they were actual images of the gods themselves is not easily answered. One of the figurines is nude, and that fact eliminates it as a god or goddess; in the long tradition of Semitic religions gods and goddesses were always represented fully clothed in rich garments appropriate to their station.

Even the clothed figurines may not be gods. Some of them are very full-breasted, others have swollen bellies—clearly they represent pregnant women. These features suggest that the little figurines were statues representing the petitioners, not the gods. They were carrying messages to the gods, pleas for answers to prayers. "Make me fertile," they seem to say; "ensure the safe delivery of my child."

Once placed in a shrine and dedicated to a god, a

clay figurine became a holy object, the property of
the god. It could not be destroyed. Over many decades—perhaps centuries—the pile-up in a small
shrine must have been extremely awkward. How
some of the figurines were disposed of at Sarepta was
discovered by Pritchard when his team dug through
the plaster floor of the shrine. There, carefully buried in a rectangular excavation, were nearly 30 of
them—three-dimensional prayers, one might almost
call them, preserved for some 2,500 years.

Sarepta may also hold the answer to another important question about Phoenician religious life: the
nature of Phoenician temples. There are indications
that a far larger structure—as yet unexcavated—lies
alongside the little shrine just described. Pritchard
can scarcely wait to get at this larger building, for up
to now knowledge of Phoenician temples has been

meager. Elsewhere in Phoenicia several temple sites
have been discovered, but all of them exist only as
foundation outlines, their walls nowhere more than
a few feet high. But they do follow so regular a pattern that it begins to be possible to describe the floor
plan of a "typical" Phoenician temple.

It was an oblong building with three rooms: first a
small anteroom, then a large main hall, finally a small
holy-of-holies at the back. The latter was reached by
a short flight of steps and contained an altar and an
idol, or whatever object was worshiped there. Sometimes it was simply a sacred stone called a *betyl*.
Pritchard's small shrine at Sarepta apparently had
a *betyl* standing directly before the altar; there is a
place for it there in the floor, but the stone has long
since been wrenched out and carted away.

A Phoenician temple probably was a rather high,

narrow, boxlike building with a tall entrance door. Steps went up to this door, which was flanked on either side by a free-standing column of wood, stone or bronze. The columns seem to have had names and distinct personalities of their own, and conceivably godlike properties.

The most detailed description of a Phoenician temple is in the Bible. It is not a direct piece of evidence since it describes a building commissioned by Solomon in Jerusalem and intended for Hebrew worship. Nevertheless, it was designed by Tyrian architects and built by Tyrian craftsmen. It fits the overall three-room model, even to the flights of steps and the columns at the front door, and adds many other details of a distinctly Phoenician flavor. It was made of heavy blocks of dressed stone, finished off inside with cedar, to which a good deal of gold ornamentation was added. It had large wooden doors, whose flanking columns were made of bronze by a Tyrian metalworker who also fabricated a number of bronze water troughs and other containers for use both inside and outside the temple. Despite fundamental differences in the two faiths, the similarities of some of the temple details are remarkable.

An important aspect of the Phoenician religion was belief in an afterlife. Evidence to this effect is abundant and varied and shows strong Egyptian influences. The Egyptians took great care to preserve the bodies of the dead. They became master embalmers, employing methods and materials that are not entirely understood today. Embalmed bodies were sometimes put in wooden mummy cases shaped like human bodies and with the owners' faces painted on them, sometimes in bulky coffins hollowed out of solid blocks of stone, which were also body-shaped and had faces carved on their lids. Archeologists call the body-shaped cases "anthropoid" coffins.

At some point in their history the Phoenicians, who had previously been using large clay burial urns or tombs built up of brick or stone, began adapting the anthropoid models of the Egyptians. A few have shown up in Phoenicia East, notably a superb black basalt coffin that was used for the burial of the Sidonian king Tabnit. It was discovered, along with some other extraordinary finds, in a burial ground outside Sidon in 1887. The find was unusual because it had not been broken into previously and looted by grave robbers.

For more than 2,000 years Sidon has been plagued by tomb robbers. Worse in a way, local vandalism and the need for handy blocks of stone to build houses, walls, sheds for animals, even to pave roads and make gutters has done irreparable damage to a vast honeycomb of underground tombs that was a thousand years abuilding. So rich was the store of dressed stone buried in the ground that local farmers had long made a practice of renting out their fields to anyone who wanted to come and quarry them.

Sidon was a city as old and rich as Tyre. Through a good part of its later history its prominent people were using two kinds of coffins. One was roughly house-shaped and was supposed to provide a domicile for the corpse after death. The other, an anthropoid coffin, was a substitute body in case the one inside decomposed completely. Efforts to prevent decomposition were taken by borrowing embalming methods from the Egyptians. Since the Phoenicians had long been supplying the Egyptians with cedar oil for embalming purposes, it is a near certainty that they were thoroughly familiar with Egyptian techniques. However, no method of embalming could be depended upon to counteract the dampness of the coastal climate in Phoenicia and the slow seepage of water into a tomb and, finally, through its cracks into the coffin itself. The few Phoenician mummies so far recovered are, with one exception, badly decomposed, and the linen bands that they were wrapped in have almost entirely rotted away. What bits of bone or cloth have been found are all from stone sarcophagi. If the coffin was made of wood—and many probably were—then coffin, along with body, disappeared long since.

At Sidon the cemeteries were in the low hills surrounding the city. There shafts were sunk into the ground and chambers for the coffins led off from them. Sometimes these chambers were vaulted with stone blocks, sometimes cut from the mother rock. Often several were connected to a single shaft, branching off at different levels. Steps were cut into the sides of the shafts so that the grave workers could get up and down. When a sarcophagus was finally in place, the chamber was walled off and the shaft sealed at its entrance with stone and then completely covered with earth.

The Sidonian stone sarcophagus that came into being about the Fifth Century B.C. was an extraordinary object. It took the Egyptian anthropoid shape, with a human face carved on the lid, but that face was in the Greek style. The result was a unique form of sculpture, not limited solely to Sidon but nevertheless peculiarly and characteristically Sidonian. Of the few score recovered from throughout the Phoenician world and now in museums in Europe and the Near East, nearly every one comes from Sidon.

Clues to the nature of Sidonian burial practices be-

gan to surface in the middle of the last century. At the time Sidon, like other coastal Lebanese cities, had resident foreigners. Many of them were amateur archeologists, and there was a lively clandestine traffic in grave objects and statuary not only among some of the foreigners but also between local dealers and collectors in Europe. I say "clandestine" because the graves were nominally the property of Turkey. What is now Lebanon was then part of Turkey—the once-great Ottoman Empire in the last stages of imperial decay. Places like Sidon were of little interest to the corrupt and listless sultans rotting in their capital at Constantinople (now Istanbul) some 600 miles north. The sultans were either powerless to hinder the steady despoilment of Sidonian treasures or unconcerned by it. As early as 1860 this indifference began to frustrate European archeologists working in the area. One, the Frenchman Ernest Renan, explored more than a hundred tombs at one necropolis, only to find that all had been looted, their sarcophagi smashed and their carved stone ornaments hacked off and carted away. Within seven years the necropolis itself had been totally vandalized, with most of the stones that made up its vaults showing up in new buildings in downtown Sidon. A fascinating historical site had disappeared.

In that same year an American missionary and antiquarian, William Eddy, was sitting at his home in Sidon one evening when local workmen burst in to tell him of a stunning discovery, a number of extra-large and beautifully ornamented sarcophagi in a series of connected chambers at the bottom of a shaft that was a full 20 feet across. Eddy went immediately to the site, had himself lowered down the shaft and by the light of a lantern examined the coffins.

Poking about in mud and dripping water, and nearly asphyxiated by bad air, he was able to explore five separate chambers with no less than seven sarcophagi in them. One was a black Egyptian design, a couple were of the Phoenician anthropoid type. But the others were of Hellenic design, far outstripping in richness of detail anything previously found at Sidon. They were large marble caskets, their sides richly decorated with figures in high relief.

After recording as careful a description of them as he could under the circumstances, Eddy was hauled up again and a message sent to Constantinople. Luckily, the director of antiquities for the museum there was a French-educated, honorable official named Hamdy Bey. Instead of allowing the finds to be broken up and trickle into the black market, he went immediately to Sidon, posted round-the-clock guards and in the name of the sultan took possession of everything at the site. Eventually all the sarcophagi found a safe resting place in the Imperial (or Topkapi) Museum at Istanbul, where they may be examined by scholars today.

The superb Hellenic-style coffins represent the last gasp of Phoenician art as it surrendered to the overpowering influence of Greek esthetics. As to who commissioned them or who ultimately occupied them there can be only conjecture. They date from about 300 B.C. and were obviously made for very important people, perhaps for the local dynasts or governors who inherited this part of Alexander's empire after his death. They are made of Pentelic and Parian marble of the highest quality, the former imported from mainland Greece, the latter from one of the Aegean Islands. But they probably were carved on the spot by Phoenician craftsmen. As in everything else they came in contact with, the Phoenicians down to their very last days were still adapting either the materials or the artistic innovations of others—sometimes both—and turning them to their own use.

Getting the sarcophagi out of their underground chambers was a difficult job because of the delicacy of their carvings and their great size and weight. One —now known as the Sarcophagus of Alexander because its friezes show the Macedonian king in combat and on a lion hunt—is 11 feet long and weighs 15 tons. Hamdy Bey solved the problem of removal by digging a slanting tunnel into the hillside and hauling out the sarcophagi on rollers, one at a time. While he was underground supervising this work he happened to glance at the ceiling of one of the chambers and noticed that some time in the past a small hole had been cut there by tomb robbers. Forcing his way up through the hole, he found himself in another chamber at the bottom of a second and entirely unsuspected tomb shaft about 20 feet away from the other larger one. This was not as deep as the other and was entirely unconnected to it. It, too, had its separate burial chambers. The one that Hamdy Bey had crawled into was empty; tomb robbers had cleaned it out. But by some fluke they had not noticed that one of the walls had been bricked up. Hamdy Bey ordered the bricks removed and found another room with a floor made of thick, close-fitting flagstones. He ordered them pried up, only to find another layer of flagstones and beneath them a third layer. Below it was a great stone slab. Apparently somebody—or his heirs—had taken great pains to make sure he would not be disturbed.

That somebody turned out to be a Sidonian king. When the last slab was removed and Hamdy Bey was

The versatility of Phoenician sculptors is revealed
in this sarcophagus, one of eight magnificent Greek-
style specimens found in 1887 at Sidon. This one
is known as the "Lycian" because it follows a style of
funerary art practiced in Lycia in southwestern
Anatolia: an exaggeratedly arched lid and scenes of
bear and lion hunts running around the sides. Its
occupant is unknown. Date: about 400 B.C.

able to shine a lantern into yet another chamber, he
found himself staring at the black basalt face of an
Egyptian anthropoid sarcophagus. When it was tak-
en out of the vault, it proved to have carved on it a
long inscription in the Phoenician language. It identified itself immediately:

> "I, Tabnit, priest of Astarte, King of Sidon, the son of
> Eshmunazar (who was also) priest of Astarte and King
> of Sidon, am lying in this (coffin). Whoever you are
> who might find this (coffin), don't, don't open it and
> don't disturb me, for no silver has been given me, no
> gold, no jewelry whatever has been given me. Only I
> myself am lying in this (coffin).
> "Do not open it, do not open it, do not disturb me,
> for such a thing would be an abomination to Astarte.
> But if you do open it and if you do disturb me, may
> you not (have any descendants) among the living un-
> der the sun, nor any rest (with the dead)."

This inscription recalls others that have been taken
from Phoenician tombs and coffins. It is clear from
the sorry record of Phoenician tomb desecration that
such a curse almost never worked. But in this case it
did. When Tabnit's sarcophagus was opened, there
lay King Tabnit inside. He was stretched out, almost
intact, on his back on top of a sycamore board with a
depression carved in it as a resting place for his head.
His body had been strapped to this board with rope
laced through six silver rings attached to the board.
Two of the rings were still in place and there were
bits of rope still in the coffin. Both body and board
were floating in an oily brownish liquid.

Here, at last, was a chance to learn something
firsthand about the secrets of Egyptian and Phoenician embalming, for Tabnit was extraordinarily

The Sarcophagi of Kings Tabnit and Eshmunazar

One of the most stunning Phoenician archeological finds ever came in 1855 with the discovery of a black basalt sarcophagus *(far right)* buried in a hillside near Sidon. An inscription carved on it in Phoenician characters identified it as the coffin of King Eshmunazar, son of Tabnit, King of Sidon. But who was Tabnit, and where was he buried? Why did the son have so magnificent a coffin when there was no sign of the father?

The answer came 32 years later. In a tomb a mile away, a matching sarcophagus was found, inscribed with Tabnit's name. Nearby was a second, empty coffin upon which no face was carved. Scholars believe it was intended for Tabnit's wife.

The experts are still arguing, however, about how the three sarcophagi got to Sidon, particularly since Tabnit's obviously was secondhand: it had the name of an Egyptian general, Pen-Ptah, inscribed on it. Was Pen-Ptah a military resident in Sidon who ordered three coffins made in Egypt for himself and members of his family —the last one never finished because he did not know who might occupy it? Was he later forced to flee Sidon, leaving his property to be confiscated? More likely, Tabnit scented a bargain during the Persian conquest of Egypt and ordered an agent to snap up the three handsomely crafted, ready-to-use sarcophagi for the royal family.

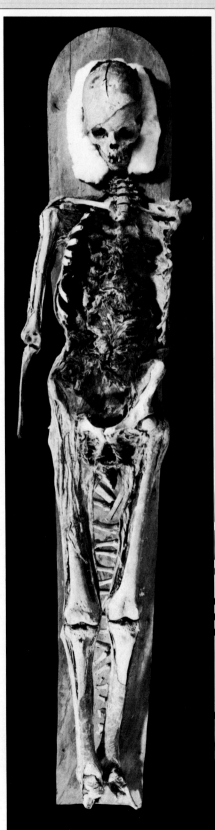

The coffin of King Tabnit is Egyptian down to its last detail, even including the name of the man who originally owned it, Pen-Ptah. When the sarcophagus was first opened in 1887, Tabnit's mummy (right) was inside it. Still soaked by the oily, brownish embalming liquid and lying on a plank of sycamore wood, Tabnit was extraordinarily well preserved. His remains, though now deteriorated, may still be seen at the Archeological Museum in Istanbul, where the coffin too is on display.

The sarcophagus of Tabnit's son, King Eshmunazar, is a near twin of the father's, but covered with Phoenician writing. Now on display in the Louvre, the coffin is actually not as wide as it looks here; the foreshortening was caused by the hard-to-photograph location of the sarcophagus.

well preserved. He was a slender but strongly muscled man about five feet five inches tall. His skin was still intact, soft to the touch, and revealed that he had had smallpox. He had a large aquiline nose, a prominent chin and wavy reddish-brown hair that showed signs of having been tinted. An incision had been made in his chest to remove his stomach. The eyes were missing. Otherwise, except for bits of his nose, lips and chest that had been exposed to the air, his body was in remarkably good shape. Even more surprising, the organs were also in good condition. That strange oily fluid, plus a quantity of fine sand in which Tabnit's body was partially embedded, had done a good job of preservation.

Hamdy Bey supervised the careful rolling-out of Tabnit's sarcophagus through the tunnel he had dug, then went off to lunch. While he was gone some overzealous members of the work crew succeeded in upsetting the coffin. All the fluid ran out onto the ground and was lost. With it went the secret of Tabnit's preservation.

Tabnit was the son of the Sidonian king Eshmunazar—his coffin inscription makes that clear. He was also the father of another Eshmunazar who was buried nearby in another black basalt sarcophagus that is now in the Louvre. The sarcophagus of the second Eshmunazar has a very long inscription on it that confirms descent from his father, Tabnit. It also contains the interesting information that his mother, Tabnit's wife, was also Tabnit's sister, a priestess of Astarte. Here again is that strong suggestion of the close linkage between priestly and royal power in Phoenicia, and of the attempts to keep as much as possible of both in the hands of a single family.

Two Eshmunazars and a Tabnit. Three names are added to the list of Sidonian kings, bringing the known total to 18. But they are sprinkled over a thousand-year span and show once again how sparse our knowledge is of the details of Phoenician city history. The typical Sidonian anthropoid coffin—that marble object with an Egyptian shape and a Greek face—is of no help in enriching that history, for it never carried any inscription at all. It was simply an oblong block of marble, vaguely body-shaped and with a removable lid. It was turned up at the foot, Egyptian style, and in some instances actual feet were carved there. Usually the face was stylized to a certain degree but, as the examples on page 116 show, attempts were made at portraiture.

Looking at those calm, smooth countenances with their staring eyes, we do get glimpses of the individuals who lay beneath them. And that individuality and a sense of lifelikeness were once far stronger than they are now, for the Phoenicians—again following Greek tradition—carefully painted the statues. Traces of color remain on many of them. One in particular, dug up at Sidon, has its paint extraordinarily well preserved. The hair is dark red, a pale flesh tint has been given the face and the lips are red. The eyes have been done with great care: brown iris and black pupil, very pale blue for the white of the eye, a dot of red in the corner, and individual eyelashes—painstakingly painted in. This sarcophagus was jarringly lifelike when found and was the gem among a memorable hoard of 11 anthropoid coffins unearthed in a network of two tomb shafts near Sidon in 1901. Although work has continued sporadically at Sidon ever since and many further finds have been made, nothing compares to this single haul or to the spectacular Tabnit-Alexander finds of 1887.

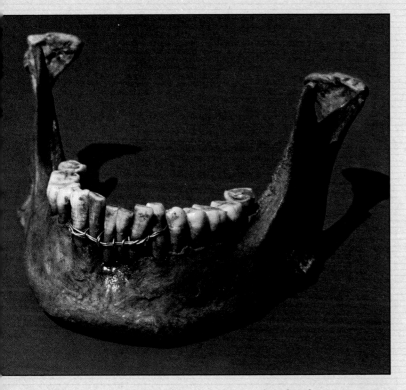

Evidence that the Phoenicians were
skilled dentists crops up in this jaw of
a man found in an anthropoid coffin
at Sidon. As a result of pyorrhea, his
front teeth had loosened and were
fastened together with a gold wire. The
device apparently served its wearer
well for many years; parts of the wire
were covered by salivary deposits.

A curious fact revealed by the excavations at Sidon is that the Phoenicians were expert dentists. The upper jaw of a woman found in one sarcophagus had two teeth from another individual neatly fastened to her own with gold wire. Whether the dental work was for cosmetic purposes (the new ones were front teeth) or to give her something to bite with is not clear. But in the case of a man found in another sarcophagus the utilitarian nature of his dental work is obvious (page 119). He was suffering from pyorrhea and was faced with the loosening or loss of six of his teeth. All these were held in place with a single strand of gold wire woven most dexterously among and around adjacent firmer ones. Their owner wore this device for years, for the teeth are well worn down, showing extended use.

Although the fashion for anthropoid coffins flourished in the east, it never caught on in Carthage and other western Phoenician cities. Only a few scattered examples have been found in these places. What Carthage did do was to take the tomb shaft west and develop it. Some shafts in burial grounds in and around Carthage are as much as 100 feet deep and reflect the efforts to which people went to keep their graves from being disturbed. There usually are only three or four coffin chambers in each of these monster shafts, indicating that accommodation of large numbers of corpses was not their purpose.

Where and when the Phoenicians first turned to cremation—as a substitute for regular burial, or inhumation—is not clear. The older coastal Canaanite practice, strongly influenced by the Egyptians, was interment. Cremation seems to have crept in during the upheavals and invasions of the 12th Century B.C., for isolated instances of it crop up here and there

Anthropoid coffins from the Sidonian burial ground lie side by side in the National Museum at Beirut. They date from the Fourth and Fifth centuries B.C. Usually made of marble, they derive from Egyptian models, but their faces show the strong Greek influence that continued to crop up in Phoenician art.

throughout the Levant after that time. The practice probably was carried west to Carthage and there strengthened by contact with local North African custom, because there is a great deal more evidence of cremation in Phoenicia West than there ever was in burial sites in Phoenicia East.

Though the westerners may have lagged as makers of sarcophagi, they were very active makers of gravestones, or steles. Steles are known throughout Phoenicia East and reflect a long tradition of erecting votive shafts or commemorative stones of one kind or another. In Phoenicia West they are enormously abundant. Motya alone has produced hundreds of them; Carthage, thousands. Steles come in a great variety of sizes and shapes, but a typical one is a rough oblong of sandstone or limestone, sometimes with a pointed top, usually with some decorative elements crudely carved on its face. Many a Carthaginian stele bears the symbol of the goddess Tanit: a triangle topped by a horizontal bar and with a circle over that (page 131). These three elements easily combine to suggest a human figure dressed in a skirt. Tanit apparently also had some lunar connection, for her symbol is often surmounted by a crescent moon.

Just who Tanit was, or how she crept into the Carthaginian pantheon, is something of a mystery. When the Tyrian princess Elissa fled to found Carthage, she took with her a high priest of the goddess of Astarte and 80 young maidens. Thereafter Astarte's cult, with local modifications to absorb the names and traits of Greek and Roman gods that make the Phoenician pantheon so confusing, persisted in one way or another throughout the history of Carthage.

Tanit may even have made her way back east and into the pantheon of the eastern cities. In 1971 a car-go of small clay Tanit figurines was found scattered over the sea bottom only a mile off the coast of Israel near the ancient Phoenician city of Akka. The ship that carried them had vanished. The Israeli archeologists who made this find think that the vessel was traveling east—perhaps from Carthage, the heart of Tanit worship—and was swamped in a storm just before it could make it into a safe harbor. If it had been going west to Carthage, the archeologists reason, it would not have sunk so near the point of departure; its captain never would have left home port in the teeth of a storm.

Baal himself was carried from the east to Carthage, but emerged there with the name Baal Hammon, or "lord of the perfume altar," reflecting the great amount of incense offered up in his rites. His exact status in Carthage is muddled, for the chief male god of the mother city Tyre was Melqart, who also was transported to Carthage and worshiped there for many centuries. Indeed, in the early years of Carthaginian history a devout contingent reportedly went back to Tyre every year on a state visit for the express purpose of paying Carthage's respects to Melqart at his temple there.

Melqart, then, represents ties with the old regime back home and is thus an expression of political conservatism in the new western city. He was the patron god of the old noble families in Carthage, particularly of the Barcids, from whom a succession of brilliant generals descended: Hamilcar Barca, two Hasdrubals, a Hannibal and a Mago. We get faint echoes of political struggles within Carthage, of class against class, in the ups and downs of the gods in whose names the various factions fought with each other. In the long run the older pair—Melqart and Astarte—lost popularity to Baal Hammon and Tanit.

They also lost something in function. In time Tanit took the place of Astarte as earth mother to the Carthaginians. She became the consort of Baal Hammon in the familiar Phoenician trinity of father, mother and son. According to Gilbert and Colette Charles-Picard, Tanit's sudden surge to supremacy can be traced to a catastrophic defeat the Carthaginians suffered at Himera in 480 B.C., when they tried to drive the Greeks out of Sicily. This repulse turned Carthage inward, more and more toward Oriental and African things. In that atmosphere Tanit sprang to prominence. Some scholars believe that she had African origins and that her rise to supremacy reflects Carthage's own geographical position: a small Phoenician enclave, set down in the midst of a large native population of Libyans, Numidians and Berbers, and inevitably affected by both intermarriage and exposure to local beliefs.

However that may be, the great number of votive stones dedicated to the holy Tanit found in Carthage after about 500 B.C. attests to her supremacy from that time on. But she, in turn, had her day. Though the Carthaginian priests were determined to keep the purity and distinctiveness of their religion (not to mention their own authority), they were forced by circumstance to give ground gradually to Greek and Roman gods, who were not only overpoweringly attractive in themselves but who also bore the standards of a more progressive, more flexible and more interesting society, with livelier art forms and a more enlightened policy with respect to manufacturing and trade—and finally, in the case of the Roman gods, an overwhelming army.

In the east the Phoenician gods and the Phoenician way of life were rapidly cannibalized by Greek gods and Greek ways. By Alexander's time Melqart was already half a Heracles, as he was in Carthage too. Baal Hammon, the last of the cruel idols to whom babies were sacrificed, was absorbed into the Romans' Saturn. Mother Tanit became Mother Juno. After the fall of Carthage in 146 B.C. its priests still hung on for a few generations, turning their attentions more and more to an African constituency. They kept their language alive for a while among the Numidians, but only for a while. The great god Baal, who had spoken with a brazen clang in many cities for a thousand years, toppled. His retinue of priests faded into anonymity. The tongue in which he had been worshiped fell to a whisper, then into silence.

The Temple Built for King Solomon

Considering how the prophets of Israel hated the Phoenician god Baal and all his works, it is ironic that the best description of a Phoenician temple comes from the Old Testament. David, the warrior who united Israel in about 1000 B.C., had little time for temple-building, but his son Solomon was determined to erect a magnificent shrine to glorify both his country and his God. Unfortunately, his people lacked the necessary skills, so Solomon contracted with King Hiram of Tyre for a team of architects, masons, carpenters and smiths who, predictably, followed a design that was widespread in the area.

The temple was a narrow stone box with walls 10 feet thick. The Bible gives its dimensions in cubits—which is awkward for scholars since there were two different standards: the regular cubit (17½ inches) and the royal cubit (21 inches). Experts are now agreed that the royal cubit was employed. On that basis, King Solomon's temple had the following approximate inside dimensions: length 135 feet, width 35 feet, height 50 feet.

Thick-walled, of stone blocks which the Phoenicians laid without cement, Solomon's temple was approached by a flight of 10 steps. Two bronze columns, named Jachin and Boaz, flanked the entrance. In front was a bronze holy-water basin weighing 30 tons and supported by 12 cast-bronze bulls, symbols of the Phoenicians' own god, El.

The Interior: A Design Drawn from the Bible

A Phoenician temple had three parts: an anteroom, then a main hall, finally a secret holy-of-holies. This basic layout suited Solomon admirably since the Hebrew and Phoenician rituals had much in common, differing mainly in the insistence of the Hebrews on worshiping a single God who had delivered them from bondage in Egypt and found them a home in Canaan.

The reconstruction on these pages, again based on the Bible, has the small anteroom, or *Ulam*, at left. Temple activities took place in the main hall, or *Hekal*. Twice each day—early in the morning and at dusk—sacrificial services were held: animals were offered up outside and incense was burned inside. The 10 tripods are light stands whose lamps are being lit by assistant priests. A high priest ignites incense on the altar in front of steps leading to the holy-of-holies (*overleaf*). In the center of the hall is a low table with 12 small loaves of bread on it, one for each of the tribes of Israel. The walls of the *Hekal* are paneled in cedar, decorated with Phoenician winged sphinxes and lotus patterns.

The lofty hall, the scent of cedar and incense, the richly ornamented walls dimly illuminated through the high recessed windows—all contributed to the mystery and beauty of the temple service. The reverence was intensified by a sense of God's near presence—just up the steps and behind the doors of the holy-of-holies.

ULAM

With its coffered ceiling, inlaid floor and richly decorated walls, Solomon's temple achieved his wis

HEKAL

hat it dazzle the world. It took seven years to build, was completed about 950 B.C. and leveled by the Babylonians in 586 B.C. No trace survives.

The Holy-of-Holies: A Throne for God's Presence

The holy-of-holies was a windowless, dark cube, also paneled in cedar but less elaborately decorated than the sumptuous *Hekal*. No one could enter here except the high priest, and he only once a year, on the Day of Atonement, when he made a special blood offering as a plea to God to cleanse His people of their sins.

This reconstruction is based on a second striking difference between the Hebrew and Phoenician faiths. The Hebrews did not believe in idols, and although the presence of God dwelt in this holy room there was no statue or image of Him there, only a small box—considered God's throne —inside which were kept the stone tablets of Moses, with the Ten Commandments inscribed on them.

Guarding God's throne (known as the Ark of the Covenant because it represented the pact between God and the Hebrews that they would worship only Him) were two large sphinxes whose outstretched wings brushed the walls and met overhead. Made of olive wood, they were 17 feet high and inlaid with gold. The Bible refers to them as cherubim.

Nothing is known of what went on inside the Phoenician version of the holy-of-holies, except that the room contained whatever image the Phoenicians worshiped. It was there that the *betyl,* or holy stone, probably was enshrined. But who among the Phoenicians had access to it is a mystery.

The doors to the holy-of-holies—made of olive wood and inlaid with gold—were opened once a yea

The winged sphinx, a motif repeated on the walls and on the Ark itself, was introduced by the Phoenicians, who in turn had found it in Egypt.

The history of Phoenicia West is really the history of Carthage. Very little is known about most of the towns and trading posts that the Phoenicians scattered throughout the Mediterranean. But Carthage is different. Its origins, though shrouded in myth, have a freight of fact behind them. The flavor of its society, though veering away from Phoenicia East through centuries of separation, can be tasted. Its history, though full of gaping holes, can be traced because Carthage grew so big and powerful that its competitors, the Greeks and Romans, became obsessed by it, wrote about it and ultimately learned to hate it as only the deadliest of rivals can hate.

According to legend, Carthage was founded in 814 B.C. as a result of a struggle for the throne of Tyre between King Pygmalion and his sister, Elissa. Elissa was married to the high priest Archabus, who was not only one of the richest men in Tyre but also her uncle. Here, yet again, is that persistent hint of the interweaving of secular and priestly power—both sustained by money—that runs through the fabric of Phoenician life.

Whether Archabus, backed by a faction of aristocrats, was himself ambitious or whether he was egged on by his ambitious wife is not known. Whatever the case, King Pygmalion had Archabus murdered. He then set out to recover as much of Archabus' fortune as he could get his hands on. Luckily for Elissa, now in fear for her own life, her

This eight-inch terra-cotta figurine of a fertility goddess was unearthed on the island of Motya in 1971. Hollow inside, it has an opening in the top of the head and a hole in each breast. Before a religious rite it could be filled with liquid, which during the ceremony would appear to flow magically after the wax plugging the nipples was discreetly melted.

husband's fortune had been sequestered. This circumstance gave her just time enough—on the pretext of collecting it and turning it over to her brother—to outfit secretly a fleet of ships, load the fortune aboard, scoop up a cadre of badly frightened aristocratic supporters and flee to Cyprus. There Elissa picked up another high priest, this one dedicated to Astarte. Elissa also recruited—or shanghaied—80 maidens who, legend goes on to say, were to serve as religious prostitutes in a temple to Astarte that she would establish. So reinforced, she set sail for Carthage.

Selecting an easily defended promontory, Elissa then proceeded to bargain with the local Libyan tribesmen for its purchase. There is a nice story connected with this. The tribesmen were persuaded to agree that she might buy only as much land as could be covered with an oxhide. But, by cutting the hide into very thin strips, Elissa was able to encircle a sizable area on and around a hill, which ultimately became the stronghold of the city and was eventually named Byrsa.

What are we to make of this story? First, it is a tale told by Greeks, who saw the Phoenicians as sharp and crafty traders: a scheme like that would have been entirely in character for Elissa. Furthermore, it is a scheme the Greeks themselves might have cooked up, and there is an echo of reluctant admiration in it. Their greatest hero, Odysseus, was a trickster who got by on wiles and lies rather than on strength. Finally, there is the fact that *byrsa* is the Greek word for "hide." Does that explain the Carthaginian citadel's bearing the name Byrsa? Or is it a later attempt to explain the coincidence with a good story? Donald Harden points out that *byrsa* could also be a Greek rendering of the Semitic word for "fortress." "Carthage" itself comes from two Phoenician words: *qart* (city) and *hadasht* (new).

At any rate, things were surely hard for Elissa and her small band of nobles set down in the midst of strangers—possibly hostile strangers. Nothing is heard of them—except for two more stories—for nearly a hundred years.

The first story, and the best known, is from Homer's *Odyssey*. There Elissa, under the name Dido, emerges as a beautiful and sensual queen who dawdled away her days in an opulent palace with a young lover—a refugee from Troy named Aeneas. But Aeneas grew tired of her and left—so Dido killed herself. Homer's version is pure myth; the fall of Troy took place some 400 years before Carthage was founded. Furthermore, Dido certainly had no fine palace to dawdle in. The early Carthaginians probably were very poor for some years and quite dependent on their contacts with Tyre.

However, as will be seen, suicide did repeatedly strike a chord in the harsh soul of Carthaginian life. It was not out of character for Elissa to have killed herself, and a better reason for her having done so is given by the Roman historian Justin writing several hundred years after the fact. According to his account, while Carthage was still young and feeble, an uncouth and forbidding neighboring chieftain demanded of the city's elders that he be given the beautiful Elissa for a wife. The alternative: destruction of the struggling little colony. This put the elders in a difficult bind: sure she would refuse, they were afraid to relay this demand directly to their imperious queen and equally reluctant to relay her refusal to the chief. With what Justin called "Carthaginian artifice," they finally decided to inform her that they

themselves were being asked to go and live with the neighboring tribesmen in order to civilize them, but that they feared to do so because of the dangers and squalor of tribal life. Predictably, Elissa upbraided them for not being willing to promote the city's welfare at the expense of their own skins. As soon as she had said that, the elders revealed to her the true demand of the neighboring prince, and Elissa was trapped by the example she had attempted to impose on the elders. So she took three months to prepare a large funeral pile. On the appointed day, she sacrificed a number of individuals (Justin does not say who they were), then climbed up on the pile and stabbed herself.

Did Elissa-Dido actually live? Did she found Carthage and, if so, when? Of her existence there can be no doubt; she is known to have been the sister of King Pygmalion, and all classical historians agree that Pygmalion's sister was the founder of Carthage. Whether Elissa founded the city in panicky flight or whether the new colony was a deliberate step in a Tyrian plan to get a toehold in the west, beyond the reach of Assyrian tormentors, is another matter. With the west opening up and the metal trade beginning to boom, it would have been to Tyre's advantage to have a strong base along the trade route, halfway to Spain.

As to when this happened, Elissa's own identity provides a clue. She was the grandniece of the notorious Jezebel of the Bible, a Phoenician princess. Since it is known that Jezebel lived in about 850 B.C., Elissa would have been a mature woman about 40 years later, well able to carry out the large task of establishing a colony in Carthage. Therefore the traditional date for her having done so—814—is probably within a few years of being correct. However, that does not sit well with the awkward problem of Phoenician pottery dating.

As noted, archeological research at Carthage has given us nothing that can be dated earlier than about 735 B.C., and so we are still left with the apparent problem of accounting for that gap of almost 80 years. Here the work of James Pritchard at Sarepta may help. Carbon dating of objects 3,000 years old or less is not refined enough to tag them precisely. A 50- to 100-year error is inevitable. Pritchard feels, however, that the huge hoard of pottery shards that he has turned up at Sarepta may finally provide a precise tag. Pritchard's sequencing of shapes and styles is so extensive and precise that once he has found a "hard" object to go with his pottery—an Egyptian inscription, say, containing the name of a king whose dates are known—then he will know how old the pieces of Sarepta pottery are. Egyptian goods were handled by the Phoenicians as trade items, and may well have been stored near kilns Pritchard has found. Since the Egyptians were fond of carving names and family histories on nearly everything they made, Pritchard feels it is only a matter of time before he finds the cross check he needs.

Once that has been accomplished, he can then address himself to another enigma: the red-slip problem. Red-slip refers to a kind of pottery finish that was in wide use at Sarepta from an early date. It was the Phoenicians' way of providing a nonporous surface to the interior of a pot by painting it with a watery mixture of extremely fine, reddish clay, then using a small tool or pebble to smooth this red-slip material into the surface of the pot as it revolved on the potter's wheel. With the raw clay surface sealed by the red-slip, the pot was then fired in a kiln, and

*Bronze Punic armor, consisting of breast-
and backplate, with shoulder straps
and girdle to hold them in place, was
found in a Third Century B.C. tomb near
Carthage. The design is Italian and
suggests that the owner was an Italian
mercenary serving in Hannibal's army.*

came out with a glazed interior that is recognizable anywhere. Although nonporous pots were made long before the Phoenicians came on the scene, the particular red-slip they used appears to be uniquely Phoenician. Thus the problem now is to learn where and when Phoenician red-slip got its start. It turns up in Carthage and other western sites in large quantities. The presumption is that it was exported there from Phoenicia East. If this turns out to be so, and if the date of its first use in the east proves to be an early one, and—finally—if older Phoenician red-slip pots at Sarepta are found to match some of those found at Carthage, *then* all experts can agree with considerable relief that Carthage was (at last on archeological evidence, instead of the shakier literary evidence they have had to lean on in the past) as old as tradition claims.

From its humble start Carthage grew rapidly to become the strongest and the wealthiest of the many Phoenician outposts in the west. In its wars—initially against the Greeks and later against the Romans —it rallied its African neighbors, ran the campaigns, maintained a large war fleet and directed commercial policy. The dreams other western Phoenician towns may have had for an independent commercial destiny —such as the mother cities back east had enjoyed— were ultimately crushed by the takeover policies of Carthage, spearheaded by a succession of power-hungry generals. Carthage initially offered a unified anti-Greek front to the other Phoenician towns and trading posts, and under that banner came as close as the Phoenicians anywhere would come to creating a solidified empire.

It was a great achievement, if not always a healthy one. The Carthaginians had two problems that their eastern relatives did not have, but they also had new opportunities for experimenting in government and developing new kinds of trade relationships with their neighbors. The Carthaginians' history was on the whole violent, their religion somber and cruel, their government autocratic. They did not trust their leaders and killed many of those who failed them. Their art was undistinguished. For all that, they were a force to be reckoned with in the Mediterranean for more than 500 years. At times they controlled a large section of the then-civilized world. In fact, they were occasionally the only civilizing element in that world.

Their two special problems over the course of several hundred years were the Greeks and the native Africans. The former were the equal of the Carthaginians in adaptability, energy, intelligence and fighting skills. The two peoples became bitter commercial rivals and fought long, inconclusive wars. The Africans presented a different kind of problem. They lived roundabout in enormous numbers, and in the city's early days were strong enough to exact an annual tribute for the land that Elissa's people occupied. But as Carthage grew in strength it also grew inland, spilling out to occupy the surrounding farm country. It was extremely fertile, and the aristocratic families acquired large holdings, which they cultivated intensively. Eventually they stopped paying the Libyan tribute. The original inhabitants were driven off the land, employed as farm laborers, or they hung on as heavily taxed small farmers. They were not allowed Carthaginian citizenship, were held in low esteem, probably treated very badly. They became an unreliable element in Carthaginian society. Being much more numerous than the Carthaginians, the na-

tives posed a constant threat and on several occasions actually revolted.

The most famous revolt came after Carthage had just lost the first of three bitter wars against the Romans and had been saddled with a crushing indemnity that left it unable to pay its mercenary troops: ex-slaves, renegade Greeks, dispossessed Sicilians, tough recruits from Spain—the scum of the Mediterranean. In 241 B.C. the mercenaries rebelled and succeeded in fomenting an uprising among the Libyan population. Three and a half years of chaotic guerrilla fighting ensued, marked by chilling atrocities on both sides. Finally the revolt was put down, but it left Carthage so enfeebled that it could not resist further pressure from the Romans to give up its holdings in Sardinia.

But all this was much later. The Carthaginians' early enemies were the Greeks, who began trickling into Sicily only about 80 years after the founding of Carthage. A group came from Chalcis in 735. Another came from Corinth in 734, a third from Megara in 728. Within 50 years there were Greek settlements all over eastern and central Sicily, each entirely in-

dependent of the others and of mainland Greece as well. Little is known of Greek and Carthaginian relations during this early period. But as the Greek settlements spread, Carthage soon decided that they must be contained. It began beefing up a settlement at Motya off Sicily's western tip, eventually turning it into a walled town. Later Carthage also made an alliance with the Etruscans, a people who ruled a powerful kingdom in central Italy. With their cooperation Carthage was able to establish a presence in Corsica and gain control over a few coastal settlements on the island of Sardinia. Gradually, the Carthaginians—aided by the alliance with the Etruscans—were able to exert more and more influence over Sardinia and Corsica. This meant that the routes west to Spain, both north and south of Sicily, were in Carthaginian hands. The Greeks were effectively shut out of the wealth that trade with Spain would provide, and the Carthaginians could now devote themselves to the metal monopoly in Spain.

This they did intensively and became rich, but in an unhealthy way. Carthage treated this fountain of silver and tin much as the Spanish conquistadors a couple of thousand years later would treat the gush of gold that poured into their laps from the New World. Both regarded their discoveries simply as mines, as sources of treasure to be got cheap and sold dear, to finance armies, to enrich the aristocracy.

Similarly, Carthage initially did little with its wealth but entrench the nobility and finance the wars that the leaders were intent on waging as part of their mercantile policy. Carthage was not so much a handler and fabricator of all sorts of fine trade goods (like its mother city, Tyre) as it was a bulk dealer in metals, ivory and other raw materials. These, through trade, ultimately fell into the hands of its competitors, who often used them more creatively. Wherever Greek or Egyptian goods stood in the stalls next to those from Carthage, the former put the latter in the shade. Thus, Carthage had to control its markets not through the excellence of its products but by force—through its ability to bar competition. Its customers, unable to get anything better, had to accept a range of poor-quality goods that Carthage was peddling. The Carthaginian economy depended on tremendous volume rather than on quality, and flooded the west with its output.

It is easy to blame Carthage for not having a better imperial experiment, but judgments of this nature are foolish. People do what they can within the limits of their own experience, their own culture, and in response to specific external pressures. The Carthaginians inherited an authoritarian, aristocratic way of life dominated by a rigid religion. Since they were exposed to Greek pressures, the Carthaginians moved to contain them by utilizing the leadership produced by their traditions.

The earliest rulers of Carthage are unknown. There are references to a King Malchus, but that name probably comes from an old Semitic word for king or lord and may refer to a title and not a single man. The first Carthaginian leader whom history recognizes by name is "King" Mago. Actually Mago was a general, head of a very powerful and wealthy family of aristocrats. He won victories against the Greeks in Sicily, and around 550 B.C. established a dynasty of military leaders—the Magonids—that was to be prominent in Carthaginian military affairs for 150 years or so. Mago may or may not have been the actual head of the Carthaginian state. According to most sources, the Carthaginian generals were elected, and appear to have served at the pleasure of a council recruited from a small group of noble families. This council set mercantile policy and more or less ran the country's affairs to suit themselves. That Carthage ever had a succession of kings is doubtful. Families seem to have been the power centers, and they strove bitterly among themselves.

It is against this background that Mago emerged. He is reported to have pushed an aggressive foreign policy in Carthage, to have built up the war fleet, to have made a military alliance with the Etruscans and to have created the first mercenary army in Carthage. Mercenaries were a necessity, for there were too few honest-to-goodness Carthaginians to make up more than an officer class. But mercenaries also cost a great deal, as did the maintenance of an adequate fleet. The money was supplied largely by the metal trade, which the new military strength protected.

The new policy, together with the colony's isolation from Tyre, inevitably led Carthage away from the traditional Phoenician posture of peaceful trader

The original of this iron lance head from the Isola Lunga wreck (page 35) rusted away long ago—yet its shape could be re-created. Encrustation had covered the disintegrating metal and a cavity was formed inside. When filled with plaster, the hollow yielded the duplicate shown here.

and into the role of hard-boiled imperialist. If Carthage was to be the policeman of the western trading empire, Carthage would have to be paid for that service. As the other Phoenician settlements in the west fell under Carthaginian dominance, they ultimately found themselves with little or no direct share in the metal trade, and nothing to say about when and where wars would be fought—except that they were expected to help wage and finance them.

There were plenty of wars. At first the campaigns were generally successful and enhanced the stature of the Magonids who, according to the French historians Colette and Gilbert Charles-Picard, "managed to surround their power with a mystic aura by playing upon nationalism and religious fanaticism." The mystique required that the generals themselves act as proper models of the hard Punic faith, and they did. At least two of them are reported to have committed suicide on the field of battle when they realized that their side had lost. Here is another aspect of that same dark strain of expiatory sacrifice that required the killing of babies to wipe out national sins or failures.

The Magonid leadership, in addition to being durable, had another asset. It spoke for all of Phoenicia West, not just one city. These two factors permitted Carthage the luxury of a coherent—if not always intelligent—foreign policy, something the Greeks never achieved before Alexander the Great. The Greeks were habitually their own worst enemies. It was their chronic inability to get along with one another—especially in Sicily—that eventually led to a battle between the Magonid Hamilcar and Gelon the Greek at Himera in 480 B.C. Terrilos, also a Greek, was an ally of the Carthaginians. When Gelon became too ag-

gressive and too successful, Terrilos called upon his Carthaginian ally, Hamilcar, to help bring about the downfall of Gelon.

As it happens, this battle took place at the same time the Persians—with the help of navies from eastern Phoenicia—were invading Greece itself. Although traditional histories suggest that Carthage knew about the Persian invasion, there is little reason to believe that this influenced the Carthaginians in any way. More likely was the Carthaginian wish to keep any single Greek settlement from gaining too much control in Sicily. Whatever the case, Carthage did go to the aid of Terrilos, only to be soundly defeated in Himera, a Greek town near Palermo. After defeat, there was only one thing for the Carthaginian general Hamilcar to do, and he did it: he killed himself. The survivors struggled home in their splintered warships. The Magonid power was eroded. According to the Charles-Picards, rival groups of aristocrats took over the city and governed it through a court of magistrates. Taking stock of their situation, these new autocrats found Carthage bankrupt and nearly defenseless, and apparently decided to embark on an entirely different policy. They withdrew into a kind of shell, banned the import of all foreign goods and concentrated on expanding Carthage's African holdings and building up its resources.

They did this for 70 years, and the ruins of Carthage speak to that long program of austerity. There is a pronounced paucity within that time period of the luxury goods previously imported by the nobility. Instead, trade with internal Africa was intensified. Caravan routes picked their way south through the Sahara to certain reliable oases for an expanded traffic in gold, ivory and slaves. Marine exploration

Carefully squared stone blocks, some of them five feet long, form the base of an outer defensive wall at Motya. Inside it lay an older wall, and the space between had been filled with rubble and concrete. The finished double wall was more than 18 feet thick.

was pushed, and it was during this period that the two admirals, Hanno and Himilco, may have made their famous expeditions down the African coast and to Britain (pages 12-13).

Throughout this period, the Romans began their rise. However, the real enemy was still the Greeks. During the 70 years that Carthage turned inward, the Greeks were occupied by one internal war after another. Waves of these city-state conflicts washed as far as Syracuse, the main Greek settlement in eastern Sicily and an ally of Sparta in the many bloody battles that city had with Athens.

By 410 B.C. the Carthaginians realized that Syracuse was becoming a very powerful force in Sicily. Once again Carthage was persuaded to help one Greek city—this time Segesta—defeat another and, in so doing, weaken the power of Syracuse. The Carthaginian leader was a general named Hannibal. He is not the Hannibal best known to posterity, but one of a dozen or more famous generals who bore the name. (There is also a bewildering cluster of Hannos, Hamilcars, Hasdrubals and Himilcos littering Carthaginian history—some related, some not.) At any rate, this Hannibal landed with his armies near Motya and stormed the nearby city of Selinus for nine days. With that victory under their belts, the troops were joined by many Sicilians. Together these forces launched an attack on Himera, the very town where Hannibal's grandfather Hamilcar had been so soundly defeated 70 years before. Hannibal won this battle, too, and had the grim satisfaction of avenging his grandfather's death by sacrificing 3,000 captured Greek soldiers.

After this success Hannibal returned to Carthage and his army disbanded. A few years later, he—now quite old—was called to lead another attack on Sicily. Hannibal died in 407 B.C.—presumably of the plague—leaving his aide and possible relative Himilco in command of the army. Our knowledge of what took place over the next few years is quite sketchy. We do know that the Carthaginians continued to be active in Sicily and involved in the various internal Greek city squabbles there. The key Greek figure during this period was Dionysius, an especially ruthless general from Syracuse. As soon as Dionysius was able to consolidate his position among the many Greek settlements, he turned on the Carthaginians and struck right at the seat of Carthaginian power in Sicily: the island of Motya.

Sicily is a volcanic island made up of steep gray rocks plunging into the sea, of dusty little coastal towns, of steep valleys hidden in the hills. Much of Sicily can be so described, and this is what one sees as one goes out from Palermo toward Motya, a dot of an island perched at Sicily's extreme western tip.

Here the violent Sicilian landscape subsides. The hills sink down. Stone walls line the shore. Stone jetties stick out into the lagoon. There is an abandoned stone windmill—a great many stones here, all carefully squared, many of them in big blocks, worn and old. Opposite the saltworks—about half a mile away, floating low on the shallow bay—lies Motya. All that is visible on it from the shore is a grove of trees and a modern Italian terra-cotta villa.

Much of the worked stone on this shore was once on that island in the form of fortifications, towers, pavements and buildings. More of it came from the Punic graveyards on the near hillside. All of it bespeaks an energy and activity at Motya that is long gone. Nothing moves there now. The jetties and fields are completely deserted. The waters of the lagoon have silted up and are clogged with weeds. The surface is glassy and empty.

In 397 B.C., when Dionysius stormed the city, Motya was anything but silent. It was a humming city, completely surrounded by a thick wall, its bay full of ships. It was this busy, bristling stronghold that the Greeks felt they had to reduce. Dionysius brought an army to the shore, just north of the island, where the Motyan burial ground was. Today, looking down into the water, one can make out the remains of a causeway that the islanders had built to connect their stronghold to the mainland. Today it runs as straight as a string a foot or so beneath the surface, though it is broken in a couple of places. The Motyans tried to destroy their causeway in a last-minute effort to protect themselves. But why they should have tried, why they should have felt they could succeed, why Dionysius should have felt he needed to destroy them —all these things are hard for today's visitor to understand. From the mainland shore Motya seems as innocent and defenseless, as needless of destruction as a garden.

But row out to the island, following a twisted channel that still makes it possible for fishing boats to come and go in the lagoon, and one's view changes. This was a fortress once, a miniature Troy whose outer walls stood 30 feet high. The roots of those walls are there now, ringing the island. The thick stone structures were strengthened at intervals by still higher stone towers. The stoutest of these towers guarded the town's main entrance. There was a heavy double gate there with a stone barrier in the middle, dividing a two-way street that ran up into the town.

Masks to Exorcise Evil Spirits

Grinning masks made of terra cotta have turned up in many tombs at Carthage and other Phoenician sites located in the western Mediterranean. Carthage's trade contacts with Africa promoted the long-held belief that the masks were inspired by neighboring cultures, particularly since many bear what seem to be tattoo marks. However, this theory was exploded by the discovery in 1960 of a 13th Century B.C. mask at Hazor, an old Canaanite town near Tyre, proving that their use predates Carthage and that the practice was originally eastern.

The masks are less than life-size —too small to be worn—and are mostly found in tombs. Almost all experts agree that they were aimed at guarding the deceased by scaring off evil spirits with their grimacing expressions. Their date: 700-500 B.C.

From Tharros, Sardinia. The left ear has been restored.

From Motya

From San Sperate

From Carthage

From Carthage. The scratches in many of the masks led some authorities to conclude that they represented tattoos.

Inside was a second gate in case the first did not hold, and inside that a third, all overhung by those flanking towers, set at an angle so that a withering fire could be directed downward at any attackers who tried to cross the causeway and storm the outer gate.

Standing on top of what is left of Motya's walls —imagining oneself positioned 15 or 20 feet higher yet, well stocked with arrows, crouched behind a slot in the stone parapet, with fellow townsmen similarly deployed all along the battlement, looking down at a lagoon bristling with Carthaginian ships—one wonders how Dionysius cracked this tough nut. According to the historian Diodorus, Dionysius brought a fleet of his own to help his army clean out the Motyans. But when he arrived and saw that the causeway had been broken, he and his army went inland to capture other Punic settlements, leaving the crew of his fleet to rebuild the causeway. He had just returned to lead the attack on Motya himself when the Carthaginian navy, alerted to the danger, came pouring around the end of an outer island and up the Motya channel. Dionysius' fleet appeared to be trapped and lost. But he mobilized all his troops for a heart-straining effort of pushing in the mud, gasping in the weeds. They managed to shove his fleet through the shallow far side of the lagoon, over some shoals and even across the end of the outer island and safely to sea. The lagoon was too shallow for the Carthaginian ships to follow. They were forced to retire, leaving besieged Motya to its fate.

Dionysius went quickly to work. The lagoon that over the centuries had provided such a useful anchorage for the Motyans now revealed a fatal flaw. It was too shallow to prevent the inexorable inching up of siege engines along the causeway and against Motya's wall. What happened beneath that wall as the engines battered away at it has been pretty well worked out by archeologists. The Greeks did come up the causeway, which they had rebuilt, and launch their main attack at the town gate. A great many arrowheads and lance tips have been found there, a far heavier concentration than in any other part of the island, attesting to the desperate fighting that went on in front of the gate. Apparently the Syracusans broke through it, only to find themselves in a casbah-like maze of strongly built houses several stories high, each a fort in itself. The Motyans got up on the flat roofs and crept from one building to another to counter any concentration of Greeks below. As a result, though badly outnumbered, they sentenced the invaders to days of the nastiest kind of alley combat before resistance was broken.

Motya could have given up at once, as the eastern Phoenician towns so often did, and might well have been shown a little mercy. But there was a tenacious streak to the Phoenicians. Having once made the decision to take a siege, they would not give up, even when their cause was hopeless. Ritual suicide again —this time on a mass scale? Perhaps. Sidon suffered dreadfully in the aftermath of one siege, Tyre from three. Carthage was defended literally to the last man. And so, it seems, was Motya. It was totally crushed. The invaders went on such a rampage of killing in the alleys that the Greek commander was able to stop it only by ordering the survivors into the temples and forbidding his soldiers to go in after them. Thereupon the city was looted of all its valuables and probably put to the torch.

Today the flat area in the center of the island, once jammed with buildings, is a vineyard. Much of the old stone, as previously noted, has been carted away to make jetties on the mainland. What is left is underground. A plow occasionally bangs into a block or column. Bits of pottery are constantly turned up, and once in a while an entire vase. What else lies beneath the vineyard is really not known, for there is a great deal of work left to be done at Motya. Its systematic exploration was begun about a hundred years ago by an Englishman, Joseph Whittaker, who eventually purchased the entire island and wrote a book about his efforts there. The work is being carried on today by the Italian archeologists Sabatino Moscati and Vincinzo Tusa, as well as by a team from the University of Leeds in England. But funds are small and the work goes slowly.

Still, a great deal has been learned about Motya. For many years archeologists thought that Motya was a "pure" site in the sense that its rubble had not been turned over again and again by succeeding generations of citizens. Traditional historians relate that after its fall there were few, if any, Motyans left to rebuild it. The city was abandoned, and the survivors moved to another Carthaginian town, Lilybaeum, on a peninsula not far away. In the past few years, however, scholars have decided that Motya was reoccupied—probably as early as 396 B.C.—by Greeks and Romans. Thus it is no longer possible to classify all the ruins as Carthaginian.

That Dionysius burned Motya in 397 B.C. is evident from the great amount of ash and charred wood among the ruins. Many of the buildings that have been uncovered so far reveal foundations and probably lower stories of stone, with floors of stone or plaster. But the ash deposits suggest that the upper stories were made of wood. The main gates to the town probably were of wood also; there are sockets in the walls to show where their hinges were hung. Piles of nails and cinders have survived in the rubble at the town entrance, just where they would have been had the gates been burst open, broken up and then completely burned.

Not far inside the main gate is a potter's shop. A kiln survives, together with a stock—laid out to dry —of the yet-to-be-glazed red-slip pots that the Motyans made in large quantities. They also did a great deal of fishing, weaving and dyeing, using local murex for the latter. Although the nets and looms they used have long since disappeared, the weights employed as sinkers or loom weights have not. They are all over the place in the ruins, the cheaper ones of terra cotta, the better ones of marble.

All sorts of little whiffs of Motyan daily life come steadily on the warm air. Large stone drums have been discovered. They were first thought to be rain barrels, but later were found to have their bottoms reinforced with cement. Some had traces of iron linings. Apparently they were used to grind corn. In due course the debris in the main street leading from the outer gate was cleared away. The street has ruts ground into its paving representing centuries of travel by heavily loaded creaking Motyan carts, whose size can be calculated by measuring the distance between the ruts. Less worn are several flights of steps running down from the walls to the waterfront. At least one flight had been installed such a short time before the siege that it had no time for wear at all. Covered ever since by debris and dirt, the stone surfaces are as square and smooth as they were on the day they came from the quarry.

Greek influence is everywhere. Clearly there was

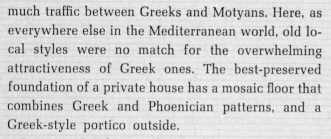

Loom weights have been found in great numbers in the rubble at Motya. Made of small bits of terra cotta or of stone, each with a hole in it, they were used to hold thread taut while weaving and were decorated with colors or designs that suggest family ownership. The one at far left bears the imprint of a running figure.

much traffic between Greeks and Motyans. Here, as everywhere else in the Mediterranean world, old local styles were no match for the overwhelming attractiveness of Greek ones. The best-preserved foundation of a private house has a mosaic floor that combines Greek and Phoenician patterns, and a Greek-style portico outside.

It seems Greeks, too, lived on Motya before and after 397 B.C.—presumably artisans and traders, but residents permanent enough to have their own temples. Even though the two peoples were long-time enemies, there apparently was considerable contact between them. Certainly there were Greeks in Motya when the siege occurred, some probably as awkwardly caught there as were Japanese businessmen in California at the outbreak of World War II. But the corrosive hatred of Greek for Greek suggests that a good many of the ones reported to have assisted in the defense at Motya were simply enemies of Dionysius, that they felt far safer with the Motyans than they did with him.

Across the island the Motyans had a second entrance to their walled town. This was the sea gate. Instead of opening onto a street, it led, via a paved ditch or canal, to a rectangular pond the Motyans had cut out of their little island. Its paved walls have now been carefully uncovered and the accumulated

silt removed. Today it looks like a large swimming pool a bit under 170 feet long and about 10 feet deep. It may have been a cothon: a man-made basin for the repair and stocking of ships, similar to those found at Carthage, but much smaller and in a better state of preservation. (Not everyone agrees with this interpretation; some specialists think that the cothon was used as a tank in which fish were stocked—perhaps to be used as a ready food supply.)

Throughout the rubble at Motya are large numbers of steles, those simple gravestones or small commemorative shafts that were a hallmark of the Punic faith. The island's cemetery itself has been located, and confirms that the early Motyans burned their dead. Later, when either the island cemetery became too crowded or when Motya became strong enough to do so, the cemetery was moved to the mainland, and cremation was abandoned in favor of inhumation. But on the island, most probably to save space, nearly all the graves that have been found thus far—in one rather crowded plot—contained a number of urns with human ashes inside them.

The Motyans apparently had a connection with an earlier, more primitive people. Whether they conquered them, elbowed them aside or moved in amicably with them is unclear. But they did absorb some of the burial customs of those earlier peoples,

who seem to have had one foot still in the Stone Age, since some of the tools and weapons that were put in those oldest graves were made of worked flint. These predecessors, though capable of making clay pots, had not refined the craft. The graves contain vases of an extremely crude nature, shaped by hand instead of on a potter's wheel.

These simple little fragments of a simpler culture are very interesting, for they suggest how it was that the Carthaginians were able to exploit their markets so successfully for so long. It can be assumed that many of the peoples with whom they came in contact —on the islands of the western Mediterranean, in Spain, in Africa and along the Atlantic coast—were similarly backward in their technology. A Carthaginian clay pot, no matter how inferior it may have been in contrast to one made in Athens or Crete or Egypt, still would have seemed a marvel of symmetry to a man who had never before seen anything like it and was therefore delighted to give up much more valuable material in order to get it.

In 1919 another burial ground was located on Motya, not far from the first one. Here the urns were very small, most of them not more than a foot tall. One after another they were opened and, like the urns at Carthage, contained the ashes of only the very young—animal and human babies. This was no or-

dinary graveyard where the dead were laid away, but a holy place, a Tophet, where the living young were sacrificed in an offering-up of one's first-born—or, as a substitute for the first-born, an animal.

That, for the present, is about all that can be said about Motya. Its abrupt end as a Carthaginian settlement in 397 B.C. makes it a fascinating place to visit, more so in many ways than two Carthaginian cities that continued in Sicily: Panormus (modern Palermo) and Lilybaeum (modern Marsala), the two bases from which Carthage continued its struggle with the Greeks for control of Sicily. That battle went on with various ups and downs for another century, with neither side able to gain a decisive edge over the other for any length of time. For Carthage it was a period of growing power and prosperity. The city was beautified and enlarged. An increasingly big hunk of African hinterland came under its control. Until the Third Punic War, which resulted in the city's fall, Carthage had been invaded only a couple of times. Its campaigns were fought overseas and it was not exposed to the recurrent rapine and pillage that had scarred many other ancient states.

Despite these advantages, Carthaginian affairs were by no means as serene as they should have been. The Sicilian wars, while waged away from home, nevertheless made themselves felt in the pocketbook. The mercenary army was always a heavy drain on the treasury, and so the prosecutors of the wars, the generals and admirals who headed up the campaigns, came under mounting criticism for their inability to win lasting victories. Being a Carthaginian general —while it may have been immensely profitable—was never a sinecure. Now it became increasingly risky. Reinforcing the built-in hostility of all Carthaginians to anyone who grew too powerful or too successful was the hostility of the court, or Council of 104. This body of narrow-minded, jealous mercantile aristocrats was unforgiving, quick to second-guess its commanders, quick to jerk them back to Carthage for trial at the first sign of failure. As time passed, the council grew harsher. By the outbreak of the first war with Rome in 264 B.C. the job of Carthaginian field commander had become positively lethal. According to legend, one military leader was crucified for having allowed himself to be captured in a surprise attack. Another lost a town and was heavily fined. A third was crucified for suffering a defeat while at sea. A general named Hasdrubal was crucified for failing to capture Palermo, and another named Hannibal was crucified by his own soldiers after a battlefield loss.

Under such circumstances, why did anyone want to be a general? For wealth, honor and social eminence, of course. But there may have been deeper reasons. Many of the men chosen for Carthaginian military leadership were smoldering hawks with a long passion for command and a dream of power. The council was not above using them to pursue the mercantile aims of its members, confident of its ability to keep them in rein. The generals, for their part,

vied for command, hoping they could keep on winning and thus stay in the council's good graces.

In the inevitable atmosphere of mutual suspicion, a consistent foreign policy became hard to maintain. Carthage's failure to find a better solution to the problem of delegating power to—and trusting—its generals partly explains why they did not succeed in driving the Greeks from Sicily, even when all of Greece was hopelessly divided in the chaotic aftermath of the death of Alexander the Great. A final Greek spasm in Sicily was contained only with the help of the Roman forces, and Carthage suddenly found itself face to face with a new and even more formidable enemy.

Now, for the first time, the essential weakness of Carthage was revealed. Roman power was based on real estate: over a good many decades a big section of Italy had been solidly welded by conquest or by treaty into a single political unit—the whole defended by a large and vigorous citizen army. The basic Carthaginian power was built around money—money to pay others to do their fighting for them. Aside from the farming areas immediately surrounding Carthage (and teeming with discontented second-class noncitizens), the empire had no property but trading posts. Its primary interest was wealth rather than imperial dreams. It regarded warfare as just another tool in the pursuit of wealth, and was willing to invest in mercenaries, as it would in any other kind of merchandise, when it felt that they were needed to ensure the continuing flow of money.

Although Carthage behaved in an imperial way, often acting as if it controlled an empire, what it really controlled was trade. The North Africans, whom the Carthaginians treated in such a high-handed manner

ATHENIAN TETRADRACHM, c.520 B.C.

LYDIAN STATER, c.570 B.C.

PERSIAN DARIC, c.480 B.C.

TYRIAN SHEKEL, c.460 B.C.

PUNIC STATER, c.350 B.C.

The introduction of coinage by others was enormously helpful to traders like the Phoenicians. The oldest coins found in the Mediterranean are Lydian and Greek. Since weight, not size, counted, the earliest were irregular lumps with a design stamped on them to guarantee value. Such a lump is the Lydian coin at top right, made of electrum, a silver and gold alloy. The Greek coin bears the letters "A θ E" to indicate it was minted in Athens. Persia first produced coins in about 480 B.C. with designs showing a running king; then Tyre some 20 years later; and Carthage 100 years later yet. At bottom right: the goddess Tanit, on a gold Carthaginian stater.

for so long, were never under secure control. Nor were the other Punic cities in the west. Nominally subservient to Carthage, they were never a "part" of Carthage. They ran themselves, picking up whatever crumbs of trade they could. Out of long dissatisfaction with the size of those crumbs, some defected when the showdown with Rome came.

It came, predictably, over Sicily after a series of petty disputes over control of that key island. In 264 B.C. war broke out. It dragged on for more than 20 years, and was decided humiliatingly for Carthage with, of all things, a naval disaster. The Romans had started the war with no knowledge of naval strategy whatsoever and no fleet; they had to use a captured galley as a model in order to build squadrons of their own. But the Romans quickly reached parity with the Carthaginians, and from that time on were certainly their equals at sea.

When the Romans finally won the First Punic War, they expelled the Carthaginians from Sicily and exacted a staggering tribute in silver over a 20-year period. It was Carthage's inability to pay both the tribute and the money due its mercenaries that led to the latter's revolt. The man who finally crushed the revolt was a tough and brilliant general of the old stamp. That man was Hamilcar Barca, founder of the so-called Barcid Dynasty. Disgusted by the scorpion-like political atmosphere at home, anxious to achieve something of the power his ancestors had enjoyed, possibly aware that if he stayed in Carthage he probably could never shake himself free of the oppressive and jealous hand of the council, Hamilcar Barca made the bold decision to return to Spain where he had led troops, and there try to establish a power center for himself. He did so in 237 B.C., with his nine-year-old son Hannibal, exacting an oath from the little boy that he would pledge himself throughout his life to the destruction of Rome.

The Barcids—five of them: Hamilcar; his son-in-law, Hasdrubal; and his three sons, Hannibal, Mago and another Hasdrubal—were extraordinary men. Of soaring ambition and incredible vigor, they vaulted right out of the narrow mercantile shell that had constricted the Carthaginian autocrats. They saw the necessity of combining mercantilism with an ongoing military and political policy. They quickly carved out a large private fiefdom for themselves that comprised almost the entire southern half of Spain, a far larger territory than that of Carthage itself. They subdued the native Iberians and developed a small but extremely able mercenary army financed by the Spanish mines, which they now controlled and whose output they expanded. The Roman indemnity was paid off. A second capital, New Carthage, was founded. This city in Spain became the independent power base that Hamilcar had long dreamed of ruling.

The Spanish enterprise was firmly established before Hamilcar was killed in battle in 229 B.C. His son-in-law, Hasdrubal, expanded it, but was murdered by an angry tribesman in 221 B.C. Hannibal inherited control at the age of 25, having been trained for the role since boyhood. He was another Alexander and endlessly inventive.

Many stories have come down to us about this particular Hannibal. One says he carried an assortment of different-colored wigs and uniforms with him so that he could go anywhere in battle without being marked down by an enemy sharpshooter. He stationed lines of elephants in swift-running rivers so that their bodies would calm the waters and enable men, horses and baggage trains to cross places where otherwise they would have been swept away. He is reported to have ordered his troops to use boiling vinegar (probably sour wine) to crack rocks high in the Alps, and thus make a narrow track down a steep descent that was hopelessly slick and icy.

Hannibal had a truly Alexandrine vision of empire. Most of the people then living in northern Italy, France and Spain were members of a huge, squabbling, semicivilized confederation of tribesmen known as the Celts. It was Hannibal's idea, having subdued many of the Spanish tribes and welded a potent army out of them, to rally all the tribes for a general uprising against the Romans. Once Rome was crushed, he would turn the entire western Mediterranean into a Carthaginian empire, which he planned to govern from Carthage. To get this plan moving he would, of course, have to deal with the Romans directly.

This posed an immense military challenge: how was he to get at them? And, if he succeeded in that, how would he beat them? They had a formidable reputation as fighters, and a large fleet. They had flattened Carthaginian armies and navies the last time around. To balance that past record Hannibal had supreme confidence in his gifts as a general and in the quality of his army, well seasoned by several years of active campaigning in Spain. Operating in the field, away from the hindrances of the Carthaginian government—a sole commander able to pursue his own policy through good times and bad —he felt he could win. He also knew he would be up against Roman generals chosen by public vote

Rome's unwitting tribute to its ancient
enemy Carthage is this relief from
Trajan's column, carved two and a half
centuries after Carthage's fall. It
shows a trireme, fully decked without
Greek-style outriggers. The inspiration
for the design seems to have been
Phoenician. According to history, when
Rome decided to become a sea power,
it copied Carthaginian warships.

This profile is believed to be that of Hannibal the Great, though some scholars attribute it to the god Melqart. It is from a Carthaginian silver three-shekel piece minted in Spain between 237 and 207 B.C., at the time Hannibal was campaigning against the Romans.

for specific campaigns, then recalled and replaced by others chosen the following year. The Roman generalship was a political plum—usually awarded to aristocrats; few of these political generals had any military experience at all.

Finally, Hannibal proposed to fight not in Sicily, not in the distant tip of Italy, not at sea but in the Roman state itself, where it would doubtlessly hurt the Romans most.

Wasting no time, he captured Saguntum, a Roman-protected town in eastern Spain, and then headed overland for Rome, fighting or temporizing with the various tribes he encountered as he went along. He accomplished the incredible feat of marching an army —with elephants—over the Alps in the fall of 218 B.C., through snowstorms, howling gales and sleet, with boulders being rolled down on him in the narrow defiles by fractious mountaineers. Most of his elephants died of cold and starvation in the mountains, and his army was in sorry shape when it reached Bologna, where he wintered and recruited new troops.

By spring Hannibal was again engaged by a Roman army, and won the first of a series of masterful battles, set pieces that are classics in military strategy even today. Knowing that the Roman generals were rash and inexperienced, all of them burning to make heroes of themselves, he slyly led them into trap after trap and obliterated entire armies. For the better part of two years he ranged over a hostile country, living off the land, fighting constantly, and had the Romans on the brink of defeat before they came sufficiently to their senses to put the command of their field forces in the hands of a wily old general named Fabius.

Fabius, nicknamed "Cunctator," the Delayer, understood that General Hannibal's principal weakness was that the longer he remained in Italy the more surely his army would shrink through illness, desertions and casualties. It was not being properly supported from Carthage; therefore, if it could be kept in a continuous state of harassment, but never engaged in large-scale combat, it would ultimately exhaust itself and have to leave.

Fabius put this strategy into effect. Hannibal, desperate for battle, dangled every lure he could think of in front of Fabius. He marched back and forth, left his camp undefended, exposed tempting detachments to be gobbled up. To no avail. Fabius watched Hannibal's supplies dwindle, meanwhile devoting most of his energies to holding off a fiery faction back in Rome that was excoriating him for cowardice. Eventually Rome replaced Fabius with a vain demagogue named Varro, who took command of the army at Cannae and within days suffered a catastrophic defeat. The strategy Fabius had advocated was hurriedly reinstated.

Through one grinding, bloody year after another Hannibal managed to maintain himself or a military force in Italy, fighting much of the time. He took a number of important Italian cities—some by storm, others by defection of the inhabitants. But slowly his initiative crumbled. The more Italian territory he controlled, the more effort he had to expend to maintain that control. Meanwhile the Romans carried the war to Spain. That all-important province, from which Hannibal derived men and money, was in turmoil. It became yet another place for him to worry about as resources stretched ever more thin. His brother Hasdrubal was killed, then his brother Mago. Both had served him well as generals.

As the war continued a Roman general finally emerged who was a match for Hannibal. His name was Publius Cornelius Scipio, himself the son of another outstanding Roman general by the same name. After several victories in Spain, Scipio returned home and announced his plan to take the war to Africa. Two years later his army won a smashing victory against the local Carthaginian army. In a panic, the Carthaginians recalled Hannibal.

Once home the grizzled military genius was smart enough to know he was badly outgunned, and he sought a parley with Scipio in the hope of working out a peace treaty. Their meeting, whether historically accurate or not, has been dramatically described by the Roman historian Livy:

"Keeping their armed men at some distance the generals, each attended by one interpreter, met, being not only the greatest of their own age, but equal to any of the kings or commanders of all nations in all history before their time. For a moment they remained silent, looking at each other and almost dumbfounded by mutual admiration. Then Hannibal was the first to speak:

" 'If it was foredained by fate that I, who was the first to make war on the Roman people and who have so often had the victory almost within my grasp, should come forward to sue for peace, I rejoice that destiny has given me you, and no one else to whom I should bring my suit. For you also, amongst your many distinctions, it will prove not the least of your honors that Hannibal, to whom the gods have given the victory over so many Roman generals, has submitted to you, and that you have made an end to this war, which was memorable at first for your disasters and then for ours. . . . Consequently we discuss terms

of peace while fortune is favoring you—a situation most ominous to us, while you could pray for nothing better.

" 'As for myself, age has at last taught me, returning as an old man to my native city from which I set out as a boy, success and failure have at last so schooled me that I prefer to follow reason rather than chance. In your case I am apprehensive alike of your youth and of your unbroken success. . . . It is not easy for a man whom fortune has never deceived to weigh uncertain chances. . . . The greatest good fortune is always the least to be trusted. In your favorable circumstances, in our uncertain situation, peace, if you grant it, will bring you honor and glory; for us who sue it is necessary rather than honorable. Better and safer is an assured peace than a victory hoped for. The one is in your own power, the other in the hands of the gods. Do not commit the success of so many years to the test of a single hour.' "

Hannibal went on to say that the Carthaginians would give up all Sicily, all Spain and all Sardinia, plus any smaller islands lying between, and would henceforth confine themselves to the African coast. His speech was a clever one but, according to Livy, it moved Scipio not at all.

When Hannibal was through talking, Scipio began. "Prepare for war," the Roman general bluntly said, "since you have been unable to endure a peace."

The two met the next morning near the inland city of Zama. Hannibal was defeated and the Second Punic War came to an end.

The loss of the war was crippling to Carthaginian ambitions. Pinned down along a narrow strip of coastal Africa, prevented by treaty with Rome from waging war, denied the wealth of Spain with which to rebuild a trading capability, the fleet burned by order of the Romans, their territory reduced to a small holding in the countryside directly around the capital, scarcely able to raise a huge annual indemnity for war damages, the Carthaginians were beset on their own back doorstep with an even graver problem. In earlier years, while the issue of the war still hung in the balance, the Romans had recruited the help of a Libyan tribal leader, Masinissa, to stir up trouble in North Africa. The end of the war found him at the head of a desert kingdom and with a large force of predatory, prowling tribesmen as his subjects. Under the terms of their peace treaty with the Romans, the Carthaginians had sworn not to take up arms against Masinissa or anyone else in Africa.

For more than four decades the Carthaginians honored this clause in the peace treaty. Time and time again a representative from Rome was required to mediate disputes. Meanwhile Masinissa became ever bolder and greedier. His raids and nibblings finally provoked the Carthaginians into a reprisal. That was all the Romans needed. Jealous of even the feeblest recovery efforts of Carthage, they fell on it again. In 149 B.C. the last of all the great sieges endured by Phoenicians both east and west was played out at Carthage. By the winter of 147-146 B.C., the inhabitants had barricaded themselves on their peninsula behind a maze of walls and defensive ditches. For some months they held off the Romans, slowly being squeezed into a smaller and smaller perimeter. Starving, hopeless, they nevertheless fought on. Finally they were penned in the fortifications atop the Byrsa Hill, where Elissa had established her citadel some 667 years earlier. There was a large temple to Eshmun on top of the hill. At the very end the handful of survivors set fire to the temple, crowded inside and burned themselves alive.

It is curious that with all the violent deaths in between—the political murders, the crucifixions of generals, the barbaric treatment of slaves and lesser people, the horrible atrocities of the mercenary war, the ritual mass slaughter of war prisoners, the sacrifice of no one knows how many infants in homage to Baal—the beginning and end of Carthage, both, should have been marked by self-destruction. Like Carthage's founder, Elissa, the last survivors of the city committed mass suicide, either in despair or in a final act of acknowledgment to their fiery gods. Carthage was in many ways a dark place, and its end seems fitting to its history.

Motya: A Key Outpost in Western Sicily

About 600 B.C., when Greek colonists were pouring into eastern Sicily, the Carthaginians decided to counter the competitive expansion by fortifying Motya, a small island at Sicily's western tip *(maps below)*. Motya was well chosen. It had an excellent anchorage, thanks to the sheltering arm of Isola Lunga to seaward. The water in the lagoon was shallow enough for the construction of a causeway to Birgi on the mainland. This shallowness ultimately proved fatal, for it enabled a Greek army to approach with siege engines in 397 B.C. and use them to pound down Motya's walls, then destroy the city. Before that, however, Motya's strategic importance was great. Relying as well on two other settlements, at Solunto and Panormus (Palermo), Carthage was able to keep the Greeks out of the western Mediterranean for more than 200 years.

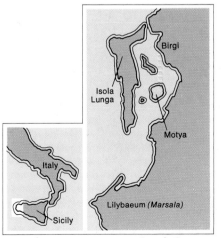

Motya's causeway, now a foot below water, is still used by Sicilian carts. Projecting stones mark its course to Birgi, one mile away.

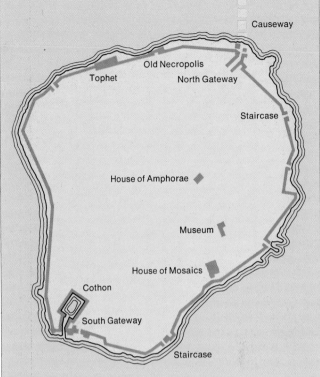

A circular island one third of a mile wide, Motya was ringed by a thick wall about 30 feet high, strengthened by towers at intervals. There were two heavily fortified entrances: a northern one, connected by a causeway to the mainland, and a southern one that served as the island's sea gate and was connected to a cothon, a man-made inland harbor. Other important archeological finds are: external staircases, an early burial ground, the Old Necropolis, with the Tophet nearby, where infant sacrifices were made, and two dwellings —the House of Amphorae and the House of Mosaics.

Motya's north entrance opened on the causeway, over which a cart is seen approaching. It was flanked by two extra-large towers angled so that they looked down on a series of gates, all of which an invader would have to break down if he hoped to enter the city using this approach. Steps to one of the towers are at left. In the center of the picture is Motya's main street, divided down the middle by the ruins of a wall that separated incoming from outgoing traffic. Ruts from Motyan carts are still visible in the paving.

Stone blocks line the entrance to Motya's cothon. Some have holes in their sides, suggesting that poles were inserted in them to hold a vessel in place while hull repairs were completed. This entrance, also, had its defensive towers. During the siege of Motya the channel was blocked with three big rocks.

Motya's cothon is the smallest but by far the best preserved of Phoenician examples. It is 168 feet long, 115 feet wide and about 10 feet deep at its maximum. It was entered by the paved channel in the foreground, some 23 feet wide, and had quays on either side for the unloading of cargo. Once inside the cothon, a ship presumably would have been tied up to a wall, preparatory to undergoing repairs, refitting and reloading.

Motya's Tophet, or sacrificial area, has been excavated to reveal some of the clay urns that still hold ashes of infants and baby animals sacrificed

there. The stone at center is a stele, or gravestone. Steles are common at Motya, and often bear the symbol of the goddess Tanit (page 131).

The House of Amphorae, so-called because of the many clay containers found in it, was excavated in 1968. It is a peculiar mixture of what may have been an old Motyan pottery works and a later structure—perhaps a private home—built by a Greek owner after the city's fall. The Greek column in the center of the picture suggests that history. Evidence for the earlier pottery works is found in the nearest corner of the excavation. The waist-high platform there may have been for the working of clay. It has a stone rim around it, a smooth top and a drain-off channel.

The House of Mosaics is named for the designs in the floor of its portico. They are made of light and dark pebbles set in mortar. The lion and bull shown here are Phoenician in character, but the edge design is Greek—another fascinating combination of styles. A cultural mix would have occurred naturally at a place like Motya, where Greek artisans and businessmen are known to have lived before and after the fall of the town.

The Emergence of Man

This chart records the progression of life on earth from its first appearance in the warm waters of the new-formed planet through the evolution of man himself; it traces his physical, social, technological and intellectual development to the Christian era. To place these advances in commonly used chronological sequences, the column at the

Geology	Archeology	Billions of Years Ago	
Precambrian earliest era		4.5	Creation of the Earth
		4	Formation of the primordial sea
		3	First life, single-celled algae and bacteria, appears in water
		2	
		1	
		Millions of Years Ago	
			First oxygen-breathing animals appear
		800	
			Primitive organisms develop interdependent specialized cells
		600	Shell-bearing multicelled invertebrate animals appear
Paleozoic ancient life			Evolution of armored fish, first animals to possess backbones
		400	Small amphibians venture onto land
			Reptiles and insects arise
			Thecodont, ancestor of dinosaurs, arises
Mesozoic middle life		200	Age of dinosaurs begins
			Birds appear
			Mammals live in shadow of dinosaurs
			Age of dinosaurs ends
		80	
			Prosimians, earliest primates, develop in trees
Cenozoic recent life		60	
		40	Monkeys and apes evolve
		20	
		10	Ramapithecus, oldest known primate with apparently manlike traits, evolves in India and Africa
		8	
		6	
		4	Australopithecus, closest primate ancestor to man, appears in Africa

Geology	Archeology	Millions of Years Ago	
Lower Pleistocene oldest period of most recent epoch	**Lower Paleolithic** oldest period of Old Stone Age	2	Oldest known tool fashioned by man in Africa
			First true man, Homo erectus, emerges in East Indies and Africa
		1	Homo erectus populates temperate zones
		Thousands of Years Ago	
Middle Pleistocene middle period of most recent epoch		800	Man learns to control and use fire
		600	
			Large-scale, organized elephant hunts staged in Europe
		400	Man begins to make artificial shelters from branches
		200	
Upper Pleistocene latest period of most recent epoch	**Middle Paleolithic** middle period of Old Stone Age		Neanderthal man emerges in Europe
		80	
		60	Ritual burials in Europe and Near East suggest belief in afterlife
			Woolly mammoths hunted by Neanderthals in northern Europe
			Cave bear becomes focus of cult in Europe
		40	
Last Ice Age	**Upper Paleolithic** latest period of Old Stone Age		Cro-Magnon man arises in Europe
			Asian hunters cross Bering Land Bridge to populate New World
			Oldest known written record, lunar notations on bone, made in Europe
			Man reaches Australia
			First artists decorate walls and ceilings of caves in France and Spain
		30	Figurines sculpted for nature worship
		20	Invention of needle makes sewing possible
			Bison hunting begins on Great Plains of North America
Holocene present epoch	**Mesolithic** Middle Stone Age	10	Bow and arrow invented in Europe
			Pottery first made in Japan

▼ Four billion years ago   ▼ Three billion years ago

▲ Origin of the Earth (4.5 billion)   ▲ First life (3.5 billion)

left of each of the chart's four sections identifies the great geological eras into which the earth's history is divided by scientists, while the second column lists the archeological ages of human history. The key dates in the rise of life and of man's outstanding accomplishments appear in the third column (years and events mentioned in this volume of The Emergence of Man appear in bold type). The chart is not to scale; the reason is made clear by the bar below, which represents in linear scale the 4.5 billion years spanned by the chart—on the scaled bar, the portion relating to the total period of known human existence (far right) is too small to be distinguished.

Geology	Archeology	Years B.C.	
Holocene (cont.)	Neolithic New Stone Age	9000	
			Sheep domesticated in Near East
			Dog domesticated in North America
		8000	Jericho, oldest known city, settled
			Goat domesticated in Persia
			Man cultivates his first crops, wheat and barley, in Near East
		7000	Pattern of village life grows in Near East
			Catal Hüyük, in what is now Turkey, becomes largest Neolithic city
			Loom invented in Near East
			Cattle domesticated in Near East
	Copper Age	6000	Agriculture begins to replace hunting in Europe
			Copper used in trade in Mediterranean area
			Corn cultivated in Mexico
		4800	Oldest known massive stone monument built in Brittany
		4000	Sail-propelled boats used in Egypt
			First city-states develop in Sumer
			Cylinder seals begin to be used as marks of identification in Near East
		3500	First potatoes grown in South America
			Wheel originates in Sumer
			Man begins to cultivate rice in Far East
			Silk moth domesticated in China
			Egyptian merchant trading ships start to ply the Mediterranean
			First writing, pictographic, composed in Near East
	Bronze Age	3000	Bronze first used to make tools in Near East
			City life spreads to Nile Valley
			Plow is developed in Near East
			Accurate calendar based on stellar observation devised in Egypt
		2800	Stonehenge, most famous of ancient stone monuments, begun in England
			Pyramids built in Egypt
			Minoan navigators begin to venture into seas beyond the Mediterranean
		2600	Variety of gods and heroes glorified in Gilgamesh and other epics in Near East

Geology	Archeology	Years B.C.	
Holocene (cont.)	Bronze Age (cont.)	2500	Cities rise in the Indus Valley
			Earliest written code of laws drawn up in Sumer
			Herdsmen of Central Asia learn to tame and ride horses
		2000	Use of bronze in Europe
			Chicken and elephant domesticated in Indus Valley
			Eskimo culture begins in Bering Strait area
		1500	Invention of ocean-going outrigger canoes enables man to reach islands of South Pacific
			Ceremonial bronze sculptures created in China
			Imperial government, ruling distant provinces, established by Hittites
		1400	Iron in use in Near East
			First complete alphabet devised in script of the Ugarit people in Syria
			Hebrews introduce concept of monotheism
	Iron Age	1000	Reindeer domesticated in Eurasia
		900	**Phoenicians popularize modern alphabet**
		800	Use of iron begins to spread throughout Europe
			Nomads create a far-flung society based on the horse in Russian steppes
			First highway system built in Assyria
			Homer composes Iliad and Odyssey
		700	Rome founded
			Wheel barrow invented in China
		200	Epics about India's gods and heroes, the Mahabharata and Ramayana, written
			Water wheel invented in Near East
		0	Christian era begins

▼ Two billion years ago

▼ One billion years ago

First oxygen-breathing animals (900 million) ▲

First animals to possess ▲ backbones (470 million)

First men (1.3 million) ▲

Credits

The sources for the illustrations in this book are shown below. Credits from left to right are separated by semicolons, from top to bottom by dashes.

Cover—Painting by Michael A. Hampshire, background photograph by Louis Goldman from Rapho Guillumette and Harry Gruyaert The Daily Telegraph Collection from Woodfin Camp & Associates. 8—Painting by Birney Lettick, background photograph by David Lees. 12,13—Map by Rafael D. Palacios. 14,15,16—Nik Wheeler from Black Star. 19—Giraudon courtesy Musée du Louvre. 22—Pierre Boulat courtesy Musée du Louvre. 25—Novosti Press Agency courtesy Pushkin Museum of Fine Arts, Moscow. 27,28,29—Courtesy University Museum, University of Pennsylvania. 30,31—Courtesy University Museum, University of Pennsylvania except far right, Herb Greer and Peter Throckmorton from Nancy Palmer Photo Agency. 32—Michael Holford courtesy of the Trustees of the British Museum. 35—Sunday Times/Honor Frost and David Singmaster. 36,37—Drawings by Ted Lodigensky. 40—Rendering by James Alexander. 43—No credit. 45,47—Drawings by Ted Lodigensky. 49 through 55—Illustrations by Fred Freeman. 56—C. M. Dixon. 59—Nik Wheeler from Black Star. 60—Frank Lerner from books in the collection of the American Museum of Natural History Library except top left, Frank Lerner courtesy The New York Public Library. 63—The Israel Department of Antiquities and Museums, Israel. 64—David Lees courtesy Museo Archeologico Nazionale, Cagliari. 69—Erich Lessing from Magnum courtesy National Museum of Lebanon, Beirut. 73—David Lees courtesy Whitaker Museum, Motya. 74—Courtesy of the Trustees of the British Museum. 75—Courtesy of the Oriental Institute, University of Chicago; David Lees courtesy Whitaker Museum, Motya; Hirmer Fotoarchiv, Munich courtesy Iraq Museum, Baghdad. 76—David Lees courtesy Museo Archeologico Nazionale, Cagliari; Courtesy of the Trustees of the British Museum. 77—David Lees courtesy Whitaker Museum, Motya—David Lees courtesy Museo Archeologico Nazionale, Cagliari. 78—David Lees courtesy Museo Archeologico Nazionale, Cagliari. 79—Courtesy of the Trustees of the British Museum. 80—Courtesy of the Trustees of the British Museum; Ashmolean Museum, Oxford. 81—David Lees, Museo Nazionale di Villa Giulia, Rome courtesy of the Soprintendenza dell' Etruria Meridionale. 82—Courtesy University Museum, University of Pennsylvania from *The Monuments of Nineveh*, Volume I, by A. H. Layard. 87—Courtesy of the Trustees of the British Museum from *The Monuments of Nineveh*, Volume I, by A. H. Layard; Courtesy of the Trustees of the British Museum. 88,89—Courtesy of the Trustees of the British Museum. 90—Courtesy of the Oriental Institute, University of Chicago. 93—Peter Davey courtesy of the Trustees of the British Museum. 94—David Lees courtesy Musée National, Carthage; Courtesy of the Oriental Institute, University of Chicago; Archives Photographiques—Boitier-Connaissance des Arts-TOP courtesy Musée du Louvre. 96,97—Erich Lessing from Magnum courtesy National Museum of Lebanon, Beirut. 98—Courtesy of the Trustees of the British Museum. 100 through 103—Mirko Toso courtesy the Hellenic Institute for Byzantine Studies, Venice. 104—Lauros-Giraudon courtesy Musée du Louvre. 107—Roger Wood courtesy Musée National du Bardo, Tunisia. 108—James B. Pritchard courtesy Musée du Louvre; Giraudon courtesy Musée du Louvre. 109—Giraudon courtesy Musée du Louvre except far left, Archives Photographiques courtesy Musée du Louvre. 111—Erich Lessing from Magnum courtesy National Museum of Lebanon, Beirut. 115—David Lees courtesy Topkapi Sarayi Archaeological Museum, Istanbul. 116—David Lees courtesy Arkeoloji Müzeleri, Istanbul. 117—Giraudon courtesy Musée du Louvre. 119—Peter Keen courtesy American University of Beirut Museum, Lebanon. 120—Erich Lessing from Magnum courtesy National Museum of Lebanon, Beirut. 123 through 127—Paintings by Don Punchatz based on material supplied by G. Ernest Wright and The Howland-Garber Model Reconstruction of Solomon's Temple. 128—David Lees courtesy Whitaker Museum, Motya. 131—Archives Photographiques courtesy Musée du Louvre. 133—Courtesy Musée National du Bardo, Tunisia. 135—Honor Frost. 136—David Lees. 138—David Lees courtesy Museo Archeologico Nazionale, Cagliari—David Lees courtesy Whitaker Museum, Motya; David Lees courtesy Museo Archeologico Nazionale, Cagliari; David Lees courtesy Musée National du Bardo, Tunisia. 139—David Lees courtesy Musée National, Carthage. 142,143—David Lees courtesy Whitaker Museum, Motya. 145—Frank Lerner courtesy American Numismatic Society. 147—Courtesy Istituto Archeologico Germanico, Rome. 148—Peter Davey courtesy of the Trustees of the British Museum. 151,152,153—David Lees. 154,155—Maitland A. Edey. 156 through 159—David Lees.

Acknowledgments

For the help given in the preparation of this book the editors are indebted to R. Tucker Abbott, du Pont Chair of Malacology, Delaware Museum of Natural History, Greenville, Delaware; American Numismatic Society, New York City; Pierre Amiet, Chief Curator, Department of Oriental Antiquities, Louvre Museum, Paris, France; Giuseppe Azzarello, Administrator, Whitaker Foundation, Palermo, Italy; Leila Badre, Assistant Curator, American University of Beirut Museum, Lebanon; Ferruccio Barreca, Superintendent, National Archeological Museum, Cagliari, Italy; Catherine Bélenger, Public Relations, Louvre Museum, Paris, France; Carmine Belluardo, Superintendency for Antiquities, Palermo, Italy; Hares Boustany, Curator, National Museum, Beirut, Lebanon; Lionel Casson, Professor of Classics, New York University, New York City; Annie Caubert, Curator, Department of Oriental Antiquities, Louvre Museum, Paris; Emir Maurice Chehab, Director-General, Department of Antiquities, Beirut, Lebanon; Necati Dolunay, Director, Archeological Museum, Istanbul, Turkey; William K. Emerson, Curator, Department of Living Invertebrates, American Museum of Natural History, New York City; Honor Frost, Director, Punic Ship Excavation, Marsala, Italy; Paul L. Garber, Professor of Bible and Religion, Agnes Scott College, Decatur, Georgia; German Institute of Archeology, Rome, Italy; Mogens Gjödesen, Curator of Greek and Roman Antiquities, New Carlsberg Sculpture Gallery, Copenhagen, Denmark; Ralph Hachmann, Professor of Ancient History, University of Saarbrücken, Germany; B. S. J. Isserlin, Professor of Semitic Studies, University of Leeds, England; Norman Kotker, New York City; Baruch A. Levine, Professor of Hebrew, Department of Near Eastern Languages and Literatures, New York University, New York City; M. I. Manussacas, Director, Hellenic Institute for Byzantine Studies, Venice, Italy; Mario Moretti, Superintendent, Villa Giulia Etruscan Museum, Rome, Italy, Sabatino Moscati, Director, Institute for Near Eastern Studies, University of Rome, Italy; Rabbi Yochanan Muffs, New York City; National Museum, Carthage, Tunisia; Francesco Pugliese, Island of Motya, Marsala, Italy; Vincenzo Pugliese, Island of Motya, Marsala, Italy; Roger Saidah, Lecturer in Archeology, American University of Beirut, Lebanon; Dr. Shawki Shaath, Department of Antiquities, Damascus, Syrian Arab Republic; Françoise Tallon, Researcher, Department of Oriental Antiquities, Louvre Museum, Paris, France; Geneviève Teissier, Department of Oriental Antiquities, Louvre Museum, Paris, France; Peter Throckmorton, Marine Archeologist, Kastella, Piraeus, Greece; Department of Western Asiatic Antiquities, British Museum, London, England; G. Ernest Wright, Parkman Professor of Divinity, Harvard School of Divinity, Harvard University, Cambridge, Massachusetts.

Bibliography

General

Bunbury, E. H., *A History of Ancient Geography*. Dover, 1959.

Burn, Andrew Robert, *Persia and the Greeks*. St. Martin's Press, 1962.

De Beer, Sir Gavin, *Hannibal*. Viking Press, 1969.

Gevirtz, Stanley, *Patterns in the Early Poetry of Israel*. University of Chicago Press, 1961.

Hammond, N. G., and H. H. Soullard, eds., *The Oxford Classical Dictionary*. Oxford University Press, 1970.

Harden, Donald, *The Phoenicians*. Penguin Books, 1971.

Hitti, Philip K., *Lebanon in History*. St. Martin's Press, 1967.

Jidejian, Nina:
Byblos Through the Ages. Dar El-Machreq Publishers, Beirut, 1971.
Sidon Through the Ages. Dar El-Machreq Publishers, Beirut, 1971.
Tyre Through the Ages. Dar El-Machreq Publishers, Beirut, 1969.

Moscati, Sabatino, *The World of the Phoenicians*. Praeger Publishers, 1968.

Olmstead, A. T., *History of the Persian Empire*. University of Chicago Press, 1948.

Singer, Charles, et al., eds., *A History of Technology*. Vols. I & II, Oxford University Press, 1967.

Snodgrass, A. M., *Arms and Armour of the Greeks*. Cornell University Press, 1967.

Tarn, William W., *Alexander the Great*. Beacon Press, 1956.

Archeology

Archaeological Discoveries in the Holy Land. Compiled by the Archaeological Institute of America. Bonanza Books, 1969.

Bass, George, *Archaeology Under Water*. Praeger Publishers, 1966.

Landay, Jerry, *Silent Cities, Sacred Stones*. McCall Books, 1971.

Pritchard, James B.:
The Ancient Near East in Pictures. Princeton University Press, 1969.
Ancient Near Eastern Texts Relating to the Old Testament, ed. Princeton University Press, 1969.
The 1972 Excavations at Sarepta. Rivista di Studi Fenici, Vol. 1, No. 1, 1973.

UNESCO, *Underwater Archaeology: a Nascent Discipline*. UNESCO, 1972.

Wright, G. Ernest, *Biblical Archaeology*. Westminster Press, 1957.

Carthage and Motya

Carpenter, Rhys, "Phoenicians in the West." *American Journal of Archaeology*, Vol. 62, 1958.

Isserlin, B.S.J.:
"Motya, a Phoenician-Punic Site Near Marsala, Sicily." *The Annual of Leeds University Oriental Society*, Vol. 4, 1962-1963.
"New Light on the 'Cothon' at Motya." *Antiquity*, Vol. XLV, No. 179, September 1971.

Picard, Gilbert and Colette, *Life and Death of Carthage*. Taplinger Publishing Company, 1969.

Warmington, B. H., *Carthage*. 1960.

Whitaker, Joseph I. S., *Motya*. G. Bell & Sons, 1921.

Ships and Shipping

Anderson, R. C., *Oared Fighting Ships*. Percival Marshall, 1962.

Bass, George:
Cape Gelidonya: A Bronze Age Shipwreck. The American Philosophical Society, 1967.
A History of Seafaring, ed. Thames and Hudson, 1972.

Casson, Lionel:
The Ancient Mariners. Macmillan Company, 1959.
Ships and Seamanship in the Ancient World. Princeton University Press, 1971.

Landström, Björn, *The Ship*. Doubleday and Company, 1961.

Morrison, J. S., and R. T. Williams, *Greek Oared Ships 900-322 B.C.* Cambridge University Press, 1968.

Ancient Writings

Bible, Revised Standard Version.

Herodotus, *Histories*. Translated by Aubrey De Selincourt. Penguin Books.

Homer, *The Odyssey*. Loeb Classical Library, Harvard University Press.

Livy, *Roman History*, Vols. 1-14. Harvard University Press.

Thucydides, *Complete Writings*. Modern Library.

Index

Numerals in italics indicate an illustration of the subject mentioned.